Assessment in Special Education

Assessment in
Special Education

William H. Berdine

Department of Special Education
University of Kentucky

Stacie Anne Meyer

Teacher, Trainable Mentally Handicapped
Booker T. Washington Elementary School
Lexington, Kentucky

Little, Brown and Company
Boston   Toronto

Copyright © 1987 by William H. Berdine and Stacie Anne Meyer

Library of Congress Cataloging-in-Publication Data

Berdine, William H.
  Assessment in special education.

  Bibliography: p.
  Includes index.
  1. Exceptional children. 2. Ability testing.
3. Exceptional children — Diagnosis. 4. Behavioral
assessment of children.   5. Observation (Educational
method) I. Meyer, Stacie A.   II. Title.
LC3969.B47   1987   371.9   86-19996
ISBN 0-316-09141-3

Library of Congress Catalog Card No. 86-19996

9 8 7 6 5 4 3 2 1

ISBN 0-316-09141-3

Published simultaneously in Canada
by Little, Brown & Company (Canada) Limited

Printed in the United States of America

Credits

p. 146, Figure 6–1: Checklist copyright Herbert C. Quay and Donald R. Peterson, 1975.
Reprinted by permission.

p. 265, Figure 9–1: From the *Adaptive Performance Instrument.* Reprinted by permission
of the College of Education, University of Idaho.

p. 321, Excerpt: From C. J. Maker, *Teaching Models in Education of the Gifted,* © 1982.
Reprinted with permission of Aspen Systems Corporation.

pp. 322–24, Excerpts: From A. Harnadek, *Inferences — A: Inductive Thinking Skills* (Troy,
MI: Midwest Publications, 1979). Reprinted by permission.

Brief Contents

Part I. Foundations of Educational Assessment in Special Education

1. Introduction to Assessment in Special Education
   William H. Berdine   3
2. Data-Collection Procedures   *William H. Berdine and Stacie Anne Meyer*   14
3. Basic Principles of Measurement and Test Development
   Donald B. Bailey   51

Part II. Cross-Categorical Assessment Considerations

4. Assessment of Language Impairments   *Arthur H. Schwartz*   82
5. Assessment in Early Childhood Special Education
   Donald B. Bailey and Susan L. Rosenthal   111
6. Assessment of Children's Social and Behavioral Problems
   Lewis Polsgrove   141

Part III.   Categorical Assessment Considerations

7. Assessment of the Mildly Handicapped Learner
   Barbara Tymitz-Wolf   184
8. Assessment of the Trainable Mentally Handicapped
   Learner   *William H. Berdine*   217
9. Assessment of the Profoundly Handicapped Pupil   *Susan C. Hupp
   and Cordelia Robinson*   252
10. Assessment of the Physically Handicapped   *John Venn and
    Mary K. Dykes*   278
11. Assessment of the Gifted Learner   *June Maker*   309

v

JUN 2 5 1987

Part IV. Epilogue

12. Synthesis of Practices and Technological Innovations
H. Earl Knowlton and Ann Boyer   333

Appendix I   355
Appendix II   357
Appendix III   370
References   389
Name Index   421
Subject Index   428

Contents

Contributing Authors   xxiii

Part I.   Foundations of Educational Assessment in Special Education

Chapter 1   Introduction to Assessment in Special Education   3

Key Terms   3
Chapter Objectives   3
Assessment Defined: Basic Principles   4
    The Settings   5
    Reasons for Testing   5
The Five-Stage Model   7
    The Levels   8
    Level One: Screening and Identification/Level Two: Eligibility and Diagnosis/Level Three: Placement and IEP Development/Level Four: Instructional Planning/Level Five: Evaluation
    Using the Model   10
Summary   11
Mastery Review   12

Chapter 2   Data-Collection Procedures   14

Key Terms   14
Chapter Objectives   14
Selecting a Data-Collection System   15
    Direct Observation   15
    Planned Schedule of Observation/Observation Settings/Environmental Influences
    Naturalistic Observation   16
    Running Records/Event Sampling/Category Sampling
    Task Analysis as an Assessment Procedure   22
    Precedural Task Analysis/Hierarchical Task Analysis/Classroom Assessment/

Prerequisites to Task Analysis/Levels of Assistance

Assessment of Learning Style   27
    Environmental Elements   27
    Emotional Elements   28
    Motivation/Persistence/Responsibility/Structure
    Sociological Elements   30
    Physical Elements   30
    Food Intake/Time
    Psychological Elements   31
    Global versus Analytical/Central Nervous System Preferences/Impulsivity versus
    Reflectivity
    Classroom Assessment of Learning Style   32

Curriculum-Based Assessment   33
    Components of CBA   33
    Implementing CBA   33
    Application of CBA to the Five-Level Assessment Model   34
    A Curriculum-Based Assessment Model/Use in Various Skill Areas/Prereferral
    Intervention

Legal and Ethical Issues in Classroom Assessment   36
    Teacher Competence and IEP Requirements   36
    Training as a Prerequisite/Issues Related to the IEP/Components of an IEP
    Issues Related to the Quality of Assessment Procedures   37
    Selection of Assessment Instrument or Procedures/Observer and Procedural Biases/
    P.L. 94–142 Requirements Regarding Quality
    Issues Relating to Nondiscrimination   41
    Cultural Pluralism in Special Education/P.L. 94–142 Safeguards/Strategies for the
    Teacher/Issues Related to Gender/Sexual Stereotyping in Assessment
    The Role of Parents in Classroom Assessment   44

Summary   46

Mastery Review   47

Chapter 3   Basic Principles of Measurement and Test Development   51

Key Terms   51

Chapter Objectives   51

How Are Tests Constructed?   52
    Item Selection   52
    Domains/Item Pools/Item Tryout
    Standardization   54
    Standard Materials/Standard Administration Procedures/Standard Scoring Procedures/
    Standard Interpretation Procedures
    Normative Sample   55
    Test Evaluation   57

Basic Principles of Measurement   58
    Criterion-Referenced and Norm-Referenced Measurement   58
    Measures of Central Tendency   59
    Measures of Variability   60
    Range/Normal Distribution Curve/Standard Deviation/Z-Score/Standard Error of Measurement
Common Raw-Score Transformations   65
    Percentile Ranks   65
    Standard Scores   66
    Deviation Score/Age Equivalents/Grade Equivalent Scores
Test Evaluation   68
    Correlation Coefficient   69
    Reliability   70
    Test-retest Reliability/Alternate-Form Reliability/Split-Half Reliability/Interscorer Reliability
    Validity   71
    Face Validity/Content Validity/Construct Validity/Concurrent Validity/Predictive Validity
Summary   73
Mastery Review   74

Part II.   Cross-Categorical Assessment Considerations

Chapter 4   Assessment of Language Impairments   82

Key Terms   82
Chapter Objectives   82
Characteristics of Language Development   83
    Aspects of Verbal Language   83
    Criteria for Normal Development/Time of Onset/Rate of Progression/Sequence of Development
    The Rule of Six   84
General Characteristics of Language Impairments   85
    Impairments in Language Content   86
    Delayed or Deficient Cognitive Development/Concepts Underlying Language Content
    Impairments in Language Form   87
    Impairments in the Use of Language   88
    Dump and Play/Assessment of Language Usage
Controversies and Issues in Language Impairments   89
    Means versus End or Assessment versus Intervention   90
    Pragmatic Approaches
    Patterns of Language Impairment   91

Differences between Delays and Disorders   91
Etiological versus Symptomatic Classifications   92
Criteria for Classification
Minimal Auditory Deficiency   92
Auditory Processing and Language Impairments   93
Bottom-up versus Top-down Approach/Complications Associated with Auditory Processing Disorders
The Role of the Special Educator   94
Classroom Assessment   95
Proactive versus Reactive Approaches
The Role of Cultural and Social Factors in Language Impairment   96
Dialects Are Not Disorders   96
Social Factors   97
Inappropriate Affect Is Often a Problem/Self-Monitoring of Language Usage/Practice Helps
Formal and Informal Assessment Formats   98
Formal Assessment Formats   98
Informal Assessment Formats   99
Screening Tests   99
Bankson Language Screening Test/Clinical Evaluation of Language Functions: Elementary Level Screening/Clinical Evaluation of Language Functions: Advanced Level Screening/Compton Speech and Language Screening Evaluation/Fluharty Preschool Speech and Language Screening Test/Hannah-Gardner Preschool Language Screening Test/Kindergarten Language Screening Test/Merrill Language Screening Test/Multilevel Informal Language Inventory/Oral Language Sentence Imitation Screening Test/Quickscreen/Stephens Oral Language Screening Test
Diagnostic Measures of Language   102
Spontaneous Language Sampling   102
Obtaining Language Samples
Evoking Conversational Speech   103
Development of IEPs
Screening of Minisamples   103
Limitations and Precautions   105
Summary   105
Mastery Review   107

Chapter 5   Assessment in Early Childhood Special Education   111

Key Terms   111
Chapter Objectives   111
Preschool Children and Setting Defined   112

Issues and Special Problems   113
   Screening and Early Identification   113
   Screening Defined/Selecting a Screening Tool/Using Screening Data
   Assessing Young Children   116
   Problems/Strategies
   Determining Instructional Targets   117
   Incorporating Two Approaches/Most Probable Next Placement
   Family Assessment   119
   Multicultural Factors in Assessment   119
   Reducing Bias
Assessment of Children with Multiple Handicaps   119
   Modifying Test Items and Procedures   120
   Techniques for Adaptation/Assessing for Critical Functions
Areas for Assessment   121
   Assessing Cognitive and Preacademic Skills   122
   Sensorimotor Skills
   Preacademic Skills   123
   Concept Development/Preferred Assessment Strategies
   Communication Skills   127
   Development of Communication/Assessing Communication Skills/Establishing Instructional Targets
   Play and Social Interaction   129
   Toy Play/Social Interactions/Play Environments/Assessing Play Skills/Considerations with Sensory or Motor Impairments
   Gross and Fine Motor Skills   132
   Assessing Gross Motor Skills/Assessing Fine Motor Skills/Reflexes, Reactions, and Tone/Muscle Tone/Assessing Reflexes, Reactions and Tone/Self-Help Skills/Eating Skills/Toileting Skills/Other Self-Help Skills
   Family Skills   135
   Parent-Child Interactions/Home Environments/Family Coping Skills
Summary   137
Mastery Review   138

Chapter 6   Assessment of Children's Social and Behavioral Problems   141

Key Terms   141
Chapter Objectives   141
Behavior Disorders Defined   142
   Behavioral-Ecological Assessment   142
   An Interactive Behavioral System/Behavioral Repertoires/Expectations of Significant Others/Internal and External Variables/Traditional Psychological Measures/Intervention Design/Ongoing Evaluation

The Behavioral-Ecological Assessment Process   144
   Screening   144
   Surveying Problem Behaviors   145
   Behavioral Excesses/Behavioral Deficits/Determining Objections to Problem Behavior/Identifying Problem Behavior Situations
   Diagnosis   149
   Identifying Antecedent Events/Identifying Consequent Events/Summarizing and Analyzing Information/Analyzing Individual Problem Behaviors
   Program Planning   157
   Selecting Target Behaviors/Classes of Behavior/Competing Behaviors/Ecological Setting/Developmental History/Influence of Adults/Selecting Appropriate Interventions/Monitoring Change Programs
Behavioral-Ecological Assessment Methods   162
   Behavior Rating Scales   162
   The Behavior Problem Checklist/The Walker Behavior Problem Identification Checklist
   Ecological Survey   163
   Direct-Observation Procedures   164
   ABC Analysis/Permanent Products/Event Recording/Duration Recording/Interval Recording/Time Sampling
   Accuracy and Reliability of Behavioral Observation   168
Behavioral-Ecological Interviewing   170
   General Interviewing Strategies   170
   Interviewing Adults   172
   Interviewing Children   173
Intervention as a Process   175
Summary   176
Mastery Review   177

Part III.   Categorical Assessment Considerations

Chapter 7   Assessment of the Mildly Handicapped Learner   184

Key Terms   184
Chapter Objectives   184
Defining the Population and Setting   185
   Educational Settings for the Mildly Handicapped   186
Issues and Special Problems   186
   Assessment of Preschool-Aged Children   187
   Assessment of Elementary-Aged Children   187
   Referrals

Assessment of Secondary-Level Youth   188
Relevant Assessment
Nondiscriminatory Assessment   189
Bias in Referrals/Testing Biases/Multiple Handicapping Conditions and Interrelated Factors/Etiological Considerations
Classroom Assessment Procedures   191
The Assessment of Learning Aptitude   192
Traditional Measures for Assessing Learner Aptitude   192
Measures of Intelligence/Measures of Adaptive Behavior
AAMD Adaptive Behavior Scale, Public School Version   196
Nontraditional Measures of Learning Aptitude   197
Attention/Memory/Learning Strategies
The Assessment of Academic Achievement   200
Three Commonly Used Tests   201
Reading   201
Issues in Reading Assessment
Formal Procedures for Assessing Reading   202
Reading Skills/Norm-Referenced Reading Tests/Criterion-Referenced Reading Tests
Informal Procedures for Assessing Reading   204
Interviews/Diagnostic Teaching/Formative Assessment
Oral Language Assessment   205
Assessment of Written Language   206
Assessment Devices/Written Language Sample/Formative Assessment
Mathematics Assessment   209
Norm-Referenced and Criterion-Referenced Tests/Work-Sample Analysis/Interviews
Summary   212
Mastery Review   213

Chapter 8   Assessment of the Trainable Mentally Handicapped Learner   217

Key Terms   217
Chapter Objectives   217
Defining the Population and Setting   218
The T.M.H. Classification Defined   220
Educational Settings Serving the T.M.H.   220
Prevalence of T.M.H. Pupils/Use of Segregated Settings
Assessment Issues in the T.M.H. Classroom   222
Considerations Regarding Assessment and Multihandicapping Conditions   222
Selecting an Instrument/Collecting Data
Classroom Assessment and Multicultural Factors   223
The System of Multicultural Pluralistic Assessment

Using Assessment Instruments versus Data-Gathering Procedures in the T.M.H. Classroom   224

Longitudinal Research Is Needed

A Priori Questions for the Teacher   225

What Should the Assessment Accomplish?/What Type of Instrument or Procedure?

Considerations in Selecting an Adaptive-Behavior Assessment Instrument for Use in a T.M.H. Classroom   226

Who Is to Be Assessed?/What Behaviors Are to Be Tested?/What Interpretative Data Are Desired?/Will a Commercially Prepared Test Be Used?

Commercially Available Adaptive-Behavior Assessment Materials   228

Vineland Adaptive Behavior Scales—Revised/Battelle Developmental Inventory/ Camelot Behavioral Checklist/Brigance Diagnostic Inventory of Early Development/ Brigance Diagnostic Inventory of Basic Skills/Learning Accomplishment Profile— Diagnostic Edition/TMR Profile

Considerations in Selecting a Direct-Observation Data-Gathering Procedure   232

Event Recording/Duration Data/Percentage Recording/Latency Data Recording/ Levels of Assistance/Time Sampling/Permanent Products

Assessing Learning-Style Preference   241

Data-Collection Questions   241

Does the Pupil Have Communicative Preferences or Requirements?/Are There Any Clearly Preferred Sensory or Perceptual Modalities?/Are There Any Clearly Preferred Reinforcers?/Does the Pupil Respond Differentially to Adults in the Classroom?/Does the Pupil Respond Differentially to Variations in Structures Built into Instructional Program Design?/Is the Pupil Unusually Distracted by Environmental Stimuli?/Does the Pupil Exhibit Unusual Response-Latency Requirements?/Does the Pupil Have Any Peer Preferences?/Does the Pupil Exhibit a Preference for Specific Forms of Instructional Activities or Settings?/Does the Pupil Respond Differentially Because of Apparent Temporal Variables?

Summary   247

Mastery Review   248

Chapter 9   Assessment of the Profoundly Handicapped Pupil   252

Key Terms   252

Chapter Objectives   252

Defining the Population and Setting   253

Functional Characteristics   254

School Settings   254

Issues and Special Problems   254

Criterion of Ultimate Functioning   255

Conditions of Instruction/Selection of Skills/Generalization

Implications of Multiple Handicaps for Assessment   256
**Adapting Assessment Procedures/Evaluating Underlying Abilities/
A Multidisciplinary versus an Interdisciplinary Approach**

Types of Assessment Procedures   259
Norm-Referenced Assessment   259
Criterion-Referenced Assessment   260
General Performance Domains
Curriculum-Referenced Assessment   261
Direct Observation of Behavior   261
Population-Specific Problems/Mechanical Recording of Responses

Selection of Assessment Instruments   263
Currently Available Instruments   264
**Adaptive Performance Instrument–Experimental Edition, 1980/Callier-Azusa Scale/
Developmental Programming for Infants and Young Children**
Analysis of Skills Assessed   268
Application of a Cognitive Model   269
**Determining Conceptual Level/Developing Task Analyses of Conceptual Level/
Analyses of Conceptual Level of Sorting Skills/Selection of Materials/Selection of
Response**

Summary   272
Mastery Review   274

Chapter 10   Assessment of the Physically Handicapped   278

Key Terms   278
Chapter Objectives   278
Defining the Population and Setting   279
Cerebral Palsy   279
Spasticity/Athetosis/Ataxia/Mixed
Spina Bifida   281
Convulsive Disorders   281
Orthopedic and Health Impairments   281
Defining the Service-Delivery Settings   282
Placement in the Least Restrictive Environment

Defining the Issues and Special Problems   283
Standardized Testing   283
Administration Procedures   284
Use of Norm-Referenced Tests   284
Intelligence Testing   285
Picture Vocabulary Tests   285
The Peabody Picture Vocabulary Test–Revised
Specialized Intelligence Tests   286
The Columbia Mental Maturity Scale, Third Edition

Assessment Team Approaches   287
Problems with Team Approaches
Assessing the Physically Impaired and Multiply Handicapped   288
Specialized Assessment Services   288
Motor and Mobility Evaluation and Management Analysis   289
Other Areas of Assessment   289
Developmental Assessment   290
**Characteristics of Developmental Assessment/Multiple Samples and Partial Credit/
Task Conditions/Multiple Presentations/Subscale Scoring/Functional Living Skills**
Task-Analytic Assessment   291
Nontraditional Assessment Procedures   292
Preparation and Intervention Procedures in Testing   292
**Primary Response Mode/Sensory Input/Degree of Motor Impairment/Positioning/
Fatigue/Medical Problems/Signs of Learning Disabilities/Recent Evaluations**
Developing a Positive Intervention Plan   297
Assessing the Physical Environment   297
Classroom Evaluation of Braces, Artificial Limbs, and Wheelchairs   297
Academic and Behavioral Assessment   301
Suggestions for Academic Assessment   301
Suggestions for Behavioral Assessment   301
Assessing Motor Ability   302
Medical Examinations/Teacher Assessment/Therapeutic Evaluation/Motor Testing
Motor-Development Assessment Instruments   303
**Stanford Functional Development Assessment/Peabody Developmental Motor Scales/
Bruininks-Oseretsky Test of Motor Proficiency**
Summary   304
Mastery Review   305

Chapter 11   Assessment of the Gifted Learner   309

Key Terms   309
Chapter Objectives   309
Concepts of Giftedness   310
Implications for Assessment   311
Defining the Setting   312
Program-Delivery Models
Levels of Assessment   313
Level One: Screening and Identification   313
Appropriate Use of Tests
Level Two: Eligibility and Diagnosis   314
Multidisciplinary Approaches/Service-Delivery Options
Level Three: Placement and IEP Development   316
Program Objectives/Assessing Goals
Level Four: Instructional Planning   317

Level Five: Evaluation 318
Out-of-Level Testing/Determining Progress
Assessment Procedures 319
Issues Related to Formal Testing 319
Limitations of Intelligence Tests/Total I.Q. Scores/Supplements to Intelligence Tests
Informal Assessment Procedures 321
Develop a High Level of Understanding of Key Concepts, Ideas, Methods, and Significant Individuals/Students Will Develop the Ability to Use Information and Evaluate It Critically Rather than Simply Knowing that Information/Students Will Develop Creative and Divergent Thinking or Problem-Solving Abilities/Students Will Become Independent, Self-Directed Learners/Students Will Develop Products that Are Similar to Those Produced by Practicing Professionals/Students Will Develop the Desire and Ability to Follow Through on Tasks or Projects They Initiate/Students Will Develop Social and Leadership Skills/Students Will Develop Self-Knowledge and Self-Understanding that Will Enable Them to Become Self-Actualized, Productive Adults
Summary 325
Mastery Review 327

Part IV.   Epilogue

Chapter 12   Synthesis of Practices and Technological Innovations   333

Key Terms 333
Chapter Objectives 333
The Role of the Special Education Teacher in the Assessment Process 335
Political Competency and the Special Education Teacher's Role 336
Screening/Diagnosis and IEP Development/Program Planning and Evaluation
Procedural Competency and the Special Education Teacher's Role 337
Screening and Diagnosis/IEP Development/Instructional Planning and Evaluation
Assessment as an Ongoing Part of Instruction 341
Instructional Planning 341
What Skills Should Be Taught?/How Does the Pupil Learn Best?/How Should Objectives Be Modified?
Program Evaluation 343
Mastery of Goals and Objectives/Current Performance Levels/Regular Classroom Functioning/Continuation in Special Education
A Summary of the Major Issues Affecting Assessment Practices 345
Prereferral Assessment and Intervention 345
Improper Test Discrimination 345
Assessment of Adaptive Behavior 346
Microcomputers and Related Technologies in Assessment 347
Microcomputer-Administered Assessment and Test-Generation

Programs   348
**Records Management/Adapting IEP Goals/Videodisk Technology/Interactive Video/
Test-Generation Programs**
Data Collection, Assessment-Analysis Programs, and IEP Development   350
Data Recording/Analyzing Assessment Data/Computer-Generated IEPs
Using Technology to Support Assessment   352
**Telecommunications Technology/Applications Where Language May Be a Factor/The
Need for More Data**

Summary   353

Appendix I Test Review Form   355

Appendix II   357
Table 1: Informal Inventories, Norm- and Criterion-Referenced Reading Tests
Table 2: Norm- and Criterion-Referenced Tests of Written Language
Table 3: Norm- and Criterion-Referenced Mathematics Tests

Appendix III   370
Introduction
Table 1: Levels of Assessment, Questions, and Information Sources
Table 2: Assessment Procedures, Indicators to Consider, and Questions
Addressed

References   389
Name Index   421
Subject Index   428

Preface

The very nature of assessment in special education is changing. At one time, assessment was an isolated event — a formal test administered by specialized personnel. Now it is conceived more broadly — a process in which various formal testing instruments and informal observation techniques are used by classroom teachers as well as by specially trained individuals. This larger view of assessment comes at a time when society as a whole is looking closely at what schools are doing and how well they are performing. One commission set up to analyze instructional issues and effectiveness, the Holmes Group, focused particular attention on educational excellence and teacher training. With this current emphasis on greater accountability and higher training and professional standards, it is critical that teachers be competent in using assessment to plan their programs, carry out effective instruction, and measure outcomes. Moreover, it is evident that teachers will be expected to conduct systematic student assessment across a wide range of abilities and behaviors.

This text examines assessment at each stage of instruction, from initial screening to program evaluation. It covers an array of assessment procedures commonly used in classroom settings with pupils with handicapping conditions. The special education classifications treated include: language impaired, early childhood, social and behavior problems, mildly handicapped, moderately handicapped, trainable mentally handicapped, severely and profoundly handicapped, physically handicapped, and gifted. While considerable variation exists within and between these pupil populations, a common denominator exists: the role of the classroom teacher as the primary assessment and data-collection agent. It is our conviction that the individual teacher must take responsibility not only for gathering information about children's past performance, but also about what is being accomplished during and as a result of the instructional process.

Assessment is examined from a broad perspective. Throughout the text, we describe methods for evaluating many different facets of pupils' performance. Such broadly based assessment is comprehensive, providing information immediately pertinent to classroom programming needs. For example, at various points in the text there are discussions of the impact of the environment on students' performance. These environmental issues vary depending on the purpose of the assessment and students being evaluated. When working with a physically handicapped pupil, an evaluation of accessibility (the presence or absence of barriers in the environment) is a critical part of the assessment process. For a behaviorally disordered pupil, it may be important to determine the antecedents for and consequences of certain behaviors.

The twelve chapters comprising this text are divided into four parts. Part I, Foundations of Educational Assessment in Special Education, consists of three chapters. In Chapter 1, we define educational assessment and introduce a five stage model for classroom assessment in special education. Direct observation procedures are discussed in Chapter 2 and the basic principles of measurement are examined in Chapter 3.

Part II, Cross-Categorical Assessment Considerations, is devoted to the assessment of developmental characteristics and behaviors found among children otherwise categorized in one or more traditional special education classification. Chapter 4 discusses the assessment of language problems that may occur in any pupil population and which often result in major instructional challenges. Chapter 5 demonstrates how to establish early assessment data bases for children across any developmental or handicapping condition. Chapter 6 describes methods of assessing specific disturbing behaviors, conduct problems, and socially inappropriate behaviors that are frequently exhibited across all special education classifications.

In Part III, Categorical Assessment Considerations, each of the five chapters considers one of the traditional special education categorical classifications. Beginning with the mild handicapping conditions (including educable mentally handicapped and learning disabilities), we go on to the trainable mentally handicapped learner, the severely/profoundly handicapped pupil, the physically handicapped pupil, and the gifted learner. Within each of these "categorical" chapters, assessment of pupil performance is related to the specific characteristics and needs of learners. Additionally, within each chapter, references are made to the methods and procedures described in Part II.

Part IV is an epilogue for the book, as well as a look to the future. The authors summarize the uses of assessment data in decision making, identify some of the major issues and problems confronting professionals, and examine implications for both summative and formative assessment in special education. Part IV concludes with a description of microcomputer innovations currently used in educational assessment and considers the implications of technology for future applications.

Assessment in Special Education has a number of distinctive features. First, the organization of chapters around the major classification areas reflects current special education practice. Second, the division of the text into cross-categorical and categorical assessment acknowledges that early childhood needs, communicative, and social and behavioral problems must be addressed in each of the traditional special education classifications. Third, application by classroom teachers of the principles and tools of assessment is emphasized throughout. Fourth, each chapter concludes with a series of questions and exercises designed to enhance mastery and application of the contents. Fifth, the contributing authors are specialists and have much experience using the assessment techniques discussed in their chapters.

This text is the result of the sustained efforts of a large number of people. We, the editors, would like to thank our contributing authors for their cooperation and understanding over the long process of producing the text. We also want to thank colleagues whose reviews were instrumental in developing this book: Cheri Hoy, The University of Georgia; John Junkala, Boston College; Mary F. Landers, Wright State University; James J. McCarthy, University of Wisconsin-Madison; Jeanice Midgett, University of Central Florida; Maurice Miller, Indiana State University; Tom Pace, Appalachian State University; Sue T. Rouse, University of South Carolina; Robert Sheehan, Cleveland State University; Paulette J. Thomas, University of New Orleans; Stanley F. Vasa, The University of Nebraska-Lincoln; and, Edward Welch, State University of New York at Albany.

We wish to extend our gratitude to Marcia Bowling who prepared all of the typed text from first draft through final edition. We also want to acknowledge the work of graduate assistants Mary Balles, Kathy Leslie, Becky Trexel, and Cathy Alig in the preparation of the text through various manuscript forms. We are particularly indebted to our editor, Mylan Jaixen, whose patience and considerable assistance have helped produce this text, and to Ellen Herman, who assisted in coordinating the book.

Contributing Authors

William H. Berdine is an Associate Professor and Coordinator, Teacher Certification Programs in Trainable Mentally Handicapped at the University of Kentucky. He has worked as a teacher of the trainable mentally handicapped in both elementary and junior high school settings. Current areas of involvement and research include secondary programs for persons developmental disabilities and personnel preparation in that area.

Stacie Anne Meyer has taught in the area of Trainable Mentally Handicapped for ten years at the elementary school level. She is currently involved in research and program development with micro-computers applied to the T.M.H. classroom setting.

Donald B. Bailey, Jr. is Director of Early Childhood Research at the Frank Porter Graham Child Development Center of the University of North Carolina at Chapel Hill. Current interests include mainstreaming, families, communication training, and the interdisciplinary team.

Arthur H. Schwartz is an Associate Professor and Director of Speech and Hearing Services at Bradley University. He has taught graduate and undergraduate courses in language development, language disorders, and diagnostic methods. His current areas of interests are the application of microcomputers to assist in the management of language disorders in children and is directing a grant to develop instructional packages on this topic.

Lewis Polsgrove has held positions as a clinical psychologist in a mental hospital and mental health center, and has served as a school psychologist, and counselor for delinquent children. He has also been a liaison counselor and a teacher of emotionally disturbed children at the Central Kentucky Re-Ed schools. He is currently a Professor in the Department of Special Education at Indiana University where he teaches behavior management and strategies for consultation in the schools, and he is the Director of the Center for Innovation in Teaching the Handicapped.

Barbara Tymitz-Wolf is an Associate Professor and Director of the Undergraduate Program for Teachers of the Mildly Handicapped at Indiana University. She has taught classes for the mildly handicapped of all ages in public school and community settings. Current interests include research on effective teaching and the infusion of quality practices in teacher education and public school programs.

Cordelia Robinson is an Associate Professor in Nursing, Special Education and Psychology at the University of Nebraska. Her involvement with severely handicapped students has included graduate instruction in teaching the S/PH pupil and direct service of evaluation, assessment, teaching, program administration, and research.

Susan C. Hupp is an Assistant Professor in the Department of Educational Psychology, Special Education Program, at the University of Minnesota. She coordinates the personnel preparation program in the area of severe handicaps. Current areas of research interest include mastery motivation of young children with moderate and severe handicaps and concept acquisition by handicapped children.

John Venn is Associate Professor in the Department of Special Education and Coordinator of personnel preparation programs in the area of the severely/profoundly handicapped at the University of North Florida. Current areas of interest include diagnostic prescriptive programming and programming for the adult handicapped.

Mary K. Dykes is a Professor of Special Education and School Psychology at the University of Florida. She coordinates the physically/multiply handicapped personnel preparation program. Current interests include appropriate assessment of children whose skills are significantly different than expected for age, integration of medical and therapy professionals and their data into education teams and programs, and education of the gifted handicapped child.

H. Earle Knowlton has been a classroom teacher in regular and special education; he has also served as a clinical diagnostician, an Easter Seals camp counselor, and a parent trainer. His current research interests at the University of Kansas include the transition process and methodological issues regarding the use of qualitative and naturalistic inquiry in special education.

Ann Boyer is a doctoral student and instructor in the Department of Special Education at the University of Kentucky. Current areas of interest include the preparation of teachers in microcomputer applications for special education students and programming and software development for limited English proficient exceptional learners.

Susan L. Rosenthal, Ph.D., currently post-doctoral fellow, Child Study Center, Yale University. Completed doctoral studies at the University of North Carolina School of Psychology/Chapel Hill.

June Maker. Associate Professor, Department of Special Education, University of New Mexico/Tempe.

Part I
Foundations of Educational Assessment in Special Education

The realities and challenges of assessing pupil performance in special education differ from those in any other educational area. Pupils with handicapping conditions that may interfere with their ability to learn often need much closer or more frequent monitoring of their progress than others. Changes in their school-related performance may be very infrequent, irregular, short in duration or rate, or barely perceptible. In order for the classroom teacher to make informed instructional decisions, assessment data must be collected frequently. The types of data, and to a large degree the procedures and methods used to collect them, are similar to those used by any educator.

Another factor affecting assessment in special education is the legal mandate set forth by Public Law 94–142. This federal law stipulates that all special education instructional programs be offered on an individualized basis and that they be monitored regularly. Classroom teachers must therefore be skilled in assessment. In the chapters that follow, we will examine the topics, practices, and issues that are crucial in the assessment of handicapped and gifted learners.

Part I describes a model for effective and efficient classroom assessment, examines procedures for collecting data through direct observation, and studies basic principles involved in measuring pupil performance and developing educational tests.

Chapter 1: Introduction to Assessment in Special Education

In this chapter, the implications of P.L. 94–142 for data collection and educational assessment are described. We then introduce a five-stage model for educational assessment, with illustrations of its application in a variety of special education settings.

Chapter 2: Data-Collection Procedures

The intent of this chapter is to familiarize you with an array of procedures for direct observation and data collection. These procedures have been found very useful in a variety of special education settings and with very diverse kinds of pupils. Examples of specific applications will be found in subsequent chapters. In addition to featuring a data-collection model, the chapter introduces a concept fairly new to special education: assessment of learning style performance. It also provides a thorough overview of the major issues in assessment confronting the special education classroom teacher.

Chapter 3: Basic Principles of Measurement and Test Development

Chapter 3 describes the principles of measurement that influence and rule assessment and testing of pupil performance. In addition to examining such topics as validity, reliability, and standardization, it looks at test materials and at norm- and criterion-reference tests. The effects of handicapping conditions on test administration and interpretation are also addressed here.

Chapter 1

Introduction to Assessment in Special Education

Chapter Objectives:

After reading this chapter and completing the Mastery Review, you will be able to:

1. Define educational assessment.
2. List and describe the five levels of the assessment model used in this book.
3. List and describe reasons why teachers should conduct educational assessment in the classroom.
4. Obtain an overview of the text's chapter topics.

Key Terms:

assessment model
cross-categorical
data collection
diagnosis
diagnostician
educational assessment
eligibility
identification
individual education plan (IEP)
instructional program planning
instructional program evaluation
multidisciplinary team
noncategorical
Public Law (P.L.) 94–142
placement
referral
screening

Assessment of pupil performance has become an accepted practice in the vast majority of our schools. The use of assessment data to prescribe, implement, evaluate, and revise instructional programs is an integral part of contemporary education, both regular and special. In special education, assessment data are required not only for prescribing programs but also for determining when pupils will enter and leave programs. Assessment of communication skills and pupil performance in academic, social, psychomotor, and self-help skills provides a basis for sound instructional decisions.

All classroom teachers must be proficient in evaluating pupils' performance and achievement in a wide variety of areas. The regular classroom teacher can typically rely on a school psychologist, a guidance counselor, or other ancillary personnel to take the major responsibility for maintaining ongoing pupil records and for conducting periodic evaluation or assessment. The special education teacher, however, is required under the provisions of Public Law 94–142 to provide instruction through individual education plans, or IEPs. Hence this legal mandate virtually prohibits the use in special education settings of many group assessment practices routinely employed in regular education. P.L. 94–142 ensures both safeguards for individual children and the appropriateness of tests and testing procedures by prohibiting:

- The use of tests or practices that may penalize a pupil through cultural or ethnic bias.
- The use of tests and/or testing procedures that have no clearly determined validity; i.e., are not supported by evidence that they test for the things they are supposed to determine (for example, a language test may not be used to establish a general intelligence level).
- The use of tests that require stimulus and response modes not readily available to the pupil because of physical or sensory disabilities (for example, testing a pupil exhibiting severe language disabilities with a procedure that requires recognition of verbal directions).

Because of the legal requirement that they make assessment data an integral part of their instructional activity, teachers in special education must be proficient in many assessment procedures.

Assessment Defined: Basic Principles

For the purposes of this text, educational assessment can be defined as follows:

> Any process of gathering intrapersonal or interpersonal performance data on a pupil's current behavior, language, or motor skills in any environment that involves a part of the pupil's current or planned educational program.

This definition recognizes data-gathering procedures used by professionals not necessarily trained in formal testing — that is, classroom teachers — as well as those of such specialists as school psychologists or psychometricians. Except in specialized graduate programs, classroom teachers have rarely had the opportunity to participate in the type of training and certification that specialists complete.

The Settings

Professional diagnosticians typically gather assessment data in highly controlled settings, often outside the classroom. The forms of assessment discussed in this text, by contrast, are procedures that classroom teachers can use with little loss of instructional time. Moreover, the procedures reach beyond the classroom into the community and the home. Contemporary teachers have come to incorporate these settings as part of the learning environment. Assessment data gathered by other professional diagnostics are not ignored by the special education teacher; they are often critical in making initial diagnostic and placement decisions. Because of the educational importance of data gathered by formal as well as by informal means, there is an interplay between the two domains.

Reasons for Testing

Special educators may use assessment data for purposes ranging from screening for suspected developmental or learning problems to developing and evaluating instructional programs. For our purposes, we can list five specific reasons for giving tests to students: screening, placement, instructional planning, pupil evaluation, and program evaluation. Barbara Tymitz-Wolf (1984) postulates that these are actually stages or levels of an assessment continuum and that they define conditions for the use of the data collected. According to Tymitz-Wolf, the process of assessing a pupil with a learning handicap can be broken down into the following steps:

1. Screening and Identification.
2. Eligibility and Diagnosis.
3. Placement and IEP Development.
4. Instructional Program Planning.
5. Instructional Program Evaluation.

Each stage of the assessment process asks a different set of questions about the learner and sets conditions for the use of the data collected. A variety of instruments and procedures may be used to answer the questions and make decisions, and the persons responsible for information gathering and decision making will vary with the stages. However, two common focal points are evident throughout the assessment process: the pupil and the teacher. Table 1–1 summarizes activities at each of the five levels of the assessment process.

Table 1–1

Levels of Assessment

· ·

Questions to Be Answered	Information Sources	Persons Responsible
Level 1: Screening and Identification		
1. Is the student's performance on standardized tests significantly different from that of peers?	Screening tests	School screening team
2. Is the student's performance and/or behavior in the classroom a cause for concern?	Classroom observations Examinations of work samples Classroom tests and grades	Regular class teacher
3. Does the student have a history of academic, behavioral, or physical problems?	Examination of student records Parent interview	Regular class teacher
4. Do modifications in the regular classroom alleviate the behavior and/or performance of concern?	Systematic modifications within the classroom	Regular class teacher
Level 2: Eligibility and Diagnosis		
1. What are the behaviors and/or skills that cause concern?	Referral	Regular class teacher
2. What are the student's present skill levels?	Standardized tests Criterion-referenced tests	Multidisciplinary tests
3. How does the student function in the regular classroom?	Classroom observation Examination of work samples, classroom tests, and grades	Regular and special educators
4. Is the student eligible for and likely to benefit from special education services?	Standardized tests Student interview	Multidisciplinary team members
5. What label should be assigned to the student?	Standardized tests	Multidisciplinary team members
Level 3: Placement and IEP Development		
1. What are the annual IEP goals and objectives?	Standardized tests Criterion-referenced tests	Multidisciplinary team members
2. Who will be responsible for accomplishing these?	Informal assessment procedures	
3. What percentage of time should the student spend in special education?	Diagnostic teaching Observations of test behavior Classroom observations	

Table 1–1

Levels of Assessment (*continued*)

. . . .

Questions to Be Answered	Information Sources	Persons Responsible
Level 4: Instructional Planning		
1. What specific skills should be taught?	Criterion-referenced tests	Regular and special educators
2. How does the student learn best?	Informal assessment procedures	
3. How should objectives be modified/ upgraded?	Continuous assessment	
	Observation of test behavior	
	Classroom observation	
	Diagnostic teaching	
Level 5: Evaluation		
1. Which goals and objectives has the student mastered?	Criterion-referenced tests	Regular and special educators
2. What are the student's current levels of performance?	Standardized tests	Regular and special educators
	Criterion-referenced tests	
3. How is the student functioning in the regular class?	Classroom grades and tests	Regular and special educators
	Examination of work samples	
	Classroom observation	
4. Should the student continue in special education?	Standardized tests	Multidisciplinary team members
	Criterion-referenced tests	
	Classroom observations	
	Teacher interview	
5. What should be the goals and objectives of next year's IEP?	Standardized tests	Multidisciplinary team members
	Criterion-referenced tests	
	Classroom observation	

. . . .

The remainder of this section will elaborate on each level as it pertains to the general field of special education. In subsequent chapters, the implications of the various levels will be examined where specifically applicable.

The Five-Stage Model

The model for educational assessment used throughout this text reflects a synthesis of established "best" practices in the field of special education. The model is not a rigid recipe but rather a frame of reference for the special educator. Multitudes of ongoing assessments are being conducted in the typical special education classroom, and a frame of reference facilitates both efficiency and effectiveness in this process. A significant advantage of the five-level model is that it not only goes beyond classroom assessment alone but also includes the entire continuum of assessment, from initial referral through instructional or intervention program evaluation.

The Levels

Level One: Screening and Identification.   The special education teacher cannot legally work directly with a pupil prior to completion of screening and identification, though an exception can be made if the pupil's parents grant permission. Even when a pupil is already placed in a special education classroom, the teacher may want to conduct screening activities to determine whether some additional learning, behavior, or developmental problem exists. A fuller description of screening procedures is provided in Chapter 4, "Assessment of Language Impairments."

During the initial pupil screening phase, assessment data are best gathered by regular classroom teachers and school educational diagnosticians. The special educator may be asked to assist in planning ways to collect information and in interpreting data pertinent to special education programming. Typically, however, direct involvement of the special educator begins after this level of assessment has been completed and a referral for special education services has been made.

Level Two: Eligibility and Diagnosis.   A referral initiated as the result of Level-One screening is not necessarily confirmation of a learning or developmental problem; the diagnosis of an educational handicap or disability may not have been made. The outcome of assessment at Level Two will be a decision about the student's actual diagnosis, eligibility for special education services, and classification in the school system's special education categories. Level Two is therefore a critical step in the process. A mistake at this point may result in an inaccurate diagnosis and an inappropriate placement that may affect the pupil's school career and potentially his or her entire life!

At this level of the assessment process, it will be determined whether a pupil needs special education. Making this important decision becomes the task of a multidisciplinary team composed of medical professionals, speech pathologists and audiologists, school psychologists and administrators, the pupil's parents or guardian and classroom teacher, and the special educator. In many cases, the pupils may take an active role in the decision-making process.

Because the principal function of the team is to confirm that a learning and/or developmental disability exists, access to a wide variety of information is vital. No one team member can make the complete diagnosis. And depending upon the specific regulations of a particular jurisdiction, a variety of instruments, including standardized tests of general intelligence, will be allowed or disallowed.

The multidisciplinary team's responsibility is to verify the pupil's need for special education or other educational services. Regardless of the pupil's eligibility for special services, the result of the process should be a more effective educational prescription. The multidisciplinary team must as a group interpret the assessment findings and make an informed decision as to whether the pupil is eligible for special education services. Ideally, such decisions are based on objective assessment data, but many other factors also influence diagnosis and eligibility decisions. For example, it has been demonstrated that individual teachers have different levels of tolerance for learning and behavior problems (Algozzine, 1976). Whether a pupil is referred may depend upon the teacher's tolerance. Cultural and ethnic factors may also have a bearing on decisions about a child's capabilities. The diversity inherent in a multidisciplinary team is generally the best assurance that the interests of the pupil are being addressed.

Level Three: Placement and IEP Development. This level of assessment does not depend on the collection of new information, it answers qualitatively different questions. Once eligibility has been determined, the team must specify an individual education plan, or IEP, for the pupil. The IEP will list instructional and behavioral goals and objectives; identify the persons responsible for their implementation; prescribe methods of evaluation and, in some instances, of intervention; and set a time frame in which the IEP is to be put into operation and evaluated.

As a member of the multidisciplinary team, the special education classroom teacher plays an important role in Level-Three activities. The teacher is familiar with resources in the classroom and the school that will be used in meeting the IEP's goals and objectives, and his or her input into writing the plan can be vital. If the teacher is not a member of the team, great care must be taken to assure that he or she is made fully aware of all assessment data, scores, interpretations of test results, and recommendations. It is, after all, considerably more difficult to implement an IEP into which one has had no input.

Level Four: Instructional Planning. It is at this level that the special education teacher is most active. The pupil's IEP provides the teacher with goals and objectives as well as suggestions for instructional programming. Because the IEP may not include specific information on performance in all targeted areas, the teacher must determine what additional data are to be collected in the classroom. Various direct-observation techniques are described in Chapter 2, and formal assessment and testing procedures are discussed in Chapter 3. The data gathered by the classroom teacher at this level will help determine how instructional programming is developed. Level Three of the assessment process provides the framework — the IEP — and Level Four adds the substance that completes that framework.

Level Five: Evaluation. P.L. 94–142 requires that each IEP be reviewed and modified accordingly on an annual basis, but most school systems stipulate that this be done more often. In addition, the special education teacher must typically conduct several procedures to gather data about pupil performance on a daily basis in order to determine the effectiveness of the ongoing instructional program. In fact, to prepare for the more comprehensive annual or semiannual IEP evaluation, the teacher will use daily achievement records. This information is critical in determining whether the pupil should continue in the current setting, change to another learning environment, or leave special services in favor of regular class placement. Unfortunately, few standards exist for evaluating either special education learning environments for individuals (Heron and Skinner, 1981) or the criteria for terminating special education placement. The role of the classroom teacher in this decision-making process — to provide accurate, representative, and current performance data — is usually best completed through the use of direct-observation procedures, adaptive behavior assessment instruments, and testing in the classroom or other natural settings.

Using the Model

Most classroom teachers do not participate in Levels One (screening and identification), Two (eligibility and diagnosis), or Three (placement and IEP development). When they are involved, they are assigned fairly specific functions, usually including that of verifying that a pupil's behavior or skill level suggests a developmental or behavioral disorder. The teacher's collaboration may also include observing the pupil in the regular class setting and examining samples of class work. Direct intervention with the pupil by a special education teacher is not usually required, but if it should be, permission must be secured from the parents. At this level of the assessment process, it is seldom necessary for the special educator to do more than observe and consult with the regular class teacher and other members of the multidisciplinary team

After a pupil has been found eligible for special education services and an Individual Educational Plan has been developed, the participation of the special education teacher becomes vital for implementing the IEP. In Levels Four and Five (instructional planning and evaluation), the classroom teacher will need to draw on a wide variety of assessment and direct-observation data-collection procedures. Depending on the pupil's classification, the available resources, the IEP contents, and the allotted time, the teacher will generally be asked to implement some of the assessment procedures discussed in subsequent chapters.

In many instances, the teacher will need to adopt a cross-categorical approach to data collection or pupil assessment. For example, it would not be unusual for a teacher working with a pupil exhibiting severe developmental impairment (see Chapter 9) to require as well the approaches described in Chapter 10, which deals with assessing the physically handicapped. Similarly, a teacher working with a gifted pupil (see Chapter 11) may find use for some of the collection procedures described in Chapter 6, "Assessment of Children's Social and Behavioral Problems." Moreover, teachers working with the mildly handicapped (see Chapter 7) and those working with the trainable mentally retarded or moderately handicapped (see Chapter 8) will find that their assessment and collection procedures overlap and that they both can make wide use of the techniques and procedures described in Chapter 4, "Assessment of Language Impairments." Regardless of the pupil's categorical classification, the content of Chapter 5, "Assessment in Early Childhood Special Education," will be useful to all classroom teachers of young children. The levels of assessment model enables teachers to determine where within the assessment process they are being asked to function.

Summary

This chapter describes the unique role of assessment in special education programs. The assessment requirements outlined in P.L. 94–142 and their impact on practices in programs for the handicapped are also discussed. A five-level model examining each stage of the assessment process is presented together with a brief overview of subsequent chapters. Points made in this chapter are:

1. The classroom teacher is a valuable participant in all phases of the assessment process.
2. The assessment of pupil performance is an integral part of special education and is an essential skill for the special education teacher.
3. P.L. 94–142 establishes guidelines for the assessment of handicapped pupils.
4. The process of assessing a handicapped pupil's educational needs includes at least five stages or levels:
    - Level One, screening and identification, is usually completed by the regular class teacher and the school educational diagnostician. Its purpose is to determine whether the pupil should be considered for special education services.
    - Level Two, eligibility and diagnosis, involves a multidisciplinary team that makes a decision about eligibility for services and a diagnosis or educational classification.
    - Level Three, placement and IEP development, establishes specific instructional goals, methods of evaluation and intervention, persons responsible, and a time frame for implementation of the IEP. The classroom teacher's involvement in these proceedings is mandated by law.
    - Level Four, instructional planning, is the primary responsibility of the classroom teacher. It is usually accomplished using a variety of assessment and data-collection procedures in the classroom setting.
    - Level Five, evaluation, includes the systematic review and modification of the IEP as well as evaluation of the effectiveness of ongoing instructional programs by the classroom teacher.
5. In many cases, assessment and data-collection procedures are applicable to several different educational classification areas and may be utilized in many, diverse special education classroom settings.

Mastery Review

I. Recall

1. List the possible members of a multidisciplinary assessment team.

   _____

   _____

   _____

   _____

   _____

   _____

2. The special education teacher most frequently becomes involved in the assessment process at what level?

   a. Level One: screening and identification
   b. Level Two: eligibility and diagnosis
   c. Level Three: placement and IEP development
   d. Level Four: instructional planning
   e. Level Five: evaluation

II. Comprehension

1. Describe each part of the definition of educational assessment given in this chapter and discuss its implications for planning and implementing classroom assessment.
2. Using the five-level assessment model, discuss in a three-to-five-page paper the role of the classroom teacher at each stage.

III. Application

Many of the application exercises in this text involve participation in an educational setting. Whatever the type of that participation, some general considerations need to be addressed before you make a classroom visit. General protocol dictates that you not disrupt ongoing activities at schools or agencies and that you maintain the confidentiality of proceedings observed. While completing the exercises, you may find it helpful to notice the many assessment activities that are constantly occurring and to look at them within the framework of the five-level model outlined in this chapter. Be aware of the total educational environment, not just the pupil or pupils with whom you are working.

Mastery Review exercises are included in each chapter of this text. The procedural considerations outlined here apply to each exercise involving direct contact with pupils and professionals.

1. Visit the administrative offices of a local school district or educational diagnostician and determine its policies for completing educational assessments at each stage of the five-level assessment model. Questions might include: Who is normally included in the multidisciplinary assessment team? Who is responsible for initial pupil screening? How are referrals processed?
2. In the library, locate a text with the complete form of P.L. 94–142. Identify those sections that deal specifically with educational assessment. Describe the specifications in each section and their possible implications for the assessment process in a three-to-five-page paper.

IV. Alternate Task

If none of the application exercises applies to your setting or circumstances, you can design two exercises of your own. They should demonstrate the application of one or more of the concepts described in the preceding chapter. Prior approval of both self-designed exercises should be obtained from your course instructor.

V. Answer Key, Sections I and II

I.   **1.**   Members of the medical professions, speech pathologists and audiologists, school psychologists, school administrators, the parents or guardian, and the classroom teacher. See p. 8.

    2.   b. p. 8

II.   **1.**   p. 4

    2.   pp. 8–10

Chapter 2
Data-Collection Procedures

Key Terms:

antecedent
baseline
category sampling
consequence
curriculum-based assessment
direct observation
duration data
event sampling
interval time sampling
latency data
learning style
levels of assistance
model
momentary time sampling
natural settings
physical prompt
prereferral intervention
running record
task analysis
verbal cue

Chapter Objectives:

After reading this chapter and completing the Mastery Review, you will be able to:

1. List and describe data-collection procedures.
2. List and describe the elements that make up learning style.
3. List and discuss basic issues in special education classroom assessment.
4. Describe procedural and hierarchical task analyses.
5. List and describe the five levels of assistance.
6. Describe curriculum-based assessment.

The special education teacher usually uses a wide variety of procedures to gather information about how successfully instructional programs are working. Finding effective ways of gathering such information can be of more concern to the special educator than to a regular class teacher for at least two reasons. First, special education pupils do not, as a rule, demonstrate rapid or readily discernible progress. Behavior and skill levels often change very slowly. Without some means of formal documentation, the teacher may not be aware of small but important improvements.

Second, the Individualized Education Plan requires that documentation of instructional programming be provided to show evidence of movement toward completion of the plan's goals and objectives. Before initiating a new instructional program, the special education teacher will generally establish the pupil's baseline performance in the targeted performance area. This makes it much easier to verify progress. Individual exit criteria are more fittingly established with accurate baseline data, and provide an integral part of the entire IEP process. The various data-collection procedures to be described in the sections that follow and the materials discussed in Chapter 3, "Basic Principles of Measurement and Test Development," can be used for baseline data collection.

An experienced teacher can in many instances make accurate decisions about a pupil without a great many data; however, data are required when IEP decisions are being made. Moreover, experienced teachers will want to corroborate their professional opinions with data that document their instructional program decisions.

Selecting a Data-Collection System

The teacher will most often need to select a data-collection system that can be readily used in the classroom. The procedure will need to be:

- relatively unobtrusive, so as not to distract the targeted pupil and others from their tasks;
- usable by instructional aides and perhaps other pupils;
- and inexpensive to use, involving minimal forms, papers, and equipment.

Direct Observation

Direct observation is defined here as any procedure that involves the systematic collection of data in natural settings. It is most commonly accomplished by the teacher or an assistant, who observes the pupil in a variety of settings selected as most likely to permit the pupil to perform skills, tasks, or behaviors relevant to the classroom assessment needs. Direct observation may also be accomplished through any mechanical process, such as videotaping or audio recording, that captures the entire setting and its major stimulus events. The use of recording equipment requires that the teacher later review and analyze the observation sessions.

Planned Schedule of Observation. Systematic data collection refers to a planned schedule of observations, as opposed to a random process. Data collected only when time permits, during unrepresentative times of day, or when a target behavior could not or normally would not be present create more instructional problems for both the teacher and the pupil than does the lack of data. Classroom teachers generally do not enjoy the luxury of extra time in the class day. If direct observation is to be accomplished smoothly and effectively, it must be planned to fit into the instructional routine and to do so in such a way that data representative of the pupil's performance are likely to be obtained.

Observation Settings. "Natural settings," as used here, refers to those settings in which the behaviors or skills to be observed would probably occur. This does not mean that the teacher must patiently wait for the pupil to exhibit a targeted skill or behavior. He or she can create a situation in the classroom — for instance, an instructional program or a planned recess — in which the pupil will have an opportunity to exhibit the skill. The teacher's involvement should not bias the pupil's performance, but simply increase the probability that a targeted behavior will occur. It is generally recommended that the teacher assign targets for observation rather than simply scheduling observations of the pupil with no specific objective in mind. A child may exhibit a rather large array of behaviors over a relatively short period, and by predetermining the target behaviors, the observer is better able to attend to the relevant task and to record the pupil's performance accurately. It is feasible to target more than one skill or behavior for observation, but the total should probably not exceed five to seven behaviors. To observe multiple targets usually requires trained personnel. A disadvantage of using multiple targets is that it tends to force the observer/recorder to focus too intensely on the pupil and insufficiently on environmental factors that may be influencing the behavior. For example, the teacher observing multiple targets may lose track of the length of time involved in the activity, but time may be a relevant variable in the pupil's behavior.

Environmental Influences. The environmental context in which a target behavior is exhibited may hold important information for the teacher. Noticing what happens immediately before a target behavior occurs (the antecedent event) may prove valuable in planning instructional programs. Similarly, the events that immediately follow a target behavior's occurrence (its consequences) may illuminate what is maintaining a behavior, what rewards the pupil responds to, or what events have a negative impact.

Naturalistic Observation

Bailey and Wolery (1984) describe three forms of naturalistic observation that fit our definitional standard for direct observation in natural settings: running records, event sampling, and category sampling. These procedures and the use of permanent products, behavior checklists, and rating scales are discussed next.

Figure 2–1

A Running Record Result Converted to Another Format for Interpretation

. . . .

Child: __Tom__   Date: __2/26__   Time: __9:15__ to __9:45__

Behavior: __Disrupting others, interrupting others__

Observer: __Ms. Andrews__   Class: __Reading__

Antecedent	Behavior	Consequence
Teacher tells students to open their books to the reading assignment.	Tom yells that his book is at home.	Students laugh.
Teacher asks a specific student to share her book with Tom.	Tom quietly moves next to student and tickles her.	Students open books to the lesson; some giggle.
Teacher asks for volunteers to start oral reading.	Tom starts reading aloud.	Students yell, "Not fair. He didn't raise his hand."
Teacher tells a child to begin reading.	Tom stops reading and goes to sharpen his pencil.	Student reads aloud, but noise from pencil sharpener distracts several other students.

. . . .

Running Records. This form of direct observation usually involves recording everything that a pupil does during a specified period of time. For example, every verbalization uttered by a pupil during the last two minutes of each hour is recorded. The running record provides data on the existence of predictable sequences of responses or patterns of behavior. Teachers often find such records useful if they are not sure whether a problem really exists. The running record provides an abundance of information that can help to determine whether more precise data collection is needed.

A major disadvantage of running records is their heavy demand on the teacher's or aide's time; therefore they must be carefully planned and structured. Bailey and Wolery also note that the data collected in running records must be recast into another format for interpretation. In their raw form, running records resemble a series of anecdotal recordings, and secondary analyses are needed to determine specific behavioral performances, rates of occurrence, percentages, patterns, and sequences. This step, too, takes time. Consequently, the teacher needs to proceed with caution when considering running records as a major form of direct observation. Figure 2–1 illustrates a running record data-collection effort.

Event Sampling. This form of direct observation typically involves a temporal dimension: it records the frequency with which a behavior occurs or the duration

Figure 2–2

Bar Graph of Total Duration of Out–of–Seat Behavior during Group Instruction

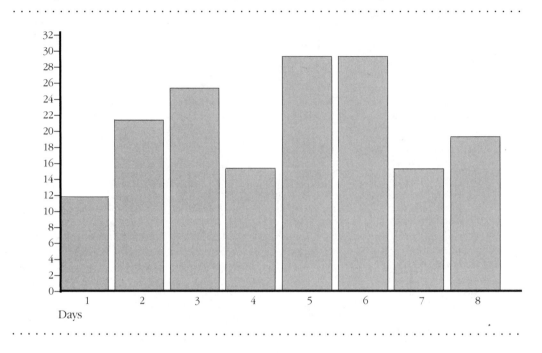

Days

of its occurrence. If a teacher is concerned about a behavior that happens quickly — for example, throwing objects on the floor — or one that is easy to verify — for example, soiling of undergarments — then a simple frequency count will accurately and efficiently yield the required data. If, however, the teacher is concerned about the length of time that a behavior continues — for instance, how long a pupil self-stimulates — an event-sampling procedure such as duration time sampling will be needed. Other useful types of event-sampling procedures include gathering duration data, latency data, interval time sampling, and momentary time sampling.

Duration data refers to the length of time required for a target behavior or skill to be fully exhibited. These data are most frequently used to record behaviors that occur infrequently but that last for a notable amount of time when they do occur. The length of time the target behavior lasts, not just its occurrence, is the critical component of the data. Duration data can be collected using nothing more than a stopwatch or a wristwatch with a second hand. The recorder starts timing when the target behavior begins and stops when it ceases. These data can be graphically illustrated in numerous ways and are readily interpretable. Figure 2–2 illustrates duration data in bar-graph form.

Latency data are those that reflect the time elapsed between the presentation of a stimulus (teacher's request) and the pupil's response. For educational pur-

Figure 2–3

Latency Data in Graphic Form

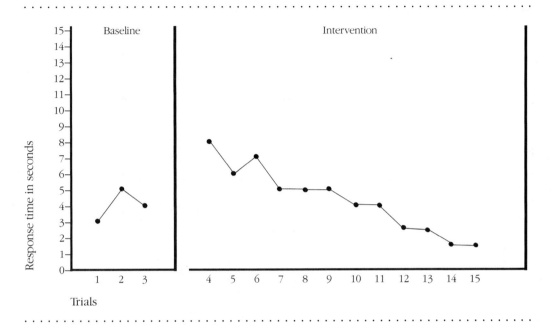

poses, it is often important that the student respond not only appropriately but also within a reasonable time span. Although latency data are most often used with moderately and severely handicapped pupils, they can be helpful in monitoring and evaluating any student's performance on specific IEP objectives and in assessing preintervention performance levels whenever reaction time is important. Figure 2–3 illustrates latency data in graphic form.

Interval time sampling is used when it is easier and more efficient to record a representative sample of a target behavior than to make a continuous recording such as a frequency count. The occurrence or absence of a target behavior can be recorded at specific, predetermined time intervals over a preset length of time, a process referred to as interval recording. For example, if a teacher is interested in determining what percentage of time a student is attending to a task, observations could be made at the fixed interval of every other 30 seconds over a 5-minute period. The teacher would then record how much time during each 30-second interval the student was attending. Fixed-interval data recording requires the teacher's complete attention during all of the prespecified intervals and is therefore somewhat inefficient.

For some target behaviors, the teacher may want to use a **variable-interval schedule**, one in which the pattern of observation intervals is irregular. For example, instead of observing during alternate 30-second periods, the teacher could

Figure 2–4

Fixed-Interval Data Recording Form for a 10-Minute Time Period

· ·

Student: _____   Date: _____

Observer: _____   Time: _____

Conditions: _____

minute	1		2		3		4		5	
	30″	30″	30″	30″	30″	30″	30″	30″	30″	30″

minute	6		7		8		9		10	
	30″	30″	30″	30″	30″	30″	30″	30″	30″	30″

Code: + = occurrence;   0 = nonoccurrence
Directions: Observe during first 30″; record during next 30″.

· ·

observe from the 15th to the 35th second in the first minute, from the 30th to the 60th second in the second minute, and so on. This schedule requires the teacher to plan ahead and adhere strictly to some form of time monitoring in order to collect accurate data. Variable-interval schedules are more efficient if the target behavior tends to be short in duration, while fixed-interval schedules generally work better when the target behavior is emitted over a long period of time and is fairly predictable. Figure 2–4 illustrates fixed-interval data recording, and variable-interval recording is shown in Figure 2–5.

Momentary time sampling is an efficient method of data collection for classroom use. In this procedure, the teacher checks for a target behavior at predetermined moments. For instance, the teacher may be interested in a pupil's correct manipulation of materials during a 30-minute workshop. By setting up a schedule of momentary time observations — in this example, every 5 minutes — the teacher creates six brief data collection periods. At the end of each 5-minute interval, he or she stops other tasks momentarily, makes the appropriate contact with the pupil to determine whether the target behavior is being exhibited, records the observation, and continues with whatever else was underway. Contact with the pupil may be visual or in some instances, depending on the target behavior, auditory. The

Figure 2–5

Variable-Interval Data Recording Form

. . . .

Student: _____ Date: _____

Observer: _____

Schedule: _____ Conditions: _____

Start time: _____ Stop time: _____ = Total time _____

	10		20		30	Comments
5		25		26		
11		14		15		
13		22		42		
7		10		16		
9		18		38		
12		26		20		
10		20		38		
12		14		20		
10		22		44		
7		26		26		
15		20		30		
11		22		42		
9		21		15		
13		10		44		

Schedule is in seconds.   Code: + = occurrence; 0 = nonoccurrence

. . . .

data gathered can be illustrated on a percentage graph (see Figure 2–6). If decisions are being made on the basis of momentary time sampling, the teacher should take care to collect enough samples over several days to insure the representativeness of the data.

It should be noted that, regardless of the time-sampling data collection procedure used, the events being observed must be fairly stable and occur reasonably frequently if the observations are to reflect the pupil's capabilities accurately.

Figure 2–6

Time Sample Data in a Percentage Graph

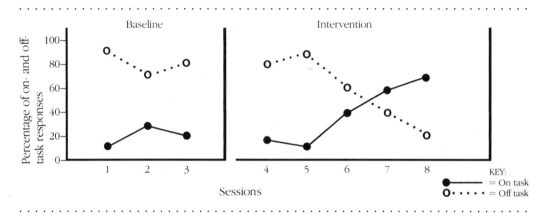

Category Sampling. In many instances, the classroom teacher will be interested in learning more about a pupil's competency in a particular area. For example, is the child exhibiting responsible social behavior, self-initiated behavior, appropriate group work behavior, or aggression towards others? The teacher is then confronted with the problem of clearly specifying which of the many possible skill behaviors in the area of interest to observe. In this system of observation, it is often helpful to describe not only instances of the behavior but also "noninstances" of it. For example, a noninstance of out-of-seat behavior would be staying in-seat for a designated period of time. This will greatly increase accuracy in the data-recording process.

Another procedural consideration for category sampling is the establishment of the most appropriate time to obtain a representative sample. It may be practical to schedule observation sessions for some behaviors in the category but not for others. For instance, it would not be logical to schedule observation sessions for "exhibiting aggression," but they might be useful for "exhibiting appropriate group work behavior." Aggression would have to be observed and recorded as it occurred.

The numerous categorical rating forms and checklists that are available can be of great help to teachers using this form of data collection. Several of these are described in later chapters. It is important that the teacher determine how clear an instrument's items are and how well it covers the behaviors of concern.

Task Analysis as an Assessment Procedure

Although it is more often used as an instructional procedure, task analysis has significant potential as an assessment tool as well. Many instructional target skills are fairly complex, involving several steps, and most teachers find task analysis an effective and easy tool for accurately assessing a pupil's ability to perform such skills. Task analysis is particularly well suited to category sampling.

Procedural Task Analysis. Task analysis means breaking a target skill or instructional task into its most basic components. For a relatively simple task like using a pair of scissors, this may involve listing all of the substeps required to complete the task. For example: Step One: Insert thumb in upper hole of scissors handle. Step Two: Insert index finger and middle finger in lower hole of scissors handle. Step Three: Bend finger to grasp scissors handles. Step Four: Move thumb away from index and middle fingers to open scissors. Step Five: Move thumb toward index and middle fingers to close scissors. This outlining of the essential procedures required to complete a task in their order of occurrence is known as "procedural task analysis."

Hierarchical Task Analysis. The teacher may analyze many higher-order skills, such as sequencing the numbers one through five, by listing substeps leading up to the successful completion of the skill. For example: Step One: Match numbers one through five in correct sequence to a number line. Step Two: Order numbers one and two correctly without a model. Step Three: Order numbers one, two, and three correctly without a model; and so on through the number five. This type of task analysis is referred to as "hierarchical," and it is quite effective in determining the component steps involved in performing complex academic skills that do not have readily apparent stages.

Most tasks can be broken down into any number of substeps. How many steps are required will vary depending on the complexity of the task involved and the pupil's abilities. Obviously, a more complex task will contain a greater number of component parts. In order for a student with a moderate or severe learning handicap to perform a task successfully, it may have to be broken down into very small, discrete steps. A pupil with a mild learning handicap may meet criterion on the same task using far fewer steps.

Classroom Assessment. A teacher can task analyze a target skill by watching someone else complete the task or by completing it themselves. The teacher should note each step as it is performed. By repeating this process or observing several different persons perform the skill, the teacher can fairly accurately determine and order its steps.

Once a target skill has been task analyzed into its component parts, the teacher may use them as a checklist with which to assess pupil performance. By carefully noting the pupil's performance on each step of the task, the teacher can pinpoint places where the pupil is experiencing difficulty as well as those in which he or she is demonstrating proficiency. This type of assessment provides data that indicate an appropriate starting point for teaching the target skill.

Prerequisites to Task Analysis. The teacher should specify the prerequisite skills for the initial step of the task-analyzed skill. If assessment shows the pupil is

Figure 2–7

Baseline Data Collection Chart Using Task Analysis

Session (Note: Date each session)

Task analysis steps		1	2	3	4	5	6	7	8	9	10
	1										
	2										
	3										
	4										
	5										
	6										
	7										
	8										
	9										
	10										

Comments:

Name of observer: _____

not capable of consistent and appropriate responses at the entry step, then the teacher should begin instruction with the prerequisite skills. This will of course require a task analysis of each of those skills.

An example of a task analysis used for a checklist is provided in Figures 2–7 and 2–8. In this illustration, the task of cutting a six-inch line is analyzed and placed on a data collection grid. A teacher can use this type of task analysis checklist by observing a pupil attempt each step of the task and noting its successful completion as well as other pertinent data, such as levels of assistance the pupil needs at various stages. A detailed assessment such as this provides precise performance data that increase the probability that subsequent instruction in the task will be successful. The checklist may also be used for posttesting mastery of instructional programming as well as for daily monitoring of instruction. Chapters 8, "Assess-

Figure 2–8

Example of a Procedural Task Analysis. Use As A Baseline Performance Checklist.

. . . .

Task: Using regular right-handed scissors, pupil will cut along a six-inch line drawn in black on a white sheet of paper.

Prerequisites: 1. Ability to attend to teacher for verbal instruction.
2. Vision to discriminate six-inch black line on white paper.
3. Ability to move thumb in opposition to middle and index fingers.

Criterion: None stated; will be grounded on baseline performance data.

Task Analysis:

1. Put thumb of dominent hand in upper hole of scissors handle.
2. Put index and middle fingers of dominant hand in lower hole of scissors handle.
3. Bend fingers around scissors handle.
4. Pick up paper with nondominant hand.
5. Move thumb up and away from index and middle fingers to open scissors.
6. Place opened scissors in line with line on paper.
7. Move thumb of dominant hand down toward middle and index fingers of same hand, closing scissors on paper.
8. Repeat step 5 and move scissors forward.
9. Repeat steps 6, 7, and 8.
10. Repeat steps 5, 6, 7, and 8 until line is cut.

. . . .

ment of the Trainable Handicapped Learner," and 9, "Assessment of the Profoundly Handicapped Pupil," elaborate the use of task analysis for assessment in classroom settings.

Levels of Assistance. In developing instructional programs, teachers are required to train pupils in entirely new behaviors or to refine and expand existing ones. To accomplish this, it is often necessary to assist the student in acquiring new response patterns. A hierarchy of forms of assistance has evolved. The forms range from very active teacher involvement to noninvolvement, or appropriate independent functioning by the pupil. The five levels of assistance described below are often used by the special education classroom teacher.

Complete physical prompting occurs when the teacher moves the student through a complete response cycle. For example, in a buttoning task, the teacher gives the command "Put the button through the hole," and then physically assists the pupil's fingers in manipulating the button through the designated hole.

Partial physical prompting is required when the student can complete only part of a response independently. The portion that the student can finish may or may not be at the beginning. Observation will determine at what point intervention

Figure 2–9

Levels-of-Assistance Data Recording Sheet

Student: _James Smith_   Code: Physical prompt = P
Verbal cue = V
Observer: _Ms. Johnson_   Modeling = M
Independent = I
Condition: _Sight word reading_

Date	Start/Stop	Cue(s)	Trial									
			1	2	3	4	5	6	7	8	9	10
2/25	9:45/10:15	stop ladies men caution exit	PM	M	V	VM	V	V	I	I	I	I
			P	P	PM	M	M	M	VM	VM	V	I
			V	V	M	I	I	I	I	I	I	I
			P	P	P	P	PV	PM	M	M	V	I
			P	P	PV	V	V	V	V	V	M	M

Summary:	2/25	x = I
	median	= P
	mode	= I

Comments: 2/25 Trouble maintaining attending

and assistance are appropriate, and careful attention is essential to maintaining errorless programming.

Verbal cuing is used when a pupil has demonstrated a correct response on an intermittent basis but still needs direction from the teacher. Using the buttoning example, it may not be necessary to assist the child physically to put the button through the hole; instead, the teacher may start the response by verbally cuing the pupil — "Now, put the button in the hole."

Modeling and imitation are teaching techniques that can reinforce and help generalize an acquired skill or behavior. For example, once the pupil has successfully acquired buttoning using a buttoning board, the teacher may then develop a program to generalize that skill to actual clothing.

Independent responding occurs when a pupil has demonstrated acquisition of the target response or behavior. The teacher can then begin the process of transferring the skill to other settings, people, and circumstances. To use the buttoning example again, the pupil will next be introduced systematically to buttons of various sizes, shapes, colors, and locations on clothing.

The importance of levels-of-assistance data for the classroom teacher is that it provides an accurate portrayal of the pupil's performance requirements. The data can be collected fairly easily through the development of symbols for the various entries (for example, vc = verbal cue, + = independent response) used during the data-collection periods. Without such data, it is very difficult for a person not thoroughly familiar with a pupil to know what level of instructional assistance is needed and what level of performance ought to be expected. Figure 2–9 illustrates a levels-of-assistance data-collection system and a simplified data encoding procedure.

Assessment of Learning Style

A direct corollary to assessing the levels of assistance a pupil may benefit from is the determination of his or her preferred learning style. The term has been defined in various ways, but for the special educator, Dunn's (1983) conceptualization of learning style as the "way individuals concentrate on, absorb, and retain new or difficult information or skills" (p. 496) seems most helpful. It should also be noted that learning style does not refer to the methods or techniques used to facilitate instruction.

Assessment of learning style is often overlooked by educators in general. In special education, teachers of gifted and talented pupils have found that determining a child's learning style can be beneficial to instructional planning (Dunn and Price, 1980; Griggs, 1984; Price, Dunn, Dunn, and Griggs, 1981; and Stewart, 1981). This kind of data ought to be an integral part of the individualized prescriptive process all special education teachers use for instructing pupils exhibiting a variety of handicapping conditions. Special educators can draw from the work of Charles (1976), Dunn (1983), Dunn and Dunn (1978), and Griggs (1984), who have developed strategies for assessing individual styles of learning, for developing individualized prescriptive instruction, and for counseling students.

Of particular interest to special educators is the work of Dunn (1983), who has described a process for analyzing learning style as it relates to the full spectrum of special education pupils' needs. The learning environment, according to Dunn, can be divided into five basic components: environmental, emotional, social, physical, and psychological. These elements are further subdivided into twenty-one interacting components that have a significant impact on the way a pupil behaves in the learning environment. Space limitations will not permit us to describe all the components; however, in the remainder of this section, we will discuss the five basic elements as they relate to developmental disabilities and learning disorders.

Environmental Elements

This component is made up of aspects of the classroom's physical environment that affect the pupil's senses and his requirements for physical structure. Four essential components are generally included in this element: lighting, temperature, sound, and physical layout or design of the learning environment. In most classrooms, the teacher can modify these factors to a limited degree, but they cannot be modified to meet all individual preferences. Temperature and lighting are particularly difficult to alter for only portions of the classroom. Sound may be adjusted through auditory blocking devices such as headphones, but the overall acoustic quality of a classroom is difficult to alter significantly.

Often the physical layout of a classroom can be modified through the placement of desks, learning centers, rest and leisure areas, and so on. By using individual carrels and room partitions, the teacher is generally able to provide considerable individual attention and can accommodate a pupil's preference for working alone or in a large group or a small one. The experienced special educator is aware that many pupils are susceptible to distraction by and perservation to irrelevant stimuli in the environment. Each pupil's sensory-environmental requirements must be known in order for effective, efficient instruction to be carried out and maintained. Through the use of a systematic data-collection method as part of the teacher's regular routine, environmental requirements of individual pupils can be met without sacrificing any aspect of instruction or radically altering the physical characteristics of the room.

Emotional Elements

Motivation, persistence, responsibility, and instructional structure or design are critical to prescriptive individualized instruction. These four elements make up the characteristic ways in which a pupil interacts with the learning environment.

Motivation. The term "motivation" as used here is synonymous with reward or reinforcement hierarchy, a concept well established as integral to special education programming. Without a thorough, up-to-date knowledge of how a pupil may respond to consequences, the teacher will often be unable to reward appropriate behavior. The effects of satiation and changes in performance requirements will alter a child's response. For example, a student may no longer need tangible rewards such as tokens, but be able to sustain performance with verbal praise. The teacher can determine what motivates a pupil by noting a pupil's selection among options given after appropriate work or behavior. By asking pupils to rank-order their favorite reward, the teacher can also determine a fairly accurate reinforcer hierarchy. Such a hierarchy can also be obtained by observing the effects of various reinforcers on the pupil's behavior. Soliciting this information from parents and former teachers can also be quite helpful. Figure 2–10 outlines two different reinforcer hierarchies.

Persistence. A pupil's ability to stay on task is often a critical factor in learning problems ranging from mild learning disabilities and behavior disorders to severe learning problems. The ability to persevere with minimal supervision until the work period is over or the task is completed is often a major long-term goal of IEPs. By using duration and latency data-collection procedures, the teacher can determine a pupil's task persistence prior to specific intervention. Subsequent in-

Figure 2–10

Two Samples of Reinforcer Hierarchies

. . . .

Emily is an eight-year-old student in an elementary TMH classroom. Her reinforcers are listed from the most to the least reinforcing.

Most reinforcing	raisins
	hugs
	tickles
	potato chips
Least reinforcing	happy faces on her work

Chad is a seventeen-year-old student in a secondary TMH classroom. His reinforcers, from most to least reinforcing, are:

Most reinforcing	a battery-operated miniature baseball game
	verbal praise
	running errands for the teacher
	free time
Least reinforcing	handshakes

. . . .

struction can then be designed to shape the pupil's persistence skills to more appropriate levels or rates.

Responsibility. Another performance area that often comprises a significant part of special education instructional programming is instruction in responsibility. Independent functioning in one's community may depend upon being able to exhibit consistently responsible behavior. Special education programming typically involves some aspect of such behavior. For example, instruction will foster the abilities to complete work on time with minimal supervision, to avoid interfering with others in the immediate work setting, to respect the property of others, to seek help when unsure of an appropriate response, and to interact cooperatively in group or social settings. The teacher is ultimately responsible for assessing each pupil's responsibility skills and for designing instructional programs that will enhance and expand proficiency in these areas.

Structure. As used here, "structure" refers to the establishment of specific performance rules for working on and completing assignments. The teacher often sets these conditions, but in many instances the work itself dictates the structure. For example, completing a math problem may require that others in the class not interrupt or otherwise bother a pupil. Another example of structure is rules the teacher establishes for classroom behavior, such as, "Raise your hand to ask a question," or, "All worksheets are due at the end of the class period." Structure in the learning environment limits the number of options available to a pupil and imposes a mode of learning, responding, or demonstrating achievement (Dunn and

Dunn, 1978). Each pupil's structural requirements may be unique. Moreover, pupils' preferences and needs for structure change as they acquire new skills.

It is critical that the teacher recognize individual performance requirements that involve structure. For example, pupils with handicapping conditions have widely varying response times. If a child is not provided with enough time to respond, it may be incorrectly assumed that he or she is unable to respond. Through the use of latency data collection the teacher can determine the pupil's requirements and use them as the basis for later instructional program design.

The teacher must maintain an ongoing data-collection system that will document pupils' preferences for instructional and learning environment structure. Appropriate and timely changes in structure can be very effective in facilitating a pupil's movement to less restrictive learning environments and more independent general functioning in the school, home, and community.

Sociological Elements

The sociological elements refers to a pupil's preferences regarding interaction with others in the learning environment. In special education, there is not one formula that will ensure success. In order for effective instruction to be sustained, the classroom teacher must group pupils according to their individual preferences as well as their skills. Grouping simply by ability level is often not the most effective procedure; in many instances it is done simply for expediency.

The teacher can often determine the most effective grouping of pupils by observing with whom they choose to work. Social preference may be utilized to influence instructional programming, and it can be incorporated into the pupil's reinforcement hierarchy. In the special education learning environment, where many pupils have a long history of school failure and frustration in addition to their developmental and behavioral handicaps, prescriptive grouping is a critical component of individualized instructional implementation.

Physical Elements

The physical elements that influence a pupil's learning style include perceptual strengths (auditory, visual, tactile/kinesthetic), food intake requirements, internal timetable, and mobility preferences.

Chapters 9, "Assessment of the Profoundly Handicapped Pupil," and 10, "Assessment of the Physically Handicapped," discuss in depth the assessment of perceptual and mobility elements in the learning environment, while Chapter 7, "Assessment of the Mildly Handicapped Learner," discusses perceptual deficits as they relate to problems in the classroom. In addition to assessment data, further valuable information can be found in the pupil's medical and health records.

It has become fairly standard practice in special education to make provisions for instructional programming and learning environment design to accommodate pupils with a wide variety of perceptual strengths and deficits. Teachers must be prepared to use multisensory instructional approaches as well as strategies that are designed to expand or to limit sensory-perceptual input.

Food Intake. Dunn (1983) observed that many individuals appear to need food when they are expending energy in problem solving or as a vehicle to break the tension that often accompanies even short periods of concentration. The use of appropriate foods as reinforcers for successful work has become an accepted facet of the special education classroom.

Like most people, pupils have definite food preferences. If, for whatever reason, eating is to occur in the classroom, the teacher must determine the pupil's preferences and limitations or restrictions. One obvious way to do this is to ask the pupils, their parents, and their former teachers. Because many pupils in special education have a wide range of metabolic, digestive, circulatory, respiratory, and allergic impairments and disabilities, it is quite important to investigate before prescribing. The special education teacher must be careful to avoid foods that are off limits to the pupil because they are contraindicated by prescribed medications.

The use of foods in the classroom may run contrary to established school system policy. The teacher in special education must always be careful not to create a learning environment that other pupils or school personnel might misunderstand.

Time. In the context of learning-style preference, "time" refers to when during the day a pupil is consistently most effective. By determining when a pupil performs not just productively but efficiently, with minimal structural requirements and teacher supervision, the teacher can make better use of limited class time. Temporal preferences can be fairly easily determined through systematically observing the pupil's work in class, and asking parents, the pupil, and former teachers.

Psychological Elements

The psychological elements Dunn (1983) refers to are global versus analytical learning-style preferences, central nervous system–determined factors, and impulsivity versus reflectivity in interpersonal style. All characterize the preferred modes of interaction that individuals may exhibit, which for the most part are not readily modifiable. The classroom teacher must learn to recognize these characteristics if effective instruction is to occur and be maintained.

Global versus Analytical. This learning style preference is the phenomenon whereby some pupils learn more efficiently if instruction is closely sequenced, as in the task analysis described earlier, while by contrast, others, are more productive if a global approach is used that includes a rationale for the task at hand, its meaning, and perhaps its uses, with illustrations and examples. The second style is more typical of the gifted or talented pupil in special education (see Chapter 11). Dunn

(1983) cautions that teachers who attempt to change these styles or intermix them will not generally experience significant success.

Central Nervous System Preferences. Pupils often exhibit an apparent preference for the use of the right or left hemisphere of the brain in learning (Dunn, Cavanaugh, Eberle, and Zenhausern, 1982). For example, Dunn (1983) notes that right-hemisphere–preferenced pupils "(a) are less bothered by sound when studying, (b) prefer dim illumination, (c) require an informal design, (d) are less motivated [in school] than lefts, (e) are less persistent, (f) prefer learning with peers, (g) prefer tactile to auditory or visual stimulation — even at the high school levels" (p. 500).

Impulsivity versus Reflectivity. Pupils may also exhibit a preference for impulsive verbal interaction (calling out an answer without being asked) as compared to one for not interacting verbally with the teacher or others in the classroom even though competent to do so. Classroom teachers will find that the reflective student does not respond well to verbal class participation. The verbally impulsive student will tend to be more productive in that environment, but may inadvertently acquire educationally, socially, and vocationally inappropriate behaviors. Assessment of this preference by teachers of the moderately and severely developmentally retarded (see Chapters 8 and 9) may be difficult because these classifications typically include a significant number of nonverbal pupils.

Classroom Assessment of Learning Style

At least three commercially available learning-style assessment devices can readily be used with minimal interference in the regular classroom routine: the Learning Style Identification Scale (Malcom, Lutz, and Hoeltke, 1981); the Learning Style Inventory of Dunn, Dunn, and Price (1979); and the Learning Style Inventory of Renzulli and Smith (1978a).

The Learning Style Inventory, or LSI (Dunn, Dunn, and Price, 1979), appears to have had sufficient research validation to warrant its use in a wide variety of special education settings. By assessing preferences across the 21 elements described above, it provides a comprehensive analysis of the conditions that pupils in grades 3 through 12 prefer in classroom settings. A two-year study completed by the National Center for Research in Vocational Education at Ohio State University found the LSI to be impressive in its reliability and both its construct and its face validity (Kirby, 1982). (Reliability and validity are defined and described in Chapter 3, "Basic Principles of Measurement and Test Development.") Predictive validity for the LSI has been documented by Krimsky (1982), Lynch (1981), Pizzo (1981), and Shea (1983).

It requires approximately 30 to 40 minutes to complete the LSI. To facilitate its interpretation, a "consistency key" is provided to help determine how accurately each respondent has answered the questions. A primary version (for grades 1 and

2) of the LSI has been developed by Perrin (1982). Reliability and validity estimates have not yet been established for this inventory.

Curriculum-Based Assessment

Much attention has been focused lately on the use of curriculum-based assessment (CBA), as a means of establishing the student's instructional needs on the basis of his or her ongoing performance in daily skills learning. Because the assessment is tied into curriculum content, it allows the teacher to match instruction to a student's current abilities and pinpoints areas where curriculum adaptations or modifications are needed. Unlike many other types of educational assessment, such as I.Q. tests, CBA provides information that is immediately relevant to instructional programming. It helps to determine where a student is functioning in relation to expected, curriculum-based criteria, and that information can be used to develop a program within a given curriculum (Tucker, 1985).

Components of CBA

Systematic evaluation of a student's performance of instructional activities is a critical diagnostic tool. Analyzing errors while building on established skills facilitates effective program planning. By helping to match the demands of instructional activities for each specific task to a student's skills, curriculum-based assessment can increase the likelihood of success. "The key to using this CBA strategy is the ability to identify and control task difficulty across various curricular assignments relative to each student's needs" (Gickling and Thompson, 1985, p. 211). Because in most curricula new skills build upon previously acquired ones, future learning difficulties can be reduced by determining which skills a student has mastered before beginning instruction.

Curriculum-based assessment is closely tied to classroom performance, and it can easily be translated into instructional programs. The very specific information it provides can help determine where to begin an instructional sequence for each student.

Implementing CBA

Blankenship (1985) has outlined the steps in implementing a curriculum-based assessment model. First, assessment procedures are developed for each skill area: component skills are listed, an objective is written for each skill, and means of testing each objective are prepared. The assessment is then administered before instruction begins. Analysis of the results will determine which students have already mastered the skill in question, which ones demonstrate competency in the established prerequisites and are ready to begin instruction, and which ones have not mastered the prerequisite skills. Instruction for each student is based on these data.

After instruction has been completed, the assessment is readministered to determine which students have now mastered the skill, which ones are demonstrating progress but need further work, and which ones are experiencing difficulty and will need to have the instructional sequence modified. This process is repeated for each student until mastery is demonstrated. Reassessing the mastered skill periodically throughout the year will help establish its long-term retention.

Application of CBA to the Five-Level Assessment Model

Curriculum-based assessment is applicable across all the levels of the assessment model presented in Chapter 1. The curriculum content provides a focus for all assessment activity. Marston, Tindal, and Deno (1982) suggest that the use of a common database for all five levels of assessment would increase efficiency, improve communication, and be more closely tied to skill areas involved in instruction.

Screening, Level One, has been defined by Salvia and Ysseldyke (1985) as the process of identifying "students who are sufficiently different from their age-mates that they require special attention" (p. 14). By comparing the current skill level of a particular student, as determined by CBA, to that of a normative sample of peers, it is possible to pinpoint students who warrant further assessment. Chapter 3 includes a detailed discussion of establishing normative samples. Marston, Mirkin, and Deno (1984) have suggested that curriculum-based assessment may help reduce bias in assessment used for screening and for determining eligibility for services.

By focusing on specific curriculum content, the information derived from this type of assessment is easily translated into specific program goals for use in an IEP. Systematic monitoring and program evaluation are built into the process.

A Curriculum-Based Assessment Model. The Montevideo Individualized Prescriptive Instructional Management System (MIPIM) is a computer-managed CBA model that covers all five levels of assessment and is currently being used in the elementary school program in Montevideo, Minnesota, to assess math and reading skills (Peterson, Heistad, Peterson, and Reynolds, 1985). Information collected every three weeks establishes which skill unit each student is currently working on in both content areas. The students in each grade level are rank-ordered by the number of skill units they have completed. A computer printout indicates the median number of units completed in each grade level and gives each student's standing. A student who falls below the 20th percentile is referred for further evaluation. If a need is indicated, such students receive remedial or special educational services. Progress norms have been gauged by computing the median number of days required to complete each skill unit, and on this basis, target dates for completion of specific program goals are established. Periodic evaluation of program data provides information on students' mastery of skill units and permits evaluation of program placement. Chapter 12 contains a more detailed discussion of the use of computers in assessment and instruction management.

Other programs using a curriculum-based assessment model have developed various criteria for determining the need for further assessment or eligibility for special educational services; among these criteria is a two-year discrepancy between a student's demonstrated skills and those of his or her peers (Marston and Magnusson, 1985).

Use in Various Skill Areas.   Curriculum-based assessment is applicable in many skill areas, including reading, math, spelling, and written expression (Marston and Magnusson, 1985). A thorough discussion of curriculum-based assessment in these areas with mildly handicapped learners is included in Chapter 7.

The Total Special Education System (TSES), developed by the Pine County Special Education Cooperative, includes procedures for across-the-board use. It focuses on discrepancies between students' performance and specific environmental demands in such areas as academics, social skills, vocational skills, and mainstreamed placement skills (Germann and Tindal, 1985). Direct observation of students in natural environments helps identify discrepancies in their behavior and current skill levels. Criteria have been established to determine eligibility for a continuum of services ranging from consultation in the regular classroom to residential treatment. The degree of discrepancy between an individual student's behavior and the established median in that student's own environment helps to determine the level of services needed, establish program goals, and define mastery criteria. Refer to Chapter 6 for a complete discussion of behavioral-ecological assessment.

Prereferral Intervention.   More attention has been addressed recently to strategies that the regular classroom teacher can use to alleviate behavioral and academic difficulties before making a formal referral. Because it is so closely tied to classroom activities, a curriculum-based assessment is a prime prereferral intervention strategy. The state of Louisiana now requires that a curriculum-based assessment of any student suspected of having a mild handicap be conducted before a formal referral is initiated. This procedure is expected to help determine whether the problems exhibited are related to a mildly handicapping condition or to the curriculum (Tucker, 1985).

The use of curriculum-based assessment is relatively new, and much work still needs to be done in this area. CBA does, however, show great promise in assessment of student progress, in screening, and in monitoring and evaluating instructional programs.

Now that we have examined various methods used to collect information, we can go on to discuss the major issues surrounding the use of assessment and data-gathering procedures. Where appropriate, the five-level model described in Chapter 1 will be incorporated into the discussion.

Legal and Ethical Issues in Classroom Assessment

The field of special education is rampant with legal and ethical issues ranging from labeling and classification to civil rights to parental rights to legislative mandates. Within the area of assessment in the classroom, the major issues seem to revolve around these general themes: teacher competence; IEP requirements; the quality of assessment procedures and decisions regarding their use; nondiscriminatory assessment materials and procedures; and parental involvement in the assessment process. Issues specific to each special education classification area concern assessment of their respective pupil populations and settings for service delivery; these will be dealt with in Part III, "Categorical Assessment Considerations." The remainder of this section will be devoted to describing the basic issues in special education classroom assessment.

Teacher Competence and IEP Requirements

The first two basic issues will be discussed together as they are closely interrelated. Traditionally, classroom teachers have not been expected to perform their own assessment activities except in documenting pupils' mastery of instructional programs. This was usually accomplished through permanent products — physical evidence — or some other data-collection procedure that facilitated the determination of a grade. In special education, particularly after the passage of P.L. 94–142 in 1975, the role of the classroom teacher in assessment activities changed significantly, and the teacher became an active member of a legally mandated multidisciplinary team. In this capacity, the teacher is involved in making decisions about a pupil's eligibility, placement, instruction, and periodic evaluation.

Training as a Prerequisite.   The vast majority of teachers can comprehend an assessment instrument's administration manual, but this ability alone will not enable them competently to administer the instrument and interpret the resultant data. They must receive specific training in appropriate assessment and data-collection procedures. One significant benefit of the teacher's involvement in a team of professionals is that it tends to increase the probability that the pupil will receive a high-quality, representative, unbiased, nondiscriminatory assessment. Because of their high rate of direct contact with pupils, classroom teachers trained in assessment and direct-observation data collection can add significantly to the process and eventual program prescription in the form of an IEP.

Issues Related to the IEP.   As mandated by P.L. 94–142, within 30 days after a pupil has been determined to be handicapped and therefore eligible for special education, an IEP must be developed. This is done by a team that typically includes a member of the school system's administration to supervise and conduct the meeting, the teacher receiving the pupil, one or both parents or the legal guardian, the student if appropriate (if he or she can comprehend meeting and add to it), and a member of the team that completed the eligibility-determination assessment or someone familiar with the team's procedure and conclusions.

Components of an IEP.   Section 121a.346 of P.L. 94–142 specifies that an IEP contain the following:

1. A statement of the child's present levels of educational performance.
2. A statement of annual goals, including short-term instructional objectives.
3. A statement of the specific special education and related services to be provided to the child and of the extent to which the child will be able to participate in regular education programs.
4. The projected date for initiation of services and the anticipated duration of the services.
5. Appropriate objective criteria and evaluation procedures and schedules for determining, on at least an annual basis, whether the short-term instructional objectives are being met.

It is quite evident that the classroom teacher must be an active participant in the data-collection and assessment process. No other professional will be as responsible for meeting the conditions of the IEP. This participation and responsibility require a highly trained person who, in addition to being an effective instructor, must also be competent in the selection, administration, and interpretation of assessments. The special education teacher must also have a background in working with other professionals involved in the IEP process. This requires training that goes well beyond that traditionally expected of classroom teachers.

Issues Related to the Quality of Assessment Procedures

It is one thing to know that you will be an active participant in data collection and assessment regarding pupils in your classroom; it may be another to know what to do, which procedure to use, and what falls outside of your responsibility. For many teachers and school administrators, these are serious problems that may affect the quality of the assessment process.

Selection of Assessment Instrument or Procedures.   In most cases, the classroom teacher will be involved in assessment at Levels Three, Four, and Five (see Table 1–1). Bailey and Wolery (1984) have developed a decision-making system (Figure 2-11) that the classroom teacher may find useful in deciding where he or she currently is in the assessment process and what questions need to be answered before moving to the next step. With the exception of those involving screening, diagnosis, and setting up an IEP-related team meeting (for which the classroom teacher is seldom solely responsible), all of the remaining steps in Figure 2–11 involve major decisions on the part of the teacher. The teacher's ability to make these decisions systematically and consistently and to answer the questions outlined in Figure 2–11 affects the quality of assessment in the classroom.

If a direct-observation data-collection procedure (as discussed earlier in this chapter) rather than an assessment instrument is selected for use, the teacher will need to make critical decisions regarding that selection. Figure 2–12 outlines a

Figure 2–11

Steps in the Assessment Process

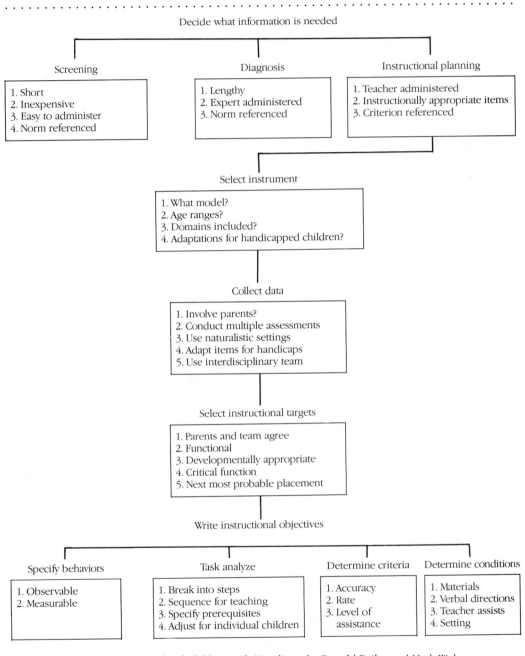

Decide what information is needed

Screening

1. Short
2. Inexpensive
3. Easy to administer
4. Norm referenced

Diagnosis

1. Lengthy
2. Expert administered
3. Norm referenced

Instructional planning

1. Teacher administered
2. Instructionally appropriate items
3. Criterion referenced

Select instrument

1. What model?
2. Age ranges?
3. Domains included?
4. Adaptations for handicapped children?

Collect data

1. Involve parents?
2. Conduct multiple assessments
3. Use naturalistic settings
4. Adapt items for handicaps
5. Use interdisciplinary team

Select instructional targets

1. Parents and team agree
2. Functional
3. Developmentally appropriate
4. Critical function
5. Next most probable placement

Write instructional objectives

Specify behaviors

1. Observable
2. Measurable

Task analyze

1. Break into steps
2. Sequence for teaching
3. Specify prerequisites
4. Adjust for individual children

Determine criteria

1. Accuracy
2. Rate
3. Level of
   assistance

Determine conditions

1. Materials
2. Verbal directions
3. Teacher assists
4. Setting

From *Teaching Infant and Preschool Children with Handicaps* by Donald Bailey and Mark Wolery, p. 45. Copyright © 1984. Reprinted with permission of the publisher, Charles E. Merrill Publishing Company.

Figure 2–12

Data-Collection Procedure Selection System

. . . .

If The Student Response Is:

1. | A permanent product | ◀ If yes, use ▶

Direct measurement
of product
A. 96 correct
B. 96 error
C. Predetermined
   qualitative
   criterion

If NO, use direct observation and assessment procedures to
determine which of the response patterns or types matches
current situation ▼

Responding at high rate, and time to observe
and record no problem   If yes, use ▶ Time sampling
procedure

▼

Short in duration and interested in rate
or frequency   If yes, use ▶ Event recording

If no, ▼

Continuous or very rapid, and teacher interested in
length of occurrence   If yes, use ▶ Duration recording

If no, ▼

Occurring almost continuously or at a high rate, and
teacher interested in both duration and frequency   If yes, use ▶ Interval recording

If no, ▼

Emitted after a specific cue or stimulus event, and
teacher interested in length of time between specific
stimulus and response   If yes, use ▶ Latency recording

If no, ▼

Indicative of accuracy or mastery, and teacher is
interested in level correct or incorrect   If yes, use ▶ Percent recording

If no, ▼

Emitted in conjunction with a physical prompt
or verbal cue card: teacher is interested in level of
of assistance needed to maintain present level of
responding   If yes, use ▶ Levels-of-assistance
recording

. . . .

decision system developed by Berdine and Cegelka (1980) that may prove useful in direct-observation data-collection procedure selection.

Observer and Procedural Biases.   Teachers using direct-observation procedures for data collection will need to be constantly guarding against both observer and procedural bias. The many advantages of direct-observation procedures for classroom use can easily deflect a teacher's attention from the negative effect his or her own biases may have on a pupil's performance. Let us look at five forms of bias that often result in observer errors. All classroom teachers need to be aware of potential biases and to control for them as much as possible.

The **halo effect** refers to the tendency consistently to over- or underrate a pupil's performance on the basis of an initial impression of or a preconceived belief about that pupil. This type of bias shows up most often in rating scales that permit subjective judgments rather than absolute ratings (behavior did or did not occur). Anecdotal data-recording procedures also tend to be influenced by the recorder's impressions or opinions (Cartwright and Cartwright, 1974). **Response-set errors** result from an observer's tendency to rate pupil performance as above average, average, or below average (high, middle, or low). These errors, too, are quite often associated with the use of either rating scales or anecdotal recording procedures. Generally, four forms of response-set error can occur:

1. *Generosity errors* are those that typically rate all pupils too high.
2. *Central tendency errors* are made by observers who almost always rate a pupil's behavior as being somewhere in between high and low, regardless of how the pupil actually behaves.
3. *Severity errors* occur when the observer tends to rate a pupil's behavior too low. Cartwright and Cartwright (1974) note that generosity errors are more common than severity errors.
4. *Logic errors* are made when the observer assumes that two separate behaviors are somehow related and therefore rates them identically. For example, if a teacher knows that a pupil is particularly polite and well behaved with teachers and adults, there may be a tendency to assume that this behavior is carried over into deportment in general, and the pupil's ratings may be elevated in all aspects of interpersonal behavior.

One additional error that can occur is **observee bias.** According to Gay (1985, p. 117), this refers to the "phenomenon whereby persons being observed behave atypically simply because they are being observed." Teachers can control for this form of bias and concomitant errors to a great extent by observing without actually collecting any data for a few sessions to accustom the pupil to being observed and by obtaining actual direct-observation data in as unobtrusive a manner as possible.

Teachers can best control for the biases and errors described above by making data collection and observation a routine part of the class, practicing the procedures to assure efficient, effective, unobtrusive use, and training all ancillary personnel assisting in direct-observation data collection. Additional suggestions for controlling for measurement errors are provided in Chapter 3, "Basic Principles of Measurement and Test Development."

P.L. 94–142 Requirements Regarding Quality. In addition to the professional decision-making factors related to quality of assessment, P.L. 94–142 prescribes specific aspects of the assessment process to help insure quality. Section 121a.532 contains the following provisions directly related to the quality of assessment:

1. Tests and other evaluation materials
    a. Are provided and administered in the child's language or other mode of communication, unless it is clearly not feasible to do so;
    b. Have been validated for the specified purpose for which they are used;
    c. Are administered by trained personnel in conformance with instructions from the producer.
2. Tests and other evaluation materials include those tailored to assess specific areas of educational need and not merely those which are designed to provide a single general intelligence quotient;
3. Tests are selected and administered so as best to ensure that when a test is administered to a child with impaired sensory, manual, or speaking skills, the test results accurately reflect the child's aptitude or achievement level or whatever other factor the test purports to measure, rather than reflecting the child's impaired sensory, manual, or speaking skills (except where those skills are the factors which the test purports to measure).
4. No single procedure is used as the sole criterion for determining an appropriate educational program for a child;
5. The evaluation is made by a multidisciplinary team or group of persons, including at least one teacher or other specialist with knowledge in this area of suspected disability.
6. The child is assessed in all areas related to the suspected disability, including, where appropriate, health, vision, hearing, social, and emotional status, general intelligence, academic performance, communicative status, and motor disabilities.

Considerable attention has been given to insuring the quality of the assessment process by legislators, educators, and advocacy groups representing the civil rights of persons with handicapping conditions. Ultimately, a large measure of the quality that goes into the assessment process and is translated into an IEP and subsequently into instructional programs is dependent upon the classroom teacher.

Issues Relating to Nondiscrimination

Ethnic and cultural factors have become a significant issue in all areas of education. With the passage of P.L. 94–142, special educators have become particularly sensitive to individual differences that may be attributed to gender, culture, subculture, or ethnic background. This federal law specifically directs special educators to assure that pupils are not assessed as handicapped and therefore eligible for special education services as a result of gender, language, cultural, or ethnic factors.

"Nondiscriminatory measurement" as used here refers to assessment and testing procedures that are not biased in any manner regarding a pupil's gender, race, culture, or language. Such measurement will result in similar, not identical, performance distributions or scores for all cultural groups regardless of their languages, dialects, value systems, information resources, and learning strategies (Alley and Foster, 1978).

Cultural Pluralism in Special Education. The fact that our student populations are made up of an ever-increasing number of cultural groups is fairly well accepted. Not so well known to the lay population is the fact that developmental disabilities and impairments are not more prevalent in any particular culture or ethnic group than in another. Special education classifications cover a representative mixture of the cultural groups that constitute American society. Killalea Associates (1980) reported at the conclusion of an extensive study for the Office of Civil Rights of forty million pupils that 15.7 percent were black and 6.7 percent were Hispanic. Within the special education classifications of educable mentally retarded, trainable mentally retarded, seriously emotionally disturbed, and gifted, blacks constituted over 38, 27, 24, and 10 percent respectively.

Blackhurst (1985) notes that the Office of Civil Rights study indicated that Hispanic groups' representation in special education classifications reflected their percentage in the general population. On a regional basis, however, Hispanic pupils are disproportionately represented among the educable mentally retarded and the gifted.

P.L. 94–142 Safeguards. Section 121a.530b of P.L. 94–142 stipulates that assessment materials and procedures must not discriminate against a student on the basis of race or culture. Moreover, Section 121a.532 requires that tests and evaluations be conducted in the "child's language or other mode of communication, unless it is clearly not feasible to do so."

Strategies for the Teacher. The classroom teacher has no ready-made solution available to avoid discrimination in assessment on the basis of cultural factors. By adhering to the mandate of those sections of P.L. 94–142 that pertain to quality of assessment and due process and by examining assessment materials and procedures carefully for potentially culturally biased items, teachers can hold the effects of cultural bias to a minimum. Turnbull, Strickland, and Brantley (1978) have developed a checklist (Figure 2–13) that a teacher can easily use to screen out the effects of bias during the administration and interpretation of an assessment procedure.

By maintaining a team approach to assessment in the classroom — involving other professionals and parents — the teacher has a good chance of reducing the

Figure 2–13

Checklist for Identification of Potential Bias During Administration

Name: _____ School: _____

Examiner: _____ Date: _____

Potential Examiner Bias   A check (√) indicates potential bias.

_____ Training (Lack of skills and/or handicapping conditions)

_____ Language/mode (Lack of language and/or mode of communication needed by the examiner with this child)

_____ Lack of experience testing similar types of children (age, cultural group, handicapping conditions)

_____ Biased attitude toward particular cultural groups

_____ Knowledge of alternative measures

Situational interference

_____ Time of day

_____ Distractions

_____ Testing materials (color, size, etc.)

_____ Inadvertent use of cues such as position cues/position of materials

_____ Length of session

_____ Comfort and accessibility of materials

_____ Order of assessment activities

Interaction between Examiner and Respondent

_____ Lack of rapport

_____ Failure to obtain and maintain attending behavior

_____ Failure to maintain child's optimum effort

_____ Inadequate communication (mode, manner, language)

_____ Dress and/or mannerisms of examiner (distracting, unique)

_____ Questionable knowledge and candor of interviewee

Checklist for Identification of Potential Bias during Scoring

_____ Ambiguous answers

_____ Unique, creative, unusual answers

_____ Other (describe) _____

Procedural Reminders to Avoid Errors

_____ Check ceiling and basal limits   _____ Check interpolation

_____ Check item credits   _____ Check age

_____ Check addition

From *Developing and Implementing IEP's* by A. P. Turnbull, B. B. Strickland, and J. C. Brantley. Developed in conjunction with G. Harbin, p. 104. Copyright © 1978 by Bell & Howell Company. Reprinted by permission of the publisher, Charles E. Merrill Publishing Company.

effects of cultural bias. Another strategy may be to use criterion-referenced assessment procedures (see Chapter 3) whenever feasible, as they do not make comparisons across pupil populations. This form of assessment focuses on the individual pupil's performance on tasks or behavior within a predetermined criterion. The teacher will need to be careful to establish or use criterion performances that reflect representative pupil performance rather than subjective criteria that may reflect teacher or instrument bias.

Issues Related to Gender. The negative effect of social discrimination on the basis of gender has been well documented. There is equally strong evidence that discrimination on the basis of sex has in special education occurred and remains a problem. Graebner (1972) and Marten and Matlin (1976) documented the underrepresentation of females as lead characters in over five hundred stories used in reading series produced by major American educational publishers. The Marten and Matlin study did note some improvements in the frequency of female main characters, but it also noted that female characters were still portrayed predominantly as passive role models.

Sexual Stereotyping in Assessment. In addition to educational materials like texts, assessment instruments and materials have also been found to discriminate against females. Mchoughlin and Lewis (1981) note that the identification of vocational occupations with stereotypic sex roles may limit pupils' choices in vocational interest inventories and aptitude assessment. Not only are the occupational roles inappropriately stereotyped, they add, but the roles assigned to females are of lower status than those assigned to males. Evidence exists to support the contention that gender discrimination in assessment is occurring in a wide variety of special education settings (Bailey and Harbin, 1980; Bernknoph, 1980; Cegelka, 1976; Salvia and Ysseldyke, 1981; and Ysseldyke and Regan, 1980).

In the chapters that follow, specific problems regarding potential discrimination against the respective special education populations will be discussed. There is no single solution to problems of sexual and cultural discrimination in educational assessment. The classroom teacher will play a significant role in any contemporary special education assessment process and as such must constantly remain alert to bias in assessment materials, procedural variables, and personal beliefs. In addition to thorough training in assessment procedures, the systematic use of a self-evaluation system like that illustrated in Figure 2–13 is recommended.

The Role of Parents in Classroom Assessment

Parents can play a vital role in determining the best data-collection procedure to use for any given behavior or within any of the five levels of assessment outlined in Table 1–1 (see Chapter 1, p. 6).

Teachers generally have direct contact with pupils for five or six hours each day; during that time pupils must share the teacher's and aide's attention. Only a fraction of class time is available for assessment activities. To insure the data collected represent a pupil's best possible performance, the classroom teacher will need to rely on knowledgeable others in the pupil's life. Parents or legal guardians can provide invaluable aid in pupil performance data collection as they generally have more frequent contact with the pupil over more varied situations and longer periods of time. In addition, parents have a legal right to participate in any assessment collection that may affect their child's IEP.

P.L. 94–142 specifically states that "before any action is taken with respect to initial placement of a handicapped child in special education, a full and individual evaluation of the child's educational needs must be conducted" (Section 121.431). To further clarify the parents' role in special education services, the statute ensures their right to due process under the law by requiring the provision for:

- Written prior notice to the parents or guardian of the child whenever the educational agency or unit:
  (i)   proposes to initiate or change, or
  (ii) refuses to initiate or change.

- The identification, evaluation, or educational placement of the child or the provision of a free, appropriate public education to the child.

The experienced teacher knows that it is considerably easier to be effective in all aspects of classroom management if the parents are an active, positive part of the instructional process. The same holds true in assessment, particularly in direct observation. However, experienced teachers will also tell you that in order to get reliable assessment data from parents, you often need to give them some basic training in appropriate procedures for observing and reporting performance data. The teacher's responsibility is to be sure that the parents have a clear notion of what target behaviors to observe, schedule times to ensure representative data, and provide for easy recording procedures. Parents should not be expected to report on behaviors that they may not fully understand themselves or that are of such an emotional nature that accurate, objective observation by a parent would easily be compromised.

Many teachers find a **parent interview** procedure to be an effective way to gather information from the home environment and avoid the many potential problems mentioned above. Such interviews can be very structured, with the teacher following a specific set of questions. Several commercially available assessment instruments make provisions for such interviews: the Denver Development Screening Test, Frankenburg et al., 1975; the Vineland Social Maturity Scale, Doll, 1983; and the American Association on Mental Deficiency Adaptive Behavior Scale, Nihira, Foster, Shellhaas, and Leland, 1974, to mention three of the more commonly used. Most of the so-called adaptive behavior rating scales are structured so that a teacher can readily administer large parts of them by interviewing the child's parents or guardians or others close to the child. Interviewing is not always the preferred procedure, but it is often the most effective procedure available.

Teachers often find that selecting a representative sample of questions or performance areas for parent corroboration is an efficient way to determine the accuracy of their own classroom observations. When using structured and typically quite extensive formal interview procedures, the teacher should be sure to give the parents some form of feedback about the overall findings as soon as possible. This could be in the form of a brief written report, ideally accompanied by direct verbal interaction with the participating parents.

Less structured approaches can be equally effective if the teacher prepares in advance a clear set of questions about behaviors, skills, or performances that the parent would have an opportunity to observe. Although less structured approaches are not less thorough, they lack the advantages of formal instructions, questions, and recording procedures, and therefore this approach is prone to more problems than its more structured counterparts. In most instances, the teacher is best advised to keep less structured interviews relatively short (20 to 30 minutes), to cover only three or four of the most pressing behavior or performance areas, and to record responses not while interviewing but as soon after the session as possible.

A thorough discussion of behavioral-ecological interviewing procedures is provided in Chapter 6, "Assessment of Children's Social and Behavioral Problems."

Summary

This chapter examines the uses of direct-observation data-collection procedures in the classroom setting. It describes in detail specific methods for collecting data using direct observation, with examples for application. An examination of the assessment of pupil learning style is also included. Many current issues in classroom assessment and data collection are discussed, with emphasis on their impact on classroom teachers, and discussion of the parent's role in the assessment process is included. Some of the chapter's major topics are:

1. Formal means of documenting pupil progress are essential in the special education classroom to measure movement toward criteria, to support IEP decisions and corroborate instructional program decisions, to establish baseline levels, and to evaluate instructional programming.
2. Data-collection methods should be unobtrusive, be easily used, and require a minimum of equipment.
3. Direct observation is defined as a number of procedures involving the systematic collection of pupil data in a representative sample of natural settings.
4. Running records involve recording everything a pupil does during a specified time period. These data can be analyzed to determine whether more precise information is required.
5. Event sampling involves recording the frequency or duration of a specific behavior.
6. The length of time it takes for a target behavior to be fully exhibited is recorded using duration data.

7. Latency data reflect the length of time elapsed between the presentation of a stimulus and the initiation of a pupil's response.

8. Interval time sampling involves recording a representative sample of a target behavior at predetermined time intervals over a specified length of time.

9. Recording momentary exhibitions of a target behavior at the end of a predetermined time period is referred to as momentary time sampling.

10. Task analysis can be used as an assessment tool, particularly to determine pupil competency in a specific performance category.

11. Listing all of the component substeps of a task in the order of their occurrence is referred to as procedural task analysis.

12. Hierarchical task analysis involves listing component steps of complex tasks in order of difficulty. One substep is often a prerequisite for the next.

13. Often teachers want to document levels of assistance the pupil requires to complete a task. These levels include complete physical prompting, partial physical prompting, verbal cuing, modeling and imitation, and independent responding.

14. Effective program prescription may include an assessment of a pupil's preferred learning style. The five major elements of a model for learning = style–preference assessment are discussed.

15. Major issues in the area of classroom assessment include teacher competence, IEP requirements, the quality of assessment procedures, nondiscriminatory assessment materials and procedures, and parental involvement in educational assessment.

Mastery Review

I. Recall

1. Direct observation is:
   a. behaviors that make up a domain.
   b. the systematic collection of pupil data.
   c. breaking target skills into basic components.
   d. interviewing others to collect data on pupil performance.

2. Verbal cuing is used when:
   a. the pupil can independently complete part of the response but not all.
   b. the pupil needs to be moved through a complete response.
   c. the pupil can respond correctly on an intermittent basis but still needs assistance.
   d. the pupil has demonstrated acquisition of the target response.

3. The preference for the use of either the right or the left brain hemisphere in learning is:
   a. a central nervous system preference.
   b. impulsivity versus reflectivity.
   c. global versus analytical.
   d. food intake.

4. Listing substeps leading to successful completion of a skill is:

   a.   procedural task analysis.

   b.   direct observation.

   c.   hierarchical task analysis.

   d.   event recording.

5. The type of direct observation that involves recording the frequency or duration of a behavior is:

   a.   running records.

   b.   time sampling.

   c.   category sampling.

   d.   event sampling.

6. Latency data are:

   a.   length of time between the presentation of a stimulus and the initiation of a response.

   b.   length of time a behavior occurs.

   c.   length of time spent in direct observation.

   d.   length of time the student spends in class.

7. Teacher techniques used to reinforce and help generalize an acquired skill are:

   a.   independent responding.

   b.   imitation or modeling.

   c.   partial physical prompting.

   d.   verbal cuing.

8. Baseline data are:

   a.   data collected on student performance after intervention or instruction is started.

   b.   data collected on student performance prior to starting intervention or instruction.

   c.   data the teacher hypothesizes and graphs.

   d.   data collected because of government requirements.

9. Data collected by recording everything a pupil does during a specified period of time are referred to as:

   a.   a running record.

   b.   time sampling.

   c.   category sampling.

   d.   event sampling.

10. Data on the length of time it takes a target behavior or skill to be fully exhibited are called:

   a.   latency data.

   b.   percent data.

   c.   duration data.

   d.   rate data.

11. Settings in which the behaviors or skills to be observed are apt to occur are referred to as:

   a.   structured settings.

   b.   natural settings.

   c. simulated settings.
   d. unstructured settings.

12. A recording system used when it is easier and more efficient to obtain a representative sample is:
   a. event sampling.
   b. duration data.
   c. interval time sampling.
   d. running records.

13. The "way individuals concentrate on, absorb, and retain new or difficult information or skills" is referred to as:
   a. reinforcer hierarchy.
   b. learning style.
   c. hierarchical task analysis.
   d. motivation.

14. Which of the following would not be a subcomponent of the environmental element of learning style?
   a. lighting.
   b. temperature.
   c. sound.
   d. food intake.

15. Motivation in learning style is synonymous with:
   a. punishment.
   b. prompting.
   c. reinforcement.
   d. chaining.

II. Comprehension

1. What factors need to be considered when deciding what type of event sampling to use in assessing a behavior?

2. **a.** Decide which of the following skills would require a procedural task analysis and which would require a hierarchical task analysis.

   Brushing teeth   _____
   Alphabetizing a list of words   _____
   Sorting blocks by color   _____
   Writing name   _____
   Tying shoes   _____

   b. Write an appropriate task analysis for one of the skills listed above that might be used for assessment.

3. Given the information on learning styles contained in this chapter, describe the importance of each of the five elements in instructional planning.

4. Describe the levels of assistance that may be required by a pupil to complete a task and why this information may be included in assessment data.

5. Discuss the impact of P.L. 94–142 on nondiscriminatory testing.

6. Discuss reasons why a special education teacher may use direct observation and how this relates to the five levels of assessment described in Chapter 1.

III. Application

1. Using the information on learning styles in this chapter, develop a learning-style profile for a fictitious mildly handicapped elementary student in a resource room. For each of the five basic elements, describe the learner's preference and at least one adaptation that might be made in the learning environment to accommodate this preference.
2. Visit an educational setting and, after conferring with the teacher, observe one student in the setting and create a running record of the student's behavior for a period of at least 20 minutes. Convert the information in this running record into a format similar to that used in Figure 2–1.

IV. Alternate Task

If none of the application exercises is relevant to your setting or curriculum, you can design two exercises of your own. They should demonstrate application of one or more of the principles or concepts described in the preceding chapter. Prior approval of both exercises should be obtained from your course instructor.

V. Answer Key

I.		II.	
1. b p. 15	**10.** c p. 18	**1.** pp. 17–21	
2. c p. 26	**11.** b p. 16	**2.** p. 23	
3. a p. 32	**12.** c p. 19	**3.** pp. 27–32	
4. c p. 23	**13.** b p. 27	**4.** pp. 25–27	
5. d pp. 17–18	**14.** d p. 27	**5.** pp. 41–42	
6. a pp. 18–19	**15.** c p. 28	**6.** pp. 15–26	
7. b p. 26			
8. b p. 15			
9. a p. 17			

Chapter 3

Basic Principles of Measurement and Test Development

Chapter Objectives:

After reading this chapter and completing the Mastery Review, you will be able to:

1. Describe how tests are developed.
2. Describe the variables to be considered when evaluating test results.
3. Describe correlation coefficients.
4. List and describe the types of reliability found in tests.
5. List and describe the basic types of validity to look for in tests.
6. Describe the major issues confronting classroom teachers using tests for educational assessment.

Key Terms:

criterion-referenced test
deviation score
domains of behavior
measurement
norm-referenced test
normative sample
normal distribution curve
raw score
reliability
standardization
standard deviation
standard error of measurement
standard score
true score
validity
variability
z-score

Fundamental to the assessment process is *measurement,* the process of quantifying abilities or behaviors. A measurement system provides teachers, administrators, and researchers with a means of analyzing data that otherwise would be too voluminous to interpret. Unfortunately, the quantification of human attributes is not an easy process. Although it is a simple task to count the number of words a child has read or the number of math problems worked correctly, it is much more difficult to measure broader constructs such as achievement, intelligence, or personality.

The purpose of this chapter is to describe the process by which tests are constructed, define various procedures by which test performance is summarized, and describe techniques for evaluating tests' adequacy by analyzing their reliability and validity.

This information is important to special education teachers for several reasons. *First,* teachers need to be able to understand and interpret various scoring systems. Each profession represented on an interdisciplinary team uses test instruments unique to that profession, but the manner in which tests are developed and test performance is evaluated is generally the same across professions. Knowledge of the properties of various scores is important for effective communication with other professionals and with parents. *Second,* teachers need to be aware of the limitations of various techniques for summarizing performance, particularly that of handicapped pupils. For example, most tests evaluate performance against that of a norm group. But does it make sense to compare a handicapped child with a group of nonhandicapped peers? In most situations, it would not be appropriate to make such a comparison; but in a special education setting or in situations in which pupils are being considered for mainstreaming into regular classes, it may be not only recommended but even desirable to make such a comparison. *Finally,* teachers need to be able to read and interpret test manuals in order to decide whether a particular instrument is useful for the intended purpose. Many tests are not worthwhile investments, and the classroom teacher will need to have the skills necessary to interpret the technical sections of test manuals to determine whether a particular instrument's design, development, and content documentation warrant its purchase and use.

How Are Tests Constructed?

Test construction can be accomplished in many different ways. Some tests are developed systematically and carefully over an extended period of time, while others are hastily put together. Some are based on a particular theoretical approach, while others are eclectic. However, there are several fundamental steps that must be taken in the development of any assessment tool; they include item selection, standardization, and evaluation.

Item Selection

What should comprise the content of a given test? The most straightforward answer is that content is determined by the *purpose* for which the assessment tool is intended. Four common purposes of tests in special education are screening, identification and placement, educational planning, and educational evaluation. In the discussion of the five-level model for educational assessment provided in Chapter 1, these four purposes were described in detail. Although all tests begin with the construction of a pool of items, the nature of that pool will vary with the purpose the test is intended to address. For example, a screening test will have only a few items, whereas a test for educational planning will probably have many.

Domains.   Once the purpose of an assessment tool has been clearly specified, the test constructor then identifies domains of behavior to be assessed. A domain may be defined as an identifiable set of related skills. For example, tasks included on an intelligence test used for identification and placement generally would be those that require varying levels of intelligent behavior and that successfully differentiate children of low intelligence from those of high intelligence. The tasks need not necessarily reflect those required in school; they need only require "intelligent" behavior. However, a good intelligence test will be based on a theory that attempts to define intelligent behavior and identify basic domains of intelligence.

An achievement test, on the other hand, is designed to indicate the extent to which a child has acquired school-related skills. Thus the tasks included in an achievement test should be representative of those required in school. Domains to be included will depend on the intended breadth of the instrument; for example, some achievement tests may assess only basic reading, math, and spelling skills, while others also include such skill areas as history, social studies, or general information.

Item Pools.   Once the domains have been identified, the test constructor develops a large pool of items to be considered for inclusion. These are items that the developer feels are appropriate given the purpose and the identified domains of the instrument. Items selected for possible inclusion should sample only the intended content, should encompass all of the domains (either equally or proportionally depending upon the importance the test developer places on each domain), and should require different levels of skill. For example, not all items should require simple memorization or recall of facts; children should also be asked to demonstrate "higher-level" thinking skills such as the ability to analyze, synthesize, apply, and evaluate what they have learned (Bloom, Engelhart, Furst, Hill, and Krathwohl, 1956).

Item Tryout.   The initial pool of items should be larger than the final pool since undoubtedly there will be problems with some of the items initially selected. Thus the next step in selection is the item tryout. Usually this is done by administering the entire pool to a representative sample of students in order to identify those items which should be included in the final version of the assessment instrument.

Criteria for final inclusion will vary according to test purpose. For example, a test that is designed to place items at different age or grade levels will retain only those passed by approximately half of the children at a given level. However, there are several criteria that would be incorporated into any analysis. First, any item that is obviously unclear or that takes too long to complete would be eliminated. Second, an item that does not differentiate between good and poor students would be eliminated. An item that almost everyone gets right or wrong might also be eliminated, depending upon the purpose of the test. Finally, overlapping items would be eliminated in order to avoid duplication.

From the remaining items, the test developer constructs the final version of the instrument. Actually, this version should be referred to as the final field-test version, as the instrument is now ready for the two other major steps in its development: standardization and evaluation.

Standardization

Standardization refers to the extent to which a test instrument specifies or standardizes test materials, administration procedures, scoring procedures, and interpretation. It is important because the less standardized the test, the less able the teacher is to compare test performance either across children or within a child across different testing periods.

Assume, for example, that a test item says, "Stack five blocks," and provides no further directions. Three different teachers might interpret that item in very different ways: one might use one-inch cubes, another wooden unit blocks, and another plastic blocks; one might provide a model, while another gives only verbal instructions; one might require a time limit and allow only one trial, while another gives unlimited time and several trials; one scores performance as correct regardless of how neat the stack is or whether it leans, while another requires a neat, symmetrical stack. Clearly, these teachers are not assessing the skill in the same way. Although adaptations and variations of skill assessment are necessary for handicapped children, as we shall discuss shortly, the interpretation of any test is based on the fundamental assumption of standardization.

Standard Materials.   Use of standard materials means that each child administered a test will receive the same materials. A test kit will often include those materials if they are not readily available or if they are unique tasks. Standardization of materials ensures that variability in children's performance is due to true differences in skill rather than to the presentation of different stimuli for testing purposes. Moreover, the use of materials designed especially for the test helps to prevent differential exposure to materials that are commercially available. For example, a test containing a commercially available puzzle would be biased in favor of children who had that puzzle in their homes.

Standard Administration Procedures.   Use of standard administration procedures means that each person administering the test presents items or tasks in the same manner. This is important to ensure that variability in children's performance is not attributable to variability in task presentation. Included in standard administration procedures are verbal instructions given by the examiner, the manner in which materials are presented and displayed, the level of examiner assistance or encouragement permitted, the number of trials allowed, and time limits.

Standard Scoring Procedures.   Use of standard scoring procedures means that each person giving the test scores performance in the same manner. For many questions, such as "What is 2 + 2?" the answer will be self-evident; but for others, particularly those involving reasoning, defining, or problem solving, a set of guidelines is generally needed for scoring. For example, if a child responds "Cry" to the question, "What is the thing to do if you fall and scrape your knee?" should that answer be considered correct? Only with a set of guidelines available in the test manual will all examiners score this response in the same fashion.

Standard Interpretation Procedures.   Use of standard interpretation procedures means that each person using a test would interpret a given level of performance in the same fashion. For example, assume that Nathaniel, who is in the third grade, correctly answers 22 of 57 items on a reading achievement test. Is this level of performance good or bad? To answer this question, the examiner needs some markers against which Nathaniel's performance can be compared. Generally a child's performance is interpreted either in relation to a normative sample or in relation to some standard of mastery. Regardless of the method used, standard interpretation procedures help ensure that performance will be interpreted fairly and equally across all children.

In general, the standardization of test materials, administration, scoring, and interpretation works in favor of children, since it protects them from inappropriate interpretation of their performance on the basis of factors other than their own abilities. However, standardization can sometimes serve as a barrier to performance for handicapped children. For example, a child with no arms is asked to manipulate blocks to create a certain design. Should the examiner be permitted to move the blocks in response to the child's verbal directions or eye gazing? For some tests, such a modification would be a violation of correct procedure. Thus the child may fail the item even if he or she has the cognitive abilities necessary to complete it successfully.

This is a fundamental issue in the assessment of exceptional children. Subsequent chapters discuss the issue in detail as it pertains to different groups of exceptional children and describe appropriate strategies for modifying or adapting test items to meet the needs of individual children.

Normative Sample

Once the standardized administration and scoring procedures have been developed, most tests are administered to a normative sample. This process results in standardized scores that can be used as norms against which an individual child's score is compared. A sample is used because it is not feasible to test every child in the United States in order to develop norms. However, in order for the sample to produce adequate norms, the characteristics of the children included must be representative of those of the population at large.

To determine whether a sample is representative, one must know who the population is and what its characteristics are. For example, if a test is developed to screen for children at risk for difficulties in local kindergarten classes, it would be appropriate for the normative sample to be representative of children in that system. If all the children come from one socioeconomic group, then the normative sample might come only from that group. This procedure precludes statements about a child's likelihood of success or failure in a setting other than that in which the test was normalized. It would also be inappropriate for any other setting to adopt this test as a screening measure. If a test is used to make diagnostic statements about the child's level of performance (e.g., level of intellectual functioning), it should have been standardized on a normative sample representative of the nation's population.

Many characteristics of the normative sample need to be considered. They include the year the testing was done and the age, race, sociocultural group, and geographic location of the children. Children's exposure to materials and expectations change over time, so norms developed many years ago may no longer be accurate. For example, on the Stanford-Binet intelligence test, the average five-year-old child in 1972 displayed skills that five-year-olds did not display in 1937. If the 1937 norms were used in 1972, the result would have been the placement of children who were functioning within the normal range in gifted-talented programs. There is not a set time period after which norms become out of date, but it is important to remain cognizant of this issue and to know what year the norms of any test used were developed.

Tests are often normed on a limited age range with the assumption that they will be administered only to children who fall within that range. Sometimes for handicapped children this issue is more complex than it originally appears. A retarded child of seven may not have the skills necessary to obtain a score on the Wechsler Intelligence Scale for Children–Revised (WISC–R), an I.Q. test generally designed for children ages 6 to 16. Although the child can pass many items on the preschool version of the WISC–R, that test was not normed for seven-year-old children, thus making it impossible to interpret the performance. In that instance, one can solve the problem by administering the Stanford-Binet, which is normed on people from two years to adulthood. However, there is not always an equivalent test to administer; for example, the retarded child of seven, if nonverbal, may not have the skills to take the Stanford-Binet since it requires many verbal responses. The Bayley Scales of Infant Development may be the test that has items representative of his or her skills. While one may choose to administer this test, interpretations of intellectual functioning would need to be made with caution since the test was normed on a different age group.

It is important to include other demographic variables such as race, gender, and sociocultural group since they are often associated with test-score differences. Insuring proportional race, gender, and economic-status balance in the normative sample allows for the examination of bias in test questions and ensures an appropriate reference group. The effect of cross-cultural factors on assessment in the classroom has been discussed in Chapter 2, "Data-Collection Procedures."

Item bias in tests can be determined by statistical measures or by expert judgment. Statistical techniques help to quantify the degree of difference between the performances of two groups on a given item. We might want to look at an item to see whether it is, for instance, biased in favor of boys. Since the purpose of the test is not to discriminate between boys and girls, we would check to see whether a statistically significantly higher number of boys than girls passes the item. Expert judgment is often used to evaluate items for bias.

If the normative sample does not include children who vary in important demographic characteristics, it is difficult to make appropriate normative interpretations. For example, an intelligence quotient of 100 on a test that was normed only on white children would not necessarily mean that a given child was average for his or her age, since a large proportion of children that age had been *systematically* excluded from the normative sample.

An additional consideration when using tests with a special population is whether or not that population has been included in the normative sample. In order for a test to be optimally appropriate for hearing-impaired children, it should have been administered to children with a full range of hearing impairments. Another important consideration is the range of experiences the special population has had. A test normed only on blind children in institutions cannot be assumed to provide information about blind children attending regular public schools. One should always keep in mind when evaluating or developing a test that the normative sample composition depends vitally on the purpose for which the test is intended. A test for physical abilities in five-year-old boys would not include 4-year-olds or girls of any age. Similarly, a test that proposes to assess handicapped children for mainstreaming might need to have any such children in the normative sample providing the instrument had been field tested to be certain that handicapped children can understand the instructions, manage the materials, and perform other behavior prerequisite to participation in the test. These provisions assure the needed nonhandicapped peer contrast.

Test Evaluation

Once test items have been identified and standard materials, administration, scoring, and interpretation procedures have been established, the test is ready for evaluation. This purpose of this phase of test development is to answer two fundamental questions about the instrument: "Is it reliable?" and "Is it valid?" The reliability issue addresses the *consistency* of the instrument, while the validity question seeks to determine how well the instrument does what it is supposed to do. In other words, how well does the instrument fulfill the purposes for which it was originally intended? Reliability and validity are evaluated by actually using the instrument with a large number of children. Specific aspects of reliability and validity and procedures for their assessment are addressed in a later portion of this chapter.

Basic Principles of Measurement

Of fundamental importance is the process of summarizing test performance. Most assessment tools attempt to quantify ability, and the quantification of ability or performance is a basic component of measurement. The special education teacher must be familiar with various procedures for summarizing test performance, must be able to read and interpret the scores of a variety of tests, and must be aware of the potential limitations of various scores. In this section we describe the differences between norm-referenced and criterion-referenced measures and discuss general concepts relating to measures of central tendency and of variability.

Criterion-Referenced and Norm-Referenced Measurement

Almost any assessment procedure yields a *raw score*. This score usually represents a simple count of the number of items performed correctly. By itself, it is not very meaningful, since no one really knows, for example, how good a score of 15 correct actually is. Thus the raw score usually is converted into another number that is more readily interpretable.

Two fundamentally different procedures are used to transform and interpret raw scores. One of these is referred to as *criterion-referenced measurement,* measurement in which a raw score is evaluated in relation to some criterion or standard of mastery. Usually criterion-referenced measures use the simplest and most easily understood transformation — percentage. Thus, if there are 25 items on a test, a raw score of 15 would be interpreted as 60 percent correct. Now we know how well the child did in relation to the total number of correct responses possible. If the items presented have been agreed upon as a standard of mastery, then we can say that the child has mastered approximately 60 percent of the content in a given area. Criterion-referenced measurement is probably the most relevant way to summarize performance in order to determine educational objectives and to evaluate a child's progress.

In *norm-referenced measurement,* a raw score is evaluated in relation to those obtained by other children. Here the question shifts from, "How well did this child do in relation to the amount to be learned?" to, "How well did this child do in relation to what other children did?" To answer this question, raw scores are transformed into one of several possible types, including percentile ranks, standard scores, age-equivalent scores, and grade-equivalent scores. Each of these compares an individual's performance to that of the "typical" child.

Much controversy has arisen in special education over the issue of criterion-referenced versus norm-referenced scores. Proponents of criterion-referenced measurement claim that it is not fair to compare a handicapped child with typical children; that such comparisons can lead to inappropriate labeling; and that norm-referenced measures, by virtue of the way they are constructed and scored, cannot be useful for planning educational objectives or evaluating educational progress. Proponents of norm-referenced measurement claim that criterion-referenced measures are situation specific and difficult to interpret: they do not tell us, for example, whether 60 percent mastery is appropriate for a given age group.

Clearly the two measurement systems are used to answer different questions, and both are important in a comprehensive evaluation of exceptional children. In this chapter we focus on the measurement properties of norm-referenced tests. This focus does not reflect a preference for these measures, however; it is simply a recognition of the complexity of interpreting norm-referenced scores and of the importance of understanding the fundamental procedures for developing and interpreting each measure's findings. In order to help you fully understand these scores, we first provide introductory sections describing measures of central tendency and of variability.

Measures of Central Tendency

Most techniques for summarizing test performance compare a child's score with those obtained by a larger, representative sample of children. Two basic measures aid in this comparison: measures of central tendency and measures of variability. Assume, for example, that Jodie has achieved a raw score of 65 on a test. What techniques would you use to relate her score to those of the rest of the children in her class? One strategy would be to obtain a measure of *central tendency* for the class. That is, you ask how well the typical child performed on the test.

The three basic measures of central tendency are, of course, the *mean,* the *median,* and the *mode.* The mean is the most frequently used measure of central tendency and is computed by adding together all of the scores in the class and dividing the sum by the total number of children taking the test. The median is the middle score and is determined simply by arranging the scores in order from highest to lowest and selecting the middle score. The mode is the most frequently occurring score in a distribution.

The median and mode have some advantages over the mean in certain instances. One extremely high or extremely low score may raise or lower the mean score, but it will not greatly affect the median or mode. For example, the mean height of players on the following basketball team is 6 feet 2 inches, even though only one person on the team is taller than 6 feet:

Mike: 6 feet
James: 6 feet
David: 6 feet
Al: 6 feet
Tom: 6 feet 10 inches

However, the mean is used almost exclusively as the measure of central tendency for computing most test scores.

Table 3–1

Computing the Mean, Median, and Mode for a Distribution of Scores

. . . .

The following represent scores on a test administered to the 25 children in Ms. Morrison's class.

45	64	71	78	82
50	65	72	79	83
53	65	75	80	83
59	68	78	80	85
60	70	78	81	90

Mean	*Median*	*Mode*
Sum of all scores = *1794*	Middle score	Most frequently occurring score
÷ no. of students 25		
Mean = 71.76	Median = 75	Mode = 78

. . . .

Table 3–1 presents a distribution of scores in a class and gives examples of computing the mean, median, and mode. As you can see, different measures of central tendency can result in different figures. Regardless of the measure used, however, we can say that Jodie's score of 65 was below that of her typical classmate since it is lower than the mean, the median, or the mode.

The mean is the simplest and most readily understood technique for summarizing a group of scores. However, if we use it without actually looking at the entire distribution of scores, we do not know how far Jodie's score was below the mean. Hence the need for measures of variability.

Measures of Variability

Measures of variability are important in interpreting test data because they expand the limited frame of reference provided by measures of central tendency. For example, if the mean number of parts assembled by workers in a sheltered workshop is 35 per hour, we know that Johnny, a prevocational student who can assemble 28 per hour, is below average in his rate, but we don't know *how far* below the mean he is. Consider the two hypothetical distributions of worker performance presented in Figure 3–1. Both have means of 35, but a rate of 28 is relatively much worse in Distribution A than it is in Distribution B. Many more of the workers whose performance is depicted in Distribution A can work faster than Johnny, while fewer of those whose performance is graphed in Distribution B are faster. The shaded area represents those whose work is slower than Johnny's.

Range. Measures of variability provide a numerical way to describe the nature of a given distribution. The range, for example, lets us know the extreme scores. If the range of rates in the sheltered workshop were 10, with extremes of 30 and

Figure 3–1

Comparison of Two Distributions with the Same Mean but Different Variabilities

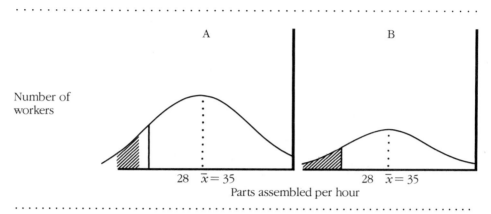

40, then we would know that Johnny's rate of 28 put him below anyone in the workshop. Thus, it may be that his fluency needs to be increased before he is placed in such a setting. If, however, the range were 20, with extremes of 25 and 45, then Johnny might fit nicely in that setting.

The problem with range is that it is limited in its usefulness because it does not give us all the information we need about a distribution. Even if we knew the mean and the range, we would not be able to say how many or what percentage of the workers were faster than Johnny. To aid us in making these decisions, we can use the *standard deviation*.

Normal Distribution Curve.   Before discussing standard deviation, however, we must describe the normal distribution curve. Many variables in nature, such as human height and weight, yield distributions that approximate the normal curve. Almost all scoring systems used in present-day educational and psychological assessment are based on the fundamental assumption that the variables dealt with in testing (e.g., intelligence or achievement) are normally distributed. The normal distribution curve, displayed in Figure 3–2, has three basic characteristics: it is bell shaped; it is symmetrical; and its mean, median, and mode all have the same value. As you can see, most people taking a test score at or near the mean. As scores deviate from the mean in one direction or another, fewer and fewer people obtain them. According to Hopkins and Antes (1978), the normal or bell curve "is not a distribution of actual scores but a theoretical distribution plotted from a mathematical equation. The normal curve is a theoretical mathematical ideal, and its importance lies in the fact that actual distributions approximate the theoretical model of the normal curve. Sets of test scores can be made meaningful by using the normal curve as a model . . . to interpret each score in relation to other scores" (p. 242).

Figure 3–2

The Normal Distribution Curve

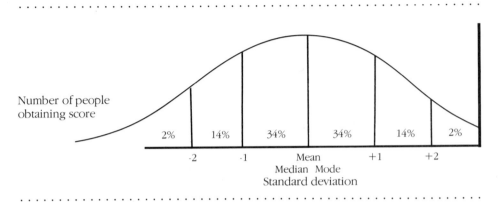

When tests' scores have the same mean, standard deviation, and distribution, the tests are viewed as comparable. Converting raw scores to standard scores achieves equal means (0) and standard deviations (1), and normalizing those scores gives their distributions the same shape (a normal curve). This is one of several attributes of the normal-curve concept.

Standard Deviation. Although a standard deviation can be computed for any distribution, we will be concerned here only with the standard deviation of a normal distribution. The standard deviation is simply a number that gives an indication of a score's relative place within a distribution. It is obtained by definition and is best understood by looking at the normal distribution curve displayed in Figure 3–2. By definition, the standard deviation describes how far away a person's score is from the mean *relative to the performance of other people*. As you can see, in a normal distribution 50 percent of people score at or below the mean and 50 percent score at or above it. By definition, one standard deviation above the mean (+1) encompasses 34 percent of the people in a group; likewise, one standard deviation below the mean also encompasses 34 percent of the population. Thus, in theory, 68 percent of all people taking a test will score within a range from −1 to +1 standard deviation units. By definition, an additional 14 percent will score between one and two standard deviations above or below the mean. And theoretically only .26 percent of the distribution will exceed three standard deviations on one side of the mean or the other.

Let's look at a relatively familiar example. Intelligence is assumed to be a normally distributed variable. The Wechsler Intelligence Scale for Children has a mean of 100 and a standard deviation of 15. This means that an I.Q. of 85 is one standard deviation below the mean and that approximately 16 percent of the population would score below 85. An I.Q. of 130 is two standard deviations above the mean, so only 2 percent of the population should score higher than this.

The standard deviation is useful not only for describing a person's performance relative to that of a group, but also for comparing scores on tests that have different means and/or standard deviations. Thus a score of 115 on a test that has a mean of 100 and a standard deviation of 15 is the same relative score as a score of 60 on a test that has a mean of 50 and a standard deviation of 10. In both cases, the student scored exactly one standard deviation above the mean, which means that in both cases the score was equal to or better than those obtained by 64 percent of all persons taking the test.

Z-Score.   Although it is relatively easy to interpret scores that fall right on the standard deviation lines, there are two basic limitations to the standard deviation:

1. How do you interpret scores that are not expressed in standard deviation integers? For example, looking again at the I.Q. test, how would you interpret an I.Q. of 93?
2. How can you compare scores on tests that have different means and/or different standard deviations?

The z-score can solve these two problems. It is an attempt to standardize scores so that they are comparable, and it consists of the deviation of a score from the mean expressed in standard-deviation units. For example, an I.Q. score of 115 has a z-score of 1 because it is one standard deviation away from the mean. The formula for obtaining a z-score for any test is simply:

$$z = X - \bar{X} / s_x$$

Where: X = subject's raw score
$\bar{X}$ = mean raw score
s_x = standard deviation of the raw scores.

Take the test score (X), subtract the mean performance on the test from it $(\bar{X})$, and divide by the standard deviation (s_x). This results in a new distribution of scores with a mean of 0 and a standard deviation of 1. Table 3–2 provides a simple way of interpreting Z = scores.

Standard Error of Measurement.   The standard error of measurement (SEM) is a critical concept in interpreting test scores. Scores on tests are assumed not to be completely accurate because of chance factors that might affect a person's performance. Instead, they are considered to be *estimates* of that person's *true score*. The true score is the score that precisely represents a person's ability to complete a given test. We will never know anyone's true score because we never know what chance factors (fatigue, poor lighting, inattentiveness, etc.) may be affecting his or her performance. The next best thing, of course, is *obtained* score, or the score actually received on a test. *The obtained score is always considered to be an estimate of the individual's true score.*

Table 3–2

Interpreting Z-Scores

. . . .

Step	**Example**
1. Convert the individual score into a z-score.	1. $\bar{X} = 100$ $s_x = 15$ (Johnny's score) $z = 105$ $z = \dfrac{105 - 110}{15} = .33$
2. Find the tenths value of the z-score in the far left column labeled "z."	2. With a z-score of .33, we would go to the fourth row, which is labeled "0.3."
3. Find the hundredths value of the z-score in the top line of the chart.	3. With a z-score of .33, we would go to the fourth column, which is labeled ".03."
4. The point at which these two values intersect is the proportion of cases between the z-score and the mean.	4. Looking at the point where column .03 and line 013 intersect, note that the proportion of cases between the z-score and the mean is .1293.
5. If the z-score is positive, *add* this proportion to .50. If it is negative, subtract it from .50. This will give you the percentage of cases in the distribution that scored less than this score.	5. Since .33 is positive, we will add .1293 to .50, getting .6293. This means that Johnny scored better than approximately 63 percent of the population.

. . . .

You might ask how confident we can be that the obtained score is close to the child's score. Many test publishers use the SEM to assist in this decision.

Let us assume that it is possible to test a child many times on the same test; let us also assume that the child's scores on these repeated administrations would not be affected by boredom, practice effects, etc. The result would be a frequency distribution of that child's scores, and it would be very similar to a normal distribution. Furthermore,

1. The mean of this distribution would be the child's true score.
2. The standard deviation of this theoretical distribution is called "the standard error of measurement."

You will recall that 68 percent of the scores on a normal curve fall between one standard deviation below the mean and one standard deviation above it. Thus we may use the standard error of measurement information provided by a test's publisher to interpret a given obtained score. Assume that Beth obtains a score of 78 on a test that has a standard error of measurement of 2. What can we say about the degree of confidence we have that 78 is an accurate reflection of Beth's true abilities? The procedure is simple. First, subtract the standard error of measurement from the obtained score. In this case, we get 76. Then add the standard error of measurement to the obtained score. In this case, we get 80. We may then say that there is a 68 percent probability that Beth's true score lies somewhere between 76 and 80.

As Hopkins and Antes (1978) suggest, "interpretation of an obtained score with the standard error of measurement permits a person to visualize a score as a *band* rather than as a *point*" (p. 282). This means that the scores that fall at the cut-off points for various diagnostic categories need to be interpreted cautiously. For example, an I.Q. of 70 is considered the upper limit at which a person can be eligible for educably mentally retarded services. However, if the standard error of measurement for the intelligence test is 4, one needs to consider that fact before labeling children with scores from 66 to 74 as educably retarded and when determining the most appropriate services for children with scores of 71 to 73.

The SEM is also useful in comparing two scores on the same test. Rather than comparing them in terms of absolute differences, the band for one score can be compared to the band for the other. Let us assume that Alecia was administered the same test twice: once in September, when she obtained a score of 57, and again in May, when she obtained a score of 61. Did she show a significant improvement in performance? The answer to this question depends in part on the SEM. If it is 3, the answer is no, since the bands for the two scores overlap.

The purpose of this section has been to describe fundamental concepts associated with measure of central tendency and variability. Because the objective is not computational, we have not described formulas for computing the standard deviation and standard error of measurement. The objective is for teachers to have a conceptual understanding of the *meaning* of these computations in order to interpret test scores more accurately.

Common Raw-Score Transformations

Percentile Ranks

Most of us have seen data presented in percentile ranks. It is one of the simplest transformations of raw scores and the easiest for most people to interpret. A *percentile rank* is defined as the point below which a given proportion of persons score. Thus a percentile rank of 70 means that the person's score exceeded those of 70 percent of the people taking a test, and a percentile rank of 30 means that the person's score exceeded those of only 30 percent of the people taking a test.

Percentile ranks are excellent tools for describing a student's present status. One potential limitation, of course, is the extent to which the comparison group possesses characteristics similar to the student's. An additional limitation is that percentile ranks should *not* be used to evaluate progress because of certain characteristics they possess. Look, for example, at Figure 3–3. Assume that raw scores on a given test are normally distributed and that one child obtains a raw score of 60 on a pretest, while another child obtains a raw score of 80. At the end of the school year, each child passes 10 additional items. Although the children's raw scores will show an equal amount of change, their percentile change scores will

Figure 3–3

Effects of Using Change in Percentile Rank as an Indicator of Program Effectiveness

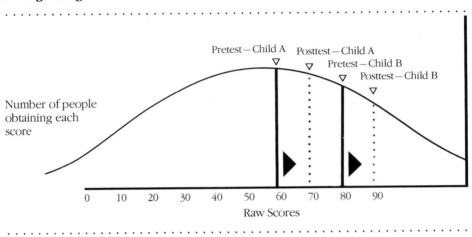

be quite different. The child who went from 60 to 70 passed many more people than did the one who went from 80 to 90. Although posttest percentile rank, once again, is a good indicator of a child's present status, the *change* in percentile rank is *not* an appropriate measure of program effectiveness since both students learned precisely the same amount of material.

Standard Scores

Another frequently used type of score is the standard score, a score that has been transformed to fit a normal curve. Two commonly used standard scores are the *T*-score and the stanine. A T-*score* has a mean of 50 and a standard deviation of 10; therefore, a child with a *T*-score of 60 would be performing at one standard deviation above the mean. *Stanine scores* range from 1 to 9 and have a mean of 5 and a standard deviation of 2; therefore, the child who obtained a *T*-score of 60 would obtain a stanine of 7. An example of a test that uses stanine scores is the Peabody Picture Vocabulary Test.

Deviation Score. A deviation score is also based on the principles of the mean, the standard deviation, and the normal curve, but it differs from a *T*-score or a stanine because the mean and standard deviation are not necessarily the same across tests. A deviation score provides information about how an individual child's score differs from the mean. In order to interpret the score correctly, however, one must know the mean and standard deviation of the individual test. An I.Q. is an example of a deviation score. As it happens, the Wechsler series, the Stanford-Binet, and the McCarthy all have means of 100; however, the standard deviation for the Wechsler tests is 15, while the standard deviations for the Stanford-Binet and the

Figure 3–4

Converting Raw Scores to Age-Equivalent Scores

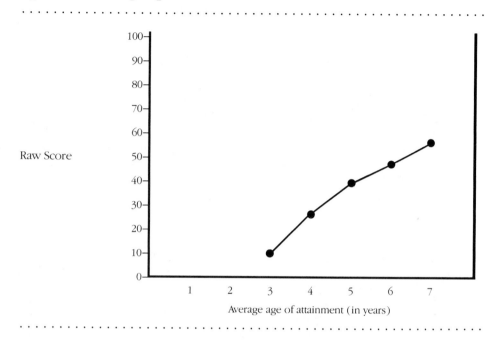

McCarthy are 16. Therefore, a child who obtains an I.Q. score of 87 is at the 19th percentile on the WISC–R but at the 21st percentile on the Stanford-Binet. This may appear to be a minor distinction, but it is easy to imagine how varied interpretations of the numbers would be if the means were different or the standard deviations more discrepant. Deviation scores do not always allow scores on different tests to be compared directly.

Rather than using deviation scores for reporting intelligence quotients, psychologists initially used ratio scores. A ratio I.Q. score is found by dividing chronological age by mental age and multiplying by 100. If a child of 6–0 (six years, zero months) had a mental age of 6–0, she would have an I.Q. of 100. One of the problems with this method is that the standard deviation scores are different for different ages, which means that an I.Q. score of 110 obtained at age five is not directly comparable to an I.Q. score of 110 obtained at age 12. These ratio scores are rarely used today.

Age Equivalents. Developmental tests often translate raw scores into age scores that are derived by giving the tests to children in the age span of interest. A test might be given to two hundred children within a few weeks of their fourth, fifth, sixth, seventh, eighth, and ninth birthdays. The mean raw score for each of these ages would be computed and graphed. Using Figure 3–4 as a guide, imagine a child who obtains a raw score of 40. This child would be described as functioning most like a five-year-old. The ages of children who obtain raw scores that do not correspond exactly to the mean for a tested age have to be approximated. If a child obtains a raw score of 45, his age score might be five years, six months.

This method of interpreting a child's score has certain advantages, particularly for interpreting developmental tests, but there are several caveats. First of all, there is no "typical child." In Figure 3–4, the raw score of 10 was derived from an average of many three-year-old children's scores. Second, raw scores may be obtained in different ways. Two children may be administered the Bayley and both obtain developmental ages of 20 months. However, one child may obtain this score with his first failure at the 14th-month level and his highest pass at the 30th-month level, while the other child may have her first failure at the 18th-month level and her highest pass at the 22nd-month level. Obviously, while these children's overall performances suggest they are functioning at the same level, the scatter of their skill levels suggests that programming would be quite different for the two. Finally, a child of three who obtains a mental age of five and a child of 12 who obtains a mental age of five on the Stanford-Binet are qualitatively different. Again, program plans for these two children would need to reflect this difference.

Grade Equivalent Scores.   Grade equivalent scores are similar to age equivalent scores and are derived in the same manner, with the children being grouped according to grade placement rather than age. Thus if a child receives a grade equivalent score of 4.7, this is interpreted as performance similar to that of the average child in the seventh month of the fourth-grade year. The issues regarding the nonexistence of a "typical" third-grader and the scatter of the child's performance again need to be looked at.

Another important consideration is the difference between local and national norms. Grade equivalency scores are often used with school achievement tests. What a child has been exposed to will be reflected in test scores, so that if a school system as a whole is advanced, a child referred for academic difficulties may be performing at grade level according to national norms. However, if the norm in that system is two grade levels ahead of grade placement, the child will legitimately have a hard time keeping up in the classroom. Conversely, if the majority of fourth-grade children in a school system have not been exposed to the "typical" fourth-grade curriculum, they may all score below the national mean.

Test Evaluation

An important component of assessing a child's performance is evaluating the measures one is going to use. It is necessary to be able to determine on the basis of a test manual whether or not the test is consistent and provides useful information. Understanding the information presented in test manuals requires a basic understanding of correlation coefficients and also of the different types of reliability and validity.

Correlation Coefficient

Reliability and validity are typically presented in test manuals in terms of a *correlation coefficient*. The purpose of the correlation coefficient is to describe numerically the strength or magnitude of a relationship. Remember that scores are not expected to be precisely the same across time — on each trial, one obtains an estimate of the "true" score. It is therefore necessary to have a method for testing the relationship between two scores obtained on separate trials. Correlation is the primary statistical method for doing this. A correlation question simply asks how one variable changes when another variable does. Take, for example, human height and weight. You might ask how weight changes as height increases. In broad terms, you would probably guess that when height increases, weight does also, but this does not tell you the *strength* of the relationship. Many short people weigh more than many tall people, so the relationship between weight and height is not always predictable.

Correlation may be visually conceptualized using a chart. The horizontal axis represents the scores of one variable as they increase from left to right; the vertical axis represents the scores of the other variable as they increase from bottom to top. Each dot that is plotted on this graph could represent a different student and could tell you that student's score on both variables. If you plotted the scores of several students, you would have a *scattergram,* or scatter plot. As Hopkins and Antes (1978) explain, "the closer the dots come to fitting a line, the higher the correlation coefficient and the more consistency within the two sets of measures. If the dots fall on a line, then the correlation of the two sets is said to be perfect" (p. 268).

Correlation coefficients can take any value from +1 to –1, but no other values. A correlation of *zero* means that there is no relationship between the two variables; knowing a person's score on the first variable does not help you at all in guessing his or her score on the second. As you move away from zero toward −1 *or* +1, we say that the correlation is increasing, or getting stronger. The negative or positive component of the correlation coefficient is not an indication of the strength of the correlation; it only refers to the *direction* of the relationship.

Correlations of +1 and –1 are known as perfect correlations. For +1 correlations, this may be interpreted to mean that for every increase in variable A, there is a corresponding *increase* in variable B. For –1 correlations, this may be interpreted to mean that for every increase in variable A, there is a corresponding *decrease* in variable B. Rarely will you find a perfect correlation between two variables. Even though we know that, generally speaking, people get heavier as they get taller, we all know of some tall people who weigh less than some short people. Most correlations tend to be somewhat less than perfect.

By way of summary, Hopkins and Antes state that "correlation is a study of the relationship between two sets of scores of variables. A student who places at about the same position in each of the two sets of scores which have been collected on the same set of subjects is considered to exhibit consistency. The correlation coefficient measures that tendency throughout the complete sets of scores" (p. 271).

Reliability

Reliability refers to the *consistency* of scores across time, similar items, or raters. It is usually measured over a short period of time without specific interventions in the meantime. Repeated administration of a test over longer periods of time (e.g., years) is usually discussed in relation to the test's predictive abilities. For example, if an I.Q. test is given to a child at six years and then again at 20 years, one can examine whether intelligence scores in childhood *predict* intelligence scores in adulthood. Repeated administration of tests with an intervention or unique experience in between assessments is measuring the impact of the intervention rather than the stability of scores over time.

Test-Retest Reliability. Test-retest reliability refers to the likelihood that two scores obtained within a short period of time will be similar. If a child obtains an I.Q. score of 97 this week, a month later we expect him or her to obtain a similar score. The 97 would be correlated with the later score to determine test-retest reliability. If a child's performance is not reliable when the test is repeated within a short period of time, it is not possible to interpret the score. Suppose it was not uncommon for a child to obtain an I.Q. of 90 today and one of 130 in six weeks on a particular test. Would you provide gifted and talented services for the child?

Simply administering a test to the same children twice within a matter of months does not mean that one is tapping the reliability of the test. Children may remember parts of the test and thus improve their performance. In a test requiring speed in putting puzzles together, remembering the successful solution could improve one's level of performance or at least insure that the level of performance was the same. A test measuring problem-solving abilities may be similarly affected by memory: the child may recall the answer and not have to work through the steps the second time. By contrast, the child may become bored with the materials and not be motivated to work with them. One solution is to have alternate forms of the test.

The problems of determining long-term reliability stability may in part be resolved by using a short (two-week) test-retest interval, plus a practical interval of one complete grading period, to demonstrate test stability over a reasonable amount of time. The former could provide a clean estimate for comparison with other tests; the latter could provide some notion of stability over practical periods of time.

Alternate-Form Reliability. Using alternate forms of the test can prevent some of the difficulties associated with administering the same test repeatedly. This is particularly helpful when evaluators want to measure the effectiveness of a program by comparing a pretest and a posttest. In order to do this, one needs to be confident that changes seen on the posttest were the result of a given intervention. Administering alternate forms of the same test is one method of checking, but in so doing one must be confident that the two forms are measuring the same construct. This agreement between forms is referred to as "alternate-form" reliability and is measured by examining the correlation between the two forms. The tests may be administered sequentially in one session or on two different occasions, and a correlation coefficient is then derived. If they are administered at different times, information about stability across time is also gathered. For example, the Peabody Picture Vocabulary Test, commonly used to screen for language skills, has two forms. The median delayed test-retest correlation for the standard scores is .77 (Salvia and Ysseldyke, 1981).

Split-Half Reliability.   By examining the correlations between two parts of the same test, one can determine its internal consistency, or split-half reliability. Sometimes the first half of the test is correlated with the second half; sometimes the odd-numbered items are correlated with the even-numbered items. For example, on a multiplication test with 20 questions, scores for 10 of the questions would be compared to those for the other 10 questions. If across many children the scores were highly correlated, the test would be considered internally consistent.

Interscorer Reliability.   The concept behind standardization is that regardless of who administers the test, the scores will remain the same. Standardized instructions, materials, and scoring procedures help to address this issue. Interscorer reliability examines whether the scoring procedures are clear and precise enough to ensure that different raters will give scores consistent with each other.

Many tests involve asking the child to respond to questions. For some of these, it is impossible to give scoring instructions that cover every possibility. To determine reliability, the scores two different teachers assign to the child's answers would be correlated to see how similar they were. Another kind of assessment requiring a measure of interscorer reliability is behavioral observation. The more complex or subjective the scoring is, the more important and the more difficult it is to establish interscorer reliability.

An important question is, What constitutes a good reliability coefficient? In general, it depends upon the test, the conditions under which it was administered, and the type of reliability sought. Some general guidelines can be useful, however. A reliability coefficient of .9 or higher is almost always viewed as adequate. A coefficient between .8 and .9 is within the range of acceptability but some people would question it. A reliability coefficient of less than .8 is generally not acceptable. It indicates that performance across time or across measures simply is not consistent, and thus interpretation of a single score is very difficult.

Because correlation coefficients can be effected by so many factors (speeded test versus a power test, test/retest interval, type of coefficient), the standard error of measurement discussed earlier is used by many for test selection purposes.

Validity

Validity questions seek to determine whether a test is useful for its intended purpose; does it do what it claims to? In order to use the results fairly and confidently, we must know that the test correlates with other indices of what it is supposed to measure — that it is valid. The measurement of validity, like the measurement of reliability, generally depends on the statistical method of correlation. In measuring validity, we are examining the relationship between the test scores and the scores on other measures. The five basic types of validity are face, content, construct, concurrent, and predictive. These will be considered separately.

Face Validity.   The measurement of face validity examines whether the test appears to measure what its publishers say it should. On the most obvious level, a language test would not have face validity if it tested multiplication skills. However, it may not always be that clear. A language test that tested a child's ability to point to objects but used *obscure* objects might not be considered to have face validity as a test of receptive language. Face validity is often the underlying construct in the assessment of content and construct validity.

Content Validity.   The measurement of content validity examines whether the items on the test are all representative of the domain that is being assessed. This involves defining what the domain one is measuring encompasses. The definition must have face validity, and the test items must be highly correlated with it. For example, a test of reading skills that tested the ability to read individual words but not the comprehension of paragraphs would not be a valid test of reading skills because the assessment of reading needs to include comprehension in order to be representative.

Content validity often is assessed through expert judgment. For example, a science achievement test might be rated by practicing scientists to determine the extent to which it adequately reflects the range and depth of appropriate scientific knowledge.

Construct Validity.   The measurement of construct validity examines the degree to which the test measures a construct or trait. As in determining content validity, a criterion must be developed that represents the construct or trait. This criterion is then used to determine the correlation between the test items and the construct. For example, a developmental test would be examined to find out how well it correlated with theories of development, while a test of visual processing skills would be examined against visual processing theories.

Concurrent Validity.   The measurement of concurrent validity examines the degree to which the scores correspond to current, similar information about the child. A reading test used to place children in remedial classes might be compared to the teacher's assessments of each child's reading skills and need for additional help. If the correlation between the two measures were high, then the test would be considered to have good concurrent validity.

Predictive Validity.   The measurement of predictive validity is the examination of the degree to which the test predicts what the developers claim it predicts. Intelligence tests are supposed to predict school achievement. The assumption is that children with lower I.Q. scores learn more slowly and need additional help. If that were not the case, then I.Q. tests would lack predictive validity, and their use for school placement purposes would have to be questioned.

Although many different techniques could be used to test validity, the correlation coefficient is the most frequently reported. Obviously, we would like for coefficients to be as high as possible. For example, if the Graduate Record Examination is to be used to select students for graduate study, one would hope that it correlated highly with actual performance in graduate school. The specification of a minimum acceptable validity coefficient is difficult, however, for several reasons. First, validity can never be higher than reliability, so the lower the reliability, the less valid a test will be. (Note that the reverse does not hold; a test could be perfectly reliable or consistent but not be at all valid for a given purpose.) Second, some decisions require a higher level of validity than others. For example, a test designed to identify and label mentally retarded children should be very valid, since the decision made on the basis of test results is a serious one. A test designed to indicate whether a child has creative tendencies, in contrast, may be a useful measure even with a relatively lower validity coefficient.

Just as there are many ways to evaluate test reliability, so too are there many ways to address validity. Ideally, a test manual should state the specific *purposes* for which the test is intended and then provide data supporting its use for *each* purpose. The informed consumer must then evaluate the instrument relative to the purposes for which he or she would like to use the information gathered.

Summary

Some of the major topics and information dealt with in this chapter include:

1. The development of any assessment tool must involve item selection, standardization, and evaluation. The content or item selection depends on the purpose of the test and domains of behavior to be assessed. Standardization involves the use not only of standard materials but also of standard administration, scoring, and interpretation procedures.
2. Administering a test to a normative sample results in standardized scores or norms to which an individual pupil's score may be compared. Characteristics of the normative sample that should be considered include the year the testing was done and age, racial, sociocultural, and geographic location factors.
3. Evaluation of tests addresses the issues of reliability and validity.
4. A raw score represents a simple count of the number of items performed correctly. The raw score is then converted into another form depending on the type of test used.
5. In criterion-referenced measurement, a raw score is evaluated in relation to a specific criterion or standard of mastery, and a percent score is often used to represent the pupil's performance.
6. A raw score is evaluated in relation to other raw scores in norm-referenced

measurement. This may include percentile ranks, standard scores, and age- or grade-equivalent scores.

7. A measure of central tendency aids in comparing a specific score with scores obtained by a larger representative sample. The three basic measures of central tendency used in educational measurement are the mean, the median, and the mode.

8. Measures of variability describe the nature of a given distribution numerically and include range (extreme scores) and standard deviation.

9. A normal distribution curve is bell shaped and symmetrical, and its mean, median, and mode all have the same value. It is a theoretical mathematical construct that graphically illustrates measurement scores along a continuum.

10. The standard deviation score describes a score's distance from the mean relative to the performance of others who have taken the same test.

11. Z-score refers to the deviation of a score from the mean in standard-deviation units and is useful in comparing such scores as I.Q.'s from different tests having different standard deviation scores.

12. Reliability refers to the consistency of scores across time, similar items, and persons administering the test.

13. Validity questions ask whether a test is useful for its stated purposes. The five basic types of validity are face, content, construct, concurrent, and predictive.

Mastery Review

I. Recall

1. A standardized test is one that:
    a. sets standards of training for persons administering the test.
    b. has norms.
    c. specifies materials and procedures for administration, scoring, and interpretation.
    d. establishes a standard criterion for performance.

2. A norm-referenced test:
    a. compares performance to a standard of mastery.
    b. is used only with normal children.
    c. reflects societal norms for appropriate behavior.
    d. compares a child's performance to that of other children.

3. A criterion-referenced test:
    a. sets specific criteria for performance on each item.
    b. compares performance to a standard of mastery.
    c. meets approved criteria for test development.
    d. cannot be used to compare performance across children.

4. Approximately two-thirds of the individuals in a normal distribution will fall between a z-score range of:
    a. $-.5$ to $+.5$.
    b. -1.0 to $+1.0$.

   c.   −1.5 to +1.5.

   d.   −2.0 to +2.0.

5. The standard error of measurement is an index of:

   a.   validity.

   b.   reliability.

   c.   internal consistency.

   d.   change.

6. The 75th percentile is the point in a distribution:

   a.   below which are 25 percent of the cases.

   b.   below which are 75 percent of the cases.

   c.   at which a student has answered 75 percent of the questions correctly.

   d.   below which 75 students score.

7. Which of the following is *not* a good use for percentile ranks?

   a.   To compare the performance of two children.

   b.   To describe a student's present status.

   c.   They are easily understood by the public.

   d.   To evaluate progress.

8. A *T*-score has:

   a.   a mean of 100 and a standard deviation of 15.

   b.   a mean of 50 and a standard deviation of 5.

   c.   a mean of 50 and a standard deviation of 10.

   d.   a mean of 10 and a standard deviation of 5.

9. Marty obtained a grade-equivalent score of 4.5. This is best interpreted as meaning that:

   a.   Marty knows about half of the skills learned in fourth grade.

   b.   Marty earned the same number of raw-score points as the average child in the fifth month of the fourth grade.

   c.   Marty is a typical fourth-grader.

   d.   Marty is above the typical fourth-grader.

10. What is the coefficient of correlation when two traits are not related?

   a.   −1.

   b.   −.5.

   c.   0.

   d.   +1.

11. The normal curve:

   a.   is bell shaped.

   b.   is a theoretical model.

   c.   has the same mean, median, and mode.

   d.   all of the above.

12. The reliability of a test refers to its relative:

   a.   validity.

   b.   power.

   c.   consistency.

   d.   appropriateness.

13. Which of the following is not a technique for determining the reliability of a test?
    a. Correlate scores on the test with those on a different test.
    b. Correlate scores on the odd-numbered items with those on the even-numbered items.
    c. Correlate scores on two different administrations.
    d. Correlate scores on two forms of the same test.

14. Which statement is true?
    a. High reliability is a sufficient condition for high validity.
    b. High validity is a necessary condition for high reliability.
    c. Validity can never be higher than reliability.
    d. Reliability can never be higher than validity.

15. If a language test required a lot of motor skills, it would be said to have low:
    a. content validity.
    b. construct validity.
    c. concurrent validity.
    d. predictive validity.

II. Comprehension

1. The mean age for third-graders in an elementary school was 8.6 years. The standard deviation for Mr. Jones's class was 1.8 and for Ms. Smith's class was 1.2. What conclusion can be drawn from this?
2. The Wechsler Intelligence Scale for Children has a mean of 100 and a standard deviation of 15. Jeremy earned an I.Q. of 125. What is his z-score?
3. Which of the following correlations indicates the strongest relationship between two variables? $+.3, +.7, -.4, -.8$.
4. A T-score of 50 is comparable to what stanine score?
5. The standard deviation of I.Q. scores on the Stanford-Binet Intelligence Scale is 16. Approximately 34 percent of students taking the test will earn scores between what two points?
6. Judy scored 72 on a test that has a standard error of measurement of 4. What does that indicate about her true score?

III. Application

Visit a school system or a university's educational assessment center and review:
a. two standardized tests of achievement.
b. two criterion-referenced instruments.
c. two norm-referenced instruments.

Use the review form in Appendix I for this purpose.

IV. Alternate Task

If none of the application exercises applies to your setting or circumstances, you can design two exercises of your own. They should demonstrate application of one or more of the principles or concepts described in the preceding chapter. Prior approval of both exercises should be obtained from your course instructor.

V. Answer Key

I.
1. c pp. 54–55
2. d pp. 58–59
3. a p. 59
4. b p. 63
5. a pp. 63–64
6. b p. 65
7. d p. 65
8. c p. 66
9. b p. 68

10. c p. 69
11. d p. 61
12. c p. 70
13. a pp. 70–71
14. c p. 73
15. a p. 72

II.
1. pp. 62–63
2. p. 63
3. p. 69
4. p. 66
5. pp. 61–62
6. pp. 64–65

Part II
Cross-Categorical Assessment Considerations

The field of special education represents a vast array of differences in handicapping conditions, developmental disabilities, and body-system impairments. The attempt to find a common denominator across the field is difficult and in many instances not fruitful in the attempt to improve services to pupils. In the area of assessment, however, there appears to be some logic in viewing early intervention, language development, and social and behavior problems as being equally important to the various special education classifications.

These three areas have in the past represented distinct training, teacher certification, and funding classifications, and they will probably continue to do so. Such distinctions are less meaningful in classroom assessment performed by a teacher; in fact, accurate, useful data collection may be hindered if the teacher is not able to utilize pupil-performance data-collection procedures relevant to each of the three areas. Logic should warn us that any child can have behavior or social problems as he or she develops and interacts with the environment. Moreover, the vital role of early intervention with persons exhibiting developmental and behavior disabilities is well documented, and the critical role of language in developing the skills needed to fulfill one's developmental potential is no longer a matter of debate. Assessment in all three of these areas must be an ongoing function of the classroom teacher.

In Part II of this book, we will look at assessment in three vital areas:

Chapter 4: Assessment of Language Impairments

This chapter describes communicative or language-impairment assessment procedures that are within the capabilities of teachers not specifically trained in speech pathology or language impairments. The role of the classroom teacher working with trained specialists in this area is also discussed. The chapter focuses on the role of the classroom teacher in screening pupils for potential language impairments and interpreting assessment data. Referral considerations are also discussed; commercially available assessment instruments are described; normal language development is reviewed; and characteristics of language-impaired pupils are listed.

Chapter 5: Assessment in Early Childhood Special Education

Five skill areas commonly addressed in early childhood assessment are examined and the role of the parents in early childhood assessment is outlined. Commercially available assessment materials appropriate for use with young children are described. The procedures discussed throughout the chapter are applicable across the array of special education classifications.

Chapter 6: Assessment of Children's Social and Behavioral Problems

We describe procedures that classroom teachers in a variety of special education settings will find useful both for determining whether a behavior problem exists and for designing effective instructional programs. Particular emphasis is given to procedures that the classroom teacher can employ to analyze the effect of the environment on the pupil and, conversely, the pupil's effect on the classroom environment. Principles of applied behavior technology as they affect assessment of behavior and social disorders are discussed. These principles have found wide use in all areas of special education assessment, program design, implementation, and evaluation.

Chapter 4

Assessment of Language Impairments

Key Terms:

auditory processing
communication game
dump and play
language formulation
language functions
language processing
language structures
minimal auditory deficiency
morphology
phonology
pragmatic model
representational deficit
rule of six
semantics
spontaneous language sampling
syntax

Chapter Objectives:

After reading this chapter and completing the Mastery Review, you will be able to:

1. Identify the characteristics of language impairments in children.
2. Develop an awareness of the importance of recognizing language impairments in young pupils.
3. Describe practical ways a special education teacher can screen and refer pupils with suspected language impairments to language specialists.
4. Describe the roles of different variables in language impairments as they affect educational programming.

Difficulties in the comprehension or expression of verbal language are a common characteristic of many exceptional children. Language impairments can interfere with a child's ability to learn, to function in a classroom, and to communicate. Throughout the day, teachers encounter frequent instances of the inaccurate, incomplete, or inefficient verbal communication that typifies the language-impaired child. The nature and characteristics of language impairments follow predictable patterns and courses of development. Knowledge of these characteristics can permit early detection, appropriate referral, better intervention, and more efficient interaction between language specialists and special educators.

Recognition of language impairments in exceptional children is important. Frequently, the first indication that a child's development is atypical is a lack of communicative development. Language-impaired children have difficulty in understanding or using vocabulary, understanding or using complete or complex sentence structures, and adjusting their communications to the appropriate person, place, and time.

Because of the frequent opportunities for communicative interactions in the classroom, teachers are in an optimal position to recognize difficulties in language use. Knowing the key attributes and major landmarks of language can help the special educator recognize a child's problem.

Characteristics of Language Development

Verbal communication is the result of an interaction of language structures and functions. Language structures involve word meanings (semantics), word patterns (syntax), word forms (morphology), and speech sounds (phonology). The functions of communication pertain to the reasons for selecting particular language structures to achieve a specific purpose.

Aspects of Verbal Language

Seven aspects of verbal language are employed in communication: semantics, phonology, morphology, syntax, purpose, contextual influences, and listener influences. Bloom and Lahey (1978) have organized these attributes into three dimensions: content, form, and use. Language content refers to the meaning or semantic aspect of a message. Phonology, morphology, and syntax are mechanisms for conveying meaning and are appropriately classified as language form. Language use encompasses the purposes of language, listener variables, and content variables. Children with language impairments have problems in using language content and form to process and/or formulate messages. A problem exists when a child's development is significantly outside the limits of that of typical children.

Criteria for Normal Development.   Many exceptional children have difficulties with one or more of the major dimensions of verbal language. Normal language development has three characteristics: time of onset, rate of progression, and sequence of development.

Time of Onset.   Most people have an intuitive idea of when children should be talking. They begin to utter their first words at around one year of age (Wood, 1981), combine words into short phrases at about 18 months (Bloom and Lahey, 1978), and are forming complex and compound sentences by age three. These milestones can be used as estimated guidelines for verbal development, and parents and teachers become concerned if a major milestone is not achieved at a particular time. Time of onset is one criterion for determining whether a child's verbal communication skills are emerging in a typical manner.

Rate of Progression.   Children's language development progresses at a predictable rate. They begin to form two-word combinations or phrases within a certain period of time after uttering their first words, though there is some leeway for time of onset and rate of progression. While concern may not be justified if a child is not uttering single words by the first birthday, it *is* appropriate if the child has not spoken a first word by the age of one year and six months. A two-year-old child is expected to advance to more complicated phrases and sentences than the two-word phrases uttered at around 18 months of age. If the child has not shown evidence of an expected milestone by a certain time or has not progressed to the next stage in the developmental sequence, concern is in order.

Sequence of Development.   Language content and form also develop in a logical and predictable sequence. Dale (1976), Bloom and Lahey (1978), Miller (1981), and Wood (1981) have summarized the developmental sequence of these aspects of verbal language. The sequence of development may be impaired in two ways. First, the child can be following the sequential progression, but at a much slower rate. This is called a "lag" or a "delay." Other children may skip some of the steps in the developmental progression. Because later stages of language are contingent on prerequisite development, skipping a step can result in fixation in the developmental progression (Morehead and Ingram, 1973). Skipping steps in the sequence of development leads to gaps and is considered disordered.

Within the special education classroom, there are likely to be several children with either delays or disorders. It is possible to determine whether language is impaired by using time of onset, rate of progression, and sequence of development as criteria. (Additional information regarding the assessment of young children's communicative skills is provided in Chapter 5.)

The Rule of Six

A handy rule of thumb to help one decide whether language content, form, and use are within the normal range is the "rule of six." Children progress from stage to stage in language development at approximately six-month intervals. Not all children begin to talk at one year or put words into phrases at one and a half; some do not start talking until 15 or 17 months of age. They may be three or four months behind their peers in progressing to the next stage of language development. It may be possible for a child to catch up on some milestone if his or her age is within six months of the typical time of emergence. If more than six months have elapsed and the milestone is not achieved (onset has not occurred) or the child has not advanced to the next stage (progression has not occurred), however, the likelihood is that development will not self-correct with maturation. The rule of six suggests that if the child is more than six months behind schedule, concern for normal development is warranted.

With this background, it is possible to define a language impairment as follows:

> Any disruption in onset, progression, or sequence of development of language content, form, or use to process or formulate meaning in communication.

Children with language impairments do not always demonstrate their communicative skills in a representative fashion. In strange situations with unfamiliar individuals, they will "clam up": verbalize as little as possible, as simply as possible, giving only what is requested and volunteering little else. Special educators are in a position to obtain valuable information about a child's language as they hear a larger and more diverse sample of communication from the child. Time and effort can be saved if special educators are able to guide the language clinician toward the language content, form, and use that the child lacks, misuses, or has difficulty using consistently. To do this requires some basic knowledge of what to listen for in a child's verbal communication.

General Characteristics of Language Impairments

As previously described, there are three major components in language — content, form, and use — and two major dimensions — processing and formulation. Children with language impairments typically show disruptions in the onset, progression, and sequence of development in the three major components. Language processing involves receiving auditory sensations, organizing the sensations into patterns, and analyzing that information. Formulation is the dimension of language involving the production of a verbal message. It includes the selection of content, coding the content into form, and organizing the form into patterns. Also known as language expression, language formulation is sometimes confused with speech (articulation), but the production of speech sounds is only one of its aspects. While many children have difficulty producing speech sounds accurately, the language-impaired child's problems center primarily on semantics, syntax, or the use of language.

A child's formulation is typically poorer than his or her processing. Because they have difficulty understanding verbal messages, language-impaired children find it hard to formulate messages. Their vocabulary lacks depth and variety, their utterances are short and incomplete, and they overuse simple sentence patterns. When they use longer or more complex sentence patterns, they seem to omit or misuse key components.

Table 4–1

**Characteristics of Impairments in the Acquisition of
Language Content**

. . . .

Vocabulary:	Reduced vocabulary size.
Variety:	Lack of variety of information in language utterances.
Context:	Content of messages involves the "here and now."
Concepts:	Difficulty understanding words that symbolize abstract concepts (e.g., if, so, then, but).
Overuse:	Overuse of a simple class of words (e.g., nouns and verbs).
Simplicity:	Difficulty following long or complex verbal directions.
Concreteness:	Problems following spoken explanations without seeing or participating in an ongoing event.

. . . .

Impairments in Language Content

Children's vocabulary represents concepts or categories of knowledge about objects and events. Many children with language impairments have difficulty either processing or formulating language content (Morehead and Ingram, 1973), which is the key building block of language structure and is considered an indicator of underlying cognitive development.

Table 4–1 highlights some common characteristics of content problems.

Delayed or Deficient Cognitive Development. The vocabulary used by language-impaired children tends to be small, superficial, and reflective of reductions in the development of underlying concepts. Bloom and Lahey (1978) suggest that content categories underlie children's vocabulary. Words represent classes of information such as existence (nouns), action (verbs), location ("here," "there"), internal state ("want," "need"), negation ("no," "not"), time, and quantity.

Language content develops through four different operations: the development of new content categories as cognitive skills mature; the subdivision of existing content categories into smaller, more refined units; the combining of content categories to form relationships; and the addition of members to content categories. Children with content impairments have problems representing objects and events by verbal symbols. A study by Morehead and Ingram (1973) indicated that poor vocabulary of language-deficient children reflected deficits in an underlying ability to represent objects, events, and relations with verbal symbols. Referring to this as a "representational deficit," they suggest that content problems in language impairment are rooted in delayed or deficient cognitive development.

Concepts Underlying Language Content. Some language-impaired children lack the cognitive development to deal with objects and events that are not of immediate personal relevance. The pupils described in Chapter 8, "Assessment of the Trainable Mentally Handicapped Learner," often exhibit this type of language

Table 4–2

Characteristics of Delay or Disorders in Language Form

. . . .

Comprehension:	Difficulty understanding long or complex utterances.
Dependence:	Reliance on short or simple sentences.
Monotony:	Lack of variety in forms used.
Overuse:	Overuse of a limited number of simple phrase or sentence patterns.
Omission:	Omission of key words or grammatical markers in sentences.
Misuse:	Misuse of verb forms in longer sentences.
Questions:	Simple or fragmented questions.
Markers:	Difficulty with tenses or plurals.
Combining:	Unable to combine tenses, plurals, verb forms, and questions accurately and completely.
Oblivious:	Unaware of the grammatical nature of utterances.

. . . .

problem. It is difficult for them to deal with things that cannot be perceptually verified or with objects and events that require a perspective other than that of their own needs.

Impaired children have a tendency to deal with objects or events in wholes rather than parts. For example, a language-impaired child may learn to call all articles of clothing that have sleeves "sleeves" rather than "shirts," "sweaters," "jackets" or "coats" because something about the sleeve is meaningful to the child. The child tends to overextend words into inappropriate contexts, for instance by labeling all liquids that can be poured into a glass "juice" as opposed to "milk," "water," or "soda." Wood (1981) noted that overextension is typical of young children but that it is outgrown as a child's cognitive skills are developed and refined. Lags and disruptions in content category development have a cascading effect on the development of form.

In brief, the concepts underlying language content are regarded as fundamentally reduced in language-impaired children, affecting further development of language form.

Impairments in Language Form

The speech of children with form problems — disruptions in the use of syntactic or morphological rules — tends to be inaccurate or incompletely organized. Long, complex sentences are difficult for language-impaired children to understand, though they may understand the same information in simple grammatical constructions. Table 4–2 illustrates some of the more common characteristics of form problems.

Some language-impaired children tend to misuse or omit key aspects of form. There is disagreement as to whether they lack the rules for processing and formulating sentences or simply do not use them. If a child forms short, simple verbal

Table 4–3

Common Characteristics of Children with Use Problems

. . . .

Oblivious:	Unaware of cues that a message was received and understood.
Rigid:	Unable to revise the content and form of a message if so requested by a listener.
Monitoring:	Difficulty recognizing that a message was inaccurately or partially received.
Roles:	Unsure about communication roles; may not respond to verbal and nonverbal cues; may interrupt speakers.
Gesture:	Relies more on gestures than on spoken language to obtain and maintain listener attention.
Tone:	Mood or affect may be inappropriate to the context or tone of the situation.
Interactive:	Seems to "send" or "receive" messages rather than interact verbally with another person.
Disinterest:	Disinterested in communicative interactions other than sending or receiving personal information.

. . . .

utterances, it is highly probable that his or her processing of long or complex information is also inadequate. Missing or misused rules for processing grammatical structure (e.g., verb tense) in a sentence can contribute to a child's misunderstanding because they lead to the inaccurate, incomplete, distorted, or inefficient gathering of information. Responses may in turn be inappropriate, incomplete, or irrelevant. Since the child may not be aware of this problem, he or she will seldom ask for repetition or rephrasing.

Impairments in the Use of Language

The ability to communicate effectively involves the selection, monitoring, and revision of language content and form. Children with language impairments frequently fail to detect the nonverbal communication cues in interpersonal interactions. Since the rules for social communication are refined in social interactions, children lacking experience in interaction may be awkward and inefficient in achieving the purposes of communication. Several of the common problems in language use are described in Table 4–3.

Dump and Play. Using language content and form involves a process that John Muma (1978) has termed "dump and play." The term "dumping" refers to the processing or formulation of words and sentences without regard to their context. Communication involves much more than "dumping" language content and form; the speaker and listener signal that communication has or has not occurred either verbally or nonverbally. The sharing of signals and any subsequent revisions in the message are what Muma calls "playing." To "play" at the communication game, a

Table 4–4

Issues and Controversies about Language Impairment in Children

. . . .

Purpose:	Is language a means to communication or an end unto itself?
Types:	Are there patterns of language impairment?
Categories:	Do the patterns of language impairment coincide with the categories of exceptionalities?
Auditory deficiency:	How does minimal auditory deficiency affect a child's language development?
Auditory processing:	How does minimal auditory deficiency perpetuate and modify language impairment?
Roles:	What are the roles of the special educator in the recognition and assessment of language impairment?

. . . .

child must be able to recognize the social aspects of the message as well as its content and form; he or she must "dump and play" both as a speaker and as a listener. Children with a use problem may be able to "dump" language content and form, but they have difficulty "playing" at monitoring and revising the message to communicate effectively.

Assessment of Language Usage.   Because many tests of language structure do not involve functional tasks, assessment of problems in the use of language is complex. Language use is best assessed in functional communicative situations such as the classroom rather than by formal tests. The data-collection procedures described in Chapter 2 have wide use in the assessment of language impairments. The use of systematic procedures focuses attention on the way a child "plays" the communication game and facilitates the speech and language clinician's gathering of valuable clinical information.

Controversies and Issues in Language Impairments

The more that is discovered about language and language impairments, the greater the number of questions that emerge. These questions have a direct influence on all disciplines concerned with language impairment. Since 1960, monumental changes have occurred in the manner in which language specialists view the nature and characteristics of language impairments, understand the variables influencing and perpetuating such impairments, and view appropriate assessment and intervention procedures. Several issues offer challenges to specialists, and these also influence the way children are tested, treated, and educated. Some of them are highlighted in Table 4–4 in the form of six questions about language impairment. Each of the areas will be elaborated in the following section of this chapter.

Means versus End or Assessment versus Intervention

One of the first major issues facing language specialists has been the realization that assessment and intervention approaches based on content and form were not achieving the goal of enabling the child to use language meaningfully. The contributions of Bloom and Lahey (1978), Chomsky (1965), Fodor and Katz (1964), and McNeill (1970) emphasized the processes and rules underlying language content and form. Entire methodologies have been developed to assess and treat deficits in the structural aspects of language. Eisenson (1972), Gray and Ryan (1973), Tyack and Gottesleben (1977), and others have developed intervention approaches that systematically shape the content and form of the child's language. It has been assumed that language structures are the tools of communication; if taught the tools, the child would automatically use them and so communicate and learn in an instructional setting.

It has become apparent that there is some conceptual or methodological flaw in structure-based approaches. Many children taught this way were meeting criterion and demonstrating proficiency in clinical situations but were still talking in short, simple, or fragmented sentences. They continued to have difficulty responding accurately, completely, and efficiently to spoken language and in generating appropriate messages in a functional situation.

Pragmatic Approaches.   New perspectives on language and language disorders, called pragmatic approaches, emerged in the mid–1970s (Lucas, 1980). Pragmatic approaches regard language as a means and communication as an end. Bates (1976), Dore (1974), Halliday (1977), and Searle (1969) described how language is used to achieve communication functions. Parallel developments in sociolinguistics provided insights into the roles of listeners, contexts, and conditions on the child's processing and formulation of language content and form.

Without a goal (communication), efforts to develop language structures would be thwarted. A child with no need or opportunity to communicate has little impetus to develop or refine content categories, syntactic rules, or morphological markers. Therapy efforts that stress structure without application to communicative contexts seldom generalize into functional situations. Children who reach criterion in therapy often have difficulty using the rules they have learned in nonclinical settings.

The communicating child attempts to exchange information either verbally or nonverbally. The means of communication may be disrupted, but the child does try to interact to a degree. Unfortunately, it is not uncommon to find language-impaired children who can parrot appropriate language structures yet are unable to communicate. These children may have been taught language structures in nonfunctional settings. What is the purpose of having the structures of language if they don't function to communicate? As we progress through the 1980s, the view that language is a means of communication has superseded the belief that the goal of language specialists should be to facilitate language structures.

Patterns of Language Impairment

A second issue, still unresolved, concerns the patterns or subtypes of language impairment. The literature in children's language has long attributed different types of language disruptions to specific causes. As early as 1954, Mykelbust introduced the concept of differential diagnosis, maintaining that there are patterns or clusters of performance on key aspects of development that typify different etiologies.

Experts have disagreed as to whether language impairments are homogeneous. Menyuk (1964, 1971) contended that language-disordered children are not "infantile speakers" functioning at a younger but intact level. She found that the types of grammatical rules they had difficulty with, their patterns of errors, and the changes that occurred in their speech over time did not resemble those of typically developing younger children. Leonard (1972) later replicated Menyuk's work and concluded that the language-disordered child has the same rules and processes as his or her chronological or matched peers but uses them significantly less frequently. He advocated the position that language-disordered children are functioning at an intact but younger level and should be regarded as delayed.

In 1973, Morehead and Ingram reported findings similar to Leonard's: grammatical rules are present in but not used by language-deficient children. Morehead and Ingram extended their investigation into the content (concepts) underlying language form and found that language-deficient children had fewer and less advanced content categories underlying the speech of language-deficient children. They suggested that these children's problem is not the application of grammatical rules but a lack of depth and variety in underlying content categories. Their problems in establishing, refining, adding to, and revising content categories are a reflection of a basic representational or cognitive deficit.

There has not been sufficient evidence to challenge Leonard's (1972) and Morehead and Ingram's (1973) position that language-impaired children are following the normal developmental sequence of content and form. Clinicians continue to maintain that they see different types of language-impaired children, different patterns of errors, and different responses to therapy. In the last three years, there has been a resurgence of interest in patterns of language impairment. While there is no agreed-upon grouping, it is becoming apparent that patterns do exist, and efforts are being made to identify them.

Differences between Delays and Disorders

The controversy surrounding the identification of subtypes of language impairment is more than an academic discussion of minutiae. If patterns could be verified, then intervention could be adjusted to meet them. Delayed children profit more from a stimulation approach in a functional context than from a remediation approach in a clinical context. The language-disordered child, however, needs to acquire prerequisite skills before efforts to move his or her language forward can be successful. Individualized remediative approaches in clinical settings are more appropriate for such a child. A stimulation approach such as that suggested for the language-delayed child would be insufficient to enable the disordered child to advance in language development.

Etiological versus Symptomatic Classifications

Somewhat related to the controversies surrounding the patterns of language impairments is the issue of the basis for classifying types of language impairments. Etiological approaches, heavily influenced by the medical model and widely held in the 1940s and 1950s, are based on the assumption that identifiable patterns of language problems can be attributed to varying underlying conditions. This approach assumes that a child with a hearing impairment will show different patterns of onset, progression, and sequence of development in language content, form, and use than will a mentally retarded or behaviorally disordered child. Traditional etiological classifications have been helpful in obtaining legislative support and educational programming for groups of children, but classifying language-impaired children by etiology may not be in their best interests.

Communication behavior is fundamental to human development and performance. It involves social, emotional, intellectual, and psychological processes. Categorizations of language impairment on the basis of etiology are of questionable value. Etiological schemas have led to categorical assessment approaches and intervention, but language-impaired children seldom fit clearly into a single etiological category.

Criteria for Classification. It is widely believed that there are different patterns of language impairment; disagreement seems to revolve around the criteria for classification. Unlike the etiological approach, the symptomatic approach is concerned with etiological conditions only as they impair intervention efforts. It focuses instead on patterns of performance in such key areas of language development as content, form, and use.

Careful observation of the comprehension and formulation of language in exceptional children indicates the following commonalities: delays in onset; delays in progression; disruptions in sequence; and problems in content, form, or use, or a combination thereof.

Combinations of these four patterns seem appropriate for categorizing children regardless of the etiology of their condition and the severity of their impairment. Particular techniques are not reserved for one specific population; the identification of patterns according to variation in the use of content and form is more appropriate.

Minimal Auditory Deficiency

Specialists working with language-impaired children have realized that relatively minor ear infections, if they occur frequently, can affect language long after they have been cleared. Repeated periods of middle-ear infection can result in gaps in the language development of children with marginal language skills. During episodes of active infection, the hearing loss filters information, resulting in a minimal auditory deficiency (Brandes and Ehinger, 1981). It is likely that many of the attentional, behavioral, and learning problems that occur cyclically are related to hearing loss. Instructions delivered verbally are distorted and/or ignored by the child with minimal auditory deficiency.

Special educators need to be concerned about the child who has a history of repeated ear infections. Recurring problems are a signal to provide special attention through preferential seating, repeating instructions, and pairing oral instructions with written or visual ones whenever feasible. The classroom teacher may first suspect this problem when a learning-style–preference profile, as described in Chapter 2, is completed. It is important to watch for changes in academic, social, or emotional behavior as documented by the profile. If the changes in a pupil's behavior are accompanied by colds, it may be that a middle-ear infection is active and that medical referral is needed. Such infections seem most likely to occur during major seasonal shifts, after a vacation to another area of the country, or when there are unseasonable weather changes in which temperatures and precipitation increase.

Auditory Processing and Language Impairments

The primary channel through which language is acquired is hearing. Hearing-impaired children show verifiable deficits in speech and language that are attributable to their impairment. Practitioners from many disciplines have long been trying to determine whether distortions in the transmission of auditory information contribute to speech, language, or learning problems in normally hearing children. Auditory processing refers to the transmission and organization of sensory information from the ear to the language centers in the brain. It involves myriad overlapping psychological processes, including discrimination, memory, figure-ground perception, and sequencing.

Bottom-up versus Top-down Approach. Aram and Nation (1982) have indicated that there are two ways of understanding the role of auditory processing in language. A "bottom-up" approach maintains that children develop language because of the perceptions they receive. For example, the ability to discriminate and remember auditory input assists the child in understanding long or complex sequences of information. That is, perception contributes to higher-level conceptual processes such as language. The opposite view, advocated by Rees (1973, 1981), is a "top-down" approach that maintains that basic cognitive-linguistic development enables an individual to process sensory information. Rees's position, which is consistent with current views on cognitive and linguistic functioning, maintains that children perceive *because* they conceptualize and utilize language. For example, they recognize or remember information about events or concepts they understand. The debate between these two viewpoints is highly active and far from resolution.

Researchers investigating auditory processing in speech-, language-, and learning-disabled children have reached different conclusions. There is as much information supporting the position that auditory processing disorders contribute to language disorders as there is opposing it. Despite the unresolved controversy, many special education teachers, speech and language pathologists, and other specialists working with children contend that their clients simply do not listen, cannot listen for long periods, or seem confused by auditory information. How is it that, though so many people concur that listening problems exist and interfere with speech, language, and academic functioning, researchers studying isolated aspects of this phenomenon fail to substantiate clinical impressions?

Complications Associated with Auditory Processing Disorders. Auditory processing disorders may not be present in every language-impaired child, but they complicate a basic language impairment when they do exist. In the child with normal language, distortions in the processing of auditory information may be compensated for by higher-level cognitive or linguistic abilities, but children cannot compensate for distortions in auditory processing if their higher-level language or cognitive skills are impaired. Distortions in auditory information processing are magnified in the language-impaired child, resulting in the inaccurate or incomplete derivation of meaning from spoken information.

As a result of their inability to understand complex verbal formulations, language-impaired children have difficulty attending. They tend to show the following characteristics: they "tune out" in the presence of competing information; in a complex listening situation, their attending skills deteriorate faster and to a greater degree than those of a normal child and remain nonfunctioning for a much longer period of time; they have difficulty "tuning in"; and they are unaware of the fact that they are "tuning in" or "tuning out." In a classroom setting, language-impaired children with auditory processing problems miss some of what is said or misinterpret aspects of what they hear. A child cannot build, refine, or extend academic skills on the basis of distorted or incomplete spoken information.

Interest in auditory processing in children with speech, language, and learning problems remains active. Lubert (1981), Tallal and Stark (1980), and Thal and Barone (1983) have continued to try to ascertain what happens when auditory information is processed by language-impaired children. While the resolution of the controversy about auditory processing is far from complete, efforts are continuing to identify and treat these children.

The Role of the Special Educator

By the nature of their training and experience, special educators have a background in the educational management of language-impaired children but do not necessarily possess training and experience in language assessment and intervention. Language clinicians, on the other hand, have had specific coursework, practica, and experience in testing and treating the communication problems of language-impaired children in clinical settings. The basic format for the interaction of speech and language clinicians and special educators should and can be complimentary. The clinician assesses and modifies language problems that are basic to the child's learning, and the teacher exploits the classroom context by screening for the presence of language problems in that setting. Combining their expertise in the recognition and treatment of the language-impaired child benefits both the child and the professionals.

Classroom Assessment

It makes little sense to waste the time and energies of the child, the classroom teacher, and the language clinician by performing the same assessments in the classroom and the therapy room. It would seem appropriate for the special educator to screen and refer and the language clinician to test and remediate. This statement is not meant to diminish the role of the classroom teacher in language assessment; it is rather a realistic observation that the assessment and treatment of language disorders require highly specialized skills. It is unrealistic to expect the classroom teacher to be competent to do more than screen the child and facilitate the work of other professionals specially trained to remediate language disorders. This is a good example of multidisciplinary teamwork.

The data-collection procedures described in Chapter 2 and the screening measures discussed later in this chapter provide information only on the possible existence of a problem. Relatively simple to administer and score, screening tests can be administered by a teacher without disrupting daily activities. Follow-up testing by a language clinician is needed for any child who fails language screening. Diagnostic testing, on the other hand, provides in-depth information about the nature and scope of a problem. These measures are time consuming, and it requires considerable effort to analyze them. If a language clinician serves the children in a special education class, he or she can and should perform both diagnostic testing and language therapy. Additional information regarding the screening of language skills in young children is provided in Chapter 5, "Assessment In Early Childhood Special Education."

The special education teacher sees the child in a variety of contexts and undoubtedly has a broader picture than the language clinician of his or her overall abilities, performance problems, and needs. Therefore, the teacher can provide the clinician with a clear understanding of what the child is doing in the classroom. Conversely, the teacher needs to understand what the clinician does with the child in therapy. The two specialists must obviously complement each other.

Proactive versus Reactive Approaches.   There is a difference between the proactive and the reactive approach to working in a classroom with the language-impaired child. In the reactive approach, the special education teacher tries to carry out what the child has learned from another specialist. The clinician, similarly, tries to extend what the child is learning in class by using class materials as a medium for focusing on language.

An alternative is the proactive approach, in which the teacher and clinician share a common base of information, with each specialist giving input into the other's activities. In order to learn in a classroom context, the child must process and formulate language content and form. If the teacher understands the necessary content and form, he or she can recognize when the child is having difficulty and identify the content and form the child lacks or misuses. In a proactive role, the special educator can save the clinician considerable time and effort by providing guidance in intervention for critical language content and form. At the same time, the clinician must be able to inform the teacher about what the child is doing in therapy, how that work can be incorporated into the classroom context, and what can be done to get the child to use language content and form.

In short, the classroom teacher can be either an aggressive participant in the child's speech and language therapy program or a passive observer. The difference between the two roles hinges on the teacher's awareness of the typical characteristics, behaviors, and patterns of linguistic performance of the child in his or her classroom who needs or is getting language therapy.

The Role of Cultural and Social Factors in Language Impairment

The general problems that cultural factors present for assessment in classroom settings were discussed in Chapter 2. For the speech and language clinician, these factors have immediate, direct impact on the assessment of language impairments. The standard language of the United States is English, but the many, varied cultural and ethnic groups that make up the country have created an equally broad mixture of English-language forms. Additional variation in language results from geographic, economic, and educational factors. All of these influences are further confounded when a handicapping condition is present that impedes an individual's communicative skills.

Dialects Are Not Disorders

Subgroups within our society differ on a variety of factors, including racial, geographic, economic, educational, and ethnic background. Members of some cultural groups use dialects, variations in standard language content and form. There has been some controversy as to whether children who speak in dialect have language impairments. This issue becomes more poignant for the exceptional child, adding to the time and effort necessary for productive language therapy.

A general set of principles for language content and form is used for instruction in school settings. Many children from microcultures — groups whose cultures differ from that of mainstream America — have language systems that seem to diverge from the standard code, yet they do not fit a definition of impaired. Throughout the 1960s, the language systems of dialect speakers were analyzed to determine whether it was an incomplete version of standard English or an intact but different system. If the language of a child is missing key concepts (content) or rules for organizing content (form), then that child needs assistance in completing the development of a language system. Adler (1979), Dale (1976), and Williams (1970) found in studies of inner-city ghetto children, children from poor rural areas, and children from diverse ethnic backgrounds that the normal child from a microculture has an intact language system that allows him or her to function adequately with other members of the microculture. In the exceptional child from a microculture, however, the combination of language impairment and dialect can give the listener the impression of inability to communicate.

Children from microcultures in the special education classroom pose unique challenges for the special educator, especially if they have language impairments. Because it is unrealistic to expect the child to master both standard and community codes, questions have been raised about the feasibility of teaching children in their restricted code rather than the standard one. This only fosters the distinction between the two codes, however. If the child needs to know the content and form of the standard code, it would seem most beneficial to assist him or her in learning to switch codes rather than to alter his or her dialect, which is not in need of remediation.

Social Factors

A child's language is affected by at least three things: the purpose of the message, the physical setting, and the person with whom the child is communicating. Bloom and Lahey (1978) refer to this aspect of language as "use." Many of the problems of language-impaired children are compounded by inexperience or lack of proficiency in adapting their language content and form to fit their purposes, context, and listener.

Inappropriate Affect Is Often a Problem.   Language-impaired children do not use language affectively; they may say the "wrong" thing at the "wrong" time or in the "wrong" way to the "wrong" person. The primary way in which normal children refine their communicative proficiency is through experience with interactions. Basic language problems, compounded by the lack of opportunity to use language, cause many special education children to have difficulty adapting their language to a specific situation and person. Thus a problem that may basically involve language content and form is compounded by inappropriate or ineffective social behaviors.

Self-Monitoring of Language Usage.   In a social situation, a child must monitor the effects of a message on the actions of listeners. If the content and form are achieving the intent, the communicators move on to other topics or information. If the listener is sending cues, either verbal or nonverbal, that the message is not understood, the child must repeat, rephrase, or adapt content and form. Language-impaired children have difficulties because they either do not attend to feedback or are unable to alter the content and form of their language. And when they fail to understand a message, they may not send the speaker cues that they do not understand. For example, the language-impaired child may follow only a segment of directions or may respond as if he or she understands what is expected when in reality the speaker's intent was lost.

Practice Helps.   Breakdowns in communication may be the result of difficulties the child has with the social aspect of language. Constant checking and verification will lead to improvement; the child needs to be encouraged to "say it a different way." The more opportunities a child has for self-expression in a variety of contexts, the more adept he or she will become at communicating. In the classroom, the special educator should watch for discrepancies between the child's academic performance and interpersonal interactions. The child who misunderstands, who responds inappropriately in an instructional context yet reacts appropriately at play with other children or adults needs special cues in the classroom. Frequently, all that is necessary is to repeat the information or to request that the child repeat it to the teacher to verify that he or she has understood. Similarly, feedback needs to be obtained as to the child's meaning. "Did you mean _____ or _____ ?" should be asked frequently.

Mastery of the social aspect of communication may be as important as the quality and quantity of language content and form. The child's age or the extent or variety of his or her intrinsic and extrinsic problems may make development of an intact structural language system impossible. In older or more impaired children, the emphasis may need to shift from the acquisition of new or more advanced content and form to assistance in the more effective use of existing content and form. This can be facilitated in the classroom setting by providing the child with opportunities to talk with a variety of individuals in different settings and for diverse purposes.

Formal and Informal Assessment Formats

Assessment of language content, form, and use should provide information about how a child processes and formulates language. The two major formats for assessing language impairments are formal and informal measures. The two employ similar data-gathering activities. Chapters 2, "Data-Collection Procedures," and 3, "Basic Principles of Measurement and Test Development," provided a detailed description of assessment and data-gathering. The section that follows will describe the specific application of these principles and procedures to the assessment of language impairments.

Formal Assessment Formats

Formal assessment measures compare a child's performance to that of some normative group in order to determine the existence and degree of deviancy. This is referred to as "norm-referenced assessment," and its general principles are discussed in Chapter 3 (p. 55). Formal measures are used to confirm the existence of a problem.

The two types of formal language assessment are screening measures and diagnostic measures. Screening measures sample a select number of communicative behaviors to enable a teacher or clinician to decide whether more in-depth assessment is warranted. They are relatively fast and simple to administer and do not require extensive training or knowledge.

Informal Assessment Formats

The second type of assessment measure examines a child's performance in relation to some criterion and is referred to as "criterion-referenced assessment"; it too was detailed in Chapter 3. Criterion-referenced measures can be used both for screening and for periodic evaluation of a child's progress. The teacher can use informal measures to determine whether a comprehensive analysis of language use is appropriate.

The majority of screening measures are relatively informal (Bankson, 1977; Compton, 1977; Fluharty, 1978; Hannah and Gardner, 1974; Hresko, Reid, and Hammill, 1981; Stephens, 1977; Zachman, Huisingh, Jorgensen, and Barrett, 1976; Zimmerman, Steiner, and Pond, 1979). Refer to Chapters 2 and 5 of this text for a broad-based discussion of screening procedures and techniques. An increasing number of screening tests is emerging for use with school-age children (Goldsworthy, 1982; Mumm, Secord, and Dykstra, 1980; Newcomer and Hammill, 1977; Semel and Wiig, 1980; Wiig and Secord, 1983).

Many of these language-screening measures are available for administration by the special educator within a classroom setting. A short description of twelve screening tests follows.

Screening Tests

Bankson Language Screening Test (N. Bankson, 1977). This screening measure samples a variety of perceptual and psycholinguistic skills fundamental to expressive language. Taking approximately 30 to 45 minutes to administer and score, the Bankson assesses semantic knowledge, grammatical rule usage, and auditory processing. The test is standardized for administration to children aged four to eight, and the data obtained can be recorded on a profile to enable the educator to identify additional areas in which diagnostic testing is needed.

Clinical Evaluation of Language Functions: Elementary Level Screening (CELF–ELS) (E. Semel and E. Wiig, 1980). The CELF–ELS is normed for children from kindergarten through fifth grade. Taking approximately 20 minutes to administer and score, it consists of 31 items that probe grammar, semantic skills, auditory memory, and word-finding skills using a "Simon-Says" game format. The derived score is compared to a criterion cut-off score for each grade level. Follow-up diagnostic testing with specific language or psychoeducational assessment measures can be directed by the results of this measure.

Clinical Evaluation of Language Functions: Advanced Level Screening (CELF–ALS) (E. Semel and E. Wiig, 1980). The CELF–ALS is designed to screen language in children from the 5th through the 12th grade. Taking approximately 20 minutes to administer and score, it probes 34 different semantic and grammatical structures to identify children who need further assessment. Using a card game rather than a sentence imitation format, the CELF–ALS provides teachers with information on key aspects of language facility. In a scoring format similar to that of the CELF–ELS, the child's performance is compared to cut-off scores for each grade level. Particularly for junior or senior high school students, this screening test can assist in selecting appropriate diagnostic tests.

Compton Speech and Language Screening Evaluation (A. Compton, 1977). A screening test for various aspects of speech and language, the CSLSE can be used to screen a kindergarten or first-grade child's communication in less than 10 minutes. Employing plastic objects, it screens the following areas of performance: articulation, vocabulary, colors, shapes, auditory-visual memory, comprehension and production of a variety of grammatical forms, fluency, and voice characteristics; it also permits inspection of the oral mechanism.

Fluharty Preschool Speech and Language Screening Test (N. B. Fluharty, 1978). Using a set of 10 picture cards, the Fluharty test screens the language of children aged two through six to identify those in need of comprehensive speech and language evaluations. The test assesses vocabulary, articulation, comprehension, and expression of grammatical constructions. The entire test can be administered and scored within 10 minutes by the classroom teacher. Scores obtained can be compared to cut-off scores in each area.

Hannah-Gardner Preschool Language Screening Test (E. P. Hannah and J. O. Gardner, 1974). Designed to screen the language of children aged three to five-and-a-half, the Preschool Language Screening Test uses objects and pictures to sample aspects of language comprehension and production. It takes approximately 25 to 35 minutes to administer and score and samples auditory, visual, motor, and conceptual tasks.

Kindergarten Language Screening Test (S. V. Gauthier and C. L. Madison, 1978). Developed for screening general language skills in five-year-old children, the KLST uses stimulus pictures to elicit a language sample. It consists of 29 items, of which a child must respond appropriately to at least 19. This screening measure also allows the teacher to judge the child's intelligibility, attention to task, willingness to communicate, and use of gestural communication. The KLST can be administered in less than 10 minutes and provides information on naming colors, counting, following multistage commands, imitating sentences, identifying body parts, and communicating spontaneously.

Merrill Language Screening Test (M. Mumm, W. Secord, and K. Dykstra, 1980). The MLST can be administered individually or to a group of children in kindergarten or the first grade. Employing three different tasks, including sentence imitation and story recall, this test evaluates receptive and expressive language, verb-tense agreement, and utterance length. It allows for consideration of dialectal variations when performance is being scored.

Multilevel Informal Language Inventory (C. L. Goldsworthy, 1982). The MILI, a probing procedure designed to assess any of 50 different syntactic constructions, enables educators and clinicians to confirm the existence of difficulty with particular types of constructions quickly and efficiently. Designed for use with children aged 4 to 12, it probes spontaneous language, imitation, and receptive language. The MILI takes approximately 45 minutes to administer and uses pictures to evoke language structures.

Oral Language Sentence Imitation Screening Test (L. Zachman, R. Huisingh, C. Jorgensen, and M. Barrett, 1976). The OLSIST is a norm-referenced screening test for expressive language. According to its authors, it can be used with children aged three to seven. Administered on an individual basis, it presents the child with sentences of varying lengths and grammatical complexities to imitate. All responses are scored on the basis of verbatim or divergent production of the model sentence. Taking less than 5 minutes to administer and score, the OLSIST differentiates borderline from failing performance.

Quickscreen (J. B. Fudala, 1981). Quickscreen identifies kindergarten and first- and second-grade children in need of further testing. Taking 15 to 25 minutes to administer and score, it samples articulation, voice, grammar, auditory memory and sequencing, auditory comprehension, and auditory integration.

Stephens Oral Language Screening Test (SOLST) (I. Stephens, 1977). The SOLST is described as a measure of simultaneously screening articulation and expressive syntax in children aged four to seven. It asks the child to repeat 15 sentences of varying length and complexity. The examiner can score the syntax on a scale of 0 to 7 according to the type of response to a sentence. Articulation is evaluated by totaling the number of errors across the sentences. Taking less than 10 minutes to administer and score, the SOLST provides information about referral for further assessment.

All of the screening measures described above can be used by a special educator to screen for language impairments. While often not as structured as the formal diagnostic measures used by language specialists, screening tests are administered according to a specific format using particular materials and stimulus items. Any time such artificial constraints are imposed on a child, it is possible that the amount and quality of language sampled may not be representative of the child's communicative abilities.

Diagnostic Measures of Language

The second group of formal measures of language is diagnostic measures. These standardized, norm-referenced tests provide in-depth assessments that are utilized to diagnose a problem and make educational decisions and placements. Typically taking more time to administer and score than informal tests, diagnostic measures are used by communication-disorder specialists to quantify the nature and extent of an aspect of a language problem, estimate the prognosis for improvement, and provide a basis for therapeutic intervention. Because of the structure these measures require for administration, they may not be practical for the special educator.

Spontaneous Language Sampling

A group of language assessment procedures can be informal as well as screening or diagnostic in nature. Known as "spontaneous language sampling," these procedures can indicate the child's level of functioning and provide information that can be used in a clinical setting. Spontaneous language sampling is the most cost-effective measure available to the special educator because it is relatively quick and simple to obtain, does not take much time to review, and provides a wealth of information about the child's use of language content and form.

Spontaneous language sampling is a flexible procedure used to evaluate the content and form of a child's language in a functional communicative context like a classroom. It involves obtaining a set of verbal utterances from the child in a conversational situation. The running-record data-collection procedure described in Chapter 2 (p. 17) can be used to record this kind of information. Since children tend to provide a more accurate picture of their language performance in conversational samples than on tests, language sampling can provide a wealth of information to special educators and language clinicians.

Obtaining Language Samples. There are two ways in which a conversational language sample can be obtained: a set number of utterances (e.g., 20 or 25) can be obtained, or utterances can be collected over a set period of time (e.g., 10 minutes). This procedure is referred to as "time sampling" and is described in more detail in Chapter 2 (pp. 18–21). A sample can be obtained either to supplement the clinician's assessment efforts or to probe the child's progress in acquiring new content or form in therapy. Ideally, the teacher should tape-record these minisamples for later replay and analysis. It is difficult to try to maintain a conversational flow and analyze language at the same time. The major purpose of the minisample in a classroom is to detect some of the child's more common content, form, and use problems (see Tables 4–1, 4–2, and 4–3).

To obtain a sample of conversational speech, set aside about 10 minutes to talk with the child in a setting away from other children or activities. Select materials, pictures, or activities that the child enjoys or likes to talk about. Converse with, but do not interrogate, the child. Any child, normal or impaired, who feels interrogated will tend to talk even less. When sampling communication, get the child to comment on objects, events, emotions, and ideas as elaborately as possible. Try to obtain descriptions of the functions of objects or events, questions about objects or events, and explanations of events or reactions.

Evoking Conversational Speech

The content and form a child uses are greatly influenced by what he or she is trying to communicate. Halliday (1977) has identified several different communicative functions. If activities are chosen according to the function they elicit, the language obtained will be diverse and reflective of the child's abilities.

Table 4–5, based on information described by Staab (1983), provides concrete ideas for activities to obtain basic communicative samples. It is recommended that two or three activities be used in a 10-minute conversation. Each activity should be from a separate category. The particular category to be sampled is based on the teacher's knowledge of the child's interests and communicative abilities. Activities involving the instrumental and regulatory functions will lead to labeling or simple utterances. Activities that are interactional, personal, heuristic, imaginative, and informational in nature lead to more elaborate utterances.

Development of IEPs.   The most productive role a special education teacher can assume with the language-impaired child is to complement the language clinician. A natural place for this cooperative relationship to occur would be in the development of a pupil's individual education plan (see Chapter 1 for a detailed description of IEP development, implementation, and evaluation). Knowledge of the characteristics of language impairments enables the teacher to recognize afflicted children in the classroom. By using miniconversational language samples, the teacher can pinpoint concerns about the use of language content and form. This information in turn provides a basis for referral to a language clinician, collaboration with the clinician, and follow-through monitoring. The types of activities described here are useful in the classroom and are not meant to supplant the special assessment procedures used by a language clinician.

Screening of Minisamples

When listening to a tape of language minisamples, focus on key content and form. Verbs, questions, tense markers, plurals, and negations are important indicators of language structures. To screen the child's content, try to determine the different

Table 4–5

Activities for Obtaining Different Language Functions during Minilanguage Sampling

. . . .

1. Instrumental Functions ("I want . . .")
   a. Requesting objects from a treasure chest.
   b. Requesting food at snack time.
   c. Requesting supplies during art activities.
2. Regulatory Functions ("Do as I tell you . . .")
   a. Role playing involving directing others.
   b. Directing placement of common objects in, around, and under boxes or cans.
   c. Giving instructions on how to participate in an activity (e.g., finger painting).
3. Interactional Functions ("Me and you . . .")
   a. Planning an activity with the teacher or clinician (e.g., going on a trip).
   b. Answering questions from clinician or another child about hidden objects.
4. Personal Functions ("I like to . . .")
   a. Discuss anomalous pictures (e.g., animals flying).
   b. Describe a favorite toy or game.
   c. Describe some interest.
5. Heuristic Functions ("Tell me why . . .")
   a. Describe activities in picture.
   b. Make up questions about a hidden object.
6. Imaginative Functions ("Let's pretend . . .")
   a. Make up a story about a TV character or show.
   b. Make wishes for a birthday or holiday.
   c. Explain wishes.
   d. Tell a fairy tale.
7. Informational Functions ("I've got something to tell you . . .")
   a. Use sequential picture cards and make up a story.
   b. Describe a family activity or holiday.
   c. Explain how two objects relate to each other.
   d. Explain what is wrong with anomolous pictures.

. . . .

types of concepts he or she is talking about (objects, attributes of objects, action words, location words, words indicating recurrence such as "more" or "another," words indicating states such as "want" or "need," and designative words such as "that one" or "this"). Bloom and Lahey (1978) have developed a useful approach to analyzing language content. Table 4–6 lists eight questions special educators should ask as they screen an audio or a videotape of a language sample. This information can be provided to the language clinician or used by the teacher carrying out a program of language therapy in the classroom.

Spontaneous language sampling is a flexible procedure and is ultimately a true reflection of the child's ability to use language in a functional situation. It enables periodic probing of a child's communicative abilities throughout the school year. Periodic language minisampling in the classroom also helps the teacher be aware of specific aspects of language content and form. Knowing what to listen for height-

Table 4–6

Key Questions for Analyzing a Minicommunication Sample

. . . .

1. What is the approximate *length* of the child's utterances?
2. Is the child using *simple verb forms* (e.g., verb + s as in "walks" or "walked")?
3. Is the child using *complex verb forms* (e.g., present progressives such as "is running" or modals such as "does run")?
4. Does the child *ask questions?*
5. Does the child use *tense markers* (past, present, future)?
6. Does the child *use language* to comment, interact, imagine, or analyze?
7. Does the child *understand explanations* of cause-effect, contingencies, or operations?
8. Can the child *explain* cause-effect relations, sequential step activities, or how things work?

. . . .

ens a teacher's awareness of the aspects of language that the child needs in order to function. This information should be shared with the language clinician to indicate progress or the need for alteration of language programs.

Limitations and Precautions

A major step in the management of language problems is the decision to refer a child for a speech and language evaluation. While most special educators can sense when a child is having difficulty communicating, they may not have a clear concept of what aspects of communication are involved. Earlier referral for special services is necessary and more appropriate than waiting for more problems to occur, referral for special services is necessary. Considerable time and effort are saved if teachers are able to specify the areas of concern or even the particular aspects and types of problems observed. Careful periodic listening to a child's language can provide the teacher, and indirectly the language clinician, with information about the child's progress or the need for alteration in therapy plans and procedures.

Summary

The assessment of language impairments, delays, and disorders and other communication problems is not usually within the training of special education teachers and may not be feasible for them to perform in light of their many other mandated instructional and IEP responsibilities. The special educator does, however, have an integral role in language impairment identification and intervention. This chapter has discussed some of the areas in which the classroom teacher and the language clinician can interact effectively. Topics and information discussed in this chapter include:

1. Language assessment by the special education teacher is primarily for screening, referral, and follow-up.
2. Language-impaired children have difficulty understanding or using vocabulary and complete or complex sentences.
3. Verbal communication is the result of an interaction of language structures (semantics, syntax, morphology, and phonology) and functions.
4. Children with language impairments often have significant difficulty with language processing and formulation.
5. The three characteristics of language development in children are time of onset, rate of progression, and sequence of language development.
6. Language delays occur when a child follows the normal sequential progression but at a much slower rate. Skipping steps in the sequence of development leads to gaps and is referred to as a language disorder.
7. Classroom teachers are in a unique position to assist the language clinician in assessing language development.
8. Language processing involves receiving auditory sensations, organizing them into patterns, and analyzing the information they contain.
9. Language formulation involves the production of a verbal message, including selecting the content, coding the content into form, and organizing the form into patterns.
10. Many children with language impairments have difficulty processing or formulating language content and have a limited vocabulary that reflects reductions in the development of underlying concepts.
11. Language-impaired children may exhibit usage problems. This is best assessed in functional communicative situations such as the classroom.
12. Issues concerning language-impaired children include questions about the purpose of language, types or patterns of language impairment, categories of impairment, the effect of auditory deficiency, the role of auditory processing, and the role of the special educator in recognizing and assessing language impairments.
13. Minimal auditory deficiency and auditory processing disorders can interfere with a pupil's ability to acquire adequate language.
14. It is appropriate for the special educator to screen and refer students with suspected language impairments. A language clinician, however, should conduct specialized language assessments and design intervention efforts.
15. Children from microcultures need experiences and opportunities in using different language codes.
16. Language-impaired children have difficulty communicating because they either don't attend to listener feedback or are unable to alter their language content and form in response to the feedback.
17. Spontaneous language sampling is the most cost-effective assessment procedure available to the classroom teacher. This procedure, which uses periodic probing of communicative abilities, is useful for screening and provides the clinician with direction for more in-depth assessment.

Mastery Review

I. Recall

1. A child who is able to express him- or herself but who has difficulty following instructions may have a problem with:
   a. language formulation.
   b. auditory processing.
   c. language processing.
   d. a and b.
   e. a and c.
   f. b and c.

2. In tapes of spontaneous speech samples, which of the following characterizes problems in the processing or formulation of language content?
   a. Misuse or omission of verb forms.
   b. Overuse of classes of vocabulary words.
   c. Overuse of short, simple utterances.
   d. Simple or fragmented questions.
   e. Difficulty understanding social roles in conversations.

3. In a language sample, utterances that are inaccurate or incomplete in organization are indicative of:
   a. problems with articulation.
   b. problems in auditory processing.
   c. problems in language content.
   d. problems in language form.
   e. problems in language use.

4. The tendency to say inappropriate things at inappropriate times or to the wrong person is indicative of a problem in:
   a. language content.
   b. language form.
   c. language use.
   d. language structures.
   e. auditory processing.

5. The principles of a pragmatic approach to language are:
   a. Function precedes structure.
   b. Language is a means of communicating.
   c. The need to communicate is the basis for acquisition of language.
   d. Structures will be acquired if there is a use for them.
   e. All of the above.

6. Deficits in concepts underlying language content characterize:
   a. children with language delays.
   b. children with language disorders.
   c. children with dialects.

    d. children with speech problems.

    e. all children with language impairments.

7. Gaps or fixations in the emergence of language content or form are regarded as:

    a. language delays.

    b. dialects.

    c. language disorders.

    d. auditory-processing disorders.

    e. differential diagnosis.

8. Approaches to language impairments that emphasize diagnosing and treating the underlying causes of the impairment are called:

    a. etiological approaches.

    b. psycholinguistic approaches.

    c. noncategorical approaches.

    d. process approaches.

    e. none of the above.

9. Language-impaired children with auditory processing problems show which of the following problems?

    a. Proficiency at tuning out irrelevant or competing background noise.

    b. Maintaining attention in the presence of other messages.

    c. Difficulty tuning in to messages.

    d. Self-awareness of when attention is wandering.

    e. All of the above.

10. The special educator can best contribute to the language assessment process by:

    a. screening and referral to language clinicians.

    b. screening and diagnostic testing.

    c. diagnostic testing and intervention.

    d. none of the above.

11. In reviewing a spontaneous language sample, the special educator should look for:

    a. occurrence of verb forms.

    b. evidence of the child's initiating communication.

    c. occurrence of plurals or tense markers.

    d. asking and answering questions.

    e. all of the above.

12. Subgroups within our society whose language code differs from the content and form of standard code are called:

    a. delayed.

    b. disordered.

    c. dialect speakers.

    d. speech disordered.

    e. none of the above.

13. A language-screening measure performs which of the following functions?

    a. Samples a select number of language behaviors.

    b. Conducts an in-depth analysis of a specific aspect of language.
    c. Gives a comprehensive evaluation of speech sound production.
    d. A and b.
    e. All of the above.

14. Informal language assessment measures:
    a. are hard to administer.
    b. require extensive training to administer and score.
    c. indicate whether further testing is needed.
    d. can only be performed by certified speech–language pathologists.
    e. none of the above.

15. In obtaining a spontaneous language sample, the special educator should try to obtain:
    a. naming or labeling behavior.
    b. answers to yes-no questions.
    c. information on following directions.
    d. descriptions and explanations.
    e. none of the above.

II. Comprehension

1. Discuss the relationship between delayed or deficient cognitive development and impairments in language content.
2. Describe the pragmatic approach to language and its implications for intervention in and assessment of language impairments.
3. Describe the role of the special education teacher in the assessment of language impairments, relating it to the multidisciplinary team and the five-level assessment model discussed in Chapter 1.
4. Explain the difference between formal and informal formats for use in assessing language impairments.
5. List some specific behaviors that may indicate language impairment in children.
6. Describe the three characteristics of normal language development discussed in this chapter.

III. Application

1. Visit an educational setting and, after conferring with the teacher, select one pupil and gather a language sample from him or her for a period of at least fifteen minutes. Use the time-sampling procedures described in Chapter 2. You may want to tape-record the language sample. Table 4–5 lists some suggested activities to facilitate obtaining different language functions in your sample. Discuss your sample in a three-to-five-page paper. Refer to Table 4–6 for some suggestions on analyzing the sample.
2. Visit a local school system or university educational assessment center and review one of the screening instruments discussed in this chapter. Use the Test Review Form in Appendix I to evaluate the instrument.

IV. Alternate Task

If none of the application exercises applies to your setting or curriculum, you can design two exercises of your own. They should demonstrate application of one or more of the principles or concepts described in the preceding chapter. Prior approval of both exercises should be obtained from your course instructor.

V. Answer Key

I.
1. f pp. 93–94
2. b pp. 86–87
3. d pp. 87–88
4. c pp. 88–89
5. e p. 90
6. a p. 86, p. 91
7. c p. 91
8. a p. 92
9. b p.94
10. a pp. 94–5
11. e pp. 103–04
12. c pp. 96–97
13. a p. 99
14. c p. 99
15. d pp. 102–03

II.
1. pp. 86–87
2. p. 90
3. pp. 95–96
4. pp. 98–99
5. pp. 86–89
6. pp. 83–85

Chapter 5

Assessment in Early Childhood Special Education

Chapter Objectives:

After reading this chapter and completing the Mastery Review, you will be able to:

1. Describe characteristics of young children that require special consideration in designing and conducting assessments.
2. Describe strategies for conducting appropriate assessments for young children.
3. Define screening and identify appropriate and inappropriate uses of data gathered using screening measures.
4. Describe five skill areas typically assessed with young handicapped children and list three important considerations in designing and conducting appropriate assessments in each area.
5. Differentiate a developmental from a functional approach to the assessment of young handicapped children.
6. Describe advantages and disadvantages of both the functional and the developmental approach to assessment with young handicapped children.
7. Define "next most probable placement" and list strategies by which early childhood special educators can identify skills children will need in future educational environments.
8. State why family involvement in the assessment process is particularly important for young handicapped children.
9. Describe at least three areas of family functioning that the early childhood special educator may need to assess.

Key Terms:

at risk
automatic reactions
concept development
criteria of the next educational
    environment
critical functions
developmental approach
fine motor skills
functional approach
gross motor skills
noncategorical setting
preacademic skills
rating scale
reactions
reflexes
self-help skills
sensorimotor skills

Most states do not require schools to provide educational services for handicapped infants and preschoolers. However, there are currently several incentives for beginning intervention early. The first and by far most convincing reason is the growing body of literature suggesting that early intervention can have a significant impact on the development of both high-risk and handicapped children (e.g., Dunst and Rheingrover, 1981; Lazar and Darlington, 1982; Simeonsson, Cooper, and Scheiner, 1982). Second, there is a growing awareness of the importance of early intervention for families of handicapped children, particularly those that have only recently learned of their child's disability. A final reason why education for handicapped children is beginning earlier is that incentive grant money for preschool programs is available through federal funding sources. Although the amount is not sufficient to cover all the costs of early-intervention programs, it is enough to make it possible for school systems to consider providing such services.

At one time, programs for very young children were viewed primarily as caretaking efforts. The adults in those programs had to be patient and caring individuals, but technical and professional teaching skills were not expected or required. Today, the successful teaching of young handicapped children demands that trained professionals be equipped with skills for dealing with their unique characteristics and needs. The educational evaluation of young handicapped children similarly requires the use of skills that differ from those required of teachers of older handicapped children. This chapter focuses on issues relevant to the educational assessment of handicapped children between the ages of three and five years.

Preschool Children and Setting Defined

Most programs for children in the preschool age range are center based or school based. Unlike the majority of services provided for older handicapped children, however, early childhood special education will typically occur in a *noncategorical* setting. It would not be at all unusual for a single preschool classroom to contain children with orthopedic handicaps, vision or hearing handicaps, social or behavioral disorders, and varying levels of mental retardation. Although larger school systems may have separate preschool classes for children with mild handicaps and those whose handicaps are more severe, most preschool classes are organized around the ages of the children served rather than around handicapping conditions. Thus the early childhood special educator must be prepared to assess the educational needs of children with many different conditions.

In addition, the early childhood special educator must be prepared to assess children with a wide range of developmental skills. Children identified as handicapped at a young age are likely to be more severely impaired than those identified after entry into public schools, since mild handicapping conditions often are not apparent until school-related demands are made upon a child. (Chapter 7 provides a more detailed discussion of assessment of pupils exhibiting mild handicapping conditions.)

The teacher of young handicapped children must be prepared to assess and teach very basic developmental skills. For example, a severely retarded three-year-old may need to work on skills that are ordinarily demonstrated during the first year of life. The teacher must also be prepared to assess important preacademic skills in mildly handicapped preschoolers; the bright five-year-old child with cerebral palsy, for instance, may need to work on skills needed for successful entry into kindergarten.

Issues and Special Problems

All age levels and handicapping conditions require some unique considerations in planning and conducting the process of educational evaluation. In assessing young handicapped children, the special educator must recognize four factors. First, they will frequently be involved in screening and early identification, and so should be aware of important considerations in using and interpreting screening data. Second, the early childhood special educator will be assessing young children, and so should be aware of age-specific characteristics that affect the assessment process. Third, the educator must find an appropriate balance between assessing developmental skills and assessing functional skills, and so should have a working knowledge of normal development as well as of daily living skills that will be required of children. Finally, the early childhood special educator must be able to work with parents in the assessment process and may need to assess the family's skills as well as the child's.

Screening and Early Identification

Many school systems now conduct early screening programs for developmental disorders in order to identify children who may be at risk for school failure. Early childhood special educators are often responsible for conducting the initial screening assessments. Children identified as high risk are referred for more thorough examination, usually by an interdisciplinary team.

Screening is based on the assumption that early intervention makes a difference. Although screening serves an important purpose, the teacher should be aware of its limitations. Interpreting screening data and making proper use of the information gleaned from them are critical in an evaluation program.

Screening Defined. Screening is the process of assessing a large number of children for the purpose of identifying those who need more thorough evaluation to determine whether or not they actually have problems. For example, a teacher might shake some noisy toys behind each child as a rough screening for hearing impairment. Those children who react slowly or not at all may need to be referred for a more thorough audiological examination to determine whether there actually is a hearing loss.

When a handicap is not readily apparent, a more formal procedure must be used for screening large numbers of children. For example, phenylketonuria

(PKU), a metabolic disorder typically resulting in mental retardation, cannot be identified simply by looking at an infant. Its effects are so devastating, however, that a urine screening for PKU is now routinely conducted for all newborns.

Selecting a Screening Tool. Several preschool screening measures are commercially available; some of the more popular ones are listed and described in Table 5–1. Some are intended to screen for broad problems such as "developmental delay" or lack of "readiness" for school, while others screen for more specific handicaps such as learning disabilities or a sensory impairment.

In selecting a screening measure, the early childhood special educator, together with other appropriate staff, should first determine the primary purpose of the screening program. What are you looking for? What will happen to children who are considered at risk on the basis of their performance on the screening measure? Are resources available for more detailed evaluations? Are interventions available for children who do need special services? Once these questions have been answered, screening measures should be evaluated according to their ability to meet your program's needs.

An effective screening measure will embody at least the following four characteristics. First, it should be accurate and valid for the intended purpose. Second, it should be short, economical, and easy to administer, since many children will be screened. Third, its form should not be aversive to children. Finally, it should not impose unusual time or transportation requirements on parents.

Many states or school systems have developed their own instruments for identifying children at risk for school failure. While these vary considerably in quality, a locally developed screening instrument may be more useful than a commercially available one since it may more accurately reflect the expectations of the local program. Locally developed measures may have drawbacks because the development of a reliable, valid measure of developmental skills is time consuming and expensive. (See Chapter 3 for a description of the instrument-development process.) Many states or school districts do not have the time, the money, or the expertise to develop an appropriate measure, and the result may be a misleading or inaccurate instrument. Therefore, it is often advisable for agencies to select a published, well-established screening tool.

Using Screening Data. Screening measures alone should not be used to determine the presence or absence of a handicapping condition; they were not developed or validated as diagnostic measures and should not be used as such. *The only valid use of screening data is to determine whether a child should be referred for further evaluation.* For example, the Denver Developmental Screening Test classifies test performance simply as "normal," "questionable," or "abnormal." Children whose performance is classified as abnormal often are referred for more extensive evaluation; those whose performance is classified as questionable are screened again after a period of time. In interpreting screening data to parents, early childhood special educators should emphasize that poor performance on a

Table 5–1

Common Preschool Screening Measures

Scale	Age Range	Time Required	Who Assesses	Method of Gathering Information
Battelle Developmental Inventory Screening Test (Newborg, Stock, Wnek, Guidubaldi, and Svinicki, 1984)	0–8	10–30 minutes	Teacher notes professional	Some parent interview Some direct test Some observation
Comprehensive Identification Process (Zehrback, 1975)	2½ 5½	25–35 minutes	Teacher or trained paraprofessionals supervised by professionals	Some parent interview Some direct test
Denver Developmental Screening Test (Frankenburg, 1975)	0–6	10–20 minutes	Teacher Nurse Social worker	Some parent interview Some direct test
Development Profile II (Alpern, Boll, and Shearer, 1980)	0–6	20–40 minutes	Teacher or Social worker	Parent interview
Preschool Attainment Record (Doll, 1966)	0–7	20–30 minutes	Teacher Social worker	Parent interview

screening measure does not necessarily mean a child has a handicapping condition.

Assessing Young Children

Naturally, the early childhood special educator will be assessing young children, whether the assessment is a screening or a more detailed educational evaluation. Anyone who has tried to assess young children can attest to the difficulties frequently encountered in the process. Teachers of young exceptional children should be aware of the factors that can complicate the assessment process and should know how to ensure that the information obtained from assessments is representative of the child's true abilities.

Problems.   Young children are particularly difficult to test for at least three reasons. First, they are easily distracted. They usually attend to stimuli that interest them and may not want to perform the task requested. Second, young children have short attention spans. Although interested in a task, a child may not be able to persist at it for long. Finally, young children often shy away from strangers. Any parent can recount numerous examples of his or her young child's refusal to perform for a stranger a task that had often been performed at home. This problem is particularly apparent in the area of communication skills, where a normally talkative child will suddenly clam up when in the presence of unfamiliar adults. This point was introduced in Chapter 4's discussion of the teacher's unique position to evoke representative language samples (p. 102).

The problems associated with assessing young children can be serious if they interfere with an accurate determination of the child's abilities. A child who refuses to perform tasks required on standardized measures will score below his or her potential and may inappropriately be labeled as handicapped. On the basis of test results, an educator may decide to teach a skill that the child can actually perform but simply did not demonstrate, thus wasting time that could have been spent working on more appropriate skills at a higher developmental level. Because of these and other possible problems, anyone involved in the assessment of young children should be familiar with strategies that increase the probability of obtaining a representative and accurate sample of the child's skills.

Strategies.   The potential for obtaining inappropriate assessment data is reduced when a familiar person such as a parent or teacher is involved in the assessment process. Optimally, the child should know the teacher and feel comfortable in his or her presence. Similarly, the teacher should know the child and be able to provide an assessment that includes individualized activities that are motivating for him or her. However, at certain times, such as when a child first enters a program or when initial screening is conducted, it may be impossible to arrange an extended period during which children and teachers can get to know each other. In such cases, one important strategy to consider is having one or both parents present during the assessment. Research generally indicates that this practice is useful in obtaining accurate skill assessments. When parents are present, however, they should be asked not to provide any assistance to the child. The parent should serve as a source of emotional support for the child but should refrain from giving any hints or other forms of help.

Several other conditions will also increase the chances of observing the child's best possible performance. First, the materials and activities selected should be those that naturally appeal to young children. Colorful materials and a gamelike atmosphere can increase the child's motivation to attend to and persist at a task. Pacing and variation are also important. Children generally perform better and for longer periods of time when tasks are presented at a fast pace, with little waiting time in between, and when seat-work tasks requiring concentration are alternated with activities allowing movement. Third, the teacher should encourage the child to persist by maintaining a high success rate and, if necessary, by reinforcing the child for his or her efforts. Knowledge of the pupil's preferred rewards is helpful (see the discussion on learning-style preference in Chapter 2, pp. 27–32). Finally, the teacher should gather information from such additional sources as third-party reporting and naturalistic observation.

An example of a standardized test well organized for young children is the McCarthy Scales of Children's Abilities (McCarthy, 1972). The first two subscales of the test require no verbal responses, thus helping to establish rapport with the shy child. Only a single-word response is required in the third subscale; it is not until the fourth subscale that the child needs to explain his or her response. Gross motor items occur in the middle of the scale, allowing children a break from seat work. Materials are colorful, attractive, and in a gamelike format. Furthermore, extra trials are permitted for many items, and only the child's *best* performance is counted.

Determining Instructional Targets

There are two fundamentally different approaches to the assessment of young handicapped children. The *developmental approach* assumes that children should be taught skills in the sequence in which they normally develop. Assessment should be conducted within a developmental framework, and instruction should proceed in accordance with developmental guidelines. For example, the normal developmental sequence for learning to walk includes such prerequisite skills as sitting, crawling, creeping, and pulling to stand. The developmental approach assumes that in order to learn an advanced skill in the sequence, a child must first master all of the skills that typically precede it. Thus, if the teacher wants Larry to learn to walk, he will first have to sit, crawl, and creep.

The *functional approach,* in contrast, assumes that children should be taught skills that are immediately useful or that will help them move to and be successful in a less restrictive placement. Assessment should seek to determine the child's ability to perform functional tasks, and instruction should focus on skills not yet demonstrated. Thus the teacher who wants Larry to learn to walk might simply conduct a *task analysis* of walking, breaking it down into a sequence of teaching steps. (Chapter 2, beginning on p. 22, provides a more detailed discussion of task analysis.)

Determining appropriate instructional targets is relatively easy for elementary school teachers since there is common agreement on the skills that should be taught in curriculum areas like reading, mathematics, and spelling. The early childhood special educator, however, is not working under similar conditions. There is still some question as to which skills have the highest probability of helping the child be more successful, independent, and happy in later life. Thus the issue of developmental versus functional targets is a very real one.

Incorporating Two Approaches.   Although the developmental and functional approaches clearly differ in a number of dimensions, teachers do not need to decide to choose one or the other. Both have merit, and both should be incorporated in a meaningful assessment of young children. On the one hand, to take a strictly functional approach might mean that the teacher would try to teach a child a skill for which he or she had none of the necessary prerequisites. On the other hand, taking a purely developmental approach might mean that the teacher would try to teach a child a meaningless skill just because it is a developmental milestone. A common item on many developmental scales, for example, asks whether the child can stack 10 blocks. Although this task is a good developmental indicator, it is not clear whether stacking blocks fulfills any important function for children. Teachers might be better off identifying related fine motor skills such as sorting or writing, which have greater usefulness.

Developmental targets and functional targets are not mutually exclusive groups of skills. Both approaches are important and should be incorporated in the assessment process. The functional approach should be used to identify critical skills to be taught, and the developmental approach should be used to identify useful instructional sequences for accomplishing those skills.

Most Probable Next Placement.   Regardless of the philosophical perspective one takes, an important strategy in determining instructional targets is to look at the requirements for successful participation in the most probable next placement setting. Vincent, Salisbury, Walter, Brown, Gruenwald, and Powers (1980) refer to this process as the identification of the *criteria of the next educational environment.* The first step is to identify the placement setting to which the child is most likely to go following the present one. For most children in early childhood programs, that placement will probably be a kindergarten or a special education classroom. Next, the skills needed in that setting are identified. Vincent et al. suggest four strategies for doing this. First, the child could spend a brief time in the setting to see what skills are needed. Second, the teachers in that setting could be asked to generate a list of survival skills. Third, the present teacher could identify by observation the skills most often required in that setting. Finally, children previously moved into the setting could be followed to determine the extent to which they were successful in the transition.

Family Assessment

All teachers, and especially teachers of handicapped children, should recognize the importance of involving families in the assessment, planning, and intervention process. First of all, the parents may be valuable sources of information about their child. More importantly, however, the family may require the early childhood special educator's assessment efforts. Most families that have only recently learned of their child's disability experience considerable stress, and they often need considerable support from schools and teachers. The teacher may assess the family's needs and address it as a partial or even primary focus of the intervention effort. Strategies for assessing family needs are discussed later in this chapter.

Multicultural Factors in Assessment

Like teachers of children of any age group and any handicapping condition, the early childhood special educator will be assessing and teaching in a multicultural, multiethnic society. In such a society, it is incumbent upon those involved in the assessment process to ensure that decisions based on assessment data are fair and appropriate for all children and families.

Bias can occur in several ways. The test instrument itself may contain content and language unfamiliar to children from certain cultural groups. The examination may be biased if the examiner is prejudiced or if the format of the testing session is not familiar to the child. The norms or other criteria for interpreting performance may also be unfair to some children. The central issues involved in nondiscriminatory assessment and the effects of cultural factors were discussed in Chapter 2 (p. 41).

Reducing Bias. To reduce the possibility of bias in the assessment process, the early childhood special educator should take several precautions. Bailey and Harbin (1980) suggest at least three broad strategies. First, major decisions should be made by a multidisciplinary team that has made an active, concerted effort to involve parents in the assessment and decision-making process. Second, to the extent possible, assessment should focus on identifying specific skills for the purpose of determining relevant educational goals rather than for the purpose of labeling and placement. Finally, assessment should be conducted from an ecological perspective: the teacher should seek to determine which skills the child will need to survive and succeed within his or her own community as well as those needed to succeed in school.

Assessment of Children with Multiple Handicaps

The appropriate assessment of children with physical or sensory impairments has always been a difficult issue for psychologists and others who assess special populations. Most measures are designed and scored on the assumption that test items have been administered according to the standard procedures specified in the test manual. Any modification of those procedures violates the integrity of the test and makes any interpretation of the scores meaningless.

Many children with sensory or motor impairments, however, cannot be tested fairly under such circumstances. For example, a bright girl with severe cerebral palsy may pass only a few items on an intelligence test because she cannot perform the required motor or speech movements. As a result, she may inappropriately be labeled mentally retarded. Chapter 8, "Assessment of the Trainable Mentally Handicapped Learner," provides a detailed discussion of other assessment issues affecting persons exhibiting moderate mental retardation. Chapter 9, "Assessment of the Profoundly Handicapped Pupil," discusses assessment of children exhibiting severe retardation and multiple handicapping conditions.

Modifying Test Items and Procedures

Fortunately, the teacher often has more flexibility than the psychologist, since educational assessments are designed primarily to identify instructional objectives rather than to determine the presence or absence of a handicapping condition. The emphasis is on the specific skills a child can or cannot perform rather than on the score obtained. The teacher can and should modify or adapt assessment procedures when appropriate to determine a child's skills. It should be emphasized that modifying a standardized assessment procedure violates the guidelines for most tests and precludes the comparison of test scores with those of a normative group.

Techniques for Adaptation.   Several ways to modify test items have been suggested. The Uniform Performance Assessment System (Haring, White, Edgar, Affleck, Hayden, Munson, and Bendersky, 1981) describes three general techniques. A *support* adaptation means that the child must be placed in a certain position or provided some general form of support before being able to pass an item. A *prosthetic* adaptation means that the child needs a specific piece of equipment such as braces or a hearing aid to demonstrate a skill. A *general* adaptation is one that does not require support or a piece of equipment but still represents a change in the basic requirements of the task or changes the utility of a skill. For example, a hearing-impaired child may need to perform communication tasks using manual signing.

McLean and Snyder-McLean (1978) describe several general adaptations. First, the teacher can modify the stimulus materials. For example, a child with motor impairments may need to have pictures cut apart and spread out in order to point to the correct choice. Second, the teacher can modify the way in which the stimulus is presented. For example, if the child cannot perform the task according to the specified procedure, the teacher may give a hint or perhaps even model the skill to determine the level of support a child needs in order to complete it.

Assessing for Critical Functions.   Several factors must be considered in deciding when and how to modify a task. The first step is to determine, if possible, the critical function being tested by a given item (White, 1980). Understanding the concept of critical function requires comprehending the basic nature of any test. Each test item is simply an indicator of a broader skill. For example, many tests require the child to complete a sentence like the following: "Fire is hot; ice is _____ ." The intent of this item is not to determine whether the child knows the answer to this particular question; it is to determine whether the child has the cognitive abilities necessary to complete opposite analogies.

Determining the critical function of an item requires the teacher to ask, "What is this item really testing?" Once this question is answered, an appropriate modification or adaptation can be designed. For example, many tests have an item such as, "Put together a three-piece puzzle." What is the critical function of this item? There are many possibilities. It could be an attempt to measure the child's motor, cognitive, visual-perceptual, or recreational skills. The modification used depends upon the critical function of the item. If it is designed to test motor skills, a child with no arms should have to perform some other motor manipulation (e.g., moving pieces with a head pointer) in order to pass the item. If it is designed to test cognitive or visual-perceptual skills, the teacher might ask the child to describe where the pieces go. If it is designed to assess recreational skills, the teacher might simply substitute a more appropriate recreational activity.

The purpose of any modification or adaptation of test procedures is to determine the level of physical or instructional assistance the child needs in order to perform a task or to determine an alternate way for the child to demonstrate the skill in question. Modifying assessment procedures is time consuming and difficult. However, for children who have physical or sensory impairments, it is a critical aspect of the assessment process and should be carefully and thoroughly planned. Additional suggestions for educational evaluation of multiply handicapped children are discussed in Chapters 8, 9, and 10.

Areas for Assessment

Because the early childhood special educator works with very young children, the skills he or she assesses differ considerably from those assessed by teachers of older handicapped children. Assessment usually centers around six broad domains: cognitive and preacademic; communication; play and social interaction; fine and gross motor; self-help; and family skills.

Many types of assessment instruments have been developed for use with young children, and they differ in both purpose and form. Some are designed primarily to determine the child's level of functioning in comparison to other children (norm-referenced), while others are designed mainly to help plan instructional programs. Some cover a wide range of skill areas; others focus on a single developmental area such as cognitive or language skills. Some assess skills through actual testing, others through direct observation in natural settings or by interviewing. It would be impossible to review all of the existing measures within the confines of this chapter, so general considerations for assessment in each developmental area will be discussed. Tables are included to provide a brief listing and description of some of the more common measures. The reader should consult test manuals for more detailed information regarding each measure or consult sources that review published tests (e.g., Buros, 1978; Doucette and Freedman, 1980; Hoephfner, Stern, and Nummedal, 1971) or entire texts devoted to assessment in early childhood special education (e.g., Bagnato and Neisworth, 1981; Darby and May, 1979; Goodwin and Driscoll, 1980; Paget and Bracken, 1983; Powell, 1981).

A large number of measures have been developed over the past 15 years to assess developmental skills across a variety of areas. Some of the more popular measures are described in Table 5–2.

Assessing Cognitive and Preacademic Skills

Skills related to basic thinking and conceptual development are generally referred to as "cognitive" skills. We cannot observe cognitive skills per se; rather, we infer their presence by observing a child's behavior. Many terms have been used to describe cognition, of which "intelligence" is perhaps the most common. Unfortunately, no label tells us very much about the specific cognitive skills a teacher should assess or teach. Therefore, considerable effort has been made to address the nature of cognition and the instructional implications of what is now known about cognitive development.

Cognitive skills in preschool children are usually divided into two major groups: the sensorimotor skills, which normally develop during the first two years of life; and the preacademic/conceptual skills, which normally develop between the ages of two and six years. The teacher of three-to-five-year-old handicapped children should be able to assess skills in both areas because many severely handicapped young children need to learn some of the basic sensorimotor skills.

Sensorimotor Skills. Cognition is a particularly difficult construct to describe in very young children. The most commonly accepted description of cognitive development during this period of life is that proposed by Piaget (1952). Assessment of the skills he proposes has been operationalized by Uzgiris and Hunt (1975) in the Ordinal Scales of Psychological Development. Although the general intelligence of infants is still assessed using such infant intelligence tests as the Bayley Scales of Infant Development (Bayley, 1969), many teachers now use the Uzgiris-Hunt scales to assess the cognitive skills of very delayed children.

The Ordinal Scales of Psychological Development assess the six basic sensorimotor skills described by Piaget. *Object permanence* refers to the child's knowledge that people or things exist even when they are not immediately present. For example, the child who has not yet learned object permanence will not search for a toy that falls from a high chair, whereas the child who tries to find the dropped toy apparently has learned that it exists even when it is out of sight. *Causality* refers to the child's ability to recognize cause-and-effect relationships. *Means-ends behavior* refers to the child's ability to try purposively to solve a problem or achieve a result by using objects or people. For example, the child might use a yardstick to obtain a toy that had rolled underneath the couch. *Spatial relationships* are those skills required in the accurate perception of objects in space and in relationship to one another. *Imitation* occurs when the child can copy the behaviors needed to explore objects and the environment in general.

Preacademic Skills

Cognitive development between the ages of two and five years is in some ways less clearly described than that of infancy. However, the major skill areas of concern to teachers are those related to the development of concepts, reading, and math.

Concept Development.   The skills associated with grouping and classification are included in concept development. The first prerequisite is simple discrimination; the child who can perform this skill can, for example, differentiate a ball from nonballs. The next prerequisite is matching, or finding objects or pictures that are alike. After matching, the child learns to sort objects into different groups. By this point, the child has the basic skills necessary for concept development. The teacher's task is to assess which concepts the child has, determine which are needed, and teach those not successfully demonstrated.

Assessment and instruction in prereading and premath skills follow directly from this stage. *Prereading skills,* of course, are those thought to be important to the development of reading, including comprehension (e.g., describing action in pictures, sequencing pictures, recalling details of a story), visual discrimination (e.g., matching letters, naming letters, reading common words on sight), and sound discrimination (e.g., identifying rhyming words, matching consonant and vowel sounds, sounding out words). *Premath skills* are those thought to be important to the development of number concepts and the performance of mathematical operations. They include basic concepts such as big/little, more/less, all/none, number recognition, counting, and matching numeral to set.

Preferred Assessment Strategies.   Of the three primary assessment strategies — direct testing, naturalistic observation, and parent interview — direct testing is preferred for assessing most cognitive skills for several reasons. First, it gives the teacher the opportunity to observe the child's responses to a variety of very specific cognitive tasks. The characteristics of the stimuli presented can be controlled, thereby allowing for a more precise description of the child's skills. Naturalistic observation is important for determining functional use of cognitive skills, but for instructional purposes the teacher should plan some systematic assessment of cognitive and preacademic skills. Although parents can also provide some useful anecdotal information (e.g., whether the child searches for people when they leave the room, an indication of object permanence), here again the teacher is limited

Table 5–2

Preschool Assessment Scales Covering More than One Developmental Area

Scale	Age Range	Cognitive/ Preacademic	Communication	Social/ Play	Fine and Gross Motor	Self-help	Other
Battelle Developmental Inventory (Newborg, Stock, Wnek, Guidubaldi, and Svinicki, 1984)	0–8	X	X	X	X	X	Attention, Personal responsibility; Expression of feelings/ affect, coping, social role, peer/adult interaction
Behavioral Characteristics Progression (Office of the Santa Cruz County Supt. of Schools, 1973)	0–Adult	X	X	X	X	X	Perception Task completion Music and rhythms
Brigance Diagnostic Inventory of Early Development (Brigance, 1978)	0–6	X	X		X	X	
Carolina Developmental Profile (Lillie, 1975)	2–5	X	X		X		Visual perception
Early Intervention Developmental Profile (Schafer and Moersch, 1981)	0–6	X	X	X	X	X	
Early Learning Accomplishment Profile (Glover, Preminger, and Sanford, 1978)	0–3	X	X	X	X	X	

	Age					
Hawaii Early Learning Profile (Furuno, O'Reilly, Hosaka, Inatsuka, Allman, and Zeisloft, 1979)	0–3	X	X	X	X	
Learning Accomplishment Profile (Sanford and Zwelman, 1981)	3–6	X	X	X	X	
Portage Project Checklist (Bluma, Shearer, Froham, and Hillard, 1976)	0–6	X	X	X	X	Infant stimulation
Rockford Infant Developmental Evaluation Scales (Project RHISE, 1979)	0–4	X	X	X	X	
Uniform Performance Assessment Systems (White, Edgar, Haring, Affleck, Hayden, and Bendersky, 1981)	0–6	X	X	X	X	
Vulpé Assessment Battery (Vulpé, 1977)	0–5	X	X	X	X	Basic Senses and Functions; Organizational Behaviors; Assessment of Environment

Table 5–3

Common Measures of Cognitive Development

. . . .

Scale	Age Range	Areas of Assessment
Bayley Scales of Infant Development (Bayley, 1969)	0–2½	Mental Motor
Griffiths Mental Development Scales (Griffiths, 1978)	0–8	Locomotor Personal-social Hearing and speech Eye and hand coordination Performance
McCarthy Scales of Children's Abilities (McCarthy, 1972)	2½–8½	Verbal Perceptual-performance Quantitative Memory Motor
Ordinal Scales of Psychological Development (Úzgiris and Hunt, 1975)	0–2½	Visual following and permanence of objects Development of means for obtaining environmental events Initiation Operational causality Object relations in space Development of schemes for relating to objects
Stanford-Binet Intelligence Scale (Terman and Merrill, 1973)	2–adult	Organized by age levels No differentiation by skill areas
Test of Early Learning Skills (Somwaru, 1979)	4–5	Thinking Language Numbers
Wechsler Preschool and Primary Scale of Intelligence (Wechsler, 1967)	4–6½	Verbal Performance

. . . .

to the cognitive skills naturally stimulated by the environment and may not get a clear picture of the broad range of the child's abilities and disabilities. A listing and description of common measures of cognitive skills in infants and preschoolers is presented in Table 5–3.

When assessing the cognitive skills of young children with sensory or motor impairments, the teacher should take care to ensure that each item is actually assessing a cognitive skill without penalizing the child for another impairment. Tasks must be modified so that the child can exhibit the true extent of his or her skills and the teacher can plan appropriate instructional programs.

Most preschool assessment scales have sections for assessing cognitive skills (see Table 5–2). These are generally the weakest sections of the instruments because of the difficulty inherent in describing cognitive development and the overlap of skills with other areas of development. Furthermore, most tests do not bother to describe the instructional implications of the items they include. In using any of the available scales, the teacher should evaluate the items to determine which critical functions are being assessed. For example, if a test includes an item such as "Responds correctly when given the following instruction: Put the pencil on the chair and then close the door," the teacher should not assume that this skill in itself should be an instructional target for the child. The critical function of this item is following two-step commands, and it is not a motor or hearing task but a conceptual and sequencing task. By identifying the critical functions of items included on assessment scales, teachers of young handicapped children can help ensure that they are designing instructional programs that are appropriate for the individual needs of the children in their classes.

Communication Skills

Communication is the process by which two individuals exchange information. The symbols used to communicate are the *language* of communication. Language may be expressed through a variety of common *modes* — speech, facial expressions, nonverbal behavior, touching — or through such *augmentative communication modes* as manual signing, communication boards, or computer-assisted communication. The appropriate assessment of communication skills requires a basic understanding of the developmental course of communication and an awareness of the major functions communication fulfills for young children.

Development of Communication. Communication skills interact with skills from several areas of development, particularly cognition. For example, communication requires a certain level of comprehension, means-ends skills (because communication can be used to achieve certain goals), imitation, and representational or symbolic thought. Communication requires some form of motor ability, of either the speech mechanism or some other. And communication is an inherently social process, requiring a certain level of social awareness.

Many different dimensions of communication development can be described, assessed, and treated. For example, the teacher could concentrate on the development of *phonology,* the speech sounds a child makes, or of *syntax,* the way in which the child orders words within a sentence. Most professionals now suggest, however, that teachers focus initially on assessing the meaning (semantics) and functions (pragmatics) of communication for young handicapped children. In this way the educator is assured of teaching communication skills that have the greatest probability of being used in the real world. (A more detailed description of language development and function has been provided in Chapter 4.)

Dore (1975) has described nine functions of communication commonly observed in young children: labeling, repeating, answering, requesting action, making other requests, calling, greeting, protesting, and practicing. Tough (1977) has identified major functions of language use in children ages three through seven. Taxonomies such as these have been offered as guidelines for assessment and instruction of young handicapped children. Thus the focus is on communication, with only secondary emphasis on syntax and phonology. This is not to suggest that syntax and phonology are not important; the point is rather that the most effective and immediately meaningful instructional approach is to stress what communication can do for children and to help them realize and learn those skills regardless of the mode in which they are expressed.

Assessing Communication Skills.   Of the three primary assessment strategies, direct observation and direct testing are the preferred methods of determining communication skills. Chapter 2 includes a detailed description of direct-observation data-collection procedures. Since communication is a social act, it is important to determine how the child uses and responds to it in a natural social environment.

Usually naturalistic communication assessments begins with a *language sample*. This is a documentation of all communicative efforts and responses by a child within a certain time frame. In collecting a sample, several guidelines should be followed:

1. The sample must be representative of the child's typical attempts to communicate. Therefore several samples should be collected.
2. The setting in which the observation takes place should maximize the probability that the child will demonstrate his or her highest level of communication. Therefore it should be a pleasant environment in which the child feels comfortable, and it should have numerous toys to stimulate communication and includes other people, both peers and adults.
3. The teacher may need to take an active role in the sampling process to encourage communication by asking open-ended questions or commenting on events in the room.
4. The context in which an utterance is made should be noted, since the same utterance may have two different meanings depending on the events immediately preceding it.

Establishing Instructional Targets.   Once the teacher has obtained a representative sample of the child's skills, instructional targets should be specified. The sample should be used to determine the range of communication functions the child uses. For example, a study of several language samples may indicate that a child never greets or answers peers. The instructional target could be to increase the number of times the child answers a direct question from a peer. The focus on communication function in the assessment process facilitates the adaptation of assessment procedures for multiply handicapped children. For example, the teacher may decide after collecting samples on all the children in the class that three children need to work on requesting. However, the manner in which each is expected to request may be quite different. Johnny may need to ask for juice verbally using a two-word sentence, Alecia may need to combine two manual signs to ask for juice, and Rebecca may need to point to a picture of juice on her communication board.

Although a language sample is the best indicator of the overall level of a child's communication skills, direct testing may also serve an important role. In particular, receptive communication skills may need to be assessed through direct testing. It is difficult to control the communication addressed to the child in a natural environment. The direct test allows the teacher to determine which specific kinds of messages are or are not understood by the child. A listing and description of common preschool language scales is displayed in Table 5–4.

Since communication is such a complex process, the early childhood special educator will need to learn to work in a multidisciplinary context to assess and plan an intervention program. A communication-disorders specialist or speech therapist or pathologist can provide important information about speech and language development, design sophisticated interventions, and offer one-to-one therapy to children who need it. Psychologists can provide important information about related cognitive skills. Children with physical impairments may need a physical therapist or an augmentative communication specialist to design an appropriate communication mode. Finally, parents should be involved in the communication assessment process to determine their priorities and needs in communicating with their child.

Play and Social Interaction

Young children spend the majority of their time playing. This time is not wasted, however; children learn and practice many things through play. In fact, many people have remarked that play is the young child's work. Teachers of young children have learned to use play as a means of facilitating the acquisition and use of many cognitive, social, self-help, motor, and communication skills. Early childhood special educators realize that careful planning of the play experience is important because many children do not have the skills necessary to make the best use of the play experience. The assessment of play skills actually encompasses three broad areas: toy play, peer interaction, and the play environment.

Toy Play.   The area of toy play addresses the child's ability to interact with toys, games, and other recreational equipment. The emphasis is on using the equipment appropriately, not on social interactions within the context of the play.

From a developmental perspective, initial toy play may be characterized as exploration. Wehman (1977) has described several levels of exploratory play. In the first, the child simply makes general orientational responses to changes in the environment. The next level is locomotor exploration of the environment. More

Table 5–4

Common Preschool Communication Measures

. . . .

Scale	Age Range	Areas Assessed	Primary Purpose
Peabody Picture Vocabulary Test (Dunn and Dunn, 1981)	2½–adult	Receptive language	Provides an overall indication of child's receptive (hearing) vocabulary A single score is reported
Preschool Language Scale (Zimmerman, Steiner, and Pond, 1979)	1½–7	Sensory discrimination Logical thinking Grammar and vocabulary Memory and attention span Temporal/spatial relations Self-image Each is assessed in both auditory comprehension and verbal ability	Screening and diagnosis of language development and language problem Scores reported for auditory comprehension and verbal ability
Receptive-Expressive Emergent Language Scale (Bzoch and League, 1970)	0–3	Receptive language Expressive language	Screening and diagnosis of language delays
Sequenced Inventory of Communication Development (Hedrick, Prather, and Tobin, 1975)	0–4	Receptive communication (a) awareness (b) discrimination (c) understanding Expressive communication (a) imitation (b) initiating (c) responsive (d) verbal output	Diagnosis of communication development/delays and planning communication interventions
Test of Auditory Comprehension of Language (Carrow, 1973)	3–6	Vocabulary Morphology Syntax	Determines levels of auditory comprehension and identifies specific areas of difficulty for planning interventions

. . . .

advanced levels include perceptual investigation (e.g., mouthing) and manipulation as well as searching for new objects. According to Weisler and McCall (1976), exploration consists of repetitive interactions with objects in order to learn about their nature.

As children become familiar with objects and advance in their motor skills, they begin to interact with toys in more sophisticated ways. Skills observed during the preschool period include more advanced manipulations of toys, taking toys apart and assembling them, using several toys together, symbolic/representational play with toys (e.g., dramatic play), and playing games with rules.

Social Interactions.   Just as developmental sequences may be observed in toy play, so too can predictable sequences of social interactions with peers. The hierarchy proposed many years ago by Parten (1932) is still used to describe social skills. Parten described six categories of social play. *Unoccupied behavior* occurs when the child is doing nothing and is not observing any one event in the classroom. *Solitary independent play* occurs when the child is playing alone and makes no attempt to play with others or at activities similar to those in which other children are engaged. When *onlooking,* the child is watching other children play. He or she may talk to others but does not otherwise enter into the play. *Parallel play* is that in which the child is engaged in activities similar to those of other children, but makes no attempt to interact with them. Usually the child is playing near others and with similar toys. *Associative play* occurs when the child plays with other children but there is little organization of the activity. The most advanced level of social play is *cooperative play,* when children play together in some form of organized activity with a purpose such as completing a game or dramatizing a certain activity.

Play Environments.   Often teachers and other professionals view the child as the only target for educational assessment, overlooking other important dimensions of educational programming. The play environment is one example. Considerable research has demonstrated that the quality of children's play is affected by the quality of the play environment (Bailey, Harms, and Clifford, in press). Recent research has also found that play environments for handicapped preschoolers are rated lower than those for nonhandicapped preschoolers (Bailey, Clifford, and Harms, 1982), suggesting that early childhood special educators should place greater emphasis on the assessment and planning of environmental provisions. In general, a good play environment is well organized, inviting, developmentally appropriate and stimulating, and promotes independent use of play materials. An example of a scale designed to measure the quality of the preschool environment is the Early Childhood Environment Rating Scale (Harms and Clifford, 1981).

Assessing Play Skills.   Of the three primary assessment techniques, direct observation is the most frequently used and most appropriate for assessing play skills. The exact nature of the observational system used will depend upon the developmental level and handicapping conditions of the children observed. If social interaction is the primary concern for a particular child, the teacher might observe the child's play for several days and record the percentage of time the child spends engaged in each of the categories of social play described by Parten (1932). If another child seems to be deficient in toy-play skills, the teacher might observe for several days and record each toy the child plays with and the manner he or she interacts with it. For example, does the child usually mouth the toy, bang it, or use it in combination with other toys?

Occasionally, certain toy-play skills may be assessed through direct testing. For example, if the child never selects certain toys, the teacher might present several of them to see what the child will do. If the child does not know what to do with the toy, the teacher might model its use and see if the child can imitate the appropriate action (e.g., spin the top or turn the crank on the jack-in-the-box).

Parents or other adults who know the child may be asked to complete a rating scale describing the child's social behavior. A *rating scale* is an assessment procedure that presents a set of questions to which response options are provided. An example of a question that might be included on a rating scale is, "How often does the child play cooperatively with other children?" The possible answers might include "never," "almost never," "sometimes," "often," and "always." A rating scale can be useful as a screening device and for giving a general indication of how a child's play or social skills compare with those of other children. However, measures such as this rarely provide enough information for designing an intervention program unless they are used in conjunction with observation and direct testing.

Considerations with Sensory or Motor Impairments.   Young children with sensory or motor impairments pose significant problems in the assessment of play and social skills. Most toys require some form of motor manipulation, particularly those for very young children. Children with severe motor impairments have typically been shortchanged in the assessment and instruction of social and play skills because of the difficulty in finding limited-motor responses for higher-level skills. Fortunately, the recent advent of microcomputers has opened up new options for children with severe impairments. Many microswitches have been designed to permit automatic activation of toys and interaction with computers to activate toys. As computers become more accessible to handicapped children and their teachers, an important assessment skill will be the ability to determine the child's potential and instructional needs for using them.

Gross and Fine Motor Skills

All observable behaviors, including communication, cognitive, and play skills, require some form of motor movement. But in many instances, early childhood special educators are interested in facilitating the acquisition and use of motor behaviors themselves. Although the formal assessment of many motor-related skills is typically conducted by a physical or occupational therapist, the teacher of young handicapped children should know sequences of motor development and be familiar with basic strategies for assessing motor skills. The teacher is usually interested in two broad categories of motor development skills: gross motor and fine motor. When working with physically handicapped children, he or she may also need to be involved in the assessment of reflexes, reactions, and muscle tone for the purpose of determining optimal body positions to facilitate performance or to determine the need for some form of adaptive equipment.

Assessing Gross Motor Skills.   Gross motor skills are those that require movement of the large muscles of the body. Examples include crawling, walking, running, skipping, throwing, climbing, swinging, and riding. The assessment of gross motor skills should follow three steps. First, the teacher should determine where the child's gross motor skills fall within the normal sequence of motor development. Usually this assessment includes a comprehensive analysis of a range of motor behaviors and a comparison of individual performance with normative developmental data. An example of a standardized assessment scale with normative data is the Peabody Developmental Motor Scale (Folio and DuBose, 1974).

Second, the teacher should determine the child's functional movement skills. Can the child perform related critical functions implied by some test items? For example, one test item might ask whether the child can walk 10 feet. A child with motor handicaps may be unable to walk but may be able to perform the critical function of that item (locomotion from one spot to another) by rolling or by manipulating a wheelchair. Third, the teacher should determine the extent to which the child's environment expects and encourages the use of gross motor skills. If they are not encouraged, then one form of intervention is to change the environmental demands.

Assessing Fine Motor Skills.   Fine motor skills are those requiring movement of the small muscles of the body. The term usually refers to the use of the hands and fingers. Examples of fine motor skills include grasping, releasing, stacking, stringing, cutting, and writing. Like that of gross motor skills, fine motor assessment should address a developmental as well as a functional framework. For example, the five-year-old with motor impairments may not be able to write his or her name but may be able to use a head pointer to type it.

Reflexes, Reactions, and Tone.   By the age of three years, most children have matured enough so that their reflexes, reactions, and muscle tone are not a consideration in educational programming. For children with motor impairments, particularly cerebral palsy, these dimensions will always be of concern. Because the early childhood special educator will typically be teaching in a noncategorical setting and in all likelihood will be responsible for instructing one or more children with motor impairments, it is important that he or she be familiar with basic assessment considerations in each area.

Reflexes are involuntary movements in response to certain stimuli. The behavior of newborns is primarily reflexive in nature, but the acquisition of volitional (voluntary) movements usually occurs very quickly. Children with cerebral palsy are often delayed, sometimes permanently, in acquiring volitional movements. It is not uncommon to see handicapped children in the three-to-five-year age range who still cannot control certain reflexes and thus are limited in their volitional movements. The presence of these uncontrollable reflexes seriously inhibits the performance of many important motor behaviors. Therefore it is important that the nature and extent of these reflexes be documented so that, when possible, adaptations can be made.

Similarly, *automatic reactions* are relatively automatic responses that assist in body alignment. For example, if you fall to one side, you automatically reach out your arm to protect yourself. Automatic reactions are not present at birth, but all of them usually appear by 18 months of age. Children with motor impairments, however, may not develop them. Again, this should be documented.

Muscle Tone. "Muscle tone" as used here refers to muscle tension. Abnormal tone may be described as *hypotonic* (loose, floppy) or *hypertonic* (tense, rigid). Again, the presence of abnormal tone should be documented since positioning strategies and adaptive equipment may be useful in helping to normalize tone in some children.

Assessing Reflexes, Reactions, and Tone. The assessment of reflexes, reactions, and tone is usually conducted by a physical therapist. Chapter 10 contains more detailed information on this topic. Teachers should not attempt to assess these skills or design modifications for afflicted children without consulting a therapist. However, early childhood special educators should be familiar with the terminology and techniques used by therapists since they will often be involved in the assessment process and will certainly be involved in carrying out any prescribed classroom interventions.

Self-Help Skills. Self-help skills are those behaviors which allow the child to perform basic, daily independent living activities. Self-help skills include feeding, toileting, and dressing as well as many other activities such as brushing teeth, making up one's bed, putting clothes away, and so forth. Young handicapped children are often delayed in the acquisition and use of such skills.

Although self-help skills do not fit typical conceptions of what teachers are supposed to teach, they often become a major focus of early intervention efforts. This focus is appropriate for several reasons. First, learning self-help skills aids a child in becoming more independent. Second, children who have not acquired basic self-help skills stand out to adults as well as to other children. Acquisition of these skills should increase the probability of successful mainstreaming and normalization. Finally, self-help skills are very important to parents. They are often parents' first priority for intervention efforts.

Eating Skills. Eating requires a variety of skills, including oral-motor movements, grasping, hand-mouth coordination, swallowing, and chewing. Many other mealtime behaviors can be identified, including food preparation, table manners and customs, and clean-up. The assessment of eating skills will vary according to the child's handicap and developmental level. In the case of more severely impaired children, the teacher may need assistance from an occupational therapist who is trained in oral-motor dysfunction. A therapist can provide useful assessment information regarding oral-motor reflexes, proper positioning for feeding, and techniques for stimulating appropriate tongue and mouth movements. Children who feed themselves to some extent will need to be assessed in the areas of advanced feeding skills (e.g., use of knife) and mealtime behaviors.

Eating skills are best assessed by observation during a natural eating time. A list of appropriate eating skills should be used to determine instructional targets for children. Standard assessment tools for eating skills have been published by Balthazar (1976) and Schmidt (1976). Bailey, Harms, and Clifford (in press) provide a list of assessment targets for mealtime behaviors.

Toileting Skills. The lack of toileting skills has historically been the single greatest skill-deficit barrier to the acceptance of handicapped persons by regular classroom teachers and probably by society in general. For children who have not acquired basic toileting skills, they should be a primary focus of assessment and intervention efforts.

The assessment of toileting skills focuses on three areas: toileting prerequisites (e.g., some bladder and bowel control), use of the toilet, and related dressing skills such as pulling down pants or using a zipper, all of which are best assessed by observation. Parents can also be asked to provide information about typical toileting or accident schedules at home.

Other Self-Help Skills. Other self-help skills such as dressing, hanging up coats, and brushing teeth are essentially motor skills performed within the context of specific daily living requirements. The preferred method of assessment is direct observation of the child's ability to perform the steps in the sequence. First the teacher must determine and prioritize the skills to be learned; next he or she should find or develop a *task analysis* (a detailed listing of the steps involved in performing the behaviors) for the skill and assess, through direct observation and testing, the child's ability to perform each step. The steps the child is unable to perform then become instructional targets. An example of a task analysis used as an assessment instrument was illustrated in Chapter 2.

Family Skills

Traditionally, educational assessment has had a singular focus on the skills of the handicapped children served by the program. Although this focus is appropriate, it overlooks other dimensions of service that may be equally important. In particular, the family of a young handicapped child may need to be included as a target of the educational and assessment process. At least three areas of family functioning should be considered: parent-child interactions, home environments, and family coping skills.

Parent-Child Interactions.   Research over the past decade suggests that the nature and quality of interactions between parents and their handicapped children may be different from that observed between parents and their nonhandicapped offspring (Ludlow, 1981). This finding may be due in part to the impaired interactional skills of the handicapped child and in part to the perceptions of the parents. Regardless of the explanation, the quality of parent-child interactions is a legitimate target for intervention when the relationship appears to be at risk. In fact, Bronefenbrenner (1974), in a review of the effectiveness of early intervention, suggested that the interaction between parent and child may be the single most important target area.

Assessment of parent-child interactions is best accomplished through direct observation of parents and children in a relatively unstructured situation. Although some parent rating forms may be used to obtain parents' perceptions of the typical interactions, direct observation over several observation periods is preferable. One way to collect data in such a fashion is to count several specific behaviors, such as the number of times the parent speaks to or smiles at the child or the number of times the child responds to parent-initiated interactions. Another way to summarize interactions is to complete a rating form such as the Parent Behavior Progression (Bromwich, 1981).

Home Environments.   Several studies have documented the importance of the home environment in facilitating a child's development (e.g., Bradley and Caldwell, 1976; Wachs, 1979). For example, Wachs (1979) found that five dimensions of the environment were positively related to cognitive growth: physical responsivity, private space, lack of overcrowding, degree of exploration possible, and degree of temporal regularity. Although teachers probably have little effect on major environmental provisions such as heat or the quality of the home itself, they can help parents address some of the dimensions described by Wachs. The home environment is best measured by direct observation. A scale commonly used to measure it is the Home Observation and Measurement of the Environment (Caldwell and Bradley, 1978), which includes items regarding the physical, social, and cognitive surroundings provided in the home. Target areas for intervention can be easily selected from the scale's checklist.

Family Coping Skills.   The third broad area of family skills is the family's ability to cope with the child. The birth of a handicapped child undoubtedly has a profound effect on the structure, functioning, and development of a family. Most families of handicapped children need strong support systems to handle the additional stress the handicap imposes. The early childhood special educator should be sensitive to the needs of parents. He or she should listen to them and in many cases should serve as their advocate and help them learn to advocate for themselves. Determining the support needs of parents requires interacting with them in a sensitive, observant fashion to determine their individual needs.

Summary

Designing and implementing an appropriate plan for assessing young handicapped children requires knowledge of normal and abnormal child development, the ability to relate well with young children, knowledge of functional skills for preschoolers, and the ability to work well with parents. Of particular importance is the ability to cooperate with other professionals on the multidisciplinary team to develop a meaningful, relevant, and *integrated* instructional program. The basis for that instructional plan should be a comprehensive assessment of the child's skills and learning styles in conjunction with an assessment of the family's needs and priorities.

This chapter has described principles and practices associated with the educational assessment of young handicapped children. The following major points were made:

1. Teachers of young handicapped children must be prepared to assess children with many different types of handicapping conditions and a potentially wide range of developmental skills.
2. Screening is an important responsibility of the early childhood special educator. He or she should be aware of the uses and limitations of data gathered by screening measures.
3. The assessment of young children requires special skills, including the ability to relate warmly and to plan and present assessment tasks in such a fashion as to keep the child interested and happy.
4. In addition to assessing developmental milestones, teachers should seek to assess and teach skills the child will need in the most likely next placement setting.
5. The first strategy for modifying or adapting any assessment task is to determine the critical function of the task.
6. The child's family should play an integral role in the assessment process both as a source of information and as a target for assessment and intervention.
7. The early childhood special educator should know normal and abnormal developmental patterns and should be competent in assessing cognitive, pre-academic, communication, toy play, social interaction, motor, self-help, and family skills.

Mastery Review

I. Recall

1. An effective screening measure does which of the following?
   a. Is of a form not aversive to children.
   b. Is short, economical, and easy to administer.
   c. Is accurate and valid.
   d. All of the above.

2. The only valid use of screening data is:
   a. to determine the presence or absence of a handicapping condition.
   b. to identify children at risk for school failure.
   c. to determine whether a child should be referred for further evaluation.
   d. all of the above.

3. Young children are often difficult to test because:
   a. they are easily distracted.
   b. they become fixated on one activity.
   c. they often shy away from strangers.
   d. a and c.

4. The functional approach to the assessment of young children:
   a. assumes assessment should be conducted within a developmental framework.
   b. emphasizes the importance of prerequisite skills.
   c. assumes children should be taught skills with immediate usefulness.
   d. is the most useful approach to use.

5. Identification of the criteria of the next educational environment may involve pinpointing required skills by:
   a. teacher observation of the educational setting.
   b. placing the child in the educational setting for a specified period of time.
   c. following up on students previously moved into the setting.
   d. all of the above.

6. Test items may be modified for multiply handicapped children by:
   a. modifying the stimulus materials.
   b. rearranging the order of test items.
   c. modifying the critical function.
   d. all of the above.

7. Cognitive skills in preschool-aged children are usually divided into what two groups?
   a. preacademic and academic.
   b. sensorimotor and preacademic.
   c. prereading and premath.
   d. causality and means-end.

8. The six basic sensorimotor skills described by Piaget include:
   a. imitation.
   b. concept development.

    c.   sorting.

    d.   discrimination skills.

9. The preferred strategy for assessing most cognitive skills is:

    a.   a parent interview.

    b.   direct testing.

    c.   naturalistic observation.

    d.   none of the above.

10. The best indicator of the overall level of a child's communication skills is:

    a.   naturalistic observation.

    b.   assessment of cognitive skills.

    c.   a parent interview.

    d.   a language sample.

11. The most advanced level of social play is:

    a.   associative play.

    b.   parallel play.

    c.   cooperative play.

    d.   solitary independent play.

12. Abnormal muscle tone described as hypotonic refers to muscle tone that is:

    a.   tense and rigid.

    b.   volitional.

    c.   loose and floppy.

    d.   reflexive.

13. Areas of family functioning that should be included in the assessment process are:

    a.   home environment.

    b.   sibling interaction.

    c.   communication skills.

    d.   a and b.

14. The best means of assessing family functioning is:

    a.   a parent interview.

    b.   direct observation.

    c.   rating forms.

    d.   direct testing.

15. Appropriate assessment of young handicapped children requires:

    a.   the ability to work well with parents.

    b.   knowledge of normal and abnormal child development.

    c.   the ability to work with other professionals.

    d.   all of the above.

II. Comprehension

1.   Describe special considerations required in the assessment of young children.

2.   Describe the developmental approach and the functional approach to assessment and explain how they may be used together.

3. List the different techniques for modifying or adapting test items and give an example of each.

4. Name the three major areas included in preacademic skills and describe what is included in each.

5. Describe the guidelines that should be followed when collecting a language sample. Give an example of how this sample can be used to develop instructional targets.

6. List the three areas of family functioning that should be considered in the assessment of a young child. Describe the importance of each area.

III. Application

1. Visit a setting with young children and, after conferring with the teacher or person in charge, select one child and document his or her social interaction play skills, using one of the direct-observation techniques discussed in Chapter 2. Determine which level of play skills the child is demonstrating, using Parten's hierarchy described in this chapter. Discuss your observations in a three-to-five-page paper and include your observational data.

2. Obtain a copy of one of the assessment instruments mentioned in this chapter from a university library or an educational assessment clinic. Select 10 items from the instrument and determine the critical function of each. Discuss each item and its implication for instruction in a six-to-eight-page paper.

IV. Alternate Task

If none of the application exercises applies to your setting or circumstances, you can design two exercises of your own. They should demonstrate application of one or more of the principles or concepts described in the preceding chapter. Prior approval of both exercises should be obtained from your course instructor.

V. Answer Key

I.
1. d p. 114
2. c p. 114
3. d p. 116
4. c pp. 117–18
5. d p. 118
6. a pp. 120–21
7. b p. 122
8. a p. 123
9. b p. 123
10. d p. 128
11. c p. 131
12. c p. 134
13. a p. 136
14. b p. 136
15. d pp. 112–13

II.
1. p. 113
2. pp. 117–18
3. p. 120
4. p. 123
5. p. 128
6. pp. 136–37

Chapter 6

Assessment of Children's Social and Behavioral Problems

Chapter Objectives:

After reading this chapter and completing the Mastery Review, you will be able to:

1. Identify major classes of disordered behavior emitted by school-aged children.
2. Provide a working definition of behavior disorders.
3. Identify at least four purposes of educational assessment with pupils suspected of having behavior problems.
4. Describe why a direct observational approach is more feasible than traditional approaches for assessing children's disordered behavior.
5. Describe steps to be followed in conducting a behavioral-ecological analysis.
6. Identify four methods of collecting observational information and describe the situations most appropriate for using each.
7. Describe how to use information from a behavioral-ecological analysis and classroom observations for planning and evaluating interventions with school-aged children.

Key Terms:

ABC analysis
antecedent stimuli
behavior class
behavior repertoire
behavioral deficit
behavioral-ecological assessment
behavioral excess
competing pairs of behaviors
consequent stimuli
differential reinforcement
ecological analysis
ecology
interobserver reliability
overt behavior
target behavior

This chapter discusses methods that will allow the reader to identify, predict, diagnose, and monitor children's social and motivational behavior problems. These skills are essential for supporting academic programs, for planning appropriate social-behavioral interventions, and for consulting with other professionals and parents. Social and behavioral disorders occur across all special education classifications, age groups, and cultural and ethnic populations. The assessment of children exhibiting these forms of behavior can occur in any school-based setting. To discuss them in the context of a single school setting or one particular special education population may be misleading.

The approach presented in this chapter will be most useful to professionals responsible for assessing children in classroom settings. It is directed primarily at special educators teaching in elementary or secondary school resource rooms who have additional responsibilities for providing consultative services to other special educators or to regular class teachers. These professionals are often identified as consulting teachers or teacher consultants.

Behavior Disorders Defined

Regardless of any other special education classification, a child's behavior may be judged disordered if it deviates from the range of behaviors that adults perceive as normal for the child's age and sex, if it occurs very frequently or intensely, or if it occurs over an extended period of time (Nelson, 1985). This definition emphasizes the problem behavior(s) being exhibited and the child's immediate environment. In this it differs from traditional definitional approaches, which place the emphasis on the child as disordered or emotionally disturbed and thereby disturbing to others. The expectations of the child's environment, particularly in interactive processes with significant others such as parents, teachers, and other children, are viewed by Nelson as playing an important role in determining whether a child's behavior is disordered or simply disturbing to those around him or her.

Often a child's behavior problems remain undetected until he or she enters school. The demands of the school routine, teachers, and forced interpersonal interactions may precipitate problem behaviors or reveal social-skill deficits (Bower, 1961; Robins, 1979). The number and magnitude of these demands depend upon the child's previous developmental history, the number of ecological stressors, and the degree to which the child's behavior deviates from developmental and cultural norms or from the expectations of significant individuals (Liebert and Wicks-Nelson, 1981).

Behavioral-Ecological Assessment

An Interactive Behavioral System. The phenomenon of development can be viewed as a process in which a child acquires patterns of behavior through his or her learning experiences in various environmental settings. With increasing age and experience, the child becomes capable of altering the environment through his or her behavior. Powerful environmental stimuli, in turn, exert considerable influence on the child's behavior. Thus the setting and the child together comprise an interactive behavioral system, an ecology. This system may include "the child, the settings, and the individuals within these settings that are a part of the child's daily life" (Hobbs, 1975, p. 114). A major facet of assessing a pupil's problem behavior therefore involves identifying and analyzing variables within the various settings that contributed to the problems.

A "behavior" may be defined for this discussion as an observable and measurable movement, an event that has a beginning and an end. This definition is often limited to behaviors that may be recorded by an external observer, primarily because internal behaviors such as an individual's thoughts, feelings, and images are inaccessible to others. Because behavior problems can be directly related to excesses or deficits in overt behavior and because changes in overt behavior can more easily and reliably be verified than changes in internal behavior (e.g., attitudes, self-concept, feelings), overt behaviors are always targeted for change as part of an intervention program.

To plan and implement an effective intervention program, it is important to collect and integrate information from a broad spectrum of a child's life. The following pages describe methods for performing such a "behavioral-ecological" assessment.* Some of the major assumptions upon which this approach is based are described below.

Behavioral Repertoires.   Considerable evidence indicates that most behavior is acquired through learning and that behavior problems stem primarily from faulty or inadequate learning experiences. Moreover, through their interaction with the external world, children develop "behavioral repertoires." These repertoires may be appropriate in some situations but inappropriate or inadequate in others. Assessing children's social and behavior problems, therefore, involves taking stock of their behavioral assets and liabilities in various situations.

Expectations of Significant Others.   In most cases, various significant individuals in a pupil's environment determine which behaviors are appropriate and which are not. Thus it is important that the teacher assessing the pupil unearth information related to the expectations and rules established by significant others.

Internal and External Variables.   The major goal of a behavioral-ecological approach to assessment is to collect information that will enable professionals to design intervention programs that weaken children's inappropriate behavior and strengthen their appropriate behavior. Because problem behaviors are usually maintained by present, ongoing internal and external variables, it is important to identify and attempt to control these variables in order to design and conduct viable intervention strategies.

---

*The author is indebted to Dr. Fred Kanfer and an early paper by Kanfer and Saslow (1969) for providing the framework for this approach.

Traditional Psychological Measures. For several reasons, information provided by traditional psychological measures such as personality tests, self-concept inventories, and projective tests is largely impractical for use in educational settings. Many of these measures suffer from technical inadequacies and yield esoteric results that are difficult to translate into treatment goals (Hersen and Bellack, 1976; Mash and Terdal, 1981; O'Leary and Johnson, 1979; Salvia and Ysseldyke, 1985). Few special educators have adequate training in using information from these measures for planning and evaluating intervention programs. For these reasons, information based on direct observation is more useful and reliable in planning and implementing behavioral change programs.

Intervention Design. Information collected from various sources in a child's environment is used to design intervention programs that involve the cooperative effort of significant adults across settings. This strategy is more effective than attempting to change behavior in one situation and hoping that treatment gains will generalize to others.

Ongoing Evaluation. Behavioral-ecological assessment is not a "one-shot" activity. Children's behavior is under the control of a variety of stimuli that exert a constant influence on behavior. These variables must be continually monitored so that their influence can be evaluated and controlled. In addition, the continual evaluation of behavior targeted for change across settings is necessary to determine the effectiveness of various intervention programs.

An important concept for all classroom teachers is that pupil performance assessment is part of an ongoing process of data gathering. While the process may seem like a series of discrete events, it must be fit into a continuum of events to be of maximum use and truly representative of the pupil's abilities. The discussion that follows will focus on basic assessment procedures involved in screening, diagnosis, program planning, and program monitoring. These procedures enable an effective assessment process to be used with pupils exhibiting social and behavioral problems.

The Behavioral-Ecological Assessment Process

Screening

Screening is an important initial step in the behavioral-ecological assessment process. The major activity in this phase involves the identification of problem behaviors. This entails surveying the range and severity of the child's problem behaviors, determining who objects to them, and identifying the situation(s) in which they occur. Information collected in the screening process will be used for planning intervention strategies. Chapter 1 (p. 8) described the process of screening as it relates to educational assessment in Level One of the educational assessment model, and a thorough discussion of screening as it relates to young children was provided in Chapter 5 (p. 113). Language screening procedures and instrumentation were described in Chapter 4 (pp. 99–103), "Assessment of Language Impairments."

Surveying Problem Behaviors

The screening process usually begins with referral to a special education teacher. The referral may be a written request by a school screening and referral committee or simply a verbal request from another teacher for the special educator to observe a particular child and suggest interventions. One of the first activities in this process includes identifying the pupil's behavioral excesses and deficits and determining the extent to which they deviate from established norms and local expectations (Kanfer and Saslow, 1969; Walker and Hops, 1976).

Behavioral Excesses.   By far the most common class of problems consists of behaviors that have such high frequencies or such severe consequences even at low frequencies that they need to be reduced or eliminated completely. These are called "behavioral excesses." Examples include physical or verbal aggression, defiance, cursing, temper tantrums, whining, complaining, stealing, lying, and disruptiveness. Almost all children periodically display inappropriate behavior, but when it becomes persistent or poses a threat to the child or someone else, intervention becomes necessary.

A quick and effective way to identify a pupil's behavioral excesses is to have supervising adults complete a checklist such as the Behavior Problem Checklist (BPC) (Quay and Peterson 1975) (see Figure 6–1), the Behavior Rating Profile (Brown and Hammill 1983) (see Figure 6–2), or the Walker Problem Behavior Identification Checklist (WPBIC) (Walker, 1983) (see Figure 6–3). Another method is simply to have the teacher list the problems that he or she would like to see reduced in frequency. Interviews with regular teachers can also be used to determine which behaviors are the most troublesome and how severe they are.

Walker and Hops (1976) used an innovative method for determining the severity of a child's problem behaviors compared to his or her peers. In one of their studies, classroom observers recorded problem behaviors of a target pupil and then immediately recorded the behavior of a nearby peer. By alternating observations between the target pupil and his or her peers, they collected data that allowed them to determine how much the target pupil's behavior deviated from that of other children in the classroom.

Behavioral Deficits.   Another task of the behavior assessor is to identify a child's behavioral deficits. These are perhaps best defined in terms of the discrepancy between a child's level of performance and a specified performance criterion, which may be in the form of task requirements, developmental or social norms, or (often) a supervisory adult's judgment (McFall, 1982). Harris, Wolfe, and Baer (1964), for example, defined "excessive passivity" as a low frequency of engaging in vigorous exercise. This definition works well when the behavior of interest involves the performance of a specific action.

Figure 6–1

Behavior Problem Checklist

· ·

Donald R. Peterson, Ph.D. and Herbert C. Quay, Ph.D.

Children's Research Center
University of Illinois
Champaign, Illinois

Copyright Herbert C. Quay and
Donald R. Peterson, 1975

Col. No.	Please complete items 1 to 6 carefully.
(1–8)	1. Name (or identification number) of child
(9–10)	2. Age (in years) _____
(11)	3. Sex _____ (Male = 1; Female = 2)
(12)	4. Father's Occupation _____
(13)	5. Name of person completing this checklist
(14)	6. Relationship to child (circle one)

a. Mother b. Father c. Teacher d. Other _____
(Specify)

Please indicate which of the following constitute problems, as far as this child is concerned. If an item does *not* constitute a problem, encircle the zero; if an item constitutes a *mild* problem, encircle the one; if an item constitutes a *severe* problem, encircle the two. Please complete every item.

Sample items follow:
Item no.

(15)	0 1 2	1. Oddness, bizarre behavior
(19)	0 1 2	5. Doesn't know how to have fun; behaves like a little adult
(24)	0 1 2	10. Steals in company with others
(29)	0 1 2	15. Social withdrawal, preference for solitary activities
(34)	0 1 2	20. Short attention span

· ·

It is more difficult, however, to identify and define social behavior deficits. Whereas excesses are represented by actual, measurable behaviors a child emits, deficits are often defined in terms of the *absence* of a particular behavior or behavior sequence or in terms of disruptions in the timing and pacing of appropriate behavior. For example, a child may display a social deficit by being unresponsive to others' social initiations: forgetting to answer questions, rebuffing offers to share, declining aid, or failing to provide social reinforcement (Hops and Greenwood, 1981). A quiet, withdrawn child may not speak at appropriate times or may talk too slowly or indistinctly to be understood by others.

The concept of behavioral deficit assumes that certain sets of social skills have been identified as appropriate in various situations, though they may be inappropriate in another setting or cultural milieu. Thus the inappropriateness of various skills and their identification as deficits may depend upon the skill of the observer in comparing a child's social behaviors to those exhibited by peers in a particular situation.

Unfortunately, little research information is available concerning which of children's social skills are most effective in various situations (McFall, 1982). Determining a child's social competence thus depends more on experience than on science. Some social behaviors have, however, been identified as important in interpersonal interchanges; they are listed on p. 152 in Table 6–1.

Determining Objections to Problem Behavior. The second step in the screening process, and a key to planning a successful intervention program for children who display social and behavioral problems, is to identify and collect information from the persons most affected by them. These individuals may include significant others in the child's life, such as teachers or parents, the child's peers, and the child him- or herself.

Such information is collected in initial interviews with these individuals. Questions should focus not only on which of the child's behaviors they consider most troublesome and why, but also on their ideas about how these behaviors should be eliminated, changed, strengthened, or established. This information is very important in determining the outcome of a treatment program.

Identifying Problem Behavior Situations. A third step in the screening process involves isolating various situations in which a child's problem behaviors occur in order to determine the extent and severity of the problem. The more situations in which the excess or deficit behaviors are shown, the more pervasive and entrenched they may be. Knowing this enables special educators to plan an intervention strategy that will span several situations and result in more rapid treatment gains. A comparison of the expectations and goals of various individuals in the child's environment with the situations in which behavior excesses or deficits occur may give clues as to whether these expectations or the child's behavior require medication.

A special education teacher can perform a situational analysis simply by noting the times of day or activities during which potential target behaviors are observed.

Figure 6–2

Behavior Rating Profile

. . . .

Linda L. Brown & Donald D. Hammill

Teacher Rating Scale

Student's Name: _____   Rater's Name: _____

Birthdate: _____   Subject Taught: _____

Grade: _____   School: _____

Date: _____

Other Relevant Test Scores:

_____

_____

_____

Teacher's Comments and Observations:

_____

_____

_____

_____

_____

_____

_____

_____

_____

_____

Raw scores may be converted into Scaled Scores by entering the table below.

Scaled* Scores	Raw Scores for Students in Grades 1–4	Raw Scores for Students in Grades 5–7	Scaled* Scores
1	0–4	0–2	1
2	5–12	3–8	2
3	13–17	9–21	3
4	18–29	22–28	4
5	30–37	29–37	5
6	38–45	38–44	6
7	46–55	45–51	7
8	57–66	52–58	8
9	67–71	59–63	9
10	72–78	64–67	10
11	79–83	68–78	11
12	84–87	79–86	12
13	88	87–88	13
14	89	89	14
15	90	90	15
16–20			16–20

*(Mean = 10, Standard Deviation = 3)

Results: Raw Score _____ Scaled Score _____

To survey problem situations across a child's entire day, one also may complete an ecological survey such as that described by Wahler and Cormier (1970) (see Figure 6–4, p. 153).

Figure 6–4 presents a comprehensive ecological survey that identifies various problem behaviors and the settings and times in the school day in which the child may display these. The survey may be completed either by the regular class teacher alone or by the consulting special education teacher on the basis of information collected from the teacher. It is recommended that a special educator collect surveys completed by several of a child's teachers and compare the results. This information can be used as a focus for interviews with various teachers. A school-based ecological survey may be augmented by a survey of problem behaviors the child emits at home or in the community completed by a significant adult in the child's life (see Figure 6–5, p. 154).

Once the teacher completes the initial screening and problem-identification

Figure 6–2

Behavior Rating Profile (*continued*)

. . . .

Instructions

This behavior rating form contains a list of descriptive words and phrases. Some of these items will describe the referred student quite well. Some will not. What we wish to know is this: Which of these behaviors are you concerned about at this particular time and to what extent do you see them as problems?

Take for example item #1, "Is sent to the principal for discipline." If the child frequently is sent to the principal's office, the rater might check the "Very Much Like" space. If the child is sent to the principal's office on an infrequent but regular basis, the rater might check the "Somewhat Like" space. If the child has been sent to the principal's office on rare occasions, a check in the "Not Much Like" space might be appropriate. If the child never has been disciplined by the principal, the "Not At All Like" space would be indicated. These ratings should reflect your perceptions of the child's behavior. Please do not confer with other teachers in completing this form.

Sample items follow:

The student	Very Much Like the Student	Like the Student	Not Much Like the Student	Not At All Like the Student
1. Is sent to the principal for discipline	☐	☐	☐	☐
18. Bullies other children	☐	☐	☐	☐
19. Is self-centered	☐	☐	☐	☐
20. Does not do homework assignments	☐	☐	☐	☐
29. Lies to avoid punishment or responsibility	☐	☐	☐	☐
30. Doesn't follow class rules	☐	☐	☐	☐
Sum of Marks in Each Column =	_____	_____	_____	_____
Multiply Sum by	× 0	× 1	× 2	× 3
Add Products	0 +	_____ +	_____ +	_____
	= _____ Total Point Score			

From Linda L. Brown and Donald D. Hammill, *The Behavior Rating Profile — Teacher Rating Scale* (Austin, TX: PRO-ED, 1983). Reprinted by permission.

. . . .

phase of the behavioral-ecological assessment process, a list of behavioral excesses and deficits is compiled. In addition, the teacher will have identified the specific situations in which these potential target behaviors are most problematic. The next step is to further clarify the variables contributing to the child's problem by collecting additional information for use in planning and designing an intervention plan. Again, it is important to recognize the ongoing fact-finding and verification activities in the behavioral-ecological assessment process.

Diagnosis

Different settings in the child's environment make different demands, and through experience, the child develops varying degrees of competence in meeting these demands. Accordingly, the major goals of behavioral-ecological assessment involve identification of the specific interpersonal and environmental variables within each

Figure 6–3

Walker Problem Behavior Identification Checklist
Revised 1983

. . . .

Profile Analysis Chart

T-Score	Scale 1: Acting Out Pre-K	Grade 1-3	Grade 4-6	Scale 2: Withdrawal Pre-K	Grade 1-3	Grade 4-6	Scale 3: Distractibility Pre-K	Grade 1-3	Grade 4-6	Scale 4: Disturbed Peer Relations Pre-K	Grade 1-3	Grade 4-6	Scale 5: Immaturity Pre-K	Grade 1-3	Grade 4-6	Total Score Pre-K	Grade 1-3	Grade 4-6	T-Score
Over 100				7-14						12-25	11-25	17-25	10-19	10-19	11-19	58-98	57-98	72-98	Over 100
100											11-25	16	9			57	56	71	100
		26								11						56	55	70	
		25			6							15			10	55	54	69	
				14										9		54	53	68	
95		24								10	9	14	8			53	52	66-67	95
		23		13											9	52	51	65	
		22														51	50	64	
90			26											8		50	49	63	90
		21	25	12	5		14			9	8	13				49	48	61-62	
		20	24			14		14				12			8	48	47	60	
85	26 25	19	23	11		13	13	13		8	7	11		7		47 46	46 45 44	59 58 57 55-56	85
	24	18	22	10	4	12	12	12					6			45 44 43 42 41 40	43 42 41 40 39 38	54 53 52 51 49-50	
80	23 22	17	21 20							7		10				39 38	37 36	48 47	80
	21	16	19	9		11	11			6	6			6		37 36	35 34 33	46 44-45 43	
75	20	15	18			10	10	11	14			9	5		6	35 34	32 31	42 41	75
	19 18	14	17 16	8				10	13		5	8		5		33 32 31	30 29 28	40 38-39 37	
	17	13	15		3	9	9	9	12						5	30 29	27 26	26 35	
70		12		7					11							28	25	33-34	70
	16		14			8	8	8		5		7	4				24	32	
	15 14	11 10	13	9		7			10		4	6		4	6	27 26	23 22	31 30	
65	13	9	12 11	6	2	6	7	7	9	4		5	3		4	25 24	21 20	29 27-28	65
	12 11	8	10	5					8		3		3		23 22	19 18	26 25	
60		7	9			5	6	6		3					3	21 20 19	17 16	24 23 21-22	60
	10	6	8 7	4			5	7			4	2			18	15 14	20 19	
	9	5	6	3		4	5	6		2	2	3	2	2	2	17 16	13 12	18 16-17	
55	8 7	4 3	5	2	1	3	4	5			1	2	1	1	1	15 14 13 12	11 10 9 8	15 14 13 12	55
50	6 5	2	4 3			3	2	3	4	1		1	1	1	1	11 10 9	7 6 5	10-11 9 8	50
	4 3	1	2	1	0	1	2	2	3		0					8 7	4 3	7 6	
45	2	0	1	0		0		1	2	0		0	0	0	0	6 5	2 1	4-5 3	45
	1		0				1	0	1							4 3	0	2 1	
40	0						0		0							2 1 0		0	40

Raw Scores

11	0	4	4	3	22

Figure 6–3

Walker Problem Behavior Identification Checklist
Revised 1983 (*continued*)

. . . .

Sample five items from 50 item checklist used to complete the Profile Analysis Chart

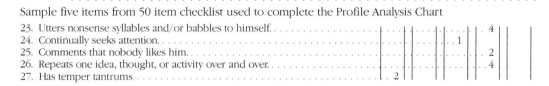

23. Utters nonsense syllables and/or babbles to himself. 4
24. Continually seeks attention. 1
25. Comments that nobody likes him. 2
26. Repeats one idea, thought, or activity over and over. 4
27. Has temper tantrums. 2

. . . .

setting that control behavior, analysis of the behavioral expectations in various settings, comparison of expectations within and across settings, and analysis of the child's behavior across settings. These activities will yield a convergence of all the child's major problem behaviors and facilitate planning interventions in which various significant individuals in the child's life may participate. For example, if a parent and teacher identify a list of the child's common problem behaviors, they can cooperate in developing a mutual program to intervene in one or more of the behaviors. Interventions that span two or more settings in which the child functions have been found highly effective in improving behavior (Hops, Beickel, and Walker, 1976).

Perhaps the most important aspect of diagnosis of a child's problem behavior is the identification of the specific variables in a particular situation that may be maintaining problem behaviors. The probability that a particular behavior will or will not occur in a specific situation is influenced by the events that precede it — the *antecedent stimuli* — and the events that follow it, the *consequent stimuli.*

Identifying Antecedent Events. Antecedent stimuli are visual, auditory, or tactile cues present in a situation that determine the occurrence and direction of a particular behavior. For example, the sight and aroma of popcorn at a moviehouse may stimulate a person to salivate, to experience hunger pangs, to initiate self-instructions to check his or her money supply, and to line up at the concession stand. In general, "external" antecedents are capable of making a sensory impression that can be verified by an outside observer (e.g., the sight and aroma of popcorn). "Internal" antecedents such as hunger, thirst, emotions, thoughts, self-instructions, and visual images are also thought to influence the form, direction, and intensity of external behavior (Bandura, 1969; Meichenbaum and Arsarnow, 1979; Skinner, 1953).

A number of antecedents naturally affect behavior, but most are learned as an individual interacts with the environment. To predict and change a child's behavior, then, we must identify the external and, in some cases, the internal antecedents that influence it. However, it is often difficult to determine the antecedents of prob-

Table 6–1

Checklist of Children's Social Skills

. . . .

Skill	Comments
_____ 1. Makes eye contact when speaking, ✓ listening.	
_____ 2. Enters activities with other children. ✓	
_____ 3. Initiates conversation with other children. ✓	
_____ 4. Responds to conversation of other ✓ children.	
_____ 5. Shares things with other children. ✓	
_____ 6. Offers to help others. ✓	
_____ 7. Spontaneously helps others.	
_____ 8. Allows others to interrupt conversation.	
_____ 9. Refrains from interrupting others' conversation.	
_____ 10. Praises others.	
_____ 11. Maintains topic of conversation.	
_____ 12. Refrains from showing offensive habits.	
_____ 13. Speaks at an acceptable volume level.	
_____ 14. Apologizes for social transgressions.	
_____ 15. Avoids displays of strange or bizarre mannerisms.	
_____ 16. Disagrees without arguing.	
_____ 17. Uses positive over negative criticism.	
_____ 18. Avoids bossing others.	
_____ 19. Ignores provocative social stimuli.	
_____ 20. Initiates or works at tasks without outside help.	

1 = Almost always   2 = Often   3 = Sometimes   4 = Almost never

. . . .

lem behavior. Careful and repeated observations are usually necessary to pinpoint external antecedents. Internal antecedents must be determined by interviewing the child about his or her reaction to various external antecedents.

Identifying Consequent Events.   Although antecedents exert an important influence over behavior, consequent stimuli are far more powerful in their effects. For example, Johnny may learn a very painful lesson through negative consequences by putting his hand on a hot tea kettle. Toni may have learned that crying before bedtime pays off in getting her parents' attention and extra TV time. Negative consequences reduce the probability that a behavior will occur again under similar circumstances, and positive consequences reinforce or increase the probability that a behavior will occur.

Figure 6–4

Student School Behavior Checklist

This checklist is designed to help you pinpoint common behavioral assets and excesses of students in various situations. To use it, first observe the student several times during the time period indicated in the left-hand column, then check the behaviors shown in the list appearing at the top of the page if the student shows them during this period.

Teacher: _____

Subject: _____

Period: _____

Date(s) recorded: _____

Student: _____

The column headings (behaviors) read:
late for class, blackmails others, threatens others, drugs, out of seat, talks to others, talks w/o permission, refuses requests, ignores requests, dawdles, defiant, argumentative, steals, lies, destroys property, complains/whines, cries, inattentive, dependent, isolates self, messy, seeks attention, distractible, avoids adults, avoids peers, quiet/sullen, acts silly, distracts class, sleeps, fights, completes work, talks about self, turns in homework, keeps things in order, seeks peer contacts, seeks adult contacts, volunteers answers, volunteers help, volunteers information, on time for class, controls anger

Morning:
Teacher explains lesson
Class discussion
Demonstration
Individual work
Class presentation
Cooperative work with other students
Before class
After class
Free time
Study hall
Lunch
Gym

Afternoon:
Teacher explains lesson
Class discussion
Demonstration
Individual work
Class presentation
Cooperative work with other students
Before class
After class
Free time
Study hall

Adapted from: Whaler, R. G., & Cormier, W. H. (1970). The ecological interview: A first step in out-patient therapy. *Journal of Behavior Therapy and Experimental Psychiatry, 1,* 279–289.

Figure 6–5

Child Community Behavior Checklist

· ·

The following checklist allows you to describe your child's problems in various situations outside the house. The situations are listed in the column at left and common problem behaviors are listed in the row at the top. Examine each situation in the column and decide if one or more of the problem behaviors in the row fits your child. Check those that fit the best, if any.

	Always has to be told	Doesn't pay attention	Forgets	Dawdles	Refuses	Argues	Complains	Demands	Fights	Selfish	Destroys toys/property	Lies	Cries	Whines	Hangs on to adult	Acts silly	Mopes around	Stays alone	Has to keep things in order	Sexual play
In own yard																				
In neighbor's yard or home																				
In stores																				
In public park																				
Downtown in general																				
In church or Sunday school																				
In community swimming pool																				
In family car																				

Adapted from: Whaler, R. G., & Cormier, W. H. (1970). The ecological interview: A first step in out-patient therapy. *Journal of Behavior Therapy and Experimental Psychiatry, 1,* 282.

· ·

Research has clearly shown that antecedent stimuli gain their control over a particular behavior because they have previously been associated with powerful consequent stimuli. Although in certain situations antecedents may initiate changes in behavior, they rapidly lose their effectiveness if positive consequences (positive reinforcers) are not forthcoming. Therefore, the most important goal in assessing children's problem behavior is the identification of the consequent stimuli that have gained functional control over their behavior.

The purpose of a behavioral-ecological assessment is to collect information that will be useful for designing effective intervention programs. It focuses on ana-lyzing moment-by-moment behavioral sequences in a specific situation in which a child interacts with the environment, and it attempts to identify the antecedent and consequent variables that control behavior. This information is then used to ma-nipulate these variables to change or maintain a particular behavior.

Four basic strategies have been found effective for maintaining and changing children's behaviors: scheduling positive consequences contingent on a particular behavior; withdrawing or withholding positive consequences to weaken a behavioral response; administering negative consequences to weaken a response; and removing or instating antecedent stimuli. As the strategies that have been previously used to control a child's behavior affect the success of current strategies, it is important to determine what disciplinary measures or behavior-change strategies have been already used and with what success.

Summarizing and Analyzing Information.   Behavioral-ecological diagnosis involves summarizing and analyzing information collected from various significant persons in a child's life, identifying variables that control his or her behavior in various situations, and identifying behavior-change strategies that have previously been used. Some important questions to ask in undertaking such an analysis are:

1. What are the variety and severity of a child's problem behaviors across various settings?
2. Who are the significant persons (siblings, peers, and adults) in each major setting in which the child functions who object to the child's behavior, and why?
3. What discrepancies exist between the child's behavior and the behavioral expectations of significant persons in each major setting?
4. What differences exist among behavioral expectations of significant persons in the various settings that may cause inconsistency in managing the child's behavior?
5. Which persons are more or less effective in managing the child's behavior in each setting?
6. What cultural norms and values prevail in various settings in the child's environment, and what discrepancies exist among these?
7. What specific antecedents and consequences in each setting appear to have the most effect on shaping and maintaining inappropriate behaviors?
8. What sources of support exist for inappropriate behavior, and what factors are operating that might sabotage a behavior-change program (including influential settings, negative social models, competing value systems, competing behavioral expectations, competing reinforcers, unreliable adults)?
9. What specific antecedents and consequences in each setting appear to have the most influence upon shaping and maintaining the child's appropriate behaviors and self-control?
10. What sources of support exist for appropriate behavior that might improve the chances for the success of a behavior-change program (including influential settings, positive social models, agreement among value systems, agreement among behavioral expectations, interested and reliable adults?

Analyzing Individual Problem Behaviors.   Another important facet of the behavioral-ecological diagnosis process involves analyzing behavior problems from the perspective of the individual child. Specifically, this process entails assessing the child's behavioral repertoire, gauging his or her awareness of academic and/or social problems and related circumstances, evaluating his or her skill at behavioral self-control, and determining his or her motivation to change.

An individual analysis addresses whether the child has acquired effective strategies and individual skills for dealing with his or her social or motivational problems. If the child has the correct concepts and the requisite skills to correctly complete an academic task or to sustain appropriate interpersonal behavior but is unmotivated to use these in a particular situation, then identifying and dispensing appropriate consequences will probably be the only intervention required. If the child has not acquired critical concepts, strategies, or skills, it is necessary to assess the extent of this deficiency and to provide appropriate training for expanding his or her behavioral repertoire.

For example, Jane is a high school sophomore who also participates part-time in a learning disabilities program. She has been diagnosed as a potential suicide risk by the local mental health center. In discussing an intervention plan for Jane with a consulting special education teacher, it is discovered that Jane is very depressed because she does not have any close friends. Jane states that although she would like to have friends, she encounters extreme difficulty in developing relationships with girls her age. Assessment reveals that, among other things, she is highly critical and complains about everything: teachers, students, and schoolwork. In addition, she lacks skill in opening conversations and making small talk. The other students tend to avoid her because of her chronic sarcasm and complaining, but Jane attributes their avoidance to snobbery and cliquishness. This, in turn, intensifies her critical behavior and allows her to justify her scorn. The treatment implications would involve getting Jane to identify her problem behaviors through discussion of her problems and teaching her skills that would compete with her obnoxious behaviors. For instance, she could be taught several ways of opening and maintaining positive, constructive conversations with others.

There are no standardized guidelines for performing an individual analysis. For the most part, the information must be collected through interviews with the child and through informal and formal observation procedures. Some of the questions to be answered in an individual analysis are:

1. What appropriate behaviors does the child have in his or her repertoire for meeting expectations in various situations?
2. How accurately does the child assess his or her appropriate and inappropriate behaviors?
3. How skillful is the child at identifying and predicting the effects of situational antecedents and consequences upon his or her behavior?
4. How accurately does the child assess his or her social skills?
5. How skillful is the child at using strategies such as task analysis, self-monitoring, goal-setting, and self-instructions for solving social problems? What problems does he or she encounter in using these strategies?
6. How skillful is the child at using strategies such as self-instructions, self-evaluation, self-reinforcement, and environmental planning for directing and main-

taining behavior? What problems does he or she encounter in using these strategies?

7. How motivated is the child to change problem behavior and how successful were previous attempts to change?
8. What positive consequences can be used to motivate the child?
9. What punishing consequences (e.g., time out, extinction) can be used to decelerate problem behaviors?
10. What opinions of supervisory adults does the child have that may affect his or her motivation?

Program Planning

Information collected and analyzed in the screening and diagnosis phases is used in the program-planning phase to design an intervention program for a particular child. This activity involves selecting specific target behaviors and determining the type of treatment that will be used to effect a positive behavioral change.

Selecting Target Behaviors.   Selecting appropriate target behaviors for change entails careful consideration of the immediate and long-range needs of the child. This procedure must also be guided by attention to environmental norms, behavioral expectations, maintaining variables, the problem history, the child's abilities, the training and motivation of the child's caretakers, and the feasibility of various treatment options. Major questions to be answered in selecting target behaviors are:

1. To what extent do problem behaviors present an immediate threat or jeopardize the future of the child and/or others?
2. To what extent do problem behaviors deviate from existing social, cultural, and/or legal norms?
3. To what extent do problem behaviors involve inappropriate or unrealistic expectations of significant others in the child's environment?
4. To what extent do problem behaviors reflect behavioral deficits of the child versus inadequacies in environmental control?
5. Can problem behaviors be easily changed in view of the developmental history, abilities of the child, capabilities of change agents, and socio-cultural factors?
6. Can problem behaviors be changed with available treatment options?

In selecting target behaviors, a special educator must carefully evaluate the various problem behaviors the pupil shows as well as the immediate and long-range needs of the pupil and others. Problem behaviors should be ranked according to their priority for intervention.

One can determine whether one behavior is more important than another by asking the question, "If a behavior is allowed to continue on its present course, what are the immediate and long-range consequences to the child and others?" Behaviors that pose an immediate physical threat should be targeted for intervention before all others. Next in line are behaviors that, if allowed to continue, would result in severe negative consequences or loss of freedom for the child or others. Of third priority are behaviors that do not have catastrophic consequences but which deviate so significantly from conventions that they produce negative reactions in others. Thus, a special educator should attempt to reduce a child's physical aggression before attempting to reduce his or her cursing; cursing and openly defying the teacher should be targeted and controlled before upgrading the child's scores on daily assignments. In turn, increasing a child's scores on completed assignments should supersede reducing his or her whining and complaining about homework.

Sometimes selecting a target behavior is complicated by a classroom teacher's unrealistic expectations. Suppose that a consultation with Mr. Jones reveals that his goals for Erica are to stop teasing other children, to stop stealing and lying, to turn in all of her work, to walk quietly about the room, to raise her hand before speaking, to line up her desk before leaving the room, and to show respect for him at all times. To plan a successful intervention program, Mr. Jones must recognize that setting too many requirements for Erica may actually intensify her misbehavior. Concentrating intervention efforts on a single, most important behavior in this case will maximize benefits and improve chances of success at changing other target behaviors later.

Classes of Behavior. Behavioral intervention approaches with children have traditionally emphasized selecting and changing only one behavior at a time. In educational settings, however, children often display a variety of behaviors that violate existing social, cultural, or legal norms. Conduct-disordered children, for example, commonly display a spectrum of aggressive behaviors (hitting, pushing, biting, kicking) in addition to numerous other behaviors such as dependency, crying, whining, and noncompliance (Quay, 1979; Walker, 1983). To complicate the matter further, school personnel often delay referring children for treatment services until problem behaviors reach intolerably high rates.

In such cases an entire class of behaviors must be changed immediately. For example, if at the slightest provocation Doug begins hitting, slapping, biting, pinching, or throwing objects at others, it would be inappropriate to target only one of his behaviors for change. A powerful intervention program such as Differential Reinforcement of Omission Behavior, or DRO (Deitz and Repp, 1983; Polsgrove and Rieth, 1983), is required in this situation. Such a program would reward Doug for going a brief amount of time without displaying aggressive behaviors. After a program has successfully changed selected target behaviors, those next highest in priority can be identified for future interventions.

Competing Behaviors. It is also helpful to select target behaviors in "competing pairs" in planning an intervention program (Sulzer-Azaroff and Mayer, 1977). If, for example, we target Doug's hitting behavior for reduction, we should also specify some "competing" prosocial behaviors to strengthen. An ideal intervention program also would entail reinforcing Doug's cooperative behavior, positive interactions with peers and others, sharing, and initiating conversations.

Ecological Setting. Problem behaviors are often maintained by inconsistencies or inadequacies of controlling variables in a particular setting. For example, in some situations, a child's problem behavior may be precipitated by inadequate antecedent control: unclear, implicit, or inconsistently applied rules; conflicting instructions; or competing cues. In other cases, inappropriate or insufficiently scheduled consequences may produce negative behavior or fail to reinforce desirable behavior. For example, Ms. Strictless, a regular classroom teacher, may require pupils to raise their hands before speaking during group discussions but is lax about enforcing this rule from period to period and from day to day. As a result, her pupils may have difficulty remembering it. If Ms. Strictless continually shakes, spanks, or slaps her pupils when they misbehave (i.e., provides conflicting cues), pupils may emulate her negative social behavior. In addition, if Ms. Strictless does not use descriptive praise for appropriate behavior, her pupils will probably not display it at desirable rates.

A major objective in designing intervention programs in Ms. Strictless's class would be to identify and eliminate sources of problematic antecedent and consequence control. A special education consulting teacher could help Ms. Strictless to clarify and consistently apply her classroom rules and to adopt a positive control strategy in dealing with her pupils' misbehavior.

Developmental History. Another consideration for selecting target behaviors concerns the child's developmental history and abilities. Learning-disabled children, because of their perceived or real inability to perform well on academic tasks, often develop a learned helplessness that reduces their motivation for undertaking schoolwork (Henker, Whalen, and Hinshaw, 1980). They may have temper tantrums when asked to undertake a task they perceive as beyond their ability. A child who has a long history of avoiding other children and has limited interpersonal skills risks further failure if required to perform a behavior that is not a part of his or her repertoire. In these cases, an intervention program should strengthen target behaviors that the child already possesses in rudimentary form. For example, to strengthen a learning disabled child's self-confidence in undertaking academic tasks, he or she may be assigned work in which he or she already has some competence. In the case of a socially incompetent child a social skill that the child can easily perform would initially be targeted for increase. As a pupil gains skill and confidence through successful intervention programs, increasingly difficult tasks may be assigned and more complex social behaviors may be targeted for change.

Influence of Adults. In selecting target behaviors, it is also important to keep in mind the degree of control that a supervisory adult may have over a behavior. In some cases, it may be extremely difficult to change a behavior without altering contributing variables in the child's environment. For example, if Doug's father, Mr. Jones, does not agree to cooperate with an intervention program designed to reduce his son's in-school aggressiveness, this may hamper a change program. If Mr. Jones refuses to give up spanking and adopt more positive forms of behavior management, or if he cannot consistently reinforce or follow through with a token program, then attempting to permanently change Doug's behavior seems futile. If a teacher fails to agree to a target behavior, it is difficult to maintain his or her interest or cooperation in a behavior management program. In these situations, to alleviate a child's problem behaviors, a special educator may have to clarify the goals of a child's caretakers and get them committed to modifying their expectations and/or behaviors.

Sometimes a child's behavior cannot be targeted for change because of a limitation in important treatment options. Suppose, for example, that immediate removal (time out) from the classroom is decided upon as an essential intervention for treating Doug's physical aggression, but the classroom teacher has no aide and the school principal refuses to isolate Doug in his office. Where outside support is limited or supervisors lack the necessary training for treating severe problem behaviors, it is advisable not to attempt to treat them in the classroom. Consideration should be given in these situations to placing the child in an alternative instructional environment such as a day school or residential program.

Selecting Appropriate Interventions.   The second step in planning a change program involves selecting an intervention that will change the behavior in the desired direction. Fortunately, research in applied behavior analysis has produced a number of effective techniques for treating children's problem behaviors in classroom settings (Nelson and Polsgrove, 1982). In general, these may be divided into behavior-accelerating procedures and behavior-decelerating procedures (see Table 6–2).

The primary activity in selecting intervention methods to change specific problem behaviors involves simply determining whether the behavior is to be increased or decreased and then matching this decision to an appropriate method. A rule of thumb, however, is to select the intervention that is the least restrictive to the pupil and the least difficult for the behavior managers to implement.

In selecting an appropriate intervention for a particular problem behavior, a special educator should choose a positive control procedure over an aversive one. For example, to control chronic whining and complaining behavior, one should first attempt to strengthen noncomplaining by socially praising a pupil who begins his or her work without complaint and by not attending to him or her for five seconds after a complaint (differential reinforcement). If this approach fails, the teacher might initiate a second program by awarding a valuable point for each task begun without complaint (positive contract). If these efforts also fail, he or she might consider giving pupils a certain number of minutes of free time and then removing these, one by one, for each instance of complaining behavior. In this way, positive control procedures are exhausted before aversive ones are initiated.

Monitoring Change Programs.   After a particular target behavior has been selected for change, it is important to monitor the pupil's progress throughout a behavior-change program. This activity has several important aspects. First, obser-

Table 6–2

Strategies for Changing Children's Behavior

. . . .

Strategy	Definition
For Increasing Behavior	
positive reinforcement	scheduling social or material consequences closely in time to a target behavior to strengthen that behavior; effects observed in terms of increases in the target behavior
negative reinforcement	providing and then removing an aversive event (e.g., noise, restriction, social criticism, timeout) contingent on increases in a target behavior
modeling	providing a social model for a target behavior and reinforcing efforts at imitating desired behavior
prompts and cues	providing physical guidance or verbal instructions *prior* to the target behavior to aid acquisition and reinforcing appropriate proximal behaviors
For Decreasing Behavior	
differential reinforcement of alternative behavior (DRA)	providing positive consequences for behaviors that directly compete with a target behavior to reduce its frequency (e.g., praising sitting to reduce out of seat behavior)
differential reinforcement of low rate behavior (DRL)	providing positive consequences following a specified time interval in which a target behavior was kept at a low frequency
differential reinforcement of omission of behavior (DRO)	providing positive consequences following a specified time in which a target behavior was omitted or absent
extinction	discontinuing or withholding a reinforcing consequence when a particular target behavior is displayed
response cost	removing positive consequences for a brief period when a target behavior is displayed
timeout	temporary removal of access to all positive reinforcement for displaying a particular target behavior
overcorrection	requiring performance of a particular behavior or a behavioral sequence as a consequence of displaying a particular target behavior (e.g., cleaning the classroom for destructive behavior, practicing competing behaviors)

. . . .

vational information is collected *before* an intervention program is initiated in order to establish a pretreatment level or "baseline" of the behavior. Second, these data are plotted in a graph so that they may be easily interpreted. Third, various aspects of the plotted data are continually evaluated to determine how the program is affecting the pupil's behavior. Fourth, the intervention program may be discontinued for a time and then reinstated to evaluate how effective it is. Behavioral intervention programs are typically monitored by analyzing a child's permanent products, or using event, duration, interval, or time sampling recording methods described below.

Behavioral-Ecological Assessment Methods

Behavior Rating Scales

The best standardized measures currently available are behavior-rating checklists that are completed by supervisory adults who simply check whether the child demonstrates behaviors listed on the measure.

While several methods of assessing a pupil's behavior in a total ecological context have been developed and are available commercially, few are supported by substantive data that verify their effectiveness. Two examples of behavior rating scales that are frequently used for assessing children's behavior problems are the Behavior Problem Checklist (BPC) (Quay and Peterson, 1975, 1983; Quay, 1977) and the Walker Problem Behavior Identification Checklist (WPBIC) (Walker, 1983) pp. 146–51. In contrast to traditional classification systems based upon clinical assumptions, for example the DSM-III (American Psychiatric Association, 1980), these scales represent attempts to quantify children's behavior disorders with statistically derived clusters of problem behaviors. Results from ratings by various significant persons in a child's ecology allow the special educator to sort his or her problems into various classes of observable behaviors and can be used to evaluate the severity of these compared to a normative sample. The results also can be used to isolate target behaviors for intervention. For example, if several raters select a particular behavior as problematic for an individual child, a special educator can use this information to develop a mutual contract among adults (e.g., teachers and parents) focused upon changing that behavior. Subsequent ratings on these scales can also be used to periodically evaluate the effect of an intervention program and to identify new target behaviors.

The Behavior Problem Checklist. The Behavior Problem Checklist (Quay and Peterson, 1975) has been widely used in a variety of settings for screening, diagnosing, and evaluating behavioral change. As it has been used in over 100 studies, a considerable database has evolved regarding its stability and utility (Quay, 1983). The latest version of the BPC, the Revised Behavior Problem Checklist (RBPC), contains 77 statements or items which have been factored into four major scales: Conduct Disorder (22 items), Socialized Aggression (17 items), Attention Problems-Immaturity (16 items), and Anxiety-Withdrawal (11 items). Two minor scales, Psychotic Behavior (6 items) and Motor Tension-Excess (5 items), complete the scale (Quay and Peterson, 1983). Correlations of the RBPC with the original version indicate a high overlap between these two scales suggesting that the extensive validation of the BPC can be extended to the new version with the exception of the Psychotic Behavior scale. As with the original version, the RBPC has considerably high reliability and concurrent validity (an overview of the process of determining assessment instrument reliability and validity is provided in Chapter 3). Although the concept of a continuous dimension of children's deviance underlies the RBPC, the scale appears especially strong in its ability to differentiate "clinical" from "normal" populations of children. In this vein it is an excellent device for quickly identifying students in need of services. The low to moderate correlations among the subscales allow the special educator to fairly accurately characterize a student's problem behaviors into one of four broad areas. Individual items from the scale can be used to identify targets for intervention. And preliminary results from at least one study indicate that it is sensitive to changes in treatment over time (Quay, 1979; Quay and Peterson, 1983).

The Walker Behavior Problem Identification Checklist. The Walker Behavior Problem Identification Checklist (Walker, 1983) is a rating scale intended primarily for use by kindergarten and elementary school teachers (grades 1–6). According to its author, "The checklist is to be used as a supplement in the total identification process rather than as an instrument to simply classify children . . . (Walker, 1983, p. 1). The instrument consists of 50 observable maladaptive behaviors which teachers must select as true or reject as false about an individual child. A teacher selecting an item as true simply circles a number listed beside that item. Problem behaviors are automatically weighted as the teacher completes the checklist and results place the child along one of five dimensions or "scales": Acting Out, Withdrawal, Distractibility, Disturbed Peer Relations, or Immaturity. Once the checklist is completed, the scores for each scale are summed and a total score across all scales is derived (see Figure 6–3). Results can be used to generate a behavior problem profile and to compare results on each scale with T-scores based on the normative sample for the instrument. Scores falling one or more standard deviations above the mean are considered a significant indication that intervention services are needed. As with the RBPC, the WBPIC results provide an excellent way to screen students for potential problem behaviors. The individual items may serve as potential targets for interventions. Continual administration of the scale can also be used as a means of evaluating a child's progress in an intervention program.

Ecological Survey

A method for determining the pattern of problem behaviors across settings is the ecological survey (Wahler and Cormier, 1970). Figure 6–4 (page 153) represents one type of ecological survey checksheet that enables an assessor to isolate the situations in which various target behaviors occur. By comparing information from similar checksheets completed by parents and others, the special education teacher can piece together some important information on the consistency and pervasiveness of a child's behavior across situations. In the example provided in Figure

6–4 (p. 153), problem behaviors commonly displayed by students have been listed across the horizontal scale and situations typical of most schools have been listed down the vertical scale. To complete this checklist for a particular child, the special educator simply locates a given behavior the child displays and places a mark in the situations in which he or she shows this problem. This same format could be used with other behaviors and different situations.

Direct-Observation Procedures

Direct observation in natural settings is perhaps the most important approach for collecting information on problem behavior. The reader is reminded of the discussion in Chapter 2, "Data-Collection Procedures," of methods generally found effective in special education settings. Five direct-observation procedures already dealt with are discussed in the following section to highlight their use with pupils exhibiting behavior problems in classroom settings.

ABC Analysis. The type of observational approach used depends upon the nature of the target behavior, the situation, and the requirements of the observer. The initial round of observations of a particular pupil's problem behavior should concentrate on identifying the antecedents (A) and consequences (C) related to a critical behavior (B). This procedure, which has been described in several sources (Cooper, 1981; Gelfand and Hartmann, 1984; Kerr and Nelson, 1983), involves first recording a pupil's behavior and then attempting to identify the antecedent events immediately preceding the behavior and the consequent events immediately following it. The purpose of this activity is to isolate problem behaviors and their potential controlling variables.

As an aid to completing an ABC analysis, the special educator can use a simple recording form such as one that appears in Figure 6–6. After the identifying information is logged in, the teacher selects an unobtrusive spot in the setting in which the behavior occurs and begins recording information. The teacher identifies a particular observable behavior, records it, and then records any salient antecedents and consequences that accompany it. By making a running record of the ABC sequences, the special educator can begin to identify possible hypotheses on which to base intervention programs.

Permanent Products. Permanent products are materials on which a child leaves a record of his or her behavior. Examples include video or audio tape-recordings, written work, and test scores. Because most classroom products are readily available and because academic progress is always a prime consideration in an intervention program, a special educator should probably collect information on the child's academic productivity even if intervention is focused on other behaviors. Permanent-product information may be recorded in the form of number of assignments completed or percentage of responses correct on written work or audiotapes. After permanent product data are collected and tabulated, graphing them provides a visual display of a child's progress.

Figure 6–6

Preliminary Assessment Form

Date: _____ Activity: _____ Mgrs. I.D. Code: _____

Setting: _____ Recorder: _____ Child's I.D. Code: _____

Time	Antecedents	Behavior	Consequences

Event Recording.   In collecting data on behaviors that do not produce permanent products, such as social behavior, a special education teacher must use an observational procedure. When target behaviors can be defined in terms of discrete movements, a teacher may keep an actual frequency count of the behavior as it occurs. In this procedure, the target behaviors are tallied on a card, tally sheet, mechanical counter, or other device. In measuring Doug's aggressive behavior, for example, the special educator would mark down the actual number of times he hit, pushed, pinched, or bit another child. Event recording is probably an ideal choice when a special educator wishes to collect data on one or two behaviors, is in close contact with the child (e.g., small-group instruction), or can set aside a period for observation.

Duration Recording.   When a behavior occurs at high rates or over lengthy periods of time or when the special education teacher is preoccupied with other duties, he or she might consider measuring it in terms of its duration from the moment it begins until it ends (Cooper, 1981). The use of a duration-recording method depends upon whether the onset and termination of the target behavior can be clearly identified. Timing the duration of a particular behavior is accomplished using a clock, a wristwatch, or, preferably, a stopwatch. Data can be collected on the duration per incidence of a particular target behavior or on the total amount of time a behavior endures (Kerr and Nelson, 1983).

Interval Recording. Another behavior-observational procedure involves observing a child for short but equal time intervals (from five to thirty seconds) and recording whether or not he or she displays target behaviors during these intervals. An interval recording method is preferred when time can be set aside specifically for observation, when there are several behaviors or children to be observed, when a behavior is difficult to define in terms of discrete movements, when a behavior occurs at high rates, and when the special educator wishes to collect information related to a child's social interactions.

To set up an interval-recording system, one first identifies the target behaviors to be observed and defines them so that the behavioral categories do not overlap. Second, one determines an appropriate interval length. Intervals should be longer than the average duration of a target behavior or, if high-rate behaviors are being observed, short enough so that more than one behavior cannot occur in one interval (Gelfand and Hartmann, 1984). Third, one determines whether individual target behaviors should take up all or part of an interval or whether they simply have to occur at any time during an interval to be scored. Fourth, one should allocate time for observing and recording the behavior (e.g., 10 seconds to observe, five seconds to record). Fifth, one should develop an audio tone tape or other signaling device that cues observers through an earplug speaker when to observe and when to record. Gelfand and Hartmann (1984) suggest making a tape-recorded message saying, "Interval one, observe (10-second silence) . . . . Record (five-second silence) . . . . Interval two, observe," and so on to prevent observers from confusing observation and recording intervals. Sixth, develop a suitable recording sheet such as the one that appears in Figure 6–7.

To use the interval observation form in Figure 6–7, an observer would first determine the time interval to be used (i.e., five seconds, 10 seconds) and then pick a time for the observation to occur. An observer might observe for 10 seconds and record for the following 10-second interval until the form was completed in the total time allocated for its use.

If an observer witnessed the target behavior occur, he or she would circle the appropriate letter during the recording interval. If Adult or Peer positive or negative consequences occurred during the observation interval, this would also be recorded.

To total the results, the percentage of various behavior categories can be calculated as a ratio of number of intervals in which a particular behavior was ob-

Figure 6–7

An Example of an Interval Recording Sheet

. . . .

Child's Name: _____ Date: _____

School: _____ Time Start: _____ Time Stop: _____

Setting: _____ Situation: _____ Observer: _____

Figure 6–7

An Example of an Interval Recording Sheet (*continued*)

. . . .

Interval:	1	2	3	4	5	6
S. Bhvr. Consq.	O X A D P A+ A− P+ P−	O X A D P A+ A− P+ P−	O X A D P A+ A− P+ P−	O X A D P A+ A− P+ P−	O X A D P A+ A− P+ P−	O X A D P A+ A− P+ P−
S. Bhvr. Consq.	O X A D P A+ A− P+ P−	O X A D P A+ A− P+ P−	O X A D P A+ A− P+ P−	O X A D P A+ A− P+ P−	O X A D P A+ A− P+ P−	O X A D P A+ A− P+ P−
S. Bhvr. Consq.	O X A D P A+ A− P+ P−	O X A D P A+ A− P+ P−	O X A D P A+ A− P+ P−	O X A D P A+ A− P+ P−	O X A D P A+ A− P+ P−	O X A D P A+ A− P+ P−
S. Bhvr. Consq.	O X A D P A+ A− P+ P−	O X A D P A+ A− P+ P−	O X A D P A+ A− P+ P−	O X A D P A+ A− P+ P−	O X A D P A+ A− P+ P−	O X A D P A+ A− P+ P−
S. Bhvr. Consq.	O X A D P A+ A− P+ P−	O X A D P A+ A− P+ P−	O X A D P A+ A− P+ P−	O X A D P A+ A− P+ P−	O X A D P A+ A− P+ P−	O X A D P A+ A− P+ P−
S. Bhvr. Consq.	O X A D P A+ A− P+ P−	O X A D P A+ A− P+ P−	O X A D P A+ A− P+ P−	O X A D P A+ A− P+ P−	O X A D P A+ A− P+ P−	O X A D P A+ A− P+ P−
S. Bhvr. Consq.	O X A D P A+ A− P+ P−	O X A D P A+ A− P+ P−	O X A D P A+ A− P+ P−	O X A D P A+ A− P+ P−	O X A D P A+ A− P+ P−	O X A D P A+ A− P+ P−
S. Bhvr. Consq.	O X A D P A+ A− P+ P−	O X A D P A+ A− P+ P−	O X A D P A+ A− P+ P−	O X A D P A+ A− P+ P−	O X A D P A+ A− P+ P−	O X A D P A+ A− P+ P−
S. Bhvr. Consq.	O X A D P A+ A− P+ P−	O X A D P A+ A− P+ P−	O X A D P A+ A− P+ P−	O X A D P A+ A− P+ P−	O X A D P A+ A− P+ P−	O X A D P A+ A− P+ P−
S. Bhvr. Consq.	O X A D P A+ A− P+ P−	O X A D P A+ A− P+ P−	O X A D P A+ A− P+ P−	O X A D P A+ A− P+ P−	O X A D P A+ A− P+ P−	O X A D P A+ A− P+ P−
S. Bhvr. Consq.	O X A D P A+ A− P+ P−	O X A D P A+ A− P+ P−	O X A D P A+ A− P+ P−	O X A D P A+ A− P+ P−	O X A D P A+ A− P+ P−	O X A D P A+ A− P+ P−

			Percentage of consequation			
Codes:	Number:	Percentage:	A+	A−	P+	P−
O = Off task	_____	_____	_____	_____	_____	_____
X = Out of Place	_____	_____	_____	_____	_____	_____
A = Aggressive	_____	_____	_____	_____	_____	_____
D = Disruptive	_____	_____	_____	_____	_____	_____
P = Prosocial	_____	_____	_____	_____	_____	_____

. . . .

served to the total intervals observed. Calculating the percentage of Adult and Peer positive and negative Consequation for each behavioral category provides an analysis of potential consequences which may be maintaining the observed behaviors.

Time Sampling. In situations in which a teacher's attention may be diverted periodically or in which a number of behaviors or pupils are to be observed with a minimum of effort, a special educator may use a time-sampling procedure. Time sampling is similar to interval recording: target behaviors are identified and carefully defined, observation sessions are divided into intervals, behavior is observed over an interval, and observation intervals are cued by a signaling device. In time sampling, however, the observation intervals are much longer than those in the interval-recording procedure. The observation periods may be divided into equal intervals (typically one to 20 minutes long), or the teacher may randomly select observation intervals within a larger time block (Kerr and Nelson, 1983).

Accuracy and Reliability of Behavioral Observation

If meaningful treatment decisions are to be made for a particular child, it is important that any information collected reflect as accurately as possible the true level of the behavior across various phases of an intervention program. Some of the ways in which a teacher may improve the accuracy of data follow.

1. Collect data at the same time of day in the same setting and situation at each session (e.g., from 8:20 A.M. to 9:10 A.M. in Ms. White's class, during math period).
2. An outside observer should select an observation site that will maximize the accuracy of all observations made and minimize the interruption of ongoing classroom activities.
3. An observer or teacher should collect data in randomly selected time blocks rather than continuously (Gelfand and Hartmann, 1984).
4. If a behavior occurs specifically during a particular time block, limit observations to this period (Gelfand and Hartmann, 1984).
5. Try to disguise interest in the target pupil's behavior: avoid staring at him or her, look at other children, and do not explain your observational activities until baseline information has been collected.
6. Define target behaviors in observable and measurable terms.
7. Collect interobserver agreement data at every phase of the intervention program.

Recommendation number 7 deserves further explanation. To make sure that the information collected is accurate, it is important to check all observations against those of another observer. The second observer may be an adult or even a pupil helper. There are essentially two ways to calculate interobserver agreement on recorded data. When using an event-recording procedure, Alberto and Troutman (1982) recommend calculating interobserver reliability by forming a simple ratio of the results of two observers. For example, if Observer A records that Doug has emitted eight aggressive acts during recess free play and Observer B records nine aggressive behaviors, the reliability coefficient is calculated by dividing the smaller by the larger number:

$$\frac{\text{Observer A: 8 aggressive acts}}{\text{Observer B: 9 aggressive acts}} = .88 \text{ (reliability coefficient)}$$

This coefficient can easily be converted into a percentage; in the example above, the interobserver reliability is 88 percent. A reliability coefficient can also be calculated for duration data by identifying the smaller total number of minutes or seconds of behavior recorded by one observer and dividing it by the larger total number recorded by a second observer (Alberto and Troutman, 1982).

If interval- or time-sampling data are used, interobserver reliability is calculated by first counting the number of intervals in which two separate observers recorded the same target behavior (i.e., the number of intervals of agreement between observers) and then dividing this number by the total number of intervals in which the target behavior was observed (i.e., the number of agreements plus the number of disagreements). For example, Observer A recorded Connie as being on task during 27 intervals observed and off task during three (total = 30 intervals); Observer B's record coincided with Observer A's for on-task behavior in 23 intervals and for off-task behavior in three intervals. The agreement coefficient in this case would be calculated:

$$\frac{\text{Number of agreements}}{\text{Number of agreements } + \text{ disagreements}}$$

$$= \frac{26}{26 + 4} = .87 \text{ (agreement coefficient)}$$

In interpreting these results, we would conclude that Observer A observed Connie to be on task (27 intervals/30 intervals × 100 =) 90 percent of the time and Observer B judged Connie to be on task (23 intervals/30 intervals × 100 =) 77 percent of the time. The observers' judgments agreed 87 percent of the time.

As Kerr and Nelson (1983) point out, there is no general consensus regarding what percentage of interobserver reliability is acceptable. For behaviors that can be defined in terms of discrete criteria (e.g., out of place, hitting, words spoken), one would expect this coefficient to be 90 percent or more. For target behaviors that are defined in terms of their function and require some subjective judgment by observers (e.g., provocative acts, positively reinforcing statements), acceptable reliability will be somewhat lower. Generally, if interobserver reliability falls below 80 percent, it is a good idea to reconsider the behavioral definitions and evaluate the observational procedures for appropriateness. Two or more interobserver reliability checks should ideally be done during baseline periods and at least one check in each phase of an intervention program.

Behavioral-Ecological Interviewing

For the most part, interviews with the child, regular classroom teachers, parents, and significant others are conducted in the screening and diagnostic phases of the behavioral-ecological assessment process. In the screening phase, they are used to collect information related to selecting target behaviors, to identify specific situations and conditions under which these occur, and to identify expectations of the child and adults in a variety of situations. In the diagnosis phase, interviews are conducted to isolate variables maintaining problem behaviors in various situations, to clarify a child's developmental history, to determine possible intervention goals, and to gauge the levels of motivation and skills of both the supervisory adults and the child for changing the problem behaviors (Atkeson and Forehand, 1981; Evans and Nelson, 1977; Kanfer and Saslow, 1969).

General Interviewing Strategies

The process of interviewing begins well before an actual interview session. An interview's success can be enhanced by advance preparation. Prior to each session, the teacher/interviewer should determine what he or she wishes to accomplish and what types of information are required at a particular point in a case.

It is also helpful for an interviewer to sketch out before each session the major questions that he or she will ask. This preliminary step structures the format of the interview and provides cues during the session that enable the interviewer to take full advantage of the allotted time.

The knowledge and integrity of the person being interviewed notwithstanding, the interviewer's skill largely determines both the quality and quantity of the data collected. The kinds of questions and the way they are asked have considerable bearing on the success of the interview. Patton (1980) provides some excellent suggestions concerning interview questions.

1. Use open-ended questions; for example:
   "What can you tell me about Doug's behavior?"
   "How would you like Connie to behave if you could change her?"
   "Doug, tell me what usually happens right before you get into a fight."

2. Avoid using questions that can be answered with a single word or phrase; for example:
   "Does Doug misbehave most during the morning or the afternoon?"
   "If Connie's like most L.D. children I've taught, I bet she often cries and complains a lot when you assign her a task. Right?"
   "Connie, tell me, do you like your teacher?"

3. Ask one question at a time; for example:
   "You wrote on your referral form that Doug has a bad attitude. What does he do that made you come to that conclusion?"
   Not:

"You said that Doug has a bad attitude. What makes you think that? Does he swear, complain, throw himself around? Things like that? Or is he one of those kids who seem to have a chip on their shoulder?"

4. Use language that is understandable and compatible with the interviewee's point of view; for example:
"Mr. Smith, it seems to me that both you and Doug think that standing up for your rights is important enough to fight over. When should a person try to avoid a fight?"
Not:
"Mr. Smith, Doug previously informed me that you place a considerable amount of emphasis on resolving interpersonal conflicts by resorting to extreme solutions, namely fighting. Wouldn't you agree that in certain circumstances interpersonal differences could be better resolved through alternative methods?"

5. Begin questions with the words "how?" "where?" "what?" and "when?". "Why?" questions unnecessarily limit the range of possible answers and may lead interviewees to manufacture responses that result in inaccurate conclusions; for example:
Q. Doug, why do you get into fights?
A. I dunno.
Q. Why don't you know?
A. I guess I'm just dumb.
Q. Why do you say that?
A. (shrugs)
Q. (with renewed insight) Well, why don't you quit fighting, then?
A. I dunno.
Q. Why?

6. Use appropriate body language, such as leaning forward, eye contact, smiles, nods, and verbal cues ("Uh hmm," "Go on") to maintain interviewee's interest and productivity.

7. Use further probes to clarify or to collect further information; for example:
"When is Doug most aggressive?"
"O.K. What happens right before Connie starts her crying and whining behavior?"
"So, Mr. Smith, just to clear things up some, what would you say or do to Doug if you found that he starts many of the fights he gets into?"

Interview information provides documentation of the classroom teacher's intervention strategy and serves as a continuing resource for planning and evaluating the effects of an intervention program. The examples above outline some basic techniques for conducting effective interviews. However, we should consider differences in interview strategy and content that exist between those conducted with adults and those conducted with children.

Interviewing Adults

A teacher should have some preliminary information concerning the child's behavioral excesses and deficits and about problematic situations before interviewing significant adults in the child's life. This information, which is obtained from informal contacts, referral forms, behavior-rating scales, screening interviews, and direct observations in various settings, is used to provide a specific focus to the general interview format presented in the problem-clarification section above. For example, in clarifying information from Question 1 above, an interviewer might ask,

"In your ratings of Doug, you indicated that he is quite aggressive sometimes. How does he show aggression?"

Follow-up questions could include:

"Which of these are most serious?"

"In which situations are his aggressive behaviors most likely to occur?"

Because it is easier to recall more immediate events, Patton (1980) advises interviewers to begin with questions about present events and to move later to questions about historical matters. For example, the third question in the "Diagnosis" section of this chapter provides a good place to begin an interview with a significant adult.

Q. Ms. White, you indicated on your referral form that Connie has a problem following directions. Could you elaborate on that?

A. Well, when I give her something to do, she usually whines about it and may even start crying if it's something she really doesn't want to do.

Q. I see. How often does this happen?

A. Just about every period, but mostly with math assignments.

Q. How would you like Connie to act when you give her an assignment?

A. Normal.

Q. Normal?

A. Yeah, like most of the other kids. Go ahead and start assignments and get them done.

Q. Now think back a moment to when you first started teaching Connie. Has this behavior changed at all since then?

A. Well, if anything, she's gotten worse!

Q. What have you done to try to get her to behave normally?

A. I've tried just about everything I can think of. Mostly, I've talked to her about it. That helped some. But lately, I've become so frustrated about it that I've yelled at her and taken away recess.

Q. What effect has this had on Connie's behavior?

A. None. She's the same.

In this dialogue, we see that the interviewer started with information taken from the teacher's rating scale and used it to focus the initial question. The interview began with a question concerning the present behavior of the child. Next, the interviewer attempted to isolate the situations in which Connie's behavior is most problematic. Then she questioned Ms. White on her behavioral expectations for Connie. Finally, the questioning focused on possible historical factors in the development of Connie's problem. The following conclusions and tentative hypotheses can be gleaned from this interview so far:

Tentative target behaviors:

1. Connie often whines and complains about assignments given to her and may even begin crying when she particularly doesn't want to do the task.
2. The alternative behavior expected by Ms. White is that Connie will begin the task immediately without complaining and see the assignment through to completion.

Potential hypotheses:

1. Connie may have used this behavior successfully in the past to avoid tasks she did not want to do.
2. Connie may perceive the math tasks, in particular, as too difficult for her. They may be inappropriate for her level of mastery.
3. Ms. White may have reinforced Connie's inappropriate behavior in the past by giving her a considerable amount of positive social attention for it; she also may be maintaining this pattern now through negative social attention.

Of course, the above hypotheses merit further review and verification through interviews and subsequent data collection. At this point, however, we can probably piece together some important information. First, Connie's inappropriate behavior may be of long duration and may have been strengthened considerably by Ms. White; thus, a powerful intervention program, one that will produce immediate improvements in Connie's behavior, will probably be needed. Second, close consideration should be given to the appropriateness of the assignments and/or the amount of work being given to Connie. Third, Ms. White may require a tactful explanation of how she may be shaping and maintaining Connie's behavior.

Interviewing Children

The above discussion illustrates how interviewing strategies may be applied to collecting information from significant adults. We also saw how such information can be used to generate hypotheses for planning an intervention. Interviews with children follow much the same format but require some modification of language and content to maximize their effectiveness.

Interviewing children presents several problems which do not arise in interviewing adults. Children rarely have the assurance and interpersonal poise of adults. Many children, especially those experiencing problems with social behavior, have limited communication skills. Often children do not readily volunteer information. And as children do not usually refer themselves for treatment, they may lack insight into their behavior problems and be unmotivated or unable to offer relevant information.

For these reasons, an interviewer must spend some time before the formal interview developing rapport with the subject. Above all, questions must be kept short, simple, and concrete. An interviewer may have to describe problem situations, the child's problem behaviors, and their consequences very clearly. He or she must stay flexible, and be able to move from open-ended questions to structured ones that have several answer choices to determine a child's opinion about specific issues.

The major purpose of interviewing a child is to determine his or her awareness of the problem behaviors and their controlling variables, degree of motivation to change, and skill at behavioral self-control. The following examples show how an interview with a child might be conducted in relation to topics taken from the "Individual Behavior Problem Analysis" section:

Example 1:

Q. Doug, we've talked some before about your problem of fighting. I'm wondering what would you do if another boy accidentally bumped into you in the hall?

A. I'd bump him back, and if he said anything smart, I'd settle it!

Q. What reason would you have for bumping him back?

A. To see if he was jus' playin' around or showing off.

Q. I see. Would you ever talk things over with another boy rather than fight?

A. Yeah, if somebody's bigger or older than you.

In the first example, the interviewer focused on identifying the circumstances in which Doug would use behavior other than fighting to resolve potential conflict situations. It was not determined whether Doug would attempt to settle a conflict with another child verbally unless he was under direct threat. Based on these tentative findings, it appears warranted to conclude that Doug needs a strong, externally oriented behavior management program that consistently reinforces prosocial behaviors and punishes aggressive ones. In addition, his father might be enlisted in helping Doug discriminate circumstances in which fighting is appropriate and those in which verbal negotiation is needed. Doug may also need training in social skills that would provide him with alternative modes of behaving.

Example 2:

Q. Connie, your teacher, Ms. White, is concerned about the way you act sometimes and asked me to talk with you about this. Can you tell me what you do to cause her to worry about you?

A. No.

Q. What do you do when she gives you a math sheet to work?

A. I work it.

Q. That's all?

A. Yeah.

Q. What happens when she gives you work that is too hard for you?

A. Sometimes when I can't do it, then I cry.

Q. What usually happens then?

A. Well, Ms. White gets mad sometimes and yells at me.

Q. When you see a math sheet that you think is too hard for you, tell me how it makes you feel or think.

A. Well, I get scared and mad because I can't do it.

Q. When do you look over work that Ms. White gives you and try to figure out how to do it on your own?

A. I don't know.

Q. How would you go about trying to figure out how to do work you didn't know how to do?

A. I would raise my hand and get help.

In the second example, the interviewer first attempted to find out whether Connie could accurately report on her inappropriate behavior. At first Connie tried to evade the questions; then she was able to provide an accurate description of her behavior and its consequences. From the remaining dialogue, it can be concluded either that Connie is not answering the questions or that she has little idea of how to analyze the requirements of a task except by enlisting the teacher's help. In this case, Connie may profit from positive social attention for starting and finishing a task. She needs to learn methods for determining the task requirements and possibly for instructing herself in working toward completing it. Having her maintain a record of her successes may provide an additional incentive.

Intervention as a Process

After information is collected concerning a pupil's performance in various settings, the classroom teacher or the consulting teacher synthesizes the data for the development of a behavioral change program. This involves enlisting the cooperation of significant adults (e.g., parents, siblings, extended family members) as well as the pupil. The behavioral change plan involves selecting an appropriate strategy for manipulating antecedents and consequences to produce the desired behavior in various settings. Once the intervention program is initiated, observational data are continuously collected to monitor its effectiveness. These data are also used to determine needed changes in intervention strategies that are required to produce the desired behavioral changes. The following steps summarize this process.

Step	Type of Data Needed
1. Collect baseline information	Observations
2. Identify problem behaviors	Observations Behavioral rating scales Interviews
3. Determine frequency of problem behaviors	Observations Interviews

Step	Type of Data Needed
4. Determine severity of problem behaviors	Observations Behavior rating scales ABC analysis
5. Select target behaviors	Observations Behavior rating scales ABC analysis Interviews

Step	Type of Data Needed
6. Develop intervention plan and select strategies	ABC analysis Interviews
7. Monitor effects of intervention	Observations
8. Alter intervention strategies	Observations Interviews
9. Evaluate overall effects of behavioral change plan	Observations Behavior rating scales Interviews

By adhering to a systematic process of data collection as outlined above and throughout this chapter, the classroom teacher will be able to consistently make both effective as well as efficient behavioral change plans. The absence of a systematic process or inappropriate use of such a system can seriously inhibit the success of any behavioral change effort by either a consulting teacher or a classroom teacher.

Summary

This chapter concentrates on presenting material to enable teachers to assess problem behaviors of children exhibiting social and behavioral problems in classroom settings. These problems may be exhibited by pupils previously classified in any of the traditional special education classifications, i.e., learning disabled, mildly handicapped, trainable mentally handicapped, physically impaired, severely/profoundly handicapped and of course behaviorally disordered. It emphasizes developing the assessment skills of individuals who will function as resource room teachers with the additional responsibility of providing consultation to other teachers. The material presented here departs somewhat from traditional approaches to assessment that employ various commercial measures. Instead, the chapter focused on the collection and analysis of specific information and skills needed for screening, diagnosis, program planning, and program monitoring. These procedures are related to designing effective intervention programs for changing children's problem behaviors. Some of the other issues and information dealt with in this chapter are:

1. Environmental settings and an individual child together comprise an interactive behavior system, or an ecology. Assessing behavior problems involves identifying and analyzing variables in the ecology that contribute to the problem.

2. Screening behavior problems entails surveying the range and severity of problem behaviors, determining who objects to them, and identifying the situations in which they occur.

3. An ecological analysis involves identifying specific interpersonal and environmental variables within each setting that control behavior, analyzing behavior expectancies within and across settings, and assessing the child's behavior across settings.

4. The most important goal of assessing problem behavior is to identify the consequent stimuli that have gained functional control over behavior in various situations.

5. Individual behavior problem analysis involves assessing the extent of a child's behavior repertoire, gauging the child's awareness of academic and/or social problems, evaluating the child's skill at behavioral self-control, and determining the child's motivation to change.

6. A major objective in designing intervention programs is to eliminate sources of problematic antecedent and consequence control.

7. An ABC analysis involves recording a behavior's occurrence and identifying the antecedent (immediately preceding) events and the consequent (immediately following) events. This can be done by using a variety of direct-observation data-collection procedures.

8. Interviews with the pupil, teachers, parents, and significant others may be essential in the screening and diagnostic phases of the behavioral-ecological assessment process.

Mastery Review

I. Recall

1. Which of the following will determine whether a specified behavior may be judged disordered?

    a. No one else in the community emits this type of behavior.
    b. One person in the student's immediate environment will not tolerate it.
    c. The behavior is developmentally inappropriate.
    d. All of the above.

2. (A) _____ is/are an overt observable and measurable movement, an event that has a beginning and an end.

    a. contingency.
    b. behavior.
    c. thoughts and feelings.
    d. all of the above.

3. Behaviors which are emitted at zero or low levels but have serious consequences regarding a child's learning are called:

   a. behavior deficits.
   b. behavior excesses.
   c. behavior acquisitions.
   d. none of the above.

4. Examples of social behavior deficits include:

   a. asking for information.
   b. not speaking at appropriate times.
   c. talking too indistinctly to be heard.
   d. all of the above.

5. The child, the settings, and the individuals within these settings that are a part of the child's daily life make up:

   a. the ecological system.
   b. the developmental system.
   c. the individual system.
   d. none of the above.

6. When doing an individual analysis, the teacher would:

   a. assess the student's behavioral repertoire.
   b. determine the student's motivation to change.
   c. neither a nor b.
   d. a and b.

7. What procedures would be used in performing an individual analysis?

   a. Standardized tools.
   b. Interviews with supervisory adults and the student.
   c. Informal and formal observation procedures.
   d. All of the above.

8. Gary curses, rips up books, bites his classmates, and does not make eye contact with the teacher. Which behavior should be targeted for change last?

   a. Cursing.
   b. Ripping up books.
   c. Biting.
   d. Lack of eye contact.

9. The most important procedure for collecting information on problem behavior is:

   a. interviewing supervisory adults.
   b. direct observation in the natural setting.
   c. standardized, norm-referenced behavior checklists.
   d. all of the above.

10. Eric cries in class, while Leigh is noncompliant. Which recording system would the teacher select to monitor both students at the same time?

    a. Event recording.
    b. Time sampling.
    c. Duration recording.
    d. Interval recording.

11. If the teacher wanted to assess on-task behavior during morning seat work in a class of 10 learning disabled students, which recording procedure would be selected?

 a. Permanent product.
 b. Event recording.
 c. Time sampling.
 d. All of the above.

12. One observer recorded Gary out of his seat 20 times and in it 10 times during a 30-interval time period. The second observer recorded 21 out-of-seat behaviors and 9 in-seat behaviors. What is their reliability coefficient?

 a. 100 percent.
 b. 39 percent.
 c. 9 percent.
 d. 8 percent.

13. What guidelines should be followed when planning an interview?

 a. Use open-ended questions.
 b. Avoid using questions that can be answered with a single word or phrase.
 c. Use language that is understandable to the person being interviewed.
 d. All of the above.

14. What does the process of screening behavior problems entail?

 a. Surveying the range and severity of problem behaviors.
 b. Determining who objects to the behaviors.
 c. Identifying the environments in which they occur.
 d. All of the above.

15. The major objective in designing intervention programs is:

 a. to satisfy IEP requirements.
 b. to satisfy school administration requirements.
 c. to eliminate sources of problematic antecedent and consequence control.
 d. all of the above.

II. Comprehension

1. Discuss the major assumptions underlying behavioral-ecological assessment outlined in this chapter.
2. Describe behavioral excesses and deficits. Give examples of each.
3. This chapter defines three steps in the screening process. List these steps and describe each one.
4. What are some important considerations in selecting appropriate target behaviors discussed in this chapter?
5. List the behavioral-ecological assessment methods described in this chapter. Give an example of each.
6. Describe an ABC analysis and give an example of how it might be completed.

III. Application

1. Working with another person who has completed this chapter, visit an educational setting and, after conferring with the teacher or person in charge of the program, select a pupil to observe for three one-hour sessions. Identify a target behavior and, working separately but using a mutually agreed-upon procedure, observe and record instances of the prespecified target behavior. Determine your interobserver agreement. Describe your project in a one- to two-page paper.

2. Working with three other persons who have completed this chapter, write a case history of a fictitious school-aged pupil already assessed as a behavior problem. Role-play the interviewing procedures discussed in this chapter, taking turns being the interviewer, the pupil, and the parents. Write a three-to-five-page paper describing the interview, your reaction to the procedure, and any observations you may have. The discussion on interview strategies in this chapter may be helpful for this exercise.

IV. Alternate Task

If none of the application exercises applies to your setting or curriculum, you can design two exercises of your own. They should demonstrate the application of one or more of the principles or concepts described in the preceding chapter. Prior approval of both exercises should be obtained from your course instructor.

V. Answer Key

I.
1. c p. 142
2. b p. 143
3. a p. 145
4. b, c pp. 145–49
5. a p. 142
6. d p. 155
7. b, c p. 156
8. c pp. 156–57
9. b p. 164

10. a p. 165
11. c p. 168
12. c pp. 168–69
13. d pp. 170–71
14. d p. 144
15. c p. 160

II.
1. p. 142, pp. 144–57
2. p. 145
3. pp. 144–49
4. pp. 157–58
5. pp. 162–75
6. p. 164

Part III
Categorical Assessment Considerations

Although the field of special education encompasses a vast array of developmental, behavioral, physical, and learning disabilities and impairments, the delivery of educational services has in the past been limited to five or six categorical areas. In this part, we deal with five special education classification areas: the mildly handicapped, including the learning disabled and the educable mentally handicapped; the trainable mentally handicapped learner; the severely or profoundly handicapped pupil; the physically handicapped pupil; and the gifted learner.

The rationale for covering the learning-disabled and the educable mentally handicapped pupil within one chapter is the similarities in their classroom performance. This organization of the material follows the logic behind special education classifications: grouping by the most common developmental and learning characteristics facilitates instructional planning, implementation, and evaluation.

Part III focuses on the variety of roles that the special education teacher may play in educational assessment: collector of data, interpreter of those data, coordinator of other data collectors, intervention planner, consultant to other professionals and parents, advocate for additional services within the pupil's community, and primary behavior-change agent for the pupil.

Chapters 7, 8, 9, and 10 address the four most widely used special education service delivery classifications. They describe classroom assessment procedures and issues with pupils exhibiting mild to profound learning, developmental, behavioral, and orthopedic problems.

The final chapter in this section, "Assessment of the Gifted Learner," completes the categorical considerations. The gifted learner is included not on the basis of historical precedent (though precedent does exist), but because this group of pupils does require educational services other than those provided in regular programs.

Chapter 7: Assessment of the Mildly Handicapped Learner

This chapter discusses pupils usually classified as mildly handicapped, including the learning disabled, the educable mentally retarded, and the mildly behaviorally disordered. Assessment procedures appropriate for various age levels are described, as are the major issues at each of these levels. Formal and informal assessment procedures are examined, including a number of commercially available assessment materials and procedures focusing on specific subject areas.

Chapter 8: Assessment of the Trainable Mentally Handicapped Learner

In this chapter we describe procedures for identifying adaptive behavior and learning problems in pupils exhibiting moderately handicapping conditions. Because of the complexity of defining this special education classification, the chapter devotes particular attention to issues in identifying the population and its developmental characteristics. A detailed discussion of direct-observation data-collection procedures used in classroom settings is provided, and the effect of multihandicapping conditions on assessment is described.

Chapter 9: Assessment of the Profoundly Handicapped Pupil

This chapter provides a detailed examination of assessment procedures appropriate for use with pupils exhibiting the most severe learning and developmental problems. The difficulties in using commercially available assessment materials for this population are discussed, with suggestions for their adaptation for use by teachers. Multihandicapping conditions, varying response modes, and functional skill assessment are also described.

Chapter 10: Assessment of the Physically Handicapped

Chapter 10 addresses assessment procedures that classroom teachers will find useful in dealing with pupils experiencing a wide range of orthopedic, muscular, and vitality problems. The more commonly occurring conditions are defined and their respective etiologies described. The limitations of commercially available assessment materials are discussed, and means are provided of adapting them for classroom use. A combined medical, therapeutic, and educational team approach — the complement of the traditional multidisciplinary team concept — is described. An environmental assessment checklist is provided that examines factors affecting a physically handicapped pupil's access to school, home, and community.

Chapter 11: Assessment of the Gifted Learner

Completing the array of special education classifications and service delivery areas is Chapter 11, which features a thorough description of the problems in defining giftedness, the variety of gifted learners, and the areas of functioning that the classroom teacher should be prepared to assess. It also surveys the impact of various handicapping conditions and learning differences that must be dealt with in the assessment process. The use of commercial assessment materials and the interpretation of their findings is discussed, as are learning styles and preferences, with particular attention to the impact of these data on instructional planning and delivery.

Chapter 7

Assessment of the Mildly Handicapped Learner

Key Terms:

academic achievement domain

adaptive behavior

attention skills

categorical classroom

categorical definitions

classroom interventions

diagnostic teaching

formative assessment

inaccurate referral

informal assessment

informal reading inventory

learning-aptitude domain

learning strategies

memory skills

mildly handicapped learner

noncategorical classroom

overreferral

prereferral

primary handicap

primary referral

process-oriented assessment

work-sample analysis

written language

Chapter Objectives:

After reading this chapter and completing the Mastery Review, you will be able to:

1. Identify the categories of learners usually termed "mildly handicapped" and explain the focus of assessment for this group.
2. Describe the unique problems of identifying learners with mild handicaps at three distinct levels: early childhood, elementary school, and secondary school.
3. Recognize sources of bias in assessment practices as they relate specifically to the mildly handicapped learner.
4. Discuss the particular considerations for the mildly handicapped learner at each of the five levels of assessment.
5. Describe the two primary domains of assessment and identify standardized instruments and informal procedures used in each of them to assess a learner.

The degree of children's learning disabilities, behavior disorders, and mental retardation ranges from mild to severe. More and more frequently, service delivery systems for the mildly handicapped are aimed at children diagnosed within three traditional categories: educable mentally retarded (E.M.R.), learning disabled (L.D.), and mildly behaviorally disordered (B.D.). The reasons for this practice are threefold. First, nonspecific definitions of E.M.R., L.D., and B.D. make precise diagnosis difficult, especially when children exhibit only mild degrees of a handicap. The child who, for example, steadfastly refuses to read and is two or three years behind his or her classmates in academic abilities might be initially labeled as any of the three but might in fact be none of them.

Second, children within these categories tend to display similar characteristics in both learning and behavior (Hallahan and Kauffman, 1978). For example, difficulties in abstract thinking, memory deficits, and disturbed peer interactions are commonly noted in all three categories, and no one characteristic is sufficient to permit definite labeling. Intelligence scores can be used as a criterion to distinguish those who are mentally retarded from those who are learning or behavior disordered, but present research suggests that when *performance* is considered, learners with these three labels are more similar than different (Gajar, 1980; Marsh, Price, and Smith, 1983).

A third reason for this broad grouping of the mildly handicapped is that teachers often use similar techniques and instructional materials in working with E.M.R., L.D., and B.D. pupils. Research supports this practice, as identical instructional arrangements have proven effective with all three categories. It is essential, however, that the special educator know the particular demands of each condition and apply proven techniques accordingly. Systematically conducted differential diagnosis and careful evaluation of performance data will reveal unique aspects of learning or behavior profiles that the special educator must address for E.M.R., L.D., and B.D. pupils exhibiting mild handicaps.

The premise of this chapter is that the primary focus of assessment must be on what the learner can and cannot do rather than on the assigned diagnostic label.

Defining the Population and Setting

Pupils in all three categories gain attention at the referral stages and during diagnosis because they are deficient in skills associated with successful continued learning. As discussed by Radabaugh and Yukish (1982), the skills that interact with instructional performance among the mildly handicapped include:

1. Difficulties in *discrimination,* i.e., locating the relevant dimensions of a stimulus (Blackhurst and Berdine, 1981).
2. Difficulties in *generalizing* information from one situation to another with similar characteristics (Payne and Patton, 1981).
3. Difficulties in *attending* to stimuli without distraction.
4. Difficulties in *using strategies* in novel problem-solving situations.
5. Difficulties in *solving abstract problems.*

6. Difficulties in benefiting from *incidental learning* — those aspects of a situation that are not centrally presented.

7. Difficulties in *memory,* especially when information is presented incidentally and there is little opportunity for overlearning.

8. Difficulties in approaching tasks with a positive *learning set;* in these pupils, either failure is expected or the task is not attempted.

9. Difficulties in developing and using *social skills* that enhance interactions at school, home, and work.

10. Difficulties in *evaluating one's own performance.*

It is probable that at some time all pupils have experienced difficulty in learning. For the mildly handicapped pupil, however, the difficulties noted here consistently interfere with learning. We do not yet have a quantitative measure of how great a handicap must be for special services to be offered, nor have we established an absolute number or combination of characteristics that must be identified before a pupil is diagnosed as mildly handicapped. But in diagnosing mild degrees of a handicap, we must bear two determinants in mind: the extent to which the child's learning or behavior deviates from what is considered to be typical for age and grade level; and the teacher's tolerance and ability to deal with the child's difficulties (Pasanella and Volkman, 1977). Criteria will vary among schools, among diagnostic teams, and even among teachers. Each decision must be based on the case at hand.

Educational Settings for the Mildly Handicapped

Public Law 94–142 states that "the removal of a handicapped child from the regular education environment occurs only when the nature or severity of the handicap is such that education in the regular classes, with the use of supplementary aids and services, cannot be achieved satisfactorily" (Section 612b). Under this mandate, there is little justification for complete removal of the pupil with mild handicaps from the regular class. In most cases, such a pupil will receive the majority of his or her instructional program in the regular class, with supplemental and remedial instruction provided by special education teachers.

In some schools, the mildly handicapped pupil who receives services outside the regular classroom is placed in a noncategorical classroom with others exhibiting mild learning or behavior problems. Other schools use a service delivery model that places each of the three categorical groups in a separate classroom. In categorical classrooms, the children served sometimes exhibit more than a mild form of the handicap. This is especially true in the areas of learning disability and behavior disorders.

Issues and Special Problems

Learners with mild handicaps are not easily identified. Their problems can be quite subtle and may go unnoticed until they exhibit unusual lags in achievement or worse, fail to achieve. Because federal legislation guarantees a free and appropriate education to handicapped people between the ages of 3 and 21, the special educator will need an understanding of the difficulties in assessing a learner suspected of mild handicaps at any age level. One problem is the possibility of bias throughout the assessment process. Attention paid by the special educator to possible biasing influences will contribute to the overall integrity of the process.

Assessment of Preschool-Aged Children

It is generally believed that early intervention contributes to the growth and adjustment of handicapped children, yet identifying young children as mildly handicapped raises special dilemmas. While moderately and severely handicapped children present obvious characteristics that aid in early diagnosis, this simply is not the case with children suspected of mild handicaps. Perhaps nowhere in the field of special education are we more likely to mislabel or identify false positives than in the case of the preschool child. Are Suzanne's delayed speech and language indicative of mild mental retardation or a pattern that is idiosyncratic to her development? There is danger in assigning labels to young children since they can create many of the negative effects — e.g., loss of self-esteem, fear of peer rejection — experienced by older handicapped children. Observation and repeated measures over time can help to clarify a diagnosis, but it is possible that the problem may intensify while we wait to intervene.

Public education of the preschool handicapped is a relatively new aspect of special education; preschool programs are not yet widespread, and only those states that provide public education at the preschool level are required to include services for the preschool handicapped. In the past, there has been considerable controversy about the screening and diagnostic instruments used to place children in existing programs. The performance data these tests yield seem to have little predictive validity for school performance and little use in planning a remediation program (Keogh and Becker, 1973). Continued research on preschool assessment has generated recommendations for reasonable practice, however. Chapter 5 provides guidelines for designing a sound identification and assessment plan for young handicapped children who exhibit mild forms of a learning or behavior handicap. The discussion of the screening and identification of pupils suspected of having a learning or developmental handicap presented in Chapter 1 (p. 8) is also relevant.

Assessment of Elementary-Aged Children

Children in the primary grades (K–4) are exposed daily to activities that require sustained attention, the ability to remember, and the application of problem-solving skills. These skills in turn enable the student to generalize and ultimately to comprehend increasingly complex abstractions usually introduced in grades 4 and above. Pupils suspected of having mild handicaps have experienced repeated failure in school tasks, especially in learning to read.

Referrals.   Referrals for educational assessment are most commonly made after the first and second grades; many teachers hesitate to refer a child before he or she is more than two grade levels behind peers, and others prefer to retain a child in the hope that additional instruction may remedy the problem. In some instances, the policies of school districts may implicitly or explicitly prohibit the referral of a child in the kindergarten or beginning elementary grades.

Regular classroom teachers are the primary referral source in most schools. The referring teacher may be asked to provide a brief behavioral description of the perceived problem. Special educators may then suggest alternative instructional strategies to use with the child (Tymitz, 1984), and these efforts may result in an improvement in the child's skills or may at least provide information that can contribute to more accurate assessment and individualized educational programming.

There is increasing concern that regular classroom teachers may be overreferring pupils who do not achieve in the curriculum they present. This results in high rates of inaccurate referral — low achievers (Ysseldyke et al., 1982) and slow learners (Belmont and Belmont, 1980) referred as learning disabled. Moreover, some teachers have come to believe that individualized instruction is the sole province of special education, so any child who requires additional help "belongs" in special education. It is hoped that the problems of inappropriate referral will be resolved by continued in-service training in classroom identification of mildly handicapped learners and in individualizing instruction.

The majority of assessment instruments developed to date are directed at elementary-school age levels. Of the literally hundreds of tests, only a few are recognized as technically adequate for diagnostic purposes. (See the discussion of test construction in Chapter 3.) It is useful to remember that a diagnosis will rarely reveal the exact cause of a learning problem. In fact, one cause of these problems is poor teaching, and to date we don't have a test for that!

Assessment of Secondary-Level Youth

Prior to the passage of P.L. 94–142, there were few secondary-level programs serving mildly handicapped pupils. Although precise data are not available, it appears that on reaching the legal age for leaving school, mildly handicapped pupils either chose to drop out of school or were absorbed into existing programs and became the lowest of the low achievers. Because of the law, programs for the secondary level mildly handicapped pupil are becoming more common.

Generally pupils are assigned to secondary-level special education programs as a continuation of elementary or junior high placements; new referrals of secondary-level pupils are infrequent. This is partly because secondary teachers are not trained to identify specific learning or behavior problems in adolescents; their training experiences and instructional approaches are as a rule oriented to subject areas — science, math, language arts, social studies. In addition, many secondary-level teachers assume that pupils who have completed approximately eight years of schooling have already had ample time to be identified. As a result, they frequently attribute poor performance to lack of motivation. (This is especially true for the mildly handicapped pupil who functions at barely acceptable performance levels in a variety of subjects.) Finally, some teachers may not refer pupils because they believe that secondary school is simply too late to help the student with learning problems. Because we know that pupils can continue to benefit from special services at this level, because we know that motivation may be part of the problem but is not all of it, and because we know that learning problems may surface or recur at the secondary level, the special educator should support the identification and referral of pupils by regular secondary-level teachers.

Relevant Assessment. The mildly handicapped secondary pupil benefits more from an assessment that is relevant to both the context and the curriculum than from one conducted for the sole purpose of assigning a label. The relevancy of an assessment may be gauged by examining:

- What policies the school abides by.

    In a secondary program in which minimum competency testing is a graduation requirement, it may be necessary to design the assessment so that the performance data will aid the special educator in preparing the pupil to complete the examination or its equivalent successfully.
- What programs the school presently offers.

    A secondary school may provide vocational or career education curricula that may or may not address the needs of handicapped pupils. Each curriculum calls for a different type of assessment.
- What information teachers are most likely to find helpful.

    Secondary-level teachers may view assessment information that describes the way the pupil approaches learning tasks as more beneficial than a set of subtest scores. They may also find criterion-referenced data more informative than norm-referenced data.

Nondiscriminatory Assessment

In Chapter 2, the negative impact of bias and sources of discrimination in educational assessment were elaborated. When we speak of bias in the assessment process, we are referring to errors that are repeatedly made by teachers, psychometrists, and other specialists when they make decisions, predictions, and inferences about members of particular groups (Duffey et al., 1981).

Children suspected of mild handicaps that fall within the diagnostic categories of E.M.R., L.D., and B.D. are particularly prone to biased assessment. Imprecise categorical definitions and broad descriptions of characteristics such as immaturity, distractibility, and aggressiveness invite a high degree of subjectivity in assessment decisions.

Bias in Referrals. Teachers should be aware that bias occurs throughout the assessment process. Because of preconceived attitudes about the way "all children should perform" in the regular classroom, children who deviate are often referred. On the surface this may seem to be a reasonable practice, but it is worthwhile for the special educator to ascertain at the onset of referral how much diversity is permitted in the regular classroom curriculum. Stereotypic content depicting race, sex, language, or cultural practice may be of little interest to minority-group pupils. In their case, learning or behavior problems may indicate as much a lack of opportunity to express diversity as they do a handicapping condition (Duffey et al., 1981; Mercer, 1972; Reschly, 1981). A careful look at the regular classroom curriculum can help to alleviate inappropriate referrals under these conditions.

The special educator should also be aware that the information that initiates the referral can bias subsequent diagnostic decisions. This is especially true for pupils referred for behavior disorders. Ysseldyke, Algozzine, Shinn, and McGue (1982) found that when school professionals studied case-history folders of children referred for behavior problems, decisions to classify them as emotionally disturbed were likely even though the professionals were not presented with any evidence to confirm behavior problems. Ysseldyke and his coworkers conclude that "even before a child utters a response to a test item, the cards may be unfavorably stacked" (p. 228). To diminish biasing effects at the referral stage, the special educator should provide the regular classroom teacher with referral forms that structure an objective description of the reasons for referral based on the pupil's performance in the available learning contexts.

Testing Biases.   Beyond referral, any child entering the testing situation may be subject to other possible biasing effects, including those that relate to technical inadequacies of the tests used; those associated with procedural deficiencies such as examiner expectations or negative testing conditions; and those that concern interpretation of results, inappropriate scoring, and incorrect calculations. For the mildly handicapped, the most dangerous bias lies in the way test data are interpreted for classification and placement decisions. Despite federal guidelines, it appears that these decisions are often influenced by the availability of funding and administrative prerogative. Tucker (1980), for example, noted that there has been a dramatic increase in the assignment of black pupils to classes for learning-disabled children even when there is little evidence of handicap. Similarly, bilingual children have been assigned to classes for the mildly mentally retarded on the basis of language acquisition or cultural differences when cognitive deficits have not been established (Weffer, 1981). Just as there is concern about mislabeling, we must be aware of bias that deprives children of the services they need. Some mildly handicapped children may require full-time special education because their problems are not likely to be remediated via a mainstreamed placement. It is therefore recommended that special educators look at the effects of prior classroom intervention strategies before making placement decisions (Christenson, Ysseldyke, and Algozzine, 1982; Tymitz, 1984).

Multiple Handicapping Conditions and Interrelated Factors.   A resource room teacher was overheard remarking to her supervisor, "Next year I'd like you to assign me all thoroughbreds — all my pupils this year are hybrids!" In her own words, this teacher was describing one of the most confounding dilemmas in identifying and serving mildly handicapped pupils. Children diagnosed as educable mentally retarded (E.M.R.), learning disabled (L.D.), or behaviorally disordered (B.D.) may also exhibit other handicaps, including speech and language disorders, sensory impairments, and physical or health disabilities. Learning-disabled children may exhibit emotional disturbance (Segal and Gold, 1982), emotionally disturbed children mirror the learning problems of the learning disabled (Kauffman, 1981), and mentally retarded pupils may also demonstrate behavior disorders (Reiss, Levitan, and Szyszko, 1982). For children suspected of multiple handicaps, assessment seeks to determine what constitutes the *primary* handicap. This decision is legally required for placement and for funding purposes (see the discussion in Chapter 1 of the uses of assessment data). Schools must abide by state and federal definitions of handicapping conditions if they choose to receive federal funds for their programs. The special educator should be aware that establishment of the primary handicap is complicated by the omission of criteria in the definitions and by variations in the way the definitions are used by professionals.

Etiological Considerations.   As an alternative approach to establishing the primary handicap, some educators have focused on identifying the etiology of suspected handicaps. For children with severe handicaps, a search for etiology has been useful in making this determination. Because of the overlapping of characteristics, the subtleties of behaviors, and the numerous causes of mild handicaps (there are over 250 known causes of retardation [Berdine, 1985]), however, establishing the etiology of the mildly handicapping condition is not as successful. It is only when an E.M.R., L.D., or B.D. is found in combination with sensory or physical impairments that etiology can be accurately determined. In contrast, consider the pupil who has serious reading problems, is subject to prolonged temper tantrums, and seems virtually incapable of age-appropriate adaptive skills. Establishing etiology in this instance is analogous to establishing the precedence of the chicken or the egg. Despite the tenuousness of the assessment, however, it is imperative that the special educator consider the interaction of learning problems and mild behavior disorders. A teacher will undoubtedly observe a pupil's behavior in the process of assessing his or her learning problems, and specific behavioral problems such as low frustration tolerance must be considered in interpreting assessment results. For example, a pupil with a reading problem may have deficient skills, a low frustration tolerance, or both. In designing an assessment, the special educator must plan to collect data that can help the educator decide whether instruction should focus on one or both problems.

Classroom Assessment Procedures

The goal of assessment is to obtain specific information that will assist teachers and others in making accurate decisions about a pupil. At each of the five levels of assessment discussed in Chapter 1, it is necessary to recognize the special considerations that pertain to the mildly handicapped learner. In addition to the IEP requirements for academic or subject-matter data collection, the teacher of the mildly handicapped pupil is also often called upon to assess both the learner's aptitude and his or her adaptive behavior.

Assessment, particularly educational assessment of mildly handicapped pupils, can include measurement of learning processes and abilities such as visual perceptual skill, visual-motor ability, and psycholinguistic abilities. The validity of this process-oriented approach to assessment and remediation is a topic of debate, and selected studies either confirm or refute its efficacy. The issue remains unresolved. The reader is referred to Kavale (1981) and Smith (1983) for further reading on this aspect of assessment.

The Assessment of Learning Aptitude

Learning aptitude refers to a pupil's ability to learn or make use of new information. A primary component of learning aptitude is assessed through the measurement of two different types of learning — intelligence, which is primarily school learning, and adaptive behavior, which includes nonacademic learning. However, these tests produce only static measures of an individual's performance at one point in time.

Any effective assessment of learning aptitude must also include a dynamic component (Feuerstein, Rand, and Hoffman, 1979). That is, the examiner must interact with the pupil, altering aspects of the testing situation and assessing which modifications enable the pupil to perform the task. Such modifications could involve helping the pupil discover better ways to assimilate and utilize new information or might include teaching learning strategies, problem-solving techniques, or self-reinforcement so that the pupil can continue to improve his or her learning aptitude (Borkowski and Konarski, 1981; Feuerstein, Rand, Hoffman, and Miller, 1980). These techniques are particularly appropriate for use during criterion-referenced assessment.

Traditional Measures for Assessing Learner Aptitude

Traditional measures of learning aptitude include intelligence tests and adaptive behavior measures. Nontraditional techniques for assessing learning aptitude serve as supplements to the more traditional assessment procedures.

Measures of Intelligence. The validity and usefulness of intelligence tests have come under fire from both psychologists and educators, and the misuse of intelligence test scores has been well substantiated. All too often, these scores dominate labeling and placement decisions (Smith and Knoff, 1981) — a practice that clearly runs counter to federal guidelines under P.L. 94–142. Despite the ongoing controversy, intelligence test scores are widely used in the diagnosis of mild handicapping conditions, and a child may be differentially labeled on the basis of an intelligence test score.

The most widely used intelligence tests measure verbal and numerical ability and abstract reasoning, but some authors suggest that these behaviors are most closely related to school learning, and that these "intelligence" tests are actually tests of academic achievement (Anastasi, 1976; Levine, 1976). Research has borne this out, showing that intelligence tests are good predictors of school performance (Wesman, 1968) but poor predictors of success in later life (Oakland, 1980). Group intelligence tests may be routinely administered to all pupils in a school district, either to provide descriptive information about pupils or as a screening device. However, group measures of intelligence do not provide valid scores for eligibility and programming decisions. Individual tests must be used in these cases.

In using any instrument, it is important to examine carefully the manuals that accompany well-developed tests. They provide additional detail and are useful in helping to determine the appropriateness of using the tests to assess intelligence of a child with suspected mild learning problems.

There are three Wechsler scales: the Wechsler Adult Intelligence Scale, or WAIS (Wechsler, 1955), is appropriate for people over 16 years of age; the Wechsler Intelligence Scale for Children–Revised (WISC–R) (Wechsler, 1974) is designed to be used with children aged 6 through 16; and the Wechsler Preschool and Primary Scale of Intelligence (WPPSI) (Wechsler, 1967) is to be used with children aged four through six and a half years.

The *WISC–R* is widely used with mildly handicapped pupils. It is composed of two scales, a verbal and a performance scale, each with six subtests. During all verbal subtests, the examiner asks questions and the pupil responds. The subtests of the verbal scale are information, similarities, arithmetic, vocabulary, comprehension, and digit span.

The performance scale is composed of six timed subtests, each of which requires the child to point to, manipulate, or rearrange objects. The subtests are Picture Comprehension, Picture Arrangement, Block Design, Object Assembly, Coding, and Mazes. Two types of scores are obtained on the WISC–R: verbal, performance, and full-scale I.Q.'s, with means of 100 and standard deviations of 15, and scaled subtest scores, with means of 10 and standard deviations of 3. (Refer to the Chapter 3 discussion of measures of central tendency, pp. 60–65.) The standardized sample and the reliability of the WISC–R appear to be adequate, though evidence for validity is limited.

A common practice with mildly handicapped populations has been to analyze subtest scatter on the WISC–R. At one level, the pupil's verbal I.Q. may be compared to his or her performance I.Q. There must be a significant discrepancy between verbal and performance I.Q.'s before conclusions can be drawn from such a comparison, and although experts disagree about what constitutes significance, a difference of 15 points seems to be a generally accepted standard (Wechsler, 1974).

Some research suggests that children with reading problems or learning disabilities often have WISC–R performance scores significantly higher than their verbal scores (Clements and Peters, 1962; Huelsman, 1970). However, you should be aware that the occurrence and magnitude of the discrepancy between verbal and performance scores may be influenced by other factors, including a pupil's full-scale I.Q. score (Kaufman, 1976a; Todd, Coolidge, and Satz, 1977), socioeconomic status (Anastasi, 1976; Kaufman, 1976b), and ethnic background (Sattler, 1974). It also happens that significant discrepancies between verbal and performance I.Q.'s are frequent among normal learners (Anderson, Kaufman, and Kaufman, 1976), so the discrepancy between a pupil's verbal and performance I.Q.'s must be interpreted with caution. It would be quite inappropriate to conclude that a child was mildly handicapped on the basis of a discrepancy alone. If a pupil does demonstrate a significant verbal-performance discrepancy, this information might best be used to generate hypotheses about his or her strengths, weaknesses, and learning style, with the understanding that these hypotheses must be verified through further assessment.

The *Stanford-Binet Intelligence Scale (SBIS)* (L. Terman and M. Merrill, 1973) may be administered to individuals age 2 through adulthood. Test items are grouped on the basis of age, increasing in difficulty at each of twenty age levels from two years, zero months, through three gradations of Superior Adult performance. Scores are determined by totalling the number of months' credit earned for success at a given level to derive a mental age, which is then converted to a deviation I.Q. calculated on a mean of 100 and a standard deviation of 16. Behaviors sampled at each age level vary, though some behaviors are sampled at more than one level. Attempts to organize the range of behaviors sampled have produced several classification systems to assist in the interpretation of the SBIS. As described by Sattler (1982), items through the age levels measure seven broad areas: language, memory, conceptual thinking, reasoning, numerical reasoning, visual-motor intelligence, and social intelligence. A diagnostic team may choose to use the SBIS as the sole measure of intelligence, but it may also use the data to supplement information derived from the WISC–R.

The most recent standardization of the SBIS occurred in 1972, using the 1960 edition of test items. The sample included 2,100 children, with approximately one hundred subjects at each level. Additional details describing the sample population are not available in the manual, nor are data available on the reliability or validity of the 1972 edition.

The 1972 edition of the SBIS has been criticized for a variety of reasons, including the unavailability of data on its technical adequacy, limited geographical standardization, and failure to adjust ages of test-takers, which presently results in children having to perform above their age levels on tasks in order to receive an average I.Q. score. The SBIS has been further criticized because of its heavy emphasis on the assessment of general intellectual ability through verbal skills.

The *Woodcock-Johnson Psychoeducational Battery* (R. W. Woodcock and M. B. Johnson, 1978) is comprised of 27 subtests divided into three components: Cognitive Ability, Tests of Achievement, and Tests of Interest. The instrument is designed for use across the ages of 3 to over 80 years of age. For intelligence testing, the following subtests would be administered: Picture Vocabulary, Spatial Relations, Memory for Sentences, Visual-Auditory Learning, Blending, Quantitative Concepts, Visual Matching, Antonyms-Synonyms, Analysis-Synthesis, Numbers Reversed, Concept Formation, and Analysis.

The Woodcock-Johnson yields a variety of derived scores, including age and grade scores, percentile rank by age and grade, instructional range, relative performance index, and functioning level. Selected subtest scores provide for cluster analysis. In addition to a preschool scale and a brief scale of broad cognitive subtests, clusters for analyzing cognitive abilities include verbal ability, memory, reasoning, perceptual speed, reading aptitude, mathematics aptitude, written language aptitude, and knowledge aptitude. Because the names of the clusters are not wholly congruent with the behaviors sampled, it is advisable to review carefully the subtests within a cluster for assessment and diagnostic purposes.

The Woodcock-Johnson Battery was normed on a stratified random sample of 4,732 subjects, the majority of whom were of school age. The manual presents data that support the instrument's reliability and validity.

The *Kaufman Assessment Battery for Children (K–ABC)* (A. S. Kaufman and N. L. Kaufman, 1983) is designed to assess the intelligence and achievement of two-and-a-half-to-twelve-and-a-half-year-old children. Four Global Scales yield standard scores with a mean of 100 and a standard deviation of 15. The scales are Sequential Processing, problem solving that requires stimuli to be arranged in a serial or temporal order (three subtests); Simultaneous Processing, problem solving that requires stimuli to be integrated and synthesized (seven subtests); Mental Processing, a combination of sequential and simultaneous scales that provides a global estimate of intellectual functioning; and Achievement, tasks that require knowledge of facts, language concepts, and school skills such as reading and arithmetic.

One additional measure, the Nonverbal Scale, can be used to evaluate the intellectual functioning of hearing-, speech-, and language-impaired children and those whose first language is not English. Directions for tasks on the scale can be presented in pantomime, and children may respond with questions.

The subtests for mental processing yield a standard score with a mean of 10 and a standard deviation of 3. The Achievement subtests yield standard scores with a mean of 100 and a standard deviation of 15. Sociocultural percentile rank norms allow for comparison of a child's performance to those of others with similar cultural and socioeconomic backgrounds.

The developers of the test state that the Mental Processing Scales measure fluid thinking, or the ability to be flexible when presented with unfamiliar problems. The Achievement Scale, however, is designed to assess crystallized thinking, or knowledge acquired through education, cultural experience, and training.

The K–ABC's mental processing and achievement scales were normed on a sample consisting of 2,000 children, 100 at each half-year of age between 2 years, 6 months and 12 years, 6 months. A stratified sample based on 1980 census data included whites, blacks, Hispanics, Asians, Native Americans, and exceptional children. Split-half reliability coefficients on the four Global Scales range from .86 to .93 for preschool children and from .89 to .97 for school-aged children. Reliability coefficients on subtests range from .72 to .93, with an average value of .83.

The K–ABC is a relatively new instrument, and validity studies conducted thus far have been primarily correlational. It is important to note that many validity studies have included sample groups of special populations. To date, evidence tends to support the publisher's construct and concurrent validity claims.

The K–ABC Interpretive Manual provides detailed information on how test profiles are to be used for educational diagnosis and planning. Efforts to assure standardized scoring and interpretation are supported through an available software program.

Measures of Adaptive Behavior. Adaptive behavior is the second area traditionally measured as part of learning aptitude. The American Association on Mental Deficiency defines adaptive behavior as "the effectiveness or degree with which the individual meets the standards of personal independence and social responsibility expected of his age and cultural group" (Grossman, 1973, p. 11). Like intelligence, adaptive behavior is a hypothetical construct that cannot be measured directly but must be inferred through the evaluation of other behaviors. Unlike intelligence tests, however, adaptive behavior instruments do not test the pupil directly. Instead, they are rating scales completed by parents or some other individual who knows the child and has observed his or her behavior in a variety of situations. The validity of the results will therefore be directly dependent upon how well the rater knows the child.

Compared to the variety of other instruments used in the assessment of mildly handicapped learners, there are relatively few adaptive behavior scales from which to choose. Most of them suffer from problems in standardization and/or validity. Two examples of adaptive behavior scales are described below.

The American Association on Mental Deficiency (AAMD) has developed an Adaptive Behavior Scale (ABS) (Nihira et al., 1969) that has been widely used with a variety of handicapped persons. This scale was revised in 1974 for use in the public schools (Lambert et al., 1975). The *AAMD Adaptive Behavior Scale, Public School Version,* consists of 95 items, grouped into two parts as illustrated below:

AAMD Adaptive Behavior Scale, Public School Version

Part I **Independent Functioning**	Part II **Violent and Destructive Behavior**
Independent functioning	Violent and destructive behavior
Physical development	Antisocial behavior
Economic activity	Rebellious behavior
Language development	Untrustworthy behavior
Numbers and time	Withdrawal
Vocational activity	Stereotyped behavior and odd mannerisms
Self-direction	Inappropriate interpersonal manners
Responsibility	Unacceptable vocal habits
Socialization	Unacceptable or eccentric habits
	Hyperactive tendencies
	Psychological disturbance
	Uses medication

The test authors recommend that the ABS, Public School Version be administered by the pupil's teacher. Each domain is assessed by several items that require the teacher to check statements applicable to the learner. Raw scores are then summed, and a percentile rank is derived for each part of the scale.

The school version of the ABS was standardized on 2,600 pupils in both regular and special education classes in California. The authors did not determine the reliability of the scale, nor has its validity been adequately tested. However, use of the scale is sometimes indicated because, unlike other adaptive measures, it uses data provided by the teacher rather than the child's parents.

The *Adaptive Behavior Inventory for Children,* or ABIC, is part of the System of Multicultural Pluralistic Assessment (SOMPA) and is appropriate for use with children aged five through eleven years. Information for the ABIC is collected through a structured interview with parents, which may be conducted in English or Spanish.

The scale is composed of 242 items arranged into six scales: family, community, peer relations, nonacademic school roles, earner/consumer, and self-maintenance. In deriving scores for the ABIC, the user first determines whether the interview results seem to be valid. (The manual provides directions for making this determination.) Standard scores are computed for each of the six scales, and a total score, or average scaled score, is also derived. A child is said to be "at risk" on a particular scale if his or her score falls below the third percentile.

Overall, the reliability of the ABIC appears to be sufficient, although reliabilities for some of the subscales are lower than desirable. The test was standardized on black, Hispanic, and white populations, but only pupils from California schools were included in the sample; thus usefulness of the norms in other areas of the country is questionable. Validity of the ABIC is not fully established, and further studies are needed.

Nontraditional Measures of Learning Aptitude

The notion that learning aptitude is alterable is enjoying renewed interest. Experimental studies conducted by psychologists and educators have demonstrated effective techniques and procedures for improving attention, memory, problem-solving, and reasoning skills. For example, it has been demonstrated that when average and learning-disabled pupils were taught two different ways to remember pairs of items, the learning-disabled pupils actually performed better than the average pupils (Cherkes-Julkowski et al., 1983). At the present time, however, the implications of such studies are difficult to translate into practice. Most of this research tends to be highly experimental; it is conducted in laboratory settings that do not necessarily resemble the classroom environment. Curricular materials designed to increase learning aptitude are practically nonexistent. Perhaps the biggest criticism of this research has been the absence of generalization effects: that is, a pupil may learn a more effective memory strategy or employ a more efficient way to solve a problem in an experiment but then fail to utilize these skills in a different context or at a different time (Butterfield, 1979). It is likely that future studies will continue to deal with such difficulties as generalization and that curricular programs for intellectual skills training will be developed for classroom settings.

The following discussion will focus on three areas that are traditionally overlooked in the assessment of learning aptitudes: attention, memory, and learning strategies. Research has amply demonstrated that performance in these three areas can be improved through instruction and that improved performance results in more efficient learning. Informal assessment strategies are used in the evaluation of these three areas because more standardized techniques have not been developed.

Attention.   Attentional difficulties are often cited as sources of learning problems (Keogh, 1973; Tarver and Hallahan, 1978). At least two different aspects of attention may be considered: focusing attention and sustaining attention. First, the pupil needs to focus on the relevant aspects of a task or situation. Research conducted by Zeaman and House (1979) demonstrated that retarded learners were able to learn a discrimination task at the same *rate* as average learners, but it took them much longer to *focus* their attention on the relevant task dimension of color or shape. This finding suggests that handicapped children might perform better if the relevant features of a lesson or task were pointed out or highlighted, as this would help focus their attention. Once attention is focused, the pupil needs to maintain that attention long enough to absorb or remember the critical features of a task. Researchers have used techniques such as verbal mediation, or talking to oneself, to help learners effectively sustain attention (Meichenbaum, 1977).

The teacher does not need to utilize separate techniques or instruments to assess and then improve a pupil's abilities in focusing and sustaining attention. Rather, close observation of the pupil's behavior in the regular class and in the assessment situation itself can help provide clues to his or her attentional processes. In both these situations, the teacher should watch for the following behaviors:

1. Does the pupil have difficulty beginning tasks? Does it seem to take a long time for him or her to settle down to work?
2. Does the pupil need help getting started with tasks? Does he or she need repeated directions in order to begin?
3. Can the pupil work on a task for an extended period of time, or does he or she seem to have a limited attention span?
4. Is the pupil easily distracted? Do normally occurring classroom events, such as someone sharpening a pencil, divert his or her attention?
5. Once the pupil is distracted, how easily does he or she return to the task?

The teacher will need to analyze the answers to these questions carefully to gain a more precise understanding of the pupil's attentional difficulties. Of course, the educator must be aware that difficulties in focusing and sustaining attention may also be due to lack of motivation. It would be best to observe the pupil's behavior in a variety of tasks, only some of which he or she finds interesting, to ascertain whether attentional difficulties decrease as motivation changes.

Memory. "He just can't seem to remember things from one day to the next!" Most teachers have heard a similar comment made about a mildly handicapped learner. Research has demonstrated that a variety of strategies may be effective for enhancing memory (Butterfield, Wambold, and Belmont, 1973). These include rehearsal, or saying something over and over again; organization, or chunking material into a group (as we all do with phone numbers); and elaboration, or putting stimuli to be remembered into a sentence or a story.

Assessment information about a pupil's memory strategies can be obtained through observations, interviews, and diagnostic teaching. First, the teacher will want to observe carefully as the pupil is confronted with a memory task during assessment activities. What does the child do? Does he or she seem to have any strategy for remembering information? Second, the teacher will want to ask the pupil about how he or she remembers things. This is best done in the context of a memory task, that is, just after the learner has attempted to remember some material. The teacher should ask the learner questions such as, "How did you remember that? Is there anything you did to help you remember?" Third, the teacher may want to teach the pupil some memory strategies, such as rehearsal, organization, or elaboration, and assess whether subsequent memory performance increases.

Tasks requiring memory skills may not arise during traditional norm- and criterion-referenced testing, so the teacher may want to structure a specific assessment situation utilizing memory skill. Some tests do include a memory subtest, and the teacher may want to use this subtest in an informal way for observation, interviewing, and diagnostic teaching. Or he or she may prefer to present an actual classroom task, such as memorizing the names of 10 states and their capitals, for assessment purposes.

Learning Strategies. "Learning strategies" refers to any purposeful activities that a pupil utilizes to increase learning efficiency. Some researchers have suggested that mildly handicapped pupils are actually poor learning strategists; that is, inefficient learners (Alley and Deshler, 1979; Torgensen, 1980). Research has demonstrated that better learners consciously use strategies such as memory, reasoning, problem solving, and decision making to enhance learning (Brown, 1978; Flavell, 1976).

The pupil's use of learning strategies can be evaluated in all assessment domains. In the area of learning aptitude, the teacher may assess the strategies used to reason and solve problems as well as those used in attention and memory tasks (as described earlier). In the academic achievement domain, the teacher should evaluate strategies used in reading and comprehending written material, spelling words, writing stories, and solving math problems. Across all tasks, the teacher should note whether the pupil monitors his or her own performance. Some relevant behaviors to watch for are:

1. Does the pupil seem to be aware of how well he or she is doing?
2. Does the pupil attempt to go back and check work or responses?

3. Does the pupil plan what to do before beginning a task?
4. Does the pupil work more slowly on more difficult tasks?

Interviews should first be used to ascertain what types of strategies a pupil uses. Diagnostic teaching may then be utilized to teach a new or more efficient strategy and to evaluate its effect on subsequent performance. A word of caution: the assessment of learning strategies should always take place in conjunction with criterion-referenced testing or informal assessment techniques. Interviewing and diagnostic teaching procedures disrupt the standardized administration of a test and invalidate the use of norm tables. For additional information on the use of learning strategies with pupils exhibiting learning disabilities, the reader is referred to Alley, Deshler, Clark, Schumaker, and Warner (1983) and Deshler and Schumaker (1986).

The Assessment of Academic Achievement

"Academic achievement" refers to the pupil's mastery of such school subjects as reading, writing, arithmetic, science, and social studies. Different tests may sample different skills within the same domain, that is, one academic achievement test might evaluate skill in decoding words, whereas another evaluates comprehension skills. Often, the same test will contain multiple forms or levels that assess different skills for pupils of different ages. For example, a test of basic skills might emphasize the assessment of decoding skills in a form designed for kindergarten through second-grade children and emphasize the assessment of comprehension for pupils in grades 6 through 8. Once again, users of academic achievement tests are cautioned to examine test items carefully to determine the match between the skills assessed and the skills taught in the school curriculum.

Academic achievement tests also vary in the way they assess similar skills. Some require verbal responses, others require the pupil to point to the correct answer, while still others require the pupil to fill in a computer-scored answer sheet. The test user should therefore also consider the response demands of a test and choose one to which the learner is capable of responding. For example, filling in the answer sheet might not be an appropriate response demand for a pupil with difficulties in fine motor coordination; a test that allows the child to point would be a better choice.

For pupils with suspected learning problems, academic achievement tests may be given at three stages in the assessment process. They are often used as screening instruments during the screening and identification stage. The tests used here are group-administered devices routinely administered to all pupils in the school (e.g., the Iowa Test of Basic Skills, the Stanford Achievement tests). Academic achievement tests are also given at the eligibility and diagnosis and the evaluation stages. In these instances, individually administered tests are used. The *Peabody Individual Achievement Test* or PIAT (Dunn and Markwardt, 1970), the *Wide Range Achievement Tests* or WRAT (Jastak and Jastak, 1978) and the *Woodcock-Johnson*

Psychoeducational Battery, Part II (Woodcock, 1978) are frequently used and will be described below.

Three Commonly Used Tests

The PIAT is a norm-referenced, individually administered test that assesses five areas of academic achievement: mathematics, reading recognition, reading comprehension, spelling, and general information. The test is appropriate for use with pupils in kindergarten through grade 12. Responses are made by reading aloud, pointing to or naming the correct item, or stating an answer. The mathematics, reading comprehension, and spelling subtests are multiple choice in format. The PIAT yields scores for the total test and for the five subtests. These scores may be expressed as age equivalents, grade equivalents, percentile ranks, or standard scores. The standardization of the PIAT is highly satisfactory, but the reliabilities of individual subtests vary considerably across age groups, so the user should consult the manual when interpreting subtest scores for an individual. The publishers provide evidence for content and concurrent validity, but the user will need to determine the test's validity for the individual pupil.

The WRAT is also a norm-referenced, individually administered academic achievement test. It has two levels, one for pupils under 12 years, another for those aged 12 and over. The WRAT assesses reading, arithmetic, and spelling skills. The reading subtest requires the pupil to read isolated words aloud, while the arithmetic and spelling subtests require him or her to write a response on the test blank. Grade ratings, percentile ranks, and standard scores may be derived for the individual subtests; a total test score is not available. The standardization and reliability of the test are weak. In addition, the validity of the WRAT is suspect because the subtests measure limited samples of skills. The reading subtest measures only skill in reading words, and the arithmetic subtest consists almost entirely of occupational problems. Given the inadequacies, why is this test so widely used? The speed and ease of administration probably account in large part for the test's popularity.

Part I of the Woodcock-Johnson, which can be used in measuring cognitive abilities, was described earlier in this chapter. The same instrument includes 10 subtests in Part II, Test of Achievement. The items sample the following: Letter-Word Identification, Word Attack, Passage Comprehension, Calculation, Applied Problems, Dictation, Proofing, Science, Social Studies, and Humanities.

All three parts (cognitive ability, achievement, and interests) of the battery were standardized on the same sample group. This offers the assessment team an instrument that is versatile across three broad areas, and it also allows performance scores to be compared within and across sections of the battery.

Reading

Regardless of the limitations or advantages of a specific test, no academic achievement measure is sufficient to provide detailed information on which to base an IEP

Figure 7–1

Reading Subskills

. . . .

Word recognition: the ability to read words
1. Word attack
    a. phonics: analyzing a word by sounds associated with each letter
    b. structure analysis: analyzing a word by root, suffix, and/or prefix

2. Sight vocabulary: automatic word recognition
3. Fluency: reading sentences and paragraphs efficiently and smoothly

Comprehension: the ability to derive meaning from print
1. Vocabulary: knowledge of word meanings
2. Literal: understanding of facts and details directly stated in text
3. Inferential: drawing inferences not directly stated
4. Evaluative: integrating information and inferences with personal experience
5. Listening: understanding text that is read aloud
6. Applications: using reading skills in real-life situations

. . . .

and to guide daily instruction. For these purposes, the teacher must acquire specific information about the pupil's skills in the various academic domains.

For the mildly handicapped learner, reading skills will frequently be an area of concern. Assessment instruments and procedures should take into account the range of reading subskills. Since any single procedure will not address all these skills, a diverse set of tests and procedures must be used.

Issues in Reading Assessment.   Reading is a complex behavior composed of many subskills, but the definition of these subskills varies depending upon one's theoretical orientation. Some specialists argue that reading is primarily decoding syllables and words (Shankweiler and Liberman, 1972), while others argue that decoding plays a minor role in the reading process (Goodman, 1970). Obviously, test authors with varying theoretical positions will develop instruments that test different skills. Although an approach that allows the learner to discover correspondences and regularities among letters and sounds might be appropriate for normal learners, mildly handicapped pupils are not particularly adept at making these connections without the benefit of instruction. In fact, some more recent theories of reading disabilities support the notion that these children have a specific linguistic deficit in areas of such correspondence (Vellutino, 1977).

Formal Procedures for Assessing Reading

The assessment approach presented in this chapter favors a direct, structured approach to reading instruction with mildly handicapped learners. This position has determined the subskills discussed and the instruments and techniques presented.

Reading Skills. Reading may be conceptualized as two broad skill areas — word recognition and comprehension — each containing several interrelated subskills. Figure 7–1 presents these subskills, with a brief definition of each.

Norm-Referenced Reading Tests. Several different norm-referenced tests are available. (A thorough discussion of norm- and criterion-referenced testing is provided in Chapter 3.) *Oral reading tests* generally assess both word recognition and comprehension skills, requiring the pupil to read a series of paragraphs and answer comprehension questions. The examiner then records and classifies the oral reading errors according to directions provided in the manual. *Reading survey tests* assess a broader range of both silent and oral reading skills; the specific skills measured vary from test to test, as is apparent in the Woodcock Reading Mastery Tests.

The *Woodcock Reading Mastery Tests* (R. W. Woodcock, 1973) are often used in the assessment of mildly handicapped learners in kindergarten through 12th grade. The five individually administered subtests are Letter Identification, which asks the pupil to read and name both cursive and manuscript letters; Word Identification, which gives the pupil a list of words to read; Word Attack, which asks the pupil to read nonsense words to test phonic and structural analysis skills; Word Comprehension, in which the pupil is shown word combinations, such as "boy-girl, mother- ——," and asked to state the missing word, and which assesses vocabulary skills through an analogies task; and Passage Comprehension, in which the pupil is shown an incomplete sentence and must supply the missing word.

Raw scores obtained on each of the five subtests may be converted to percentile ranks, grade scores, age scores, and/or standard scores. The Woodcock also provides a total test score as well as mastery scores that define a range of reading proficiency on each subtest.

The Woodcock has been adequately standardized, and its reliability appears to be sufficient. Ample evidence for validity is presented in the manual, but the user must also consider the validity of the test for an individual pupil and his or her reading program. The word comprehension subtest, for example, which tests vocabulary through an analogies format, may be invalid for the pupil who is unfamiliar with such a task.

Criterion-Referenced Reading Tests. Like their norm-referenced counterparts, criterion-referenced tests assess a variety of reading skills. Appendix II presents a list of both norm-referenced and criterion-referenced tests and the skills they assess.

An *informal reading inventory* or IRI may be developed commercially or by a teacher. It consists of a series of reading passages accompanied by comprehension questions. Both word recognition and comprehension are scored, and independent, instructional, and frustration reading levels are estimated. The IRI is an extremely flexible assessment tool; for example, it may be developed to assess a pupil's reading in content-area materials like regular class textbooks. Or, in cases where standard assessment materials do not interest a pupil and it becomes difficult to determine whether reading difficulties stem from skill deficiencies or lack

of motivation, the teacher can develop an IRI to assess the pupil in specially selected motivational material.

Informal Procedures for Assessing Reading

A wide variety of informal strategies or procedures is available for the classroom
teacher to use to gather data regarding pupils' performance. Unfortunately, not
many data exist to support these informal approaches. Three of the more widely
used are discussed below. They offer a fair representation of informal data-collection procedures about whose effectiveness and efficiency there is a degree of consensus among teachers.

Interviews.   The interview is a useful technique for exploring another's point of
view. An interview may be used during the assessment of reading skills to discover
how the pupil feels about reading and perceives his or her reading skills. Interview
questions might include, "What makes reading fun for you?" "What makes reading
hard for you?" "Tell me about all the things you did today that used reading." "What
kinds of stories do you like to read?" "What makes you a good reader?"

The teacher can also use the interview to gain an understanding of the pupil's
reading strategies and study habits. It is best to present some material to be read
and to stop the pupil at various points to question him or her about how he or she
reads. For example, when the pupil comes to a word he or she doesn't know, the
teacher might ask, "How could you figure out that word? What would you use to
help you?"

The classroom teacher may also be interviewed. This interview is an important
source of information about the reading instruction in the regular class. In interviews with both pupils and teachers, a good rapport will encourage honest
responses.

Diagnostic Teaching.   Diagnostic teaching is a dynamic assessment strategy that
provides useful instructional information about how best to teach the pupil. Hypotheses are formed about the child on the basis of assessment data. These hypotheses are systematically explored by modifying the instructional process and
evaluating the resultant effects on performance. New hypotheses may then be for-
mulated and the cycle repeated.

A teacher may hypothesize various reasons for a child's reading difficulties. For
example, assessment data may lead the teacher to believe the pupil is unmotivated.
A diagnostic teaching strategy for this pupil would require the introduction of reinforcement, and the teacher would then monitor the pupil's performance and
evaluate improvement as a result of the reinforcement condition. In initiating a
diagnostic teaching strategy, one must change only one variable at a time; otherwise
it is impossible to determine the impact of individual interventions.

Diagnostic teaching strategies depend on the characteristics of an individual
pupil and his or her instructional needs. The regular and special educator should
work together in implementing diagnostic teaching strategies in both the regular
class and special education programs. Records should be kept on all diagnostic

teaching activities, as these are relevant assessment data for future instructional planning and program evaluation.

Formative Assessment. "Formative assessment" refers to devices that can be used on a daily basis to evaluate a child's progress toward specified goals and objectives. It is therefore a critical component of instructional planning. If data indicate that performance is improving, the teacher can feel confident that the present instructional program is appropriate. However, if the pupil's performance level remains the same or decreases, the teacher must make some modifications in the program.

Researchers at the University of Minnesota (Mirkin et al., 1980) have developed and field-tested formative measures in different academic skill areas. One formative measure of reading skills may be obtained by requesting the pupil to read aloud from a reader or a word list for one minute (isolated word lists appear to be the preferable measure for pupils in grades 1 through 6). The teacher then records the number of words the child reads correctly. Daily increases in this number are a valid indication that a pupil's proficiency in word recognition and comprehension is improving (Deno et al., 1979). The authors are careful to stress, however, that their research does not imply that practice in reading words from lists is a desirable or appropriate instructional practice; rather, it is suggested as a valid formative measure of reading that the teacher may utilize in instructional planning.

Oral Language Assessment

Oral language skills are critical for effective communication both in and out of the classroom. Instruction in all academic subjects, including reading, written language, and mathematics, proceeds on the assumption that children possess skills in both expressive (speaking) and receptive (comprehending) oral language. Oral language deficiencies are often subtle, yet they may have a significant influence on the child's performance. Research indicates that language difficulties are associated with academic and social failure, social rejection, and emotional disturbance (Wiig and Semel, 1976).

A specialist trained in speech and language will probably assume primary responsibility for the assessment and remediation of oral language difficulties. However, the special educator may assist in the assessment of oral skills. First, the special educator should be alert for signs indicating potential problems in receptive and expressive oral language. They include incorrect grammar, difficulties in explaining concepts or ideas, the frequent use of indefinite phrases such as "these things" or "that stuff," unwillingness to talk, misarticulation of sounds or words, difficulty following directions, and limited oral vocabulary. In this role, the special educator is serving as a screening agent for oral language difficulties. Suspected problems should be referred to a speech and language professional. Chapter 4 described this screening process in detail.

Second, the special educator may assist in evaluating the consequences of the pupil's language difficulties for his or her academic and social growth. Both the special and the regular educator will need to be aware of the limitations that oral language difficulties might impose on a pupil's performance and to make adjustments in the curriculum or their expectations. For example, a pupil with limited vocabulary development may require a preview of vocabulary terms before reading a new social studies chapter. One with articulation difficulties may need special attention and reassurance in order to feel comfortable about speaking in class. The speech and language specialist, the special educator, and the regular educator will need to work closely to coordinate an effective instructional plan. The role of the special educator and the language clinician was discussed earlier, in Chapter 4.

Assessment of Written Language

Successful performance in written language depends on the prior acquisition of skills in oral language and reading and on the integration of skills in handwriting, spelling, punctuation, and capitalization. Mildly handicapped learners may have difficulties with any or all of these. Research has demonstrated that pupils with learning problems often use fewer and less complex words than others in written composition (Poteet, 1980) and are poorer at expressing abstract reasoning (Myklebust, 1973). Despite instruction, these pupils often seem to ignore the conventions of grammar, punctuation, and capitalization and to violate the rules of sentence structure, producing significantly more sentence fragments and/or run-on sentences (Myklebust, 1973). Spelling difficulties are often found in combination with reading difficulties and may linger after the primary reading difficulty has been remediated (Poteet, 1980). Poor fine motor coordination can likewise create problems with handwriting for mildly handicapped learners. It is little wonder, then, that written language difficulties are often an area of major concern for them.

The assessment of written language often emphasizes the more mechanical skills of handwriting and spelling and ignores the quality of a pupil's written expression, but some recently developed assessment devices do attempt to measure its quality. Teachers may also employ various informal techniques for assessing both the mechanics and quality of writing. When designing assessments, bear in mind that language arts teachers are experts in written language and should be called upon by the special educator to assist in the design and analysis of written language assessment.

Written language skills may be divided into four broad areas (Vallercorsa, Silverman, and Zigmond, 1983). The first area, generation of ideas, encompasses the quality of a pupil's written expression; while the remaining areas, handwriting and conventions on print and spelling, account for the more mechanical aspects of written language. Figure 7–2 presents the subskills to be addressed in each of these general assessment areas.

Assessment Devices.   Norm-referenced and criterion-referenced tests measure various aspects of written language skills. Survey tests provide a general measure of a broad range of skills, whereas special-skill tests assess one type of skill, such as handwriting or spelling. Table 2 in Appendix II presents 10 popular survey and specific-skill tests that assess written language skills.

One of the more widely used and thorough instruments is the *Test of Written*

Figure 7–2

Written Language Skills

· ·

   I. Generation of ideas
      A. Vocabulary
      B. Productive: number of words written
      C. Substance
         1. naming
         2. description
         3. plot
      D. Grammar

  II. Handwriting
      A. Letter formation
      B. Slant
      C. Spacing
      D. Alignment

 III. Convention of print
      A. Punctuation
      B. Capitalization
      C. Sentence structure

 IV. Spelling
      A. Phonetically regular spellings
      B. Phonetically irregular spellings
      C. Morphological rules

· ·

Language, or TOWL (Hammill and Larsen, 1978). The TOWL is appropriate for pupils in grades 3 through 8 and may be administered individually or to a group. Its seven subtests analyze the pupil's performance under both spontaneous and structured conditions. In the spontaneous condition, the pupil is directed to make up a story about three pictures provided with the test. Four subtests analyze the pupil's spontaneous story, and three others assess related written language skills. In the **Vocabulary** subtest, 25 words are selected at random from the pupil's story, and each is given a value that reflects sophistication and complexity of vocabulary. The **Thematic Maturity** subtest is an analysis of the pupil's story in relation to 20 standards of thematic maturity, such as writing in paragraphs or providing a conclusion. In the subtest called **Thought Units**, the number of meaningful sentences is determined. Each sentence must contain a subject and an identifiable verb. If the pupil's spontaneous story is written, the writing is evaluated using the 11-point **Handwriting** scale. Twenty-five words are dictated to the pupil, who receives a point for each word correct in the Spelling subtest. Skills for both phonetically regular and irregular word spellings are evaluated. The Word Usage subtest assesses the pupil's knowledge of grammatical rules, including tenses and plurals. The Style subtest assesses punctuation and capitalization skills. The TOWL yields scaled scores for each subtest that may then be compared to provide information about a pupil's strengths and weaknesses in special areas. Scaled scores may also be converted to grade equivalents.

The test's reliability appears to be adequate, although various reliability estimates were performed with small numbers of pupils. Furthermore, because some subtests seem to contain a restricted sample of items, the individual teacher will need to examine the content of test items to determine their validity for different pupils and curricula.

If difficulties are encountered on a particular subtest, the teacher should attempt to isolate the problematic subskills. For example, if a pupil earns a low score on the spelling subtest of the TOWL, it must then be ascertained whether the pupil has problems with any or all of the following subskills: phonetically regular spellings, phonetically irregular spellings, or morphological rules. Criterion-referenced tests prepared by the teacher can help obtain this more detailed instructional information by focusing on the groups of subskills he or she feels must be investigated. The teacher may develop a test that presents the pupil with a task-analyzed sequence of phonetically regular words such as: consonant-vowel-consonant (e.g., cat, set); consonant-consonant-vowel-consonant (e.g., ship, plum); consonant-vowel-consonant-silent *e* (e.g., mate, kite). By determining where in the task sequence the pupil experiences difficulties, the teacher can tell where to begin instruction. Such criterion-referenced tests may be based either on skill sequences derived through task analysis or on sequences suggested by the scope and sequence charts of regular class materials.

Written Language Sample.   The written language sample is a convenient technique for assessing all areas of written language. It is similar to the spontaneous story obtained in the TOWL except that it is tailored to an individual's skills and interests. The following guidelines should assist the teacher in gathering useful information from a written language sample.

1. The written language sample will more accurately reflect the pupil's capabilities if he or she is encouraged to write about a topic of personal interest.
2. The teacher must provide the pupil with some structure to help him or her begin writing. This will vary with a child's age and skills. The younger or less proficient writer will need more structure; for instance, two or three pictures that depict topics of interest to that child. With older or more proficient writers, the teacher may discuss several topics and allow the pupil to choose one. In all instances, the teacher should make sure that the pupil has enough information about a given topic to write at least one paragraph.
3. The teacher should encourage the pupil not to avoid words because he or she is uncertain of their spellings, but rather to make educated guesses about them. The child should be allowed as much time as he or she wishes to complete the task.
4. Upon completion of the writing, the teacher should ask the pupil to read what he or she has written and should record this verbatim. For purposes of analysis, it is critical to know what the pupil intended to write as well as what was actually written.

5. All written language samples should be dated and saved along with their verbatim transcriptions.

The written language sample is analyzed by examining the pupil's performance in relation to each of the subskills listed in Figure 7–2.

It is important to realize that the written language sample requires the pupil to utilize and integrate many skills simultaneously. Writing a composition is a complex task, and the child may demonstrate difficulties here that would not be evident in easier tasks.

Consider the case of two pupils who neglect to use capital letters in their written language samples. The teacher creates one test that requires them to identify the missing capital letters in their written language samples and another that requires them to identify the missing capital letters in 10 sentences the teacher supplies. One pupil completes the test with 100 percent accuracy, and the other obtains 0 percent. The teacher has discovered critical information about these two learners. The first pupil needs instruction in applying capitalization rules to written composition, but the second needs to learn capitalization rules.

The teacher should always follow the analysis of a written language sample with tests of his or her own design to ascertain the pupil's mastery of various subskills. Although written language competence should be defined for all learners as the utilization and integration of skills in written composition, an individual's mastery of specific subskills must dictate the individualized instruction necessary to reach this goal.

Formative Assessment.   In the area of spelling, Deno et al. (1980) have developed and field-tested a formative assessment measure that consists of a one-minute dictation of words. The selection of words is not critical; they may be taken from various grade levels or from a basal reader. The teacher scores the number of words spelled correctly in the dictation. A steady increase in this number indicates that the pupil is making progress in spelling.

Another formative measure has been developed and field-tested by Deno, Marston, and Mirkin (1982) for the assessment of written language skills. Their research indicates that the teacher may obtain a useful evaluation of a pupil's progress by directing him or her to write in response to a topic sentence for two to three minutes and then counting and recording the number of words written. A consistent increase in this number indicates growth in written language skills. The reader should keep in mind that these formative measures are offered as assessment devices only; they are not recommended as instructional techniques.

Mathematics Assessment

Traditionally, educators have been more concerned with the acquisition of reading skills than with that of mathematics proficiency. As technology advances, however, mathematical skills are increasingly important to the attainment of computer literacy (Smith, 1983), and perhaps more attention will be directed toward the assessment of mathematics proficiency in the future.

Figure 7–3

Mathematics Skills

. . . .

   I. Concepts
      A. Math readiness skills
      B. Whole-number concepts
      C. Time
      D. Money
      E. Measurement
      F. Geometry
      G. Algebra

  II. Computation
      A. Addition
      B. Subtraction
      C. Multiplication
      D. Division
      E. Computations with decimals
      F. Computations with fractions

 III. Problem solving
      A. Word problems
      B. Applications

. . . .

For assessment purposes, mathematics may be divided into three broad areas: concepts, computation, and problem solving (Silverman and Zigmond, 1983). Figure 7–3 explains the various subskills that may be assessed under each of these areas.

Norm-Referenced and Criterion-Referenced Tests. As mathematics tests vary considerably in the range of skills they assess, the teacher should first examine a test carefully for its potential to provide useful information for a particular pupil or group of pupils. Table 3 in Appendix II presents a list of norm-referenced and criterion-referenced mathematics tests and the skill areas that each assesses. The teacher may also develop criterion-referenced tests to probe a pupil's math skills in greater detail. The choice of items for such a test may be dictated by the pupil's performance on a standardized test or in interview and diagnostic teaching sessions. An example of a norm-referenced test of math skill development is the *KeyMath Diagnostic Arithmetic Tests (KeyMath)* (Connolly, Nachtman, and Pritchett, 1973).

The KeyMath is an individually administered test that samples a broad range of math skills. It may be used with pupils in kindergarten through eighth grade and is composed of 14 subtests grouped into three broad skill areas. These are:

Content: Three subtests address the pupil's understanding of numeration, fractions, and geometry and symbols. In each subtest, the pupil is shown a picture, diagram, or symbol and required to answer aloud.

Operations: Six subtests assess the learner's knowledge and application of computation skills in addition, subtraction, multiplication, division, mental computation, and numerical reasoning. Both written and oral responses are required.

Applications: Five subtests assess mathematical concepts and problem-solving ability in word problems, missing elements, money, measurement, and time. Each question presents the learner with a picture and a question to be answered in words, not figures.

Although the KeyMath was standardized on a large number of subjects, information about the composition of this sample is somewhat incomplete. Judgments about test reliability are also difficult to make because the authors report only internal-consistency reliability coefficients. The KeyMath supplies a detailed behavioral objective for each test item, which should assist the teacher in judging content validity. The order of item difficulty on the KeyMath, however, may not reflect typical curriculum practices. For example, knowledge of the percent sign is seen as an easier item than knowledge of the division sign, yet most mathematics curricula teach division before percentage. Once again, the teacher will need to examine test items in relation to an individual learner and to the school's mathematics curriculum.

Work-Sample Analysis. The analysis and interpretation of a pupil's written performance provides clues to his or her understanding of various mathematical processes. This type of analysis can also be used to determine whether a consistent pattern of errors is occurring in other academic performance areas. The regular class teacher can readily score a pupil's correct and incorrect math performances. Errors may then be categorized according to the following schema (adapted from Silverman and Zigmond, 1983):

1. Wrong operation: The pupil used an operation other than the one called for by the problems.
2. Computation errors: The pupil has made errors in basic math facts.
3. Faulty algorithm: The pupil used an incorrect or incomplete process for computing an answer.
4. Carelessness: The pupil makes an error on an operation that was previously completed correctly.
5. Not understanding the concept: The pupil's response indicates that he or she lacks the underlying concepts necessary to complete the problem.

Work-sample analyses provide suggestions for further assessment through specific criterion-referenced measures, interviews, or diagnostic teaching. The systematic collection of work samples also documents a pupil's performance and progress in the regular class. For a more detailed discussion of analyzing mathematical computation errors made by pupils and their remediation, the reader is referred to Ashlock (1982 and 1983).

Interviews.   Interviews are especially useful for gaining insight into the processes a pupil uses to solve math problems. An interview may be used to verify the results of a work-sample analysis by presenting the pupil with both correct and incorrect performances and asking him or her to explain how these problems were done. The teacher should probe as necessary for a complete description of the pupil's reasoning at each step of the problem. During the interview, the teacher must refrain from correcting erroneous reasoning. (Herbert Ginsburg's book *Children's Arithmetic* [1977] provides fascinating descriptions of math interviews with children of all ages.)

Interviewing is also a relevant technique for assessing the pupil's attitude and motivation toward mathematics. A variety of interview topics might be explored with an individual pupil, such as: "How do you feel about math? Do you like or dislike it? Why?" "How do you do in math? Do you think you should do better? How?"

Diagnostic teaching offers the opportunity to try out various teaching techniques and strategies with the individual learner. The following list suggests some diagnostic teaching strategies appropriate for mathematics assessment.

1. Can the pupil complete problems when provided with a written model to follow?
2. Can the pupil perform more accurately if required to estimate an answer prior to solving the problem?
3. Can the pupil complete problems when given manipulative materials or aids such as blocks or a calculator?
4. Can the pupil complete problems if they are first read to him or her?
5. Can the pupil complete problems if changes are made in his or her motivation and/or reinforcement?

Appropriate diagnostic teaching strategies for the individual learner will depend upon the results of previous formal and informal assessment. Therefore, records should be kept of all diagnostic teaching attempts and their outcomes.

Summary

Assessment of the mildly handicapped learner is a complex, multifaceted process. A well-designed assessment should reflect awareness of the critical issues involved in the assessment of this population. These include the recognition that:

1. No specific criteria exist for the diagnosis of a mild learning handicap. There are no guidelines for determining when a pupil's learning problem warrants individualized assessment and possible placement in special education. This decision must be made on an individual, case-by-case basis.
2. Since the definitions of mild handicaps are so vague, this population is especially vulnerable to bias before, during, and after assessment. The multidisci-

plinary team must be aware of potential sources of bias and should monitor the assessment process so that objective information is collected and nondiscriminatory decisions are made.

3. The characteristics of mildly handicapped learners vary considerably at different age levels. For example, the preschooler has significantly different traits and instructional needs from the elementary or high school pupil. An age-appropriate assessment that carefully considers these distinctive differences must be designed.

4. In most cases, the mildly handicapped learner spends a significant part of the school day in regular classes. During assessment, information about the pupil's performance in the regular class must be collected. Instructional goals and objectives must be targeted at improving performance in the regular class.

5. The special educator and regular educator must work as a team to conduct an appropriate, effective assessment and remediation plan for the mildly handicapped learner.

6. Assessment must address two domains of behavior, learning aptitude and academic assessment. A comprehensive assessment of the mildly handicapped learner will always include the measurement of skills *and* performance.

7. A variety of standardized and criterion-referenced instruments is available for the assessment of mildly handicapped learners. However, it is necessary to examine the technical adequacy of any test administered.

8. The use of informal testing procedures will provide information useful in making placement and instructional decisions that will benefit the mildly handicapped learner.

Mastery Review

I. Recall

1. Miss Hoola feels that assessment at the end of the semester is adequate for her teaching purposes. Which practice of assessment is Miss Hoola omitting in her teaching performance?

   a. Standardized assessment of learner aptitude.
   b. Informal assessment of learner aptitude.
   c. Formative assessment of learner aptitude.
   d. Traditional assessment of learner aptitude.

2. When attempting to identify the effect of instruction on a student's learning strategies, the assessment procedure would follow what sequence?

   a. Diagnostic teaching, interviewing, performance evaluation.
   b. Interviewing, diagnostic teaching, performance evaluation.
   c. Performance evaluation, interviewing, diagnostic teaching.
   d. Performance evaluation, diagnostic teaching, interviewing.

3. Planning an assessment for the mildly handicapped secondary student that is relevant to the _____ is more beneficial than conducting an assessment for the purpose of _____ .

   a. determining age appropriate instruction —— vocational success.
   b. curriculum —— assigning a label.
   c. assigning of a label —— curriculum.
   d. vocational success —— determining age appropriate instruction.

4. Assessment of mild handicaps at the preschool level is confounded in most instances by:

   a. uncooperative parents.
   b. unavailability of test instruments for preschool-aged children.
   c. individual variation in developmental rates of learning and behavior skills.
   d. absence of federal mandates to support preschool education of the handicapped.

5. Children with mild mental retardation, mild learning disabilities, and mild behavior disorders are often grouped together for services because:

   a. precise diagnosis of mild handicaps in these three categories is difficult.
   b. learners in these three categories tend to display similar characteristics in learning and behavior.
   c. identical instructional arrangements have proven effective with all these categories.
   d. all of the above.

6. Assessment of mathematics should be comprised of instruments that can measure:

   a. concepts, problem solving, computation.
   b. problem solving, memory, speed.
   c. computation, memory, problem solving.
   d. speed, concepts, computation.

7. Assessment to enhance a direct, structured approach for reading instruction with mildly handicapped learners would include instruments that:

   a. sample a range of subskills.
   b. sample broad skill averages such as word recognition and comprehension.
   c. are congruent with research findings on strengths and deficits in reading abilities of those with mild handicaps.
   d. all of the above.

8. In the case of mildly handicapped students with multiple handicaps, establishing the role of etiology is most successful with children who present:

   a. profiles of learning disability.
   b. profiles of mild mental retardation.
   c. profiles of mild behavior disorders.
   d. profiles of sensory or physical impairments.

9. A critical dimension to counter bias in the assessment process with mildly handicapped learners is to:

   a. analyze the referral form in depth.
   b. review the intervention strategies attempted with the student prior to referral.
   c. identify the socioeconomic status and income level of parents or guardian.
   d. review any past record of behavior incidents that may or may not be on file.

10. High rates of inaccurate referral may be attributed to which of the following?

   a. Belief that individualized instruction can be provided only in the special classroom.

b. Confusion among teachers as to which behaviors are indicative of mild handicaps.
c. A and b.
d. None of the above.

11. Students with mild handicaps experiencing difficulty in locating the relevant dimensions of a stimulus would demonstrate lowered performance in:
a. generalization skills.
b. discrimination skills.
c. learning-set skills.
d. memory skills.

12. A written language sample offers valuable assessment data because:
a. it can be written about a topic of personal interest, thus providing a positive motivational condition.
b. it is highly structured, thus providing the student with guidelines for performance.
c. it is timed and therefore allows the student an opportunity to pace the task accordingly.
d. it is designed so that the student writes on a designated topic, and it measures the ability of the student to use relevant and accurately spelled vocabulary.

13. Assessment of written language often emphasizes _____ and ignores the _____ of a student's written expression.
a. grammar —— spelling difficulties.
b. mechanical skills —— quality.
c. spelling difficulties —— grammar.
d. quality —— mechanical skills.

14. The Woodcock Reading Mastery Test would be best described as:
a. a norm-referenced test that primarily assesses oral reading skills.
b. a criterion-referenced test that assesses silent and oral reading skills.
c. a norm-referenced test that assesses both silent and oral reading skills.
d. a criterion-referenced test that primarily assesses silent reading skills.

15. The purpose of conducting assessment of skills such as memory or attention is:
a. to identify learner aptitudes that, with instruction, contribute to raised performance levels.
b. to determine the degree to which memory or attention skills diminish achievement test results.
c. to extend the range of standardized tests administered for a more complete learner profile.
d. to establish the discrepancy between memory and attention for adaptive behavior scores.

II. Comprehension

1. Considering the discussion in this chapter on the overreferral of students with mild handicaps, describe the role of the special education teacher in Level One of the assessment model, Screening and Referral, with mildly handicapped students.
2. Discuss the importance of assessing learning aptitude in mildly handicapped learners, keeping in mind the information on learning style presented in Chapter 2.

3. This chapter examines the use of interviews, work-sample analyses, and diagnostic teaching for assessing student performance. Describe how these may be used to assess performance in reading, mathematics, and written language, giving an example for each subject area.

4. A diverse set of tests and procedures should be used in assessing reading skills with mildly handicapped learners. Describe each of the following as mentioned in this chapter: oral reading tests, reading survey tests, and informal reading inventories.

5. An error analysis of a work sample in mathematics might uncover what five types of errors? Give an example of each type.

6. Explain why students suspected of mild handicaps that fall within the diagnostic categories of E.M.H., L.D., and B.D. are particularly prone to biased assessment.

III. Application

1. Visit a local university library or educational testing center and examine and review a copy of the AAMD Adaptive Behavior Scale, Public School Version, or the Adaptive Behavior Inventory for Children. Use the test review form in Appendix I for your review.

2. During a visit to an educational setting, after conferring with the teacher or person in charge, obtain a written language sample from a student and evaluate it as described in this chapter. It might be helpful to examine the seven subtests contained in the Test of Written Language for ideas on possible formats. Write your evaluation and observation in a three- to five-page paper, giving emphasis to the implications for instruction.

IV. Alternate Task

If none of the Application exercises applies to your setting or curriculum, you can design two exercises of your own. They should demonstrate application of one or more of the principles or concepts described in the preceding chapter. Prior approval of both exercises should be obtained from your course instructor.

V. Answer Key

I.
1. c p. 205
2. b pp. 199–200
3. b pp. 188–89
4. c pp. 187–88
5. d pp. 185–86
6. a p. 209
7. d pp. 201–03
8. d pp. 190–91
9. b p. 190
10. c pp. 189–90
11. b p. 198
12. a pp. 206–9
13. b p. 206
14. c p. 203
15. a pp. 198–99

II.
1. p. 188, p. 8
2. p. 192
3. pp. 200–12
4. p. 205, p. 203, p. 204
5. p. 211
6. pp. 189–91

Chapter 8

Assessment of the Trainable Mentally Handicapped Learner

Chapter Objectives:

After reading this chapter and completing the Mastery Review, you will be able to:

1. Describe the learning characteristics of school-aged pupils educationally classified as trainable mentally handicapped (T.M.H.).
2. Describe issues and problems related to conducting classroom educational assessments with T.M.H. pupils.
3. Describe the major components of the clinical-prescriptive model for educational program design and delivery.
4. List and describe at least five commercially available instruments and systems found to be effective for educational assessment and program planning with the T.M.H.
5. List and describe at least 10 procedures for direct observation of pupil behavior in classroom settings.
6. Describe the process for translating educational assessment data into individualized education plans.

Key Terms:

adaptive behavior
continuum of special education
    services
data-recording system
developmental period
general intellectual functioning
mainstream
movement cycle
multiply handicapped
normalize
significantly subaverage
System of Multicultural Pluralistic
    Assessment (SOMPA)
T.M.H.

This chapter examines issues and techniques specific to the classroom assessment of trainable mentally handicapped learners. The educational classification term "trainable mentally handicapped" (T.M.H.) is used throughout this chapter in place of the more generic term "moderately handicapped learner" in order to preclude problems of overinclusiveness in this classification area. "Moderately handicapping" may apply to a wide range of conditions or performance deficits, including orthopedic, behavioral, communication, and learning deficits occurring singly or in combination.

The term "moderately handicapped" offers the educator little performance information. The term "T.M.H." has evolved over several years to identify a person who has moderate cognitive or learning problems. Such persons may have other developmental and behavioral disabilities as well, but their primary special needs are in learning and adaptive behavior, with self-help skill development typically a primary area. Secondary to but closely linked with the learning and self-help deficits are typically communication and motor skill problems. In addition, the T.M.H. pupil often exhibits health and vitality disabilities and impairments that compound learning problems. Assessment techniques useful to the classroom teacher of T.M.H. pupils will be discussed in this chapter.

Defining the Population and Setting

The term "T.M.H." refers to the pupil who specifically fits into the educational classification outlined by the American Association on Mental Deficiency (AAMD) in its definition of mental retardation (Grossman, 1983). The AAMD definition of mental retardation is

> significantly subaverage general intellectual functioning resulting in or associated with concurrent impairments in adaptive behavior and manifested during the developmental period.

For the teacher of T.M.H. pupils, this definition has significant implications. Its importance is highlighted when one examines the AAMD's definition of the key terms of the new definition:

> *General intellectual functioning* is operationally defined as the results obtained by assessment with one or more of the individually administered standardized general intelligence tests developed for that purpose.

This definition is important for the classroom teacher because it sets clear standards for use of the classification. The requirement of a standardized test of general intelligence adds an empirically verifiable component. Moreover, because most teachers are not trained or certified to administer standardized intelligence tests, their sole responsibility in determining a pupil's eligibility for classification as mentally retarded is removed. The AAMD's statement continues, "*Significantly*

Table 8–1

Levels of Retardation Determined by I.Q. Range

. . . .

Level of Retardation	I.Q. Range
Mild mental retardation	50–55 to approximately 70
Moderate mental retardation	35–40 to 50–55
Severe mental retardation	20–25 to 35–40
Profound mental retardation	Below 20–25

From H. Grossman, *Manual on Terminology and Classification in Mental Retardation.* Copyright 1983 by the American Association on Mental Deficiency. Reprinted by permission.

. . . .

subaverage is defined as an I.Q. of 70 or below on standardized measures of intelligence." The significance of this aspect of the definition for the classroom teacher is that it identifies parameters for each of the accepted levels within the mental retardation classification. With an upper I.Q. limit of 70 for the classification of T.M.H., a pupil would have to score at least two standard deviations (SDs) below the mean score on most if not all of the currently accepted standardized tests of general intelligence in order to qualify for the label. For example, the revised Stanford-Binet Intelligence Scale (Terman and Merrill, 1973) uses a mean of 100 and an SD of 16, and the Wechsler Intelligence Scale for Children (WISC) (Wechsler, 1974) also uses a mean of 100 but has an SD of 15. The use of a range of scores to begin and end the classifications would help to account for the typically varied performance characteristics of pupils taking I.Q. tests, and it would help to account for the scoring differences among the various intelligence tests. Table 8–1 outlines the five levels of retardation as determined by I.Q. scores.

The T.M.H. classification described earlier is generally subsumed under the AAMD's moderate mental retardation I.Q. parameters of 35–40 to 50–55. This range of intelligence measurement is generally accepted among educators as representing one critical variable that must be documented before the term "T.M.H." is used. A second, concomitant variable that is generally required for use of the term is measured adaptive behavior deficits, discussed in the following section.

> *Impairments in adaptive behavior* are defined as significant limitations in an individual's effectiveness in meeting the standards of maturation, learning, personal independence, and/or social responsibilities that are expected for his or her age level and cultural group as determined by standardized clinical assessment scales.

This provision of the 1983 AAMD definition of mental retardation has great significance for the T.M.H. classroom teacher. With the exception of persons in the pupil's home setting, no other person has as much opportunity to observe and assess a pupil's adaptive behaviors. Moreover, as licensure or certification is not required for administration of most adaptive behavior scales, classroom teachers can readily be trained to be competent in their use and interpretation. This provision permits the teacher to become a full partner in decisions regarding classification for mental retardation.

Developmental period is defined as the period between conception and the eighteenth birthday. Developmental deficits may be manifested by slow, arrested, or incomplete development resulting from brain damage, degenerative processes in the central nervous system, or regression from previous normal states due to psychological factors.

The significance for the classroom teacher of this aspect of the revised AAMD definition is that it provides a mechanism for documenting developing deficits that warrant special education services. In many instances, children will be identified during their school careers as behaving so abnormally that classification in a special education area may be the best means of making appropriate educational services available. The classroom teacher can and should play a vital role in the identification, documentation, and prescriptive process.

The T.M.H. Classification Defined

For the classroom teacher and especially for users of this text, the following definitional statement summarizes the preceding discussion.

A school-aged person may be classified as T.M.H. if the performance conditions outlined by the AAMD for moderately mentally retardation have been met. The person must have a measured I.Q. of between 35–40 and 50–55, with concomitant moderate deficits in assessed adaptive behavioral functioning.

This definition is extrapolated from a more general definition of mental retardation. It should be used in full recognition of the limitations and liabilities inherent in any definitional attempt to describe human performance. And it should be considered the necessary minimal conditions for use of the term "T.M.H." for a school-aged child but not as a complete, accurate description of that person's behavior.

Educational Settings Serving the T.M.H.

A wide variety of educational service delivery options is available for the T.M.H. pupil. Figure 8–1 illustrates a continuum of special education services. The T.M.H. pupil often enters this continuum at Level 6, full-time special class. The less restrictive settings, 5 through 1, are often inappropriate. The contemporary trend in special education is to provide the T.M.H. pupil with a full-time special class located

Figure 8–1

Continuum of Special Education Services

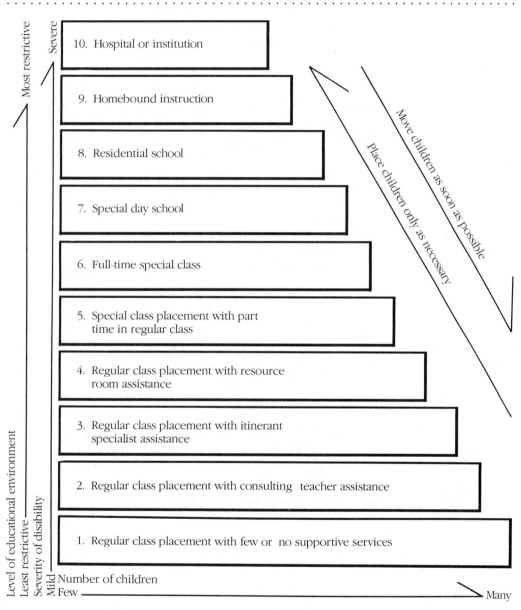

From William H. Berdine and A. Edward Blackhurst eds. *An Introduction to Special Education* 2nd ed., p. 57. Copyright ©1985 by William H. Berdine and A. Edward Blackhurst. Based on figures from M. Reynolds "A Framework for Considering Some Issues in Special Education", *Exceptional Children* 28 (1962) and E. Deno, "Special Education as Developmental Capital", *Exceptional Children* 39 (1973). Reprinted with permission.

in a regular school program. The T.M.H. class is mainstreamed into the school's ongoing ancillary and support offerings — the cafeteria, physical education department, and music department. In schools that have a comprehensive array of services, T.M.H. pupils may be further mainstreamed into classrooms for the educable and/or mildly handicapped in subjects in which they have the competence to gain additional skill. Level 7, special day school, is becoming less available as a service option because of the high cost of operating a separate school building for what is usually a low enrollment.

Prevalence of T.M.H. Pupils.   The estimated prevalence of persons with mental retardation is only 1 percent of the total population (MacMillan, 1982; Tarjan et al., 1973). It has been reported that the trainable mentally retarded make up about 20 percent of this group (Berdine, 1985).

Use of Segregated Settings.   The challenge of meeting the mandate of P.L. 94–142 has not only involved professional programmatic changes to effect more "normalized" services, but also created significant questions regarding the economic feasibility of services for persons with one of the low-incidence handicapping conditions. P.L. 94–142 has necessitated a number of service delivery changes for these conditions: in addition to lessened use of separate school facilities, there has been a general reduction in the use of residential schools, homebound instruction, and hospital or institutional settings. In many instances in which these options are used, the pupil's health or vitality dictates such restrictive measures or the parents have made a specific, private request. (An excellent discussion of the contemporary continuum of services in special education is found in *An Introduction to Special Education* [Berdine and Blackhurst, 1985].)

Assessment Issues in the T.M.H. Classroom

All the problems and issues discussed in Chapters 1 and 2 usually arise when one undertakes educational assessment in a T.M.H. classroom. The classroom teacher of the T.M.H. often encounters additional difficulties in accounting for multihandicapping conditions, conducting reliable assessment of culturally different pupils, and identifying appropriate, well-validated assessment instruments or direct-observation data-gathering procedures.

Considerations Regarding Assessment and Multihandicapping Conditions

The T.M.H. pupil population is characterized not by homogeneity in its developmental and behavioral characteristics but rather by heterogeneity. Because other handicapping conditions so often occur in conjunction with the primary moderate learning handicap, the teacher of the trainable multiply handicapped must be prepared to make use of commercial adaptive-behavior assessment instruments that account accurately for the pupil's performance in the targeted skill or behavioral areas. Few instruments are able to account reliably or accurately for multiple handicapping conditions without violating their own standards for administration and scoring. For the classroom teacher, this means that if a commercial adaptive-behavior instrument is used, it must be used in an adapted or modified manner, and that the data collected may be unreliable or invalid as measures of the targeted assessment areas.

Although no formula exists that can overcome the problems presented by multiply handicapped T.M.H. pupils, the teacher can competently perform classroom-based assessment of their learning and adaptive behavior. Figure 2–11 in Chapter 2 outlines a series of steps in the decision-making process in assessment. Regardless of a pupil's classification, the teacher adhering to these steps can adequately assess multiply handicapped pupils in the classroom.

Selecting an Instrument.   The teacher should attempt to locate an instrument that has been constructed to account for the handicapping conditions presented by the pupil, or at least one that notes provisions for handicapped children in its user's manual. If no such instrument can be found, the teacher will need to decide whether such provisions can be made independently without completely invalidating the use of the data collected in later decision making. It may well be decided that a direct-observation data-collection procedure will provide more acceptable information.

Collecting Data.   For the classroom teacher, this is the most critical stage of assessment of children exhibiting multiple handicaps. By attending to parental involvement, conducting multiple assessments, utilizing naturalistic settings, adapting assessment procedures to fit the stimulus/response characteristics of the pupil, and making use of other professionals, the teacher increases the probability of making classroom assessment worthwhile for all involved. Adherence to these procedures will help reduce the probability of measurement errors, particularly those caused by assessor bias, as the teacher is making ample provision for a variety of informed input.

Classroom Assessment and Multicultural Factors

Strategies for assessing children from varied cultural and ethnic groups were discussed in Chapters 1 and 2. Because multiple handicaps are so often present in the T.M.H. population, cultural assessment problems are perhaps even more difficult with this population. Again, few commercially prepared adaptive-behavior instruments specifically account for cultural factors in assessment in any setting, home, community, or institution. The System of Multicultural Pluralistic Assessment, however, has received considerable attention and research.

The System of Multicultural Pluralistic Assessment (SOMPA) (J. R. Mercer and J. F. Lewis, 1971). This instrument and its accompanying *Adaptive Behavior Inventory for Children* (ABIC) may be of some assistance to teachers in T.M.H. classrooms. SOMPA is intended to provide comprehensive, nondiscriminatory assessment of public-school pupils between the ages of 5 and 11 (Salvia and Ysseldyke, 1981). A pupil's performance is assessed on three models: medical, sociosystem, and pluralistic (Mercer and Lewis's redefinition of the traditional score of general intelligence or learning potential). Three groups were included in SOMPA's norm population: Hispanic, black, and white. Chapter 7 urged caution in using SOMPA outside of California, where the norm population was obtained and the instrument standardized. This is because inaccuracies have been reported in the instrument's technical manual, reliability scores are low or unreported, and validities for some of the instrument's components have not been established.

The best procedure for the teacher of the T.M.H. to follow in dealing with cultural factors may be to adhere to the policies discussed above in regard to multi-handicapping conditions. These procedures can be particularly important when attempting to account for cultural factors. Parents and/or other family members familiar with the pupil can provide excellent resources for assessing adaptive behavior, and with training they can be very reliable data collectors. The importance of multiple assessments in naturalistic settings cannot be overlooked by the classroom teacher striving to obtain accurate and representative pupil performance data.

Using Assessment Instruments versus Data-Gathering Procedures in the T.M.H. Classroom

The major problem in selecting procedures and/or instrumentation for educational assessment in the T.M.H. classroom is determining their utility for prescribing instructional programs and their appropriateness for the pupil being assessed. The selection problem is focused mainly on adaptive-behavior assessment rather than on the determination of I.Q., which is rarely the job of the classroom teacher. Adaptive behavior assessment, in contrast, is a task that the classroom teacher is uniquely qualified to perform. With the passage of P.L. 94–142 in 1975 and the AAMD's definitional revisions regarding mental retardation in 1977 and 1983 to include the use of adaptive-behavior assessment data, a veritable avalanche of assessment instruments and procedures for direct observation of behavior has been thrust into the educational marketplace.

Longitudinal Research Is Needed. The recency of the requirement for adaptive-behavior assessment has not permitted the rigorous longitudinal research necessary for empirical validation. Berdine (1985) notes that one of the most widely used adaptive behavior assessment scales, the Public School Version (Lambert et al., 1975) of the AAMD's Adaptive Behavior Scale (ABS) (Nihira et al., 1974) has been severely criticized for its lack of reliability and validity, its use for classification purposes, and its use outside of California, where it was developed (Helton, Workman, and Matuszek, 1982). With the legal mandate for adaptive-behavior assessment and continued pressure from professional educators for improvement in instrument documentation, positive changes should occur. Helton, Workman, and Matuszek (1982) note that an existing, well-documented instrument, the Vineland Social Maturity Scale (VSMS) (Doll, 1983), has already responded to these demands by documenting improvement in its reliability and validity and in the representativeness of the norm population.

A Priori Questions for the Teacher

Before beginning any form of assessment in the classroom, the teacher should ask two very basic questions. What do I plan to accomplish with the assessment? Can I most effectively complete the assessment with a commercially available instrument or with a professionally validated data-collection procedure?

What Should the Assessment Accomplish?   In Chapter 1, five levels or stages of assessment were described: One, Screening and Identification; Two, Eligibility and Diagnosis; Three, Placement and Development; Four, Instructional Planning; and Five, Evaluation. To decide what the assessment should accomplish, determine which levels fit the circumstances. Classroom teachers are rarely solely responsible for Level One or Two, and they typically contribute to Level Three, IEP development, as part of a team. For the most part, teachers will be interested in pupil performance data as they pertain to Levels Four and Five, the planning and evaluation of instructional programs.

Most T.M.H. classroom schedules include little time especially for assessment. More often than not, assessment data must be collected amidst an array of other instructional and management needs.

Another reality of assessment in an ongoing T.M.H. classroom is that it may be more efficient for the teacher to attend simultaneously to more than one level of assessment and in some instances to more than one pupil. For example, he or she may need to evaluate two or three pupils in similar instructional programs to assess their current progress as well as their eligibility for movement to another instructional classification. The experienced teacher will also be using these data for further program development.

What Type of Instrument or Procedure?   In the T.M.H. classroom, pupil-to-teacher ratios vary considerably. Most often, the teacher and one classroom aide are responsible for managing between 7 and 12 pupils. This ratio and the diversity of the T.M.H. population often dictate that the teacher use more than one type of data-gathering process. The use of a number of different assessment procedures should not be a major problem as long as it does not detract from the accuracy of the data gathered or from ongoing instructional effectiveness. In many instances, adequately documented commercially available instruments may fit the classroom teacher's needs quite well; in others, a data-gathering procedure like those described in Chapter 2 may be more appropriate. Considerations in selecting either a direct-observation data-gathering procedure or an adaptive-behavior assessment instrument are described next.

Considerations in Selecting an Adaptive-Behavior Assessment Instrument for Use in a T.M.H. Classroom

Chapter 2 provided a description of the various types of adaptive-behavior assessment instruments and procedures, and basic procedures and problems in data collection and interpretation were discussed in Chapter 2. Problems the teacher of the T.M.H. may have with adaptive-behavior assessment instrument selection differ little from those of any classroom teacher. The following section outlines some of the major considerations that should be addressed before any adaptive behavior instrument is selected for use in a T.M.H. classroom setting.

Salvia and Ysseldyke (1985) pose four questions that they believe ought to be answered prior to the administration of any test for educational data gathering. These questions can readily be adapted for use by the T.M.H. classroom teacher selecting an adaptive behavior assessment instrument.

Who Is to Be Assessed? In most situations, the classroom teacher will be assessing one pupil at a time. If more than one student is to be assessed with the same adaptive-behavior instrument, the teacher will need to be sure that it is appropriate in type, topic, and administration procedure for simultaneous use with more than one person. Can the instrument be readily scored for two or more separate performances? Are there time constraints that cannot be met if more than one person is being assessed? Are the pupils in question functioning similarly enough to assure that they can be assessed with the same instrument?

Many secondary handicapping conditions are very common in the T.M.H. pupil population, so that the pupils often exhibit a wide variety of stimulus and response needs. For example, it is common to find T.M.H. pupils with both gross and fine motor handicaps, a wide range of expressive and receptive communicative disorders, and a tremendous variety of deficits in self-help skills — all of this on top of wide discrepancies in primary handicaps. This variation will influence the manner in which the teacher makes requests (stimuli for responses) of different pupils. Individual pupils' response modes may also vary. Consequently, many teachers of the trainable mentally handicapped find it most suitable to assess only one pupil at a time in a specific performance domain such as dressing skills or counting to 10 using objects. Comprehensive assessment of a wide variety of adaptive behavior performance areas with more than one person at a time is very difficult to complete reliably and probably should not be attempted.

The presence of single or multiple sensory deficit or loss may contraindicate the use of a commercial instrument or dictate that it be altered. In the latter case, the teacher must note the alteration in the preliminary section of any report because it may invalidate the use of those data in an official individualized education plan. Again, because of the multiplicity of secondary handicapping conditions, alteration is not an uncommon practice. Few commercially available adaptive-behavior assessment instruments have been designed for use with persons with major sensory or motor handicapping conditions. The Callier-Azusa Scale (1978), for use with deaf-blind children, and the Bruininks-Oseretsky Test of Motor Proficiency (1978), for use with motor-handicapped children, are two notable exceptions. (Chapter 9 provides additional information on the Callier-Azusa Scale, and Chapter 10 includes a discussion of the Bruininks-Oseretsky Test.)

What Behaviors Are to Be Tested?   In any assessment, the assessor should have a clear notion as to the goal of the assessment process. It is not enough to state that you are interested in a pupil's self-help skills; those skills need to be specified. For example, there are numerous types of dressing skills: buttoning, zipping, shoe-lace-tying, putting on shoes and socks. Within each of these types are at least two general levels, with assistance and without. The classroom teacher must achieve this level of specificity if reliable data are to be gathered and efficiently put to use. If the targeted behavior is an academic area such as arithmetic skill, the same attention to the specific skill is required; for example, two-column addition without carrying or counting to twenty by rote.

What Interpretative Data Are Desired?   Having carefully answered the question, "What behaviors are to be assessed?" the teacher will be able to answer this one quickly. This will usually involve deciding whether to use a criterion-referenced or a norm-referenced assessment instrument. It is critical to remember that criterion-referenced assessment generally involves the use of an instrument designed to determine how well a child performs in a particular domain or domains. For example, following an instructional unit on recognition of printed common safety words such as "EXIT," "STOP," "WAIT," "GO," and "POISON," the pupil's performance on an instrument that assesses recognition of these words would provide the teacher with documentation of skills mastered, skills in need of further instruction, and skills to be programmed for generalization or maintenance activities. A percentage criterion for successful completion of the unit may be established, but the basic purpose of criterion-referenced assessment is to determine mastery of specific performance areas. Criterion-referenced instruments typically provide a sampling of sequential skills, "enabling a teacher not only to know the specific points at which to begin instruction but also to plan those instructional aspects that follow directly in the curricular sequence" (Salvia and Ysseldyke, 1985, p. 30).

Norm-referenced adaptive-behavior instruments would rarely be used by a T.M.H. classroom teacher. As you will recall from Chapter 3, norm-referenced assessment compares performance areas. In special education, norm-referenced adaptive-behavior instruments are typically used for screening to determine eligibility for services, specify placement in a program, and evaluate a program's efficacy. The AAMD's Adaptive Behavior Scale (Lambert et al., 1975) is probably the best-known norm-referenced adaptive-behavior scale, but as noted, problems in accounting for the vast heterogeneity of all handicapped populations have raised serious questions about its widespread use.

Will a Commercially Prepared Test Be Used? For most classroom teachers, including the teacher of the trainable mentally handicapped, this question will be decided on the basis of decisions about what behaviors to assess and what interpretative data are desired. The availability of funds for purchasing commercial materials is also a factor. Most school systems that expect classroom assessment to be complete will make the necessary funds available.

The assessment objectives or targets will obviously have great bearing on the selection of an instrument. Closely related will be the decision to use a criterion- or a norm-referenced instrument.

Almost all commercially available adaptive behavior instruments are standardized in their administration and scoring. And because they are commercial products, attempts are made to make them as widely usable as possible. If a teacher wants to use only a portion of an instrument, for example independent toilet skills, the standards for the test's use and possibly its scoring will be violated, prohibiting the use of these data in any official capacity. Before purchasing or using a commercial instrument, the teacher should examine the technical manual carefully to determine whether the material would be generally useful. It may very well be decided that the teacher could construct a reliable criterion- or even norm-referenced assessment instrument. This is particularly likely if the assessment targets are closely linked to an established, ongoing instructional program. The major advantage of using commercially available material is often that it reduces the time expended on noninstructional activities such as test construction.

Commercially Available Adaptive-Behavior Assessment Materials

The teacher of the trainable mentally handicapped has a wide array of commercially available adaptive-behavior assessment materials to select from. We will profile six of these in this section. Chapters 5, "Assessment in Early Childhood Special Education," and 7, "Assessment of the Mildly Handicapped Learner," also describe several assessment instruments that may be appropriate for use with the T.M.H. pupil. Table 5–1 outlines four preschool screening devices, Table 5–2 outlines 11 developmental assessment instruments, Table 5–3 lists seven instruments that focus on cognitive development, and Table 5–4 outlines five communication assessment materials. The Kaufman Assessment Battery for Children (K–ABC), the American Association on Mental Deficiency's Adaptive Behavior Scale (ABS) Adaptive Behavior Inventory for Children (ABIC), and the Woodcock-Johnson Psychoeducational Battery, all discussed in Chapter 7, have been found quite effective in the T.M.H. classroom. Finally, Chapter 10, "Assessment of the Physically Handicapped," offers descriptions of materials that assess not only a pupil's physical and motor competency but also environmental barriers that may impede his or her access to the school and community.

The following assessment materials are commercially available and have been found useful in the T.M.H. classroom.

Vineland Adaptive Behavior Scales–Revised (S. S. Sparrow, D. A. Bala, and D. V. Cicchetti, 1984). This assessment tool focuses on personal and social sufficiency from birth to adulthood and is applicable to both nonhandicapped and handicapped individuals. It requires a respondent who is familiar with the target individual's behavior. There are three versions of the revised Vineland: the Survey Form, the Expanded Form, and the Vineland–D. The first two measure adaptive behavior across four domains — communication, daily living skills, socialization, and motor skills — and the Vineland–D is intended for use in diagnostic evaluations, program planning, and research.

The Survey Form contains 297 items providing a general assessment of adaptive behavior and takes between 20 and 60 minutes to administer. The items are arranged along a developmental continuum to permit norm-referenced assessment. It is designed for use with individuals from birth through age 18 years, 11 months, and with developmentally "low-functioning" adults.

The Expanded Form contains 577 items and thus provides a more comprehensive measure of adaptive behavior; the authors claim that it is useful in IEP development. Administration time is between 60 and 90 minutes. The Classroom Edition of the Expanded Form, for use in the classroom, contains 244 items, some of which pertain to academic performance. It is appropriate for pupils aged 3 years to 12 years, 11 months. Administration involves the teacher completing a questionnaire and takes approximately 20 minutes.

The instrument's manual reports median reliability figures based on the standardization sample for the Survey Form ranging from .83 in the motor skills domain to .90 in the daily living skills domain. The Expanded Form is documented as having median reliability of .86 in the motor skills domain to .95 in the maladaptive behavior domain. Reported median reliability figures for the Classroom Edition range from .82 in the motor skills domain to .91 in the daily living skills domain.

The concurrent and construct validity of the instrument's three forms was established through correlation with similar instruments, factor analysis, and documentation of performance across the instruments' domains and subdomains. Content validity is not specifically dealt with by the instrument's developers, but because the instrument's items were selected using appropriate procedures and practices, content validity does not appear to be an issue.

Battelle Developmental Inventory (J. Newborg, J. R. Stock, and L. Wnek, 1984). The BDI is a standardized, individually administered assessment battery based on developmental milestones for children from birth to eight years of age. The 341 test items are grouped into five domains: personal-social, adaptive, motor, communication, and cognitive. Ninety-six of the items are designed to be used as a screening test, while the full battery permits a more complete evaluation of functional abilities. The scoring system takes into account both emerging and fully developed skills. The BDI provides normative data on the basis of which eligibility and placement decisions can be made. It can also be adapted for use with children with single and multiple handicapping conditions. The screening test can be administered in 10 to 30 minutes, depending on the age of the pupil, and administration of the entire BDI requires between one and two hours.

The authors claim reliability and validity figures that substantiate the instrument's use with the moderately and severely mentally retarded pupil as well as with nonhandicapped populations. The BDI is particularly useful for the identification of children at risk for developmental delay, for use in team assessments and IEP development, and for the monitoring of short- and long-term goals of student programs.

The examiner's manual of the BDI is a model that similar assessment instruments should adopt. It is easy to read, informative, and relatively simple to use. The authors report overall test-retest and interrater reliabilities of .99. Reliability figures for each of the five domains and within all 29 subdomains across all age ranges (0 to 5 months through 84 to 95 months) are also provided. The BDI examiner's manual provides a thorough chart outlining both construct and content validity. Overall, the BDI appears to be a very well designed, revised, and produced assessment instrument.

Camelot Behavioral Checklist (R. W. Foster, 1979). The CBC is a standardized teacher- or paraprofessional-administered checklist that may also be completed by anyone familiar with the pupil's home, school, and community behavior but school personnel will need to be involved because it contains a large number of school-related items. The 399 items are behavioral descriptions grouped into 10 domains and arranged in order of difficulty. The domains are self-help, physical development, home duties, vocational behaviors, economic behaviors, independent travel, numerical skills, communication skills, social behavior, and responsibility. The CBC was designed to identify specific training objectives and to provide a score based on these objectives. A Skill Acquisition Program Bibliography is provided that can be used to develop programs and curricula to improve targeted objectives, skill areas and behaviors.

On the basis of 1974 studies, the CBC manual reports a reliability coefficient of .93 for the total instrument and satisfactory construct validity.

Brigance Diagnostic Inventory of Early Development (A. H. Brigance, 1978). The Brigance IED was developed to assess development in children from birth to seven years. It is criterion-referenced and norm-referenced and covers the following domains: psychomotor, self-help, communication, general knowledge, comprehension, and academic skills. Ninety-eight skill sequences are task analyzed and may be useful in instructional program planning, and the IED can be used for pre- and posttesting. The instrument focuses on skills acquisition but does include a list of objectives that may be useful for IEP development. Administration time for the test is variable depending on the age and any handicapping conditions of the pupil.

Brigance Diagnostic Inventory of Basic Skills (A. H. Brigance, 1977). The Brigance IBS was developed and field-tested as an evaluation instrument for assessing specific areas of educational need for handicapped children from kindergarten through sixth grade. The IBS provides a systematic performance record for diagnosis and evaluation and presents the skill areas of readiness, reading, language arts, and math in developmental and sequential hierarchies. The instrument is comprehensive and simple to administer and interpret. It can also be used in program development for junior high and secondary students requiring special education programming at an elementary school level. The IBS can be administered in part or in its entirety without a great deal of difficulty and through either direct testing in the skill areas being assessed or naturalistic observation. Time of administration is variable depending on the number of skill areas being used, the shortest time for a single skill area being approximately 15 minutes. The IBS is criterion-referenced and not norm-referenced. It is a valuable tool for assessing and recording pupils' achievement and progress and for developing individualized curricula, programs, or objectives.

The publisher provides no information regarding reliability for either of the two Brigance inventories, but the contents of both were developed using appropriate test item selection procedures, and their content validity is considered very acceptable.

Learning Accomplishment Profile–Diagnostic Edition (D. W. LeMay, P. M. Griffin, and A. R. Sanford, 1977). The LAP–D was developed to provide a reliable, objective method of assessing a pupil's progress in instructional programs and the effects of those programs. The LAP–D is appropriate for use with individuals from birth to age seven years. It serves three primary functions: evaluating a pupil's entry skills, evaluating a pupil's exit skills, and validating the intervention program used. The LAP–D is criterion-referenced and developmentally based. A task analysis model is utilized in the presentation of skill statements (ascending in order of skill complexity), and instructional objectives and strategies can readily be developed from the LAP–D's administration. A thorough discussion of hierarchical task analysis is provided in Chapter 2.

Areas assessed include fine motor, gross motor, cognitive, language/cognitive, and self-help skills. Each item describes the behavior to be observed, the procedures to be followed in eliciting the desired response, and the criteria for acceptable responses. The test can be used by anyone who can observe the pupil directly and who has a minimal orientation to the material included in the LAP–D kit. The instrument can be used in conjunction with the Learning Accomplishment Profile (LAP), Revised (A. R. Sanford and J. G. Zelman, 1981) and the Learning-Accomplishment Profile for Developmentally Young Children (LAP–E, 1978), (M. E. Glover, J. L. Preminger, and A. R. Sanford, 1978) for individuals between birth and age three. Neither of these tests shares the LAP–D's diagnostic profile characteristics.

The LAP–D examiner's manual (LeMay, Griffin, and Sanford, 1977) reports that "the minimal reliability coefficient encountered via the retest procedure was .82; most of the scales and their totals however, showed a minimal reliability of .90" (p. 36). The manual also provides total reliability coefficients for all twelve scales and subscales. While it does not discuss any specific data regarding validity, the procedures for item selection and test construction meet acceptable standards. The authors of the LAP–D utilized an extensive field-testing and user/professional critique procedure that appears to have resulted in an assessment instrument fairly useful to teachers of young handicapped pupils. The examiner's manual, however, seems to be designed only for those with considerable training in testing and measurement, a serious flaw in an otherwise well-developed instrument.

TMR Profile (A. J. Dinola, B. P. Kaminsky, and A. E. Sternfield, 1968). The TMR Profile is an evaluative scale for pupil performance based on teacher observations. It was developed to identify the pupil's performance level in a wide variety of daily-living skill activities. Present performance can be compared to past performance, and the pupil can be measured against prior profile performance. The TMR Profile is intended for use with pupils already classified as exhibiting moderate mental retardation but is not norm-referenced for that population. The instrument is designed to permit a teacher to record observations of performance efficiently, illustrate these observations graphically on a form provided, and maintain a cumulative record of performance of the six daily-living skills included in the profile. Areas assessed are social behavior, self-care, communication, basic knowledge, practical skills, and body usage. Each area has five performance levels, within each of which performance statements are provided. The observer scores the profile by identifying the performance statement that best suits the pupil. The TMR Profile can be used in a wide array of school-based settings, ranging from preschool to secondary.

The TMR Performance Profile Teacher's Manual does not report any data regarding either its reliability or its validity. This is a serious drawback to the instrument's use for anything other than program prescription and monitoring. Employment of the instrument for diagnosis, referral, or placement is not recommended.

Considerations in Selecting a Direct-Observation Data-Gathering Procedure

If the teacher decides that the best procedure for data gathering is to use a direct-observation data-gathering procedure, many options are available. Figure 8–2 demonstrates a data-collection selection system that outlines a process teachers may find helpful in determining which of the several available procedures to use.

Direct-observation data-collection procedures can be used in a T.M.H. classroom to establish baseline, or preinstructional, pupil performance; to monitor pupil progress; and to evaluate instructional programs. Some of the procedures fit

Figure 8–2

Data-Collection Procedure Selection System

. . . .

If The Student Response Is:

1. | A permanent product | ◀ If yes, use ▶

| Direct measurement of product
A. 96 correct
B. 96 error
C. Predetermined qualitative criterion |

If NO, use direct observation and assessment procedures to determine which of the response patterns or types matches current situation ▼

| Responding at high rate, and time to observe and record no problem | If yes, use ▶ | Time sampling procedure |

▼

| Short in duration and interested in rate or frequency | If yes, use ▶ Event recording

If no, ▼

| Continuous or very rapid, and teacher interested in length of occurrence | If yes, use ▶ Duration recording

If no, ▼

| Occurring almost continuously or at a high rate, and teacher interested in both duration and frequency | If yes, use ▶ Interval recording

If no, ▼

| Emitted after a specific cue or stimulus event, and teacher interested in length of time between specific stimulus and response | If yes, use ▶ Latency recording

If no, ▼

| Indicative of accuracy or mastery, and teacher is interested in level correct or incorrect | If yes, use ▶ Percent recording

If no, ▼

| Emitted in conjunction with a physical prompt or verbal cue card: teacher is interested in level of of assistance needed to maintain present level of responding | If yes, use ▶ Levels-of-assistance recording

From *Teaching the Trainable Retarded* by William H. Berdine and Patricia T. Cegelka, p. 116. Copyright © 1980. Published by Charles E. Merrill Publishing Company and reprinted by permission of the authors.

. . . .

more easily than others the typical structure of a T.M.H. classroom and the pupils described earlier in this chapter. The teacher's selection of a procedure will depend on the amount of time available for data collection, the materials and personnel available to assist in the classroom, and the type of information being sought. These factors will vary over time, and several different direct-observation procedures will be used in the classroom simultaneously. Some of the most frequently used direct-observation procedures for data collection in the T.M.H. classroom are discussed in the following section.

Event Recording. In many instances, a teacher is interested in recording the number of times a targeted behavior occurs within a specific period. For example, an instructional goal for Jack may be that during a specific workshop period he will raise his hand when it is necessary to seek help rather than using inappropriate methods such as calling out the teacher's name or leaving the assigned work site. Utilizing a check-mark system or a counting device, the teacher may use event recording to note the number of times Jack exhibits the targeted behavior, hand raising, during the workshop period.

These data can be used to establish baseline, to monitor the behavior after intervention has begun, and to determine when the pupil has met the criterion established as the goal. They can be collected by any of the classroom staff or by pupils trained to use the system if the targeted behavior has clearly observable beginning and end points. Event-recording data are relatively quick, easy, and unobtrusive to collect (see Figure 8–3).

Several discrete behaviors can be observed and recorded simultaneously by setting up a checklist for each of them. Target behaviors that are fairly similar or that do not have obvious beginning and ending points probably should be dealt with separately.

Duration Data. For some targeted behaviors, it is more important that the teacher know how long the behavior lasts than how often it occurs. For example, he or she may wish to monitor how long the pupil is on task during an instructional period or how long it takes the pupil to complete a specific manipulative task. To determine the duration of the behavior, the teacher must establish its movement cycle. This term refers to a description of the time the targeted behavior begins and ends, and its observable or measurable parameters. For example: The target behavior begins when the student is seated correctly, buttocks on the seat of the chair, facing front, feet on floor, eyes on appropriate task stimulus, and hands manipulating stimulus material correctly. The target behavior ends when the pupil is no longer seated correctly, moves eyes away from appropriate task stimulus, or manipulates task materials inappropriately. Noting the amount of time between the beginning and end of the targeted behavior will establish its duration. These data are recorded each time the behavior occurs during the observation period. If the observation periods are consistent, the total amount of time the behavior was exhibited can be illustrated in graphic form; but if they vary, the data must be translated into percentages for interpretation. This is accomplished by dividing the total

Figure 8–3

An Example of Data Collection Using Event Recording

. . . .

Student: _S. R._____   Observer: _Ms. Andrews_____

Date: _3/12/87_____   Behavior: _hand raising_____

Start time: _9:00 a.m._____ + Stop time: _9:30 a.m._____ = Total time _30 min.____

	Comments
9:00 9:05	Yelled for teacher four times
9:05 9:10	Yelled for teacher six times
9:10 9:15	Sat quietly
9:15 9:20	Sat quietly
9:20 9:25	Sat quietly
9:25 9:30	No hand raising observed but yelled for teacher seven times
Data summary	N = 8

Directions: Record a ( ) each time the target behavior occurs.

. . . .

amount of time the behavior occurred by the length of the observation period. The only materials needed for duration data recording are paper, a pencil, and a time-piece. Duration data recording is somewhat more demanding of staff than event recording, but it is generally quite effective and also fairly unobtrusive. Figure 8–4 illustrates a data-collection form for duration data.

Percentage Recording.   In many instructional programs, the teacher presents a specific number of trials to a pupil and requires a response each time. For example, the teacher may present the pupil with a colored object and ask, "What color is this?" The pupil may make a correct response by naming the color, make no re-sponse, or make an incorrect response. If he or she records the responses, the teacher can determine the percentage correct by dividing the number of correct responses by the number of trials presented.

Percentage data recording is probably the most frequently used data-collection procedure for both preacademic and academic instructional programs. It can be used for manipulative tasks (for example, the percentage of objects correctly sorted) and for paper-and-pencil tasks (for example, the percentage of addition

Figure 8–4

An Example of Duration Data Recording

. . . .

Student: _C.K._____   Target behavior: _Packaging_____

Observer: _Ms. Long_____   _nuts & bolts_____

Date: _3/15/87_____   Behavior description: Seated at table,
feet on floor, open bag in lap, picks
Start time: _10:15 a.m._____   up 2 nuts and 2 bolts, drops in bag,
closes bag.
Stop time: _10:30 a.m. =_____

Total time: _15 min._____

Directions: Start the stopwatch when the behavior begins and stop it when the behavior ends. Record the elapsed time.

Behavior No.	Duration	Comments
1.	15″	
2.	5″	
3.	6″	
4.	25″	
5.	1″	
		After packaging 6 bags, left the work area
N = 6	52″	= Total duration
Target N= 30		

. . . .

problems correctly completed) and for group and individual programs. Percentage data can be gathered by either a teacher or an aide as part of the ongoing instructional program. Figure 8–5 illustrates a data-recording procedure using percentage data. Some additional time is needed to compute the figures after each program session, but the actual expenditure of time is not great considering the detailed data compiled.

Latency Data Recording.   Because of the high rate of motor handicaps in the T.M.H. population, the classroom teacher often deals with response time or reac-

Figure 8–5

An Example of Percentage Data Recording

. . . .

Student: __T.C._____   Date: __3/11/87_____

Observer: __Ms. Long_____   Condition: __ID. red/blue_____

Start time: __10:45 a.m._____   Stop time: __11:00 a.m._____ = Total time: __15 min._____

Trial	Response Correct	Incorrect	Comments
1. red	✓		
2. red	✓		
3. blue		✓	Trials #3, 4, 5: picked up object
4. red		✓	on left consistently.
5. blue		✓	
6. blue	✓		
7. blue	✓		
8. red	✓		
9. blue	✓		
10. red		✓	Trial #10 touched correct object but
11. red		✓	then picked up blue object.
12. blue	✓		
13. blue	✓		Trials #11, 16, 18, 19: continued to
14. red	✓		pick up first object on left.
15. blue	✓		
16. red		✓	
17. blue	✓		
18. red		✓	
19. red		✓	
20. blue	✓		
Data summary	N = 12	N = 8	
N/total =	60%	40%	

. . . .

tion time to environmental stimuli. In order to be functional, many behaviors must be exhibited within a reasonable amount of time after they are called for. The definition of "reasonable amount of time" will vary according to the behavior in question and the pupil's handicapping conditions.

To monitor response latency, the teacher records the amount of time elapsed between the presentation of a stimulus and the beginning of the pupil's response; the correctness of the response is not necessarily recorded. For example, the pupil given the task request "Look at me" may take quite a lot of time to respond and

Figure 8–6

An Example of Latency Data Recording

. . . .

Student: R.P.

Observer: Ms. Long

Condition attending:
"Look at me." (within 5'')

Date: 3/13/87

Start time: 1:15 p.m.   Stop time: 1:30 a.m.   = Total time: 15 min.

Direction: Start stopwatch after presentation of verbal stimulus; stop once student begins the response. Record elapsed time.

Trials	Latency	Comments
1.	10''	Made eye contact with peer
2.	3''	
3.	15''	Looked at floor first
4.	8''	
5.	5''	
6.	4''	
7.	20''	Closed eyes and refused to open
8.	18''	Looked out window
9.	5''	
10.	5''	
Data summary	93''	= Total Latency

. . . .

establish eye contact. This not only interferes with instruction, it also increases the amount of time required to complete all instructional activities that require visual contact with the teacher or aide. An instructional objective for such a pupil may be that he or she establish eye contact, upon request, within five seconds. By recording response latency systematically, the teacher can easily monitor progress on this objective. See Figure 8–6 for an example of latency data recording. This technique is often used in T.M.H. classroom settings; and while it is expensive in terms of staff time, use of timing devices, and strict attention, it is invaluable in monitoring many instructional programs.

Levels of Assistance. Very often during instructional activities the teacher will assist the pupil in making a response through modeling, physically prompting some part of the response, or verbally or gesturally cuing. This occurs particularly when a previously nonexisting skill is being developed and in many self-help skills

Figure 8–7

An Example of Levels-of-Assistance Data Recording for Spreading Butter on Bread. Latency of Response Is also Recorded.

Trials/Steps	Response	Assistance	Latency	Comments
1. Pick up knife	+	V	5″	
2. Put butter on knife	+	M	10″	Looking out window
3. Position over bread	+	V	5″	
4. Bring butter side down to bread	+	V	5″	
5. Move knife across bread	+	P	15″	Tore bread, dropped knife
6. Place knife on table	+	I	2″	
Data summary	+ = 6 − = 0	V = 3 M = 1 P = 1 I = 1	42″	= Total latency in seconds
			Code:	+ = correct − = incorrect V = verbal cue M = model P = physical guidance I = independent ″ = second

that require several steps for a correct response. Since most instructional objectives specify that the pupil be able to demonstrate criterion performance independently, it is important for the teacher to monitor the amount and kind of assistance being provided. In working on a skill involving several steps, such as shoe tying or hanging up a coat, the teacher may choose to task-analyze the skill and use this analysis as a checklist with which to establish baseline performance and monitor the pupil's progress. (See Chapter 2 for a detailed discussion of the uses of task analysis.) Recording the amount of assistance required at each step provides the teacher with an accurate portrayal of the pupil's current performance.

A more elaborate recording system is needed to pair levels-of-assistance data recording with other direct-observation recording systems such as latency data paired with levels of assistance. However, this type of data collection provides the teacher with large amounts of otherwise unavailable performance data. The time involved in designing the recording procedures and identifying the critical performance components is far outweighed by the benefits accrued. Figure 8–7 illustrates one approach to levels-of-assistance data recording.

Figure 8–8

Recording Time-Sample Data

. . . .

Two One-Minute Observation Sessions

Minutes	Session 1	Session 2
1	+	+
2	−	−
3	−	+
4	−	+
5	+	+
6	+	−
7	−	−
8	+	−
9	−	+
10	+	−
11	−	−
12	−	+
13	+	+
14	−	+
15	+	=

Occurrence of target = + = 16
Nonoccurrence of target = − = 14

. . . .

Time Sampling. Most of the data-collection systems described above require the teacher to record every instance of the targeted behavior during the observation period. In the T.M.H. classroom, this is not always feasible, practical, or in the best interest of other instructional programming occurring in the room. By using time-sampling procedures, the teacher may monitor a behavior while performing other classroom activities. To do this, he or she divides the observation period into equal intervals. At the end of each, he or she records whether the targeted behavior is occurring. This periodic monitoring provides a fairly representative portrayal of the occurrence of the target behavior and maintains other classroom activities simultaneously.

For instance, if the teacher wanted to record the percentage of time Jessica correctly manipulated material during a 30-minute workshop, he would begin by dividing the period into equal intervals — perhaps 15 one-minute intervals. At the end of each, regardless of what else he was doing, he would make a visual check on Jessica to determine and record whether she was exhibiting the behavior under observation. At the end of the 15-minute period, the teacher would divide the number of intervals in which he saw the behavior by the total number of intervals and multiply the result by 100. This would give him a percentage figure that could be used for ongoing graphic illustration.

Figure 8–8 illustrates a time-sampling data-recording procedure. Time sampling is relatively easy for the teacher to use and it provides fairly reliable performance data with minimal distraction of other classroom activities. Time sampling does require the teacher to be disciplined in attending to the intervals, and therefore it is difficult to maintain over multiple target behaviors.

Permanent Products.   As a part of determining instructional effectiveness, all teachers, including teachers of the T.M.H., rely upon and need permanent products. Some instructional objectives involve products such as name writing, cutting along a line, or buttoning buttons. By systematically monitoring the products produced for a given objective and comparing them to preestablished criteria, the teacher and the pupil can easily determine progress. The teacher can readily tell whether a pupil is experiencing difficulty or regressing to an earlier level of performance, when criteria for completion need to be changed, and when a criterion has not been met. Permanent-product data collection is not obtrusive and requires little extra staff time.

While the seven direct-observation data-recording systems described above are generally useful in T.M.H. classroom settings, this does not preclude the usefulness of any of the others described in Chapter 2. The key to selecting a data-collection procedure seems to be the teacher's interest in using data to prescribe, monitor, modify, and evaluate instructional programming in the classroom. The value of direct-observation data-collection systems or procedures is that they can easily be tailored to meet the needs of teachers and most classroom situations.

Assessing Learning-Style Preference

In Chapter 2, "Data-Collection Procedures," a process for assessing a pupil's preference in environmental stimuli was discussed. Teachers of the T.M.H. pupil may find learning-style preference a valuable additional source of information that will facilitate the pupil's learning new skills and behaviors. In addition to the Learning Style Inventory discussed in Chapter 2, the classroom teacher may use other, less formal assessment procedures to help him or her understand what environmental stimuli may facilitate or impede a pupil's learning process. It is reasonable to assume that if a teacher is able to match an instructional approach to a pupil's preferred style of learning, the learning process will be both more efficient and more effective. This individualized, prescriptive approach to instruction is one thing that differentiates special education from regular education.

Data-Collection Questions

The procedures for determining informally a pupil's preferred style of learning may take a number of forms, depending on the time available for assessment, the teacher's access to persons who know about the pupil's interaction with the environment, the pupil's level of communication skill, and the existence of multiple handicapping conditions that may impede clearly identifiable interactive prefer-

Figure 8–9

Data-Collection Questions Regarding Pupil Learning-Style Preference

. . . .

Pupil's name: _____

1. Does the pupil have communicative preferences or requirements?

Date(s) of data collection: _____

Observation site(s): _____

Data collector(s): _____

2. Are there any clearly preferred sensory or perceptual modalities?

Date(s) of data collection: _____

Observation site(s): _____

Data collector(s): _____

3. Are there any clearly preferred reinforcers?

Date(s) of data collection: _____

Observation site(s): _____

Data collector(s): _____

4. Does the pupil respond differentially to adults in the classroom?

Date(s) of data collection: _____

Observation site(s): _____

Data collector(s): _____

Figure 8–9

Data-Collection Questions Regarding Pupil Learning-Style Preference (*continued*)

. . . .

    5. Does the pupil respond differentially to variations in structures built into instructional program design?

    Date(s) of data collection: _____

    Observation site(s): _____

    Data collector(s): _____

    6. Is the pupil unusually distracted by environmental stimuli?

    Date(s) of data collection: _____

    Observation site(s): _____

    Data collector(s): _____

    7. Does the pupil exhibit unusual response-latency requirements?

    Date(s) of data collection: _____

    Observation site(s): _____

    Data collector(s): _____

    8. Does the pupil have any peer preferences?

    Date(s) of data collection: _____

    Observation site(s): _____

    Data collector(s): _____

Figure 8–9

Data-Collection Questions Regarding Pupil Learning-Style Preference (*continued*)

. . . .

9. Does the pupil exhibit a preference for specific forms of instructional activities or settings?

Date(s) of data collection: _____

Observation site(s): _____

Data collector(s): _____

10. Does the pupil respond differentially because of apparent temporal variables?

Date(s) of data collection: _____

Observation site(s): _____

Data collector(s): _____

Other observations and comments:

. . . .

ences. An efficient approach to informal assessment of learning-style preference is the use of questions that cover those basic variables in a learning environment that can be readily managed, manipulated, or altered by the teacher. Figure 8–9 illustrates a data-collection chart for nine questions relating to learning-style preference that are generally applicable to the T.M.H. pupil population. The remainder of this section of the chapter will elaborate on those questions.

Does the Pupil Have Communicative Preferences or Requirements?
Another aspect of the great heterogeneity of T.M.H. pupils is their communication requirements and preferences. It is not unusual for a teacher of the T.M.H. to be confronted with pupils whose communication abilities range from nonoral to competent oral or verbal skills. With the nonoral, the teacher must both learn to use manual communication and teach the pupil to use it in a total communication approach that combines manual gestures with oral communication. The total communication approach facilitates the pupil's use of existing verbal skills and promotes the acquisition of new ones.

Language competence also quite often affects the way a pupil interacts with the learning environment. (Chapter 4, "Assessment of Language Impairments," described in detail the complexity of this area of behavior.) The language requirements of the T.M.H. pupil are varied, but quite often the teacher must use simple command statements. Typically, complex or multiple commands will not be responded to consistently. Teachers are required to adjust their verbal instruction to accommodate this language style while continuing to expand pupils' language capabilities and repertoires. The early determination of communication preferences is essential to the development of effective instructional programs and should be the first priority of the classroom teacher.

Are There Any Clearly Preferred Sensory or Perceptual Modalities?

A critical factor in teaching any pupil exhibiting moderate learning problems is the achievement of stimulus control. The teacher must be able to control the pupil's stimulus input consistently and predictably while engaging in instructional activities. Any sensory or perceptual preferences that can be matched to instructional approaches or activities should be noted, as should any sensory or perceptual deficits — for example, low-vision, or aversion to bright lights. Appropriate instructional planning should be done to remove or reduce the impact of environmental variables that the pupil finds significantly distracting or aversive.

Are There Any Clearly Preferred Reinforcers?

The process of determining a reinforcer hierarchy has been discussed in Chapter 2 and is illustrated in Figure 2–9. It should be remembered that the values of reinforcers change with repeated use, and a reinforcer's effectiveness usually diminishes when it has been used over long periods of time. The teacher of the T.M.H. pupil will need a variety of reinforcers, including primary rewards such as food and secondary rewards such as verbal praise or tokens. Also, pupils will generally have preferences for varying types of reinforcers for different types and levels of instructional activity. For instance, in one task setting a token may have a greater effect than verbal praise, whereas in another, verbal praise when classmates are in attendance may be the preferred reinforcer. A variety of reinforcers used contingently will be a significant asset to any instructional activity.

Does the Pupil Respond Differentially to Adults in the Classroom?

No official standard exists for the number of adults or professionals required to staff a classroom for the T.M.H. Most classrooms have one certified teacher, an instructional aide, and quite often also a volunteer. In many instances, pupils will respond differentially to the adults in the classroom. The certified teacher is trained to provide effective instruction, but this is no guarantee that all pupils will respond positively to him or her. When another adult with competent instructional skills is available and to whom a pupil is responsive, the teacher should attempt to utilize this relationship to further facilitate instructional activities. The key consideration is that a certified T.M.H. teacher must be responsible for IEP decisions, for supervising the classroom's operation, and for making decisions about instructional program changes. The teacher's recognition of interpersonal preferences on the part of the pupil can be a significant asset to effective and efficient instructional programming.

Does the Pupil Respond Differentially to Variations in Structures Built into Instructional Program Design? Routine, practice, tightly controlled learning environments, and contingency management are common practices in the T.M.H. classroom. Unfortunately, these practices often overlook subtle individual preferences for differing degrees of structure. The great heterogeneity of pupils classified as T.M.H. in learning ability, perceptual-motor competence, and communication skill often makes grouping of pupils more a convenience to the teacher than a facilitator of instruction. Each pupil's requirements and preferences for routine, teacher/pupil ratio, and contingency management should be determined before any attempt at instruction is made. Where pupils' preferences for instructional structure are compatible, their grouping is more likely to be productive.

Is the Pupil Unusually Distracted by Environmental Stimuli? After the initial exposure to the wide variety of sounds, odors, sights, and textures of a classroom, most pupils exhibit an ability to remain on task and are not distracted by extraneous environmental stimuli. Many pupils classified as T.M.H., however, do not readily adjust to distracting environmental stimuli, and their instructional programs will be negatively affected if the teacher is unable or unwilling to engineer the classroom to meet their requirements. Inexpensive room partitions, carrels, directional lighting fixtures, and auditory control devices such as headphones are usually well within the resource capabilities of teachers of the T.M.H. Temperature preferences, while more difficult to accommodate, can often be met through the use of extra clothing, a permissive dress code, and small fans with child-proof blades.

Does the Pupil Exhibit Unusual Response-Latency Requirements? As described earlier, the T.M.H. pupil often exhibits inappropriate response time to instructional commands as well as to environmental stimulus events. This may involve either responding earlier than desired or taking too long to respond for effective instruction to be maintained. Early determination of pupils' response characteristics is essential for effective ongoing instruction in the T.M.H. classroom. The pupil without a fairly extensive acceptable response-latency repertoire will experience significant limitations and difficulties in the community and later in vocational settings.

Does the Pupil Have Any Peer Preferences? The ability to exhibit responsible behavior in regard to peers is often a direct instructional requirement. It is important for the teacher to know about pupils' peer preferences as classroom contingency management plans are being developed and instructional grouping is being planned. The best of friends may or may not be the best of pupils when placed together. Knowledge of a pupil's peer preferences will preclude grouping for instruction that would have a high probability of an aversive or even aggressive response.

Does the Pupil Exhibit a Preference for Specific Forms of Instructional Activities or Settings?   The use of individualized instructional approaches should encourage the determination of pupil preferences. Individualized instruction may vary significantly and include one-to-one direct instruction, individualized teacher intervention in small-group settings, individual seat work, activity sheets, auto-instructional kits, tape-recorded programs, and whole-class instruction with pupils receiving individualized attention as required. Knowledge of pupils' preferences and performance in a variety of settings and activities will help the teacher maintain a vigorous instructional program for each one.

Does the Pupil Respond Differentially Because of Apparent Temporal Variables?   Like most individuals, pupils classified as T.M.H. have periods during the day when they are more alert, responsive, congenial, or ready for interaction. Instructional planning and particularly scheduling will be greatly enhanced if pupils are scheduled for instruction during periods when their temporal preferences are compatible with the planned instructional activity.

The assessment of pupils' learning-style preferences need not be an elaborate or time-consuming process. The learning-style preference response characteristics described in depth in Chapter 2 can be determined through fairly routine direct observation in natural settings or through interviews with people who have had prior experiences with the pupil. Knowledge of a pupil's learning-style preferences will evolve quickly over the first few weeks and months of experience in the classroom. Instruction must begin before these preferences are known, but it can be modified as new knowledge is gained.

This prescriptive application of learning-style preference data is well within both IEP requirements and ongoing classroom demands. However, the teacher may not always be able to accommodate the learning-style preferences of all pupils. This is simply not feasible, and it is not expected. The adjustment of programs to facilitate instruction based on individual learning-style preferences must be accomplished on the basis of the resources and time available to the teacher. It can be hypothesized that the more learning style is considered during instructional planning, implementation, and evaluation, the more the pupil will learn.

Summary

Educational assessment of pupils classified as trainable mentally handicapped is a complex and demanding task. The classroom teacher's role in assessment is clearly significant, as many of the data used in it require direct observation in a variety of settings and circumstances. Confounding the process of assessment is the rather broad array of developmental, behavioral, and physical disabilities and impairments that are commonly found in the T.M.H. pupil population. The classroom teacher must be knowledgeable about a wide range of commercially available assessment materials as well as about basic direct-observation data-collection procedures. The ability to determine a pupil's preferred learning style has recently been shown to be important in documenting his or her performance needs and characteristics. Like other special education teachers, the teacher of the T.M.H. must be able to modify available assessment materials and procedures to fit each pupil's specific assessment needs and performance characteristics.

Some of the major topics of discussion in this chapter were:

1. The label "T.M.H." refers to members of the mentally retarded population with deficits in learning, self-help, communication, and motor skills. The label "T.M.H." requires a measured I.Q. between 35–40 and 50—55 with concomitant moderate deficits in assessed adaptive behavioral functioning.
2. Issues in assessment in the T.M.H. classroom include multihandicapping conditions, cultural factors, data-gathering procedures, and selection of adaptive-behavior assessment instruments.
3. Direct-observation data-gathering procedures used in the T.M.H. classroom include event recording, duration recording, percentage recording, latency recording, levels-of-assistance recording, time-sampling recording, and permanent-product collection.
4. Assessing learning-style preference in the T.M.H. classroom necessitates taking into consideration communicative requirements, sensory or perceptual modalities, reinforcers, instructor preference, preferred degree of structure, distracting environmental stimuli, response-latency requirements, peer preference, forms of instructional activities or settings, and temporal variables.
5. Commercially available instruments effective for assessment and program planning for the T.M.H. pupil include the Vineland Adaptive Behavior Scales–Revised, the Battelle Developmental Inventory, the Camelot Behavioral Checklist, the Brigance Diagnostic Inventory of Early Development, the Brigance Diagnostic Inventory of Basic Skills, the Learning Accomplishment Profile–Diagnostic Edition, and the TMR Profile.

Mastery Review

I. Recall

1. The term "T.M.H." refers to the:
   a. severely handicapped learner.
   b. moderately handicapped learner.
   c. mildly handicapped learner.
   d. orthopedically handicapped learner.

2. According to the AAMD definition of mental retardation, "significantly subaverage" is defined as an I.Q. of:
   a. 50 or below.

    b. 20 or below.

    c. 70 or below.

    d. 90 or below.

3. "Significant limitations in meeting demands of a designated age level and cultural group as determined by standardized clinical assessment scales" refers to:

    a. impairments in adaptive behavior.

    b. developmental period.

    c. subaverage intellectual functioning.

    d. moderate mental retardation.

4. The developmental period is the:

    a. time between the first and the fifth birthdays.

    b. time between conception and the 18th birthday.

    c. time between the 1st and the 18th birthdays.

    d. time between conception and the fifth birthday.

5. The T.M.H. student often enters the educational setting services at the _____ level.

    a. 8th, residential school.

    b. 4th, regular classroom placement, resource room assistance.

    c. 1st, regular classroom placement, few or no supportive services.

    d. 6th, full-time special class.

6. The prevalence of T.M.H. pupils is:

    a. 1 percent of the population.

    b. 20 percent of the mentally retarded population.

    c. 1 percent of the mentally retarded population.

    d. 20 percent of the population.

7. A description of when a target behavior begins and ends and its observable parameters is:

    a. a task analysis.

    b. a movement cycle.

    c. duration.

    d. latency.

8. To determine the percentage of correct responses, the teacher can:

    a. divide the number of correct responses by the number of trials presented.

    b. multiply the number of correct responses by the number of trials presented.

    c. subtract the number of correct responses from the number of trials presented.

    d. add the number of correct responses to the number of trials presented.

9. The time elapsed between the presentation of a stimulus and the beginning of a response is referred to as:

    a. duration.

    b. latency.

    c. rate.

    d. percent.

10. When the teacher records the occurrence or nonoccurrence of a behavior at the end of a specified time interval, this is referred to as:
    a. duration recording.
    b. time sampling.
    c. percent recording.
    d. event recording.

11. Using manual gestures in combination with oral communication is referred to as:
    a. total communication.
    b. verbal cuing.
    c. signing.
    d. verbal description.

12. Language requirements of the T.M.H. pupil often entail the use of:
    a. complex command statements.
    b. multiple directions.
    c. simple command statements.
    d. two-step verbal directions.

13. The T.M.H. population is characterized by its _____ .
    a. homogeneity.
    b. similarity.
    c. uniformity.
    d. heterogeneity.

14. The most critical stage of assessment of multiply handicapped students by the teacher is:
    a. selection of an instrument.
    b. data collection.
    c. identification of the handicaps involved.
    d. determination of the etiology of the handicaps.

15. Assessing a pupil's preference regarding environmental stimuli would *not* include:
    a. communicative preference.
    b. sensory or perceptual modalities.
    c. preferred reinforcers.
    d. handicapping conditions.

II. Comprehension

1. Give the AAMD definition of mental retardation and define each of its component parts.
2. List the four questions that the T.M.H. classroom teacher should address before selecting and using any adaptive-behavior instrument. Discuss the major issues for each question.
3. Select a target behavior for which duration data could be collected and establish a movement cycle for it.
4. Given the information in the previous chapter on assessing students with mild handicaps, discuss how it differs from assessing T.M.H. students.
5. Discuss the importance of assessing adaptive behavior skills in the trainable mentally

handicapped and the role of the classroom teacher in this assessment. Describe one commercial assessment instrument mentioned in this chapter that may be used.

6. Describe the continuum of special education services discussed in this chapter.

III. Application

1. Visit an educational setting serving T.M.H. pupils and, after conferring with the teacher or person in charge, collect data on a specific behavior for a period of at least 25 minutes using an appropriate direct-observation method. Discuss your observation and data in a three-to-five-page paper. Be sure to explain your rationale for selecting the observation procedure used.

2. Visit an educational setting serving T.M.H. pupils and, after conferring with the teacher or person in charge, complete the form on pupil learning-style preference contained in this chapter. Discuss your observations in a three-to-five page paper, giving emphasis to implications for instruction.

IV. Alternate Task

If none of the Application exercises applies to your setting or curriculum, you can design two exercises of your own. They should demonstrate application of one or more of the principles or concepts described in the preceding chapter. Prior approval of both exercises should be obtained from your course instructor.

V. Answer Key

I.				II.		
	1. b p. 218	**8.** a p. 235		**1.**	pp. 218–20
	2. c p. 218, p. 219	**9.** b pp. 236–37		**2.**	pp. 226–28
	3. a p. 219	**10.** b p. 240		**3.**	pp. 234–35
	4. b p. 220	**11.** a p. 244		**4.**	Chapter 7
	5. d p. 220	**12.** c p. 245		**5.**	pp. 226–32
	6. a p. 222	**13.** d p. 222		**6.**	pp. 220–22
	7. b p. 234	**14.** b p. 223			
		15. d pp. 245–47			

Chapter 9

Assessment of the Profoundly Handicapped Pupil

Key Terms:

assessment of developmental
   potential
basic skills
cognitive-developmental model
cognitive level
"criterion of ultimate functioning"
criterion-referenced assessment
curriculum-referenced assessment
environmental analysis
generalization
interactions
norm-referenced assessment
operational definition
reliability
severe and profound handicaps
task analysis

Chapter Objectives:

After reading this chapter and completing the Mastery Review, you will be able to:

1. Give a definition of the category "severely or profoundly handicapped" and discuss the implications of component parts of that definition.
2. Describe the learning characteristics of the severely or profoundly handicapped pupil.
3. Discuss the implications of multiple handicaps for assessment of the severely or profoundly handicapped pupil.
4. Identify and describe major educational assessment approaches and discuss the benefits and limitations of each approach with reference to the severely and profoundly handicapped population.
5. Identify the "criterion of ultimate functioning" and discuss its implications for the education of the severely or profoundly handicapped pupil.
6. Describe the rationale for using an analysis of assessment and instructional tasks according to their cognitive requirements.
7. Identify and describe several instruments developed specifically for the severely or profoundly handicapped population.

The initial impetus for serving the severely and profoundly handicapped learner in the public school system is frequently attributed to the *Mills versus Board of Education of the District of Columbia* decision of 1972, which instructed the board that "a free and suitable publicly supported education regardless of the degree of the child's mental, physical or emotional disability or impairment" (Abeson, 1973, p. 3) be provided to each child of school age. Public Law 94–142 was passed in 1975, and rules and regulations regarding how "free and appropriate" education is to be provided were issued subsequently. The inclusion in this volume of a chapter on the assessment of the severely and profoundly handicapped pupil is in large measure a consequence of that legislation.

Defining the Population and Setting

Like all complex concepts, that of severely or profoundly handicapped has different meanings for different people. Thompson (1974), director of the Program for Severely Handicapped Children and Youth, Special Education Programs, U.S. Office of Education, defines the severely handicapped pupil as one who,

> because of the intensity of his physical, mental, or emotional problems, needs educational, social, psychological, and medical services beyond those which have been offered by traditional regular and special educational programs, in order to maximize his full potential for useful and meaningful participation in society and for self-fulfillment (p. 73).

While the definition of "severely handicapped" permits the inclusion of a person with any type of severe disability, the majority of work in the field of education of severely and profoundly handicapped persons pertains to the person who functions in the range of severe to profound retardation when assessed with standardized psychometric or developmental schedules. According to the definition of degrees of retardation offered by the American Association on Mental Deficiency (Grossman, 1983), severe retardation is evidenced by an I.Q. in the range of 40 to 25, and profound retardation by an I.Q. of less than 25. In addition, in a group of persons who function as severely or profoundly retarded, one will find a high incidence of other disabilities including problems in audition, vision, and tactile-kinesthetic reception; processing abnormalities; seizure disorders; behavior disorders; and physical disabilities resulting from abnormalities of the neurological and musculo-skeletal systems. Interactions among these disabilities in their origins and impact upon development in any given individual will be complex. One class of severely and profoundly handicapped pupils might be composed of children with severe quadraplegic cerebral palsy who are also severely retarded and have significant vision and hearing handicaps and, frequently, uncontrolled seizure disorders. A second class of severely and profoundly handicapped learners might be composed of severely retarded, emotionally disturbed, or autistic pupils, a high percentage of whom are likely to have seizure disorders and visual or (often un-diagnosed) auditory processing disorders.

Functional Characteristics

While severely and profoundly handicapped pupils may exhibit varying sets of dis-abilities, it may be most fruitful to attend to the effects these disabilities have on their functioning. Sontag, Burke, and Yorke (1973) have offered a definition of the severely and profoundly handicapped pupil by describing their probable func-tional characteristics:

> This includes pupils who are not toilet trained, aggress towards others; do not attend to even the most pronounced social stimuli; self-mutilate, ruminate, self-stimulate, do not walk, speak, hear or see; manifest durable and intense temper tantrums; are not under even the most rudimentary forms of verbal control, do not imitate, manifest minimally controlled seizures; and/or have extremely brittle medical existences (p. 73).

School Settings

The typical school setting for this population will vary with the size of the school district. In larger districts with more than one or two classes of severely and pro-foundly handicapped pupils, there may well be a special school for the population. It may be the school where orthopedically handicapped children were served be-fore the mainstreaming impetus created by P.L. 94–142, or several classes for se-verely and profoundly handicapped pupils may be located in a regular school. If the number of children is sufficient, they will frequently be grouped by the tradi-tional levels, primary, intermediate, and secondary.

In a sparsely populated area or among small districts, several school districts may join together in a cooperative program to serve children with "low-incidence" handicapping conditions. In such situations, a teacher may face substantial vari-ability among the pupils in their cognitive functioning level and, consequently, in their instructional needs.

Issues and Special Problems

Given the mandate to provide an educational program for severely and profoundly handicapped pupils, many educators, special educators, and school systems have struggled with the challenge it presents to the traditional framework of education. Sontag, Smith, and Sailor (1977) have suggested that education for the severely and profoundly handicapped emphasize the development of basic skills that precede academic instruction. These skills include acquisition and use of a communication system, self-care skills, and the development of early cognitive, motor, perceptual, and social skills. For example, texts on instructional methods for the severely and profoundly handicapped, such as Snell (1978, 1983), are organized around themes like "basic skill development" (sensorimotor, language, motor, self-care, and social skills) and "preacademic remediation" (math skills, functional reading, and daily living training through pictorial instruction).

Criterion of Ultimate Functioning

Perhaps the primary instructional issue facing the teacher of severely and profoundly handicapped pupils is that of anticipating future settings in which the pupils will need to function and determining which specific skills they will require in those settings. These considerations are critical because children who function in the range of severe and profound retardation have difficulties with the acquisition, maintenance, and generalization of learning, and therefore they do not have time to learn skills that will not prepare them directly for independent functioning.

Toward this end, Brown, Nietupski, and Hamre-Nietupski (1976) have proposed that teachers apply the "criterion of ultimate functioning" when selecting instructional goals. This guideline means that instructional settings should have the same demand characteristics as the "real" environment; that is, pupils should learn skills that they actually need to perform. Instructional settings should not involve simulation unless it has been validated empirically as an effective means of instruction for this population of pupils. Additionally, instructional goals should be functional and age appropriate. Several guidelines can serve to highlight the application of the "criterion of ultimate functioning" in assessment.

Conditions of Instruction.   The conditions under which a pupil can perform a behavior should be assessed in the same way they must be performed. Borrowing an example provided by Certo (1983), consider a pupil who was taught to perform janitorial or cleaning work in a simulated setting. In simulation, he or she learned to approach sweeping by moving a set of classroom furniture to one side of the room and then sweeping the vacated space. Once in the actual setting, the teacher found that space constraints did not permit moving furniture. Clearly, a direct assessment of the pupil's performance of the skill in the real-life environment would have been a more efficient approach to designing instruction.

Selection of Skills.   The selection of skills and materials should be guided by the student's age and developmental level. For example, leisure activities assessed should reflect a pupil's age and developmental level. One way to do this is to perform a content analysis of age-appropriate leisure skills and select those skills for which (a) the pupil knows the basic components, (b) the pupil could be taught the basic components, or (c) the pupil could learn suitable functional alternatives (Williams and Fox, 1977) for components he or she cannot perform. An example of this type of content analysis is found in a leisure skills curriculum by Wehman and Schleien (1979), in which each skill is analyzed according to its cognitive, motor, and behavioral components.

Generalization.   The degree to which a pupil can generalize learning from one situation to another must be assessed. One of the typical characteristics of severely and profoundly retarded pupils is that they do not generalize learning spontaneously. If they learn to drink from one glass, they may not know how to drink from others. If they can put on a shirt at school, they may not know how to put on a shirt at home. In fact, their performance is remarkably inflexible. One of the assumptions underlying many traditional assessment procedures, especially norm-referenced assessments, is that it is assumed that the pupil can perform the skills passed in the test in other situations that were not tested. We cannot make this assumption with severely and profoundly retarded learners; very little information about them can be derived from presentation of one or two trials on a given task. We cannot predict from a brief sample of behavior with a severely or profoundly handicapped pupil in the same way that we can with someone who is less handicapped.

While the "criterion of ultimate functioning" serves as a valuable guideline, it should not be carried to the extreme of denying the pupil activities that are at a manageable level of conceptual difficulty simply because most of the materials that are readily available for that activity are not age appropriate. It is imperative that the teacher assess the type of activity in which the pupil seems most ready to engage and translate that activity into one that is more appropriate. For example, a fifteen-year-old pupil may enjoy playing with wind-up toys. A translation of that skill would be to assess whether he or she can turn on televisions, radios, and cassette players, objects at the same level of conceptual ability that are more age appropriate.

One difficulty in applying the "criterion of ultimate functioning" in assessment is determining the real-life settings that will be available to the pupil in the future. These settings will probably change by the time today's pupils are adults. Considering current trends, we must assume that severely and profoundly handicapped pupils will participate and be welcome in all public settings in their communities in coming years. Consequently, our assessments must be designed to assess the ability of the pupil to function in the settings of the future.

Implications of Multiple Handicaps for Assessment

It was noted in the definitions and descriptions of severely and profoundly handicapped pupils that one sees a high incidence of multiple handicaps among them, and that the interactions among specific disabilities are likely to be complex. The term "interaction" is used to describe the effects of a combination of handicaps not likely to be simply additive in nature, particularly if, as is highly probable among severely and profoundly handicapped persons, those disabilities were present from birth or a very early age. Almost all standardized assessment procedures are based on the assumption that the person performing has no significant sensory or physical impairments.

There are, of course, some instruments that have been specifically developed and normed on persons with a given disability. These include the Hayes adaptation of the Binet scales (Hayes, 1943; Davis, 1980), the Maxfield-Bucholz (1958) adaptation for blind persons of the Vineland Social Maturity Scales, and the Hiskey Scales (1966) for deaf persons. Each of these scales has been developed on the premise that one can analyze the performance demands of existing tests and make adaptations so that persons with a given disability are taken into account. While the concept is easier in principle than practice, the instruments cited have been demonstrated to have reasonable reliability and validity, and the normative frame of reference for the individual case is based on other persons with the same handicapping condition. Useful reviews of these instruments may be found in Sabatino and Miller (1979).

Adapting Assessment Procedures.   There is a tradition almost as old as the testing movement itself that recognizes the limitations of testing persons with specific sensory or physical disabilities for intellectual potential. Individual clinicians using adapted instruments over a period of years will develop some degree of accuracy in making relative judgments about individual cases. Some of the factors that are likely to have an impact on their judgments are the pupil's age at the onset of the disability and his or her experiential background. Still, an experienced and wise clinician will recognize that it is difficult to know the full impact and limitations a disability imposes on the ability to learn. When there are multiple disabilities, the tendency is to try to look at the impact of each disability in isolation. The view that the impact of each is isolated is ludicrous, particularly in the face of much evidence that development is integrated and organized across developmental domains (Sroufe, 1979). For example, our perception of spatial relationships is based, at least in part, on a foundation of multiple opportunities to view the same object from different perspectives. Our development of language comprehension is partly built on opportunities to see, hear, and touch materials in our environment. Our understanding of physical causality appears to be built on opportunities to manipulate materials actively. Analysis of almost any skill called for in independent daily living will reveal that its performance is dependent on the integration of multiple sources of information. This point must be considered in any assessment and instructional effort with severely and profoundly handicapped persons. Impairments in the ability to manipulate and to observe the effects of those manipulations are profound in their combined effects on development. (Additional information on adapting assessment instruments and procedures to meet the performance requirements of multiply handicapped young children was provided in Chapter 5.)

Evaluating Underlying Abilities.   Assessment approaches used with multiply handicapped persons should be designed to evaluate their underlying abilities despite the presence of specific disabilities, an approach advocated by Haeussermann (1958) in her book *The Developmental Potential of Preschool Children*. Briefly, she looks at the conceptual requirements of a typical task used in assessment; then the actual task requirements are modified to assess the supports needed for successful performance by a child with a given disability or disabilities. Types of modification include adaptations in stimuli, such as an increase in size or the use of concrete rather than abstract materials, and adaptations in response modality, such as pointing with one's hand or "eye pointing" rather than verbal expression.

Of central importance in this approach is an analysis of the conceptual requirements of a task (level of classification, memory, discrimination of likeness and differences, seriation, etc.). The manner in which the understanding of a basic concept is demonstrated, that is, the actual physical response, will be determined by the person's degree of physical impairment, but the physical response is not a critical indicator of the pupil's conceptual understanding of the task. Some additional examples of this approach to assessment have been described (Robinson and Robinson, 1978, 1983; Robinson and Fieber, in press; Krenzer, 1980).

Other areas of assessment can be approached in the same manner. In the development of nonoral communication, a number of centers are working on micro-computer-based assessment techniques for use with the physically disabled person. The premise of this approach is similar to that of the adapted cognitive assessments; that is, the same function (communication) can take place in different forms (verbal, sign language, communication boards, electronic communication devices). Assessment of a pupil's ability to perform a function should be designed to accept whatever form of response the pupil is capable of performing.

A Multidisciplinary versus an Interdisciplinary Approach. Throughout this book, the term "multidisciplinary" has been used to describe the team of professionals working in concert to meet the needs of developmentally disabled pupils. Fewell and Cone (1983) make the distinction, as have others before them, between an interdisciplinary and a multidisciplinary approach. The advantage of an interdisciplinary approach is the emphasis it places on *integration* of the information each discipline brings to the development of an IEP. Information about and implications of the pupil's level of functioning in the various domains (gross and fine motor development, communication, cognition, and social maturity) are shared among the team members.

The high incidence of multiple handicaps among severely and profoundly handicapped pupils would seem to indicate that their educational needs will best be met by an interdisciplinary approach. Decisions regarding priorities among objectives are made on the basis of the collected information and the needs of the pupil as a person, the goal for whom should be the maximum possible independence in functioning.

The strength of an interdisciplinary model, if it is actually implemented, is that it permits the team members to be sufficiently informed about the goals and techniques of each others' disciplines so that they will be able to identify ways of integrating daily instructional activities to maximize instructional efficiency. Thus, for example, fine motor goals will be integrated into cognitive tasks; the development of a communication board will be a collaborative effort, not just the task of the speech pathologist. Everyone on the team will be knowledgeable about the pupil's likes and dislikes and will take them into consideration in planning the instructional program. One way to make this determination would be to have a learner preference inventory completed prior to or early in an intervention program, as discussed in Chapters 2 and 8.

In many settings, the differences between multidisciplinary and interdisciplinary team functions are negligible. The key to determining what kind of team is operating or available is to examine its specific functions and services; the name alone may prove misleading.

Types of Assessment Procedures

There is a variety of types of assessments available to evaluate the performance of severely and profoundly handicapped pupils. Different types are designed for different purposes, such as monitoring a child's progress, selecting goals to be taught, and evaluating the effectiveness of programs. A major difference among assessments is the selection of items that are included (Popham, 1978). Items may be more or less directly relevant to instructional programming; or an assessment may include a set of items that sample an area of instructional interest more or less completely.

According to Popham, assessment tools created for one purpose often cannot satisfactorily be used directly for another. Therefore, it is important to consider the purpose for conducting an assessment before selecting assessment tools and interpreting their results. In general, the purpose of psychoeducational assessment is to plan and monitor a pupil's progress. Thus, it is important to select tools that enable the teacher to understand how well a pupil comprehends a unit of learning. Tests designed for other purposes may not include a sampling of items appropriate for planning instruction and must be used with care.

Norm-Referenced Assessment

Norm-referenced devices are the most widely used tools in educational assessment for the majority of special education pupils. If appropriately constructed, they permit comparison of a given individual's performance with that of a normative group. (The process of establishing a normative sample was described in Chapter 3.) Such a comparison, however, is irrelevant to the assessment of skills and instruction of pupils who are severely or profoundly handicapped. The primary limitation on the use of normed instruments for comparative and predictive purposes is that it is not possible with this population to meet the assumptions necessary to allow a valid inferential comparison. The practical reason for not using these instruments relates to their lack of utility in informing the instructional process in many instances.

Fewell and Cone (1983) point out that, although the use of normed assessments has been extensively criticized, most states rely on them as the basis for entry into special education. The requirement for using such an assessment process with severely and profoundly handicapped persons is gratuitous, and it is even potentially damaging for several reasons: The examiner is placed in the untenable position of having to administer an assessment under invalid circumstances in order to provide the pupil with access to special services. Administration of the normed instrument in the standardized manner may damage the examiner's credibility with the people closest to the pupil, the parents and teachers. Even if the content of the assessment seems relevant to the pupil's educational needs, it is likely that the circumstances under which it is administered (stimuli, response time, response mode, etc.) will not be reasonable if the pupil has sensory or physical handicaps (Robinson and Fieber, in press).

Although we are arguing for caution in the interpretation of norm-referenced instruments, most pupils will have been administered such instruments during the initial referral process and at systematic intervals thereafter. Performance on such an instrument may be used by the teacher as a source of hypotheses regarding the pupil's potential strengths and weaknesses. These hypotheses can then serve as the basis for further testing. For example, a pupil may have failed many items on a cognitive assessment that entail the use of fine motor skills. In this event, the teacher would want to assess his or her fine motor abilities.

Criterion-Referenced Assessment

Perhaps the most valuable type of assessment for use with severely and profoundly handicapped pupils is the criterion-referenced test. The purpose of such tests is to "compare a pupil's performance to a specified level of mastery or achievement" (McLaughlin and Lewis, 1981, p. 16). This basis of comparison is a decided advantage for severely and profoundly handicapped pupils who are learning skills not part of traditional curricula. Criterion-referenced assessments can be used in multiple ways, two of which are of concern to the teacher of severely and profoundly handicapped pupils.

First, a pupil's performance can be compared to a criterion that the teacher has determined indicates competence. One way to set performance criteria is to apply the "criterion of ultimate functioning." For example, the teacher may determine that the pupil should be able to demonstrate specific skills in the swimming pool in order to be able to use a community recreation center.

Second, with criterion-referenced measurement a teacher can judge a pupil's progress over time by evaluating changes in skill acquisition, dependence on prosthetic devices, and dependence on instructional cues, among other variables. For example, a change from walking down the hall trailing the wall to walking without trailing could be documented.

General Performance Domains. When using criterion-referenced assessments, it is important to consider the overall validity and reliability of different tests. Problems with validity may occur when a test does not include an adequate number of items to cover the range of skills a pupil should demonstrate in an area. Problems with reliability may occur when the individual's performance is highly variable. In this case, the pupil's performance may vary on different days of testing.

It is also possible that test items may be written unclearly or that the criterion level of performance is not described adequately. In these cases, different testers may judge the pupil's performance to be at different levels.

When using a tool with specific domains, the teacher should be able to interpret results fairly directly. However, when using a tool with more general domains (e.g., motor), he or she will need to determine what the specific domains are (e.g., basic reflexes, head control, rolling, sitting, walking) and to classify the items according to the subdomains they represent. Unless a teacher takes the time to conceptualize the test items in this way, he or she may be inclined to teach "splinter skills" without relating them to the total skill sequence they represent. This helps a teacher to understand why he or she should teach a particular skill rather than merely teaching it because the pupil got a minus score in it during assessment. For example, in a gross motor assessment, the skill of pulling oneself to stand using furniture or similar objects may be conceptualized as a step in learning to walk. Once the value of this item has been determined, the teacher will probably realize that it is an important skill to teach. However, consider the pupil who failed an item of dressing up in adult clothes. This item will probably be considered an example of representational play. Is it a valuable skill for the pupil to learn? Considering the "criterion of ultimate functioning," the teacher may well decide that it is not a valuable skill to teach even if the pupil failed the item on the assessment. If the pupil would benefit by experience with learning representational play skills, more appropriate instances can be selected.

Curriculum-Referenced Assessment

Curriculum-referenced assessments are very similar to criterion-referenced instruments; in fact, some consider them to be a subset of the latter. The major distinction between the two is that curriculum-referenced instruments are intended for direct translation into curriculum objectives, and one should be able to assume that the sequences of items they contain are valid for instruction. Criterion-referenced instruments, by contrast, may or may not be intended for direct translation into objectives, and the sequences they present are not necessarily ordinal. Aside from this distinction, the information presented about criterion-referenced instruments holds for curriculum-referenced instruments as well.

Direct Observation of Behavior

Besides employing typical methods of assessment, the teacher of severely and profoundly handicapped pupils should be able to design and use formats for direct observation. This skill is especially critical for the teacher of severely and profoundly handicapped pupils because of the paucity of well-designed assessments for this population. Observational systems can be designed to gather a variety of types of information. A teacher may wish to record what behaviors are antecedents to tantrums or the types of communication, such as gestures or changes in activity level, a pupil uses to obtain attention or to indicate a desire to stop an activity. The skills and strategies of direct observation of behavior described in Chapters 2 and 8 are applicable here as well.

Direct observation is most useful when several types of information are recorded. First, the exact behavior of the pupil should be described. Second, the conditions under which the behavior is performed should be noted. As is mentioned in the discussion of generalization, the behavior of severely and profoundly handicapped pupils may vary from one situation to another. The situational differences that cause different behavior may be very slight. Consequently, if one is relying on systematic direct observation of behavior as an assessment strategy, it will be necessary to be very precise in the specification of the environmental conditions, the directions given (antecedent events), and the type of consequences used.

Population-Specific Problems.   In working with pupils who are severely or profoundly handicapped, the strategy of direct observation may be used in conjunction with other tools such as curriculum-referenced assessments. For example, a curriculum-referenced assessment may have been chosen for use with a class because it is applicable in its present form to the majority of the pupils. However, some pupils in the class may have specific physical disabilities that require modification in the tool. It is at this point that the teacher will need to utilize the specific skills of direct observation to modify the assessment in order to make it applicable to all.

In other cases, an individual pupil's combination of disabilities may be such that there are no other appropriate assessment strategies. Often in these circumstances, direct observation cannot be used as a primary or exclusive strategy because it may be too time consuming for a teacher since it is so highly individualized. The highly individualized characteristic makes it less suitable for overall program evaluation, since it lacks the basis for comparison across pupils.

Mechanical Recording of Responses.   Mechanical recording of responses entails the use of equipment, such as a microcomputer, that can be designed to record a pupil's responses automatically. For example, a toy to be manipulated, which is connected to the input channel of a microcomputer, may be placed before a pupil. Each time he or she interacts with the toy, the computer receives a signal and records the interaction. This process can also be designed as a system of "dynamic assessment," in which the pupil's ability to learn to perform the task presented can be determined by the amount of time or number of trials required to perform it appropriately.

At this time, use of microcomputers is not a very practical classroom strategy because their application has not been developed sufficiently. The availability of effective, inexpensive hardware and software is, however, increasing daily, and computer literacy is becoming a requirement for educators at all levels. Although pupils' access to much of the current technology requires preacademic readiness skills, the availability of instrumentation to permit handicapped persons whose cognitive level is less than that of a two-year-old to control devices in their environments is increasing (Brinker and Lewis, 1983; Burkhardt, 1982; Rosenberg and Robinson, 1983).

The primary emphasis in the development of these approaches at the sensorimotor level has been to give pupils, especially physically disabled pupils, increased control over their environment and also preparatory experience for the use of communication devices. The addition of equipment that will record responses and consequences greatly increases the utility of such an approach. The greatest potential of this approach is that it allows for productive educational time for the pupil without requiring the teacher's individual attention. However, the danger in giving a pupil a means of controlling environmental events without a system for monitoring whether the equipment is functional is inconsistency in information feedback, which can have overall negative effects on performance. Providing a pupil with mechanical devices without keeping them in good working order is worse than no instruction at all.

Selection of Assessment Instruments

It should be apparent that the most useful assessment for designing instructional programs and monitoring individual and group progress with severely and profoundly handicapped pupils is the use of a criterion-referenced approach. The emphasis is on skills required in age-appropriate community environments in which the pupil will function.

In selecting instruments, there are several issues which the teacher should consider (Fieber and Robinson, 1982). Instruments reflect the premises of the people who develop them. Their discipline, theory, and concepts of development may or may not be valid and applicable across situations, so the assumptions they make should be explicitly stated.

An instrument's appropriateness is also affected by the population for which it was developed. For example, the older severely or profoundly handicapped pupil requires more emphasis on self-help and daily living skills in his or her assessment and curriculum than does a severely or profoundly handicapped infant. Look for a statement regarding the population for whom the authors feel the instrument is appropriate. Additional characteristics that should be described for the population are the presence and type of vision, hearing, and motor handicaps and what, if any, accommodations are made for the impact of these handicaps on the validity of the assessment. For example, if the instrument is described as appropriate for severely and profoundly handicapped pupils who have significant vision impairments, it should include modifications of assessment procedures and interpretations that take vision impairment into account. This should include variations in the order of acquisition of typical milestones of behavior, variations or discrepancies in the age or stage at which they appear, and a discussion of which behaviors commonly included in checklists are inappropriate criteria and suggested substitutes.

In the area of communication, any instrument for severely and profoundly handicapped persons should include assessment of prelinguistic communication behaviors and appropriate alternative modes of communication. Instruments designed to assess program effectiveness with respect to motor development should reflect goals such as the containment of deformity, the maintenance of mobility, and respiratory and circulatory functioning, in addition to developmental goals.

Although there are a number of instruments available, none, in our opinion, adequately meets all the needs of professionals working with severely and profoundly handicapped pupils. Whether the purpose is diagnostic or prescriptive assessment or program evaluation, the population of severely and profoundly handicapped pupils is an extremely complex one, and instrument development is a tremendous challenge. In fact, it may be argued that no assessment tool could be designed to evaluate severely and profoundly handicapped pupils adequately without significant modification of procedures. Because of the unique needs of each pupil, tools selected for use with different pupils may vary according to the areas to be assessed, the type of data obtained (e.g., norm referenced, criterion referenced), and the kinds of procedures that must be implemented to obtain valid results. Time spent searching for a perfect tool may be time poorly spent. Time might be better allocated to developing assessment strategies that guide the wise selection, implementation, and interpretation of assessment tools. One such system designed for use with multiply and severely and profoundly handicapped pupils has been developed by Hupp and Donofrio (1983).

Currently Available Instruments

The purpose of the following section is to acquaint you with a few of the currently available instruments. They are reviewed with reference to the stated selection criteria (Fieber and Robinson, 1982). The instruments have been selected as illustrative of what is currently available. These reviews are adapted from Seitel, Jung, and Fieber (1982).

Adaptive Performance Instrument–Experimental Edition, 1980 (Department of Special Education, College of Education, University of Idaho, Moscow, Idaho [D. Gentry]). The API was developed by a group of special educators, the Consortium on Adaptive Performance Evaluation. It is an evaluation tool for assessing the functioning of children developmentally between birth and two years of age and is most appropriate for use with individuals under the chronological age of nine. It is particularly valuable with children who exhibit sensory and/or motoric handicaps and is appropriate for children who are severely or profoundly handicapped. Over seven hundred skills in the domains of reflexes and reactions, gross and fine motor, sensorimotor, socialization, and communication are assessed utilizing small increments of behaviors. Targets are organized as equivalent behaviors, hierarchical behaviors, task-analyzed behaviors, or single behaviors. Refer to Figure 9–1 for a sample of the motor area of the API.

The API may be administered by classroom teachers, therapists, and psychologists. Observation, direct testing, and report are the assessment strategies utilized. The majority of the behaviors included can be assessed through observation in the

Figure 9–1

Adaptive Performance Instrument (API) Domains, Strands, and Targets

. . . .

Area: Motor

Domain: Fine motor

Strand: Reach for objects

1. Child fully extends the a) right arm in all directions and b) left arm in all directions.
2. Child extends the arm(s) toward an object without making contact with the object using a) both arms together, b) right arm, and c) left arm.
3. Child extends the arm(s) and makes contact with an object using a) both arms together, b) right arm, and c) left arm.
4. Without locomotion, the child contacts objects that are not contacting the body.

Strand: Voluntary grasp

1. Child voluntarily grasps a cylindrical object that is too large for the fingers to wrap around completely using a) the right hand and b) the left hand.
2. Child voluntarily grasps a thin cylindrical object with the right hand using a) ulnar-palmar grasp, b) radial-palmar grasp, c) radial-digital grasp, d) inferior pincer grasp, and e) superior pincer grasp.
3. Child voluntarily grasps a thin cylindrical object with the left hand using a) ulnar-palmar grasp, b) radial-palmar grasp, c) radial-digital grasp, d) inferior pincer grasp, and e) superior pincer grasp.
4. Child voluntarily grasps a hand-sized object with the right hand using a) ulnar-palmar grasp, b) radial-palmar grasp, c) radial-digital grasp, d) inferior pincer grasp, and e) superior pincer grasp.
5. Child voluntarily grasps a hand-sized object with the left hand using a) ulnar-palmar grasp, b) radial-palmar grasp, c) radial-digital grasp, d) inferior pincer grasp, and e) superior pincer grasp.
6. Child voluntarily grasps a pellet-sized object with the right hand using a) ulnar-palmar grasp, b) radial-palmar grasp, c) radial-digital grasp, d) inferior pincer grasp, and e) superior pincer grasp.
7. Child voluntarily grasps a pellet-sized object with the left hand using a) ulnar-palmar grasp, b) radial-palmar grasp, c) radial-digital grasp, d) inferior pincer grasp, and e) superior pincer grasp.
8. Child obtains objects of various sizes that are within reach.

. . . .

natural environment. The API is program oriented in that it assesses educationally relevant behaviors.

Child performance data can be analyzed by completing a form that summarizes an individual child's performance across all critical skills. Computer analysis is also available from the University of Idaho. Because of the complexity of the instrument, the examiner should receive training before conducting assessments. The API is currently being field tested, and revisions may follow. This instrument reflects an

innovative approach to devising an assessment model based on the combined expertise of professionals from diverse sites and professional roles.

An important advantage of the API is the process it advocates for adapting
assessment procedures throughout the instrument for children with motoric
and/or sensory handicaps. This feature of the design permits a more comprehensive and accurate evaluation. Consistency of performance is also considered in
rating each target; thus information relevant to programming for skill generalization may be obtained. The data-collection system is set up to permit the compilation of results across children and across programs, yielding information pertinent
to the development and refinement of the instrument as well as to the monitoring
of individual children's progress (Anderson, 1982).

Callier-Azusa Scale (R. Stillman [Ed.], 1978). This instrument is a developmental scale specifically designed to aid in the assessment of deaf-blind and severely and profoundly handicapped children. It is particularly comprehensive at
early developmental levels. The scale is not intended as a curriculum-referenced
tool; its stated purpose is to provide assessment information necessary to synthesize developmentally appropriate activities for a child. Scale items are not meant
to be translated directly into curriculum objectives. In addition to being used in
assessment, the scale may be employed to evaluate an individual child's developmental progress or to compare children in a program. Because the scale has been
revised several times, it is important to identify the edition used for pre- and posttest measures and to check item numbers between editions.

The scale includes 18 subscales in five domains: Motor Development, Perceptual Development, Daily Living Skills, Cognitive Communication, and Social Development. Cognitive tasks include items at the sensorimotor and preoperational
levels. Communication includes some prelinguistic forms such as understanding
tactually presented signals, anticipating the next movement in a routine sequence,
and the use of reaching, pointing, and gesturing as communication strategies. Social development includes items such as the differentiation of familiar and unfamiliar adults and gaining, maintaining, or seeking an interaction. Examples are
given for many items based on behaviors that have been observed in deaf-blind
children functioning at a given level. These behavioral examples take into account
the sensory, motor, language, and social deficits typically found in deaf-blind and
severely and profoundly handicapped children, which may differ from behaviors
observed among normal children.

The Callier-Azusa scale must be administered by individuals familiar with the
pupil's behavior, and it is suggested that he or she be observed for at least two
weeks before the scale is used. The scale was designed to be used in classroom
settings for the observation of typical spontaneous behaviors or behaviors in familiar contexts. The most accurate results are obtained if several individuals who
have close contact with the pupil (teachers, aides, parents, specialists) evaluate the
child on a consensus basis. A step on a subscale is credited only when behaviors
described within that step are integrated components of the pupil's behavioral repertoire, appearing spontaneously and appropriately generalized. The teacher

should note behaviors that are emerging and thus occur only after prompting or in specific situations.

A summary score sheet provides age equivalencies for items, which are based on the normal child-development literature. These are intended only as a rough means of comparing functioning in different areas of behavior. It is important to note the sequence in which behaviors occur. The score sheet provides a way to look at a pupil's progress on subsequent reassessment. Reliability and validity data are available from the editor.

Although this instrument would provide a useful "umbrella" assessment, teachers and therapists will want to supplement it with more detailed assessment in specific areas — for example, oral-motor problems, functional vision, and hearing. In the cognitive section, sensorimotor items derived from the various subscales of the Ûzgiris-Hunt Ordinal Scales (1975) are meshed into one sequence, and users are advised to look at each subscale area separately. Further information in the test manual on adapting tasks for motor-handicapped pupils would be helpful. When a person is severely visually impaired or blind, certain cognitive and motor behaviors that occur concurrently in developmental sequence among normal persons do not always develop at the same time. Thus when one assesses a blind pupil, one needs to be aware of such possible variations in sequence and possible selective delays. For example, cognitive performances regarding spatial relationships and categorization may be delayed as much as two years in blind children of normal intelligence as compared to sighted children.

This assessment is one of the best choices currently available for multihandicapped children who are severely or profoundly handicapped. Its successful use in the development of curricula will require expertise with deaf-blind and other sensory-impaired children together with adequate support from specialists in the fields of vision, hearing, deaf-blind, and motor handicaps (Fieber, 1982).

Developmental Programming for Infants and Young Children (D. S. Schafer and M. S. Moersch, 1977). This instrument consists of a three-volume assessment tool and guide and was designed to be used by multidisciplinary teams, including parents, with combined skills in motor, language, and cognitive development. A major goal of the instrument is to provide a link between assessment and programming for infants and children functioning on developmental levels from birth to 36 months. The tool was developed in the context of an early intervention program and is most appropriately used with children who are chronologically six years of age and younger.

Part 1 is a manual that explains a step-by-step transition from assessment to curriculum; that is, interpreting assessment findings, developing and writing behavioral objectives, and translating these objectives into activities. The manual provides very complete instructions for using the materials and points out some important considerations in interpreting the assessment findings and using the activities.

Part 2 is a criterion-referenced instrument consisting of six scales that provide developmental norms in the perceptual/fine motor, cognitive, language, social-emotional, self-care, and gross motor development areas. The 274 items, which are either original or taken from other well-known tests, yield a comprehensive profile of developmental functioning by identifying specific strengths and weaknesses in the pupil's performance. A developmental age equivalent in each area may be derived, but the method for determining it is somewhat complicated, and the authors caution that this derivation can result in the loss of useful information about a child's performance. Scoring on this instrument is pass (P); fail (F); pass-fail (P-F), to denote emerging skills; and omission (O), to denote a task that may be omitted because of a handicapping condition. Scores in each domain are transferred to a profile graph that visually depicts the child's performance in each of the six function areas.

Part 3 provides ideas for implementing specific behavioral objectives. The activities are grouped into the six areas tested in Part 2. Within each developmental range, there is a set of short-term goals, with suggested activities to assist in achieving each. Moreover, specific adaptations are suggested for three categories of handicapped children (visually impaired, hearing impaired, and motorically involved), and cautions are given to the user regarding activities that are not appropriate for children with these specific handicaps.

This instrument is meant to supplement, not replace, standardized psychological, motor, and language evaluation data. The authors caution that it is not intended for diagnosing handicaps, nor for predicting future development. The instrument has several advantages over many other criterion-based devices currently available: in addition to being comprehensive and well based on current developmental theory in motor, cognitive, and social domains, it emphasizes the generalization of concepts and developmental processes rather than training isolated (i.e., splinter) skills. Alternative assessment and intervention strategies for infants with various handicapping conditions are also provided, and the suggestions for working with motorically impaired children are particularly helpful. The ideas for adapting activities for visually impaired children are somewhat weaker and tend to oversimplify issues that need to be taken into consideration (Rose, 1982).

Analysis of Skills Assessed

While the instruments described above will assist a teacher in determining skills that should be assessed, he or she will have to decide whether specific skills that were failed should be taught and how to teach them. Educators of severely and profoundly handicapped pupils may vary somewhat in the terminology they use, but there is a considerable degree of consensus in the field regarding the critical areas of curriculum content. Certo (1983), for example, suggests that instructional content should be referenced against:

> functional, age-appropriate skills required for performance in integrated environments selected from at least the following domains: domestic living, vocational, stores/services, transportation, mobility, and leisure (p. 13).

The emphasis on functional, age-appropriate skills and the demands of community settings as the framework are all consistently advocated by educators of the severely and profoundly handicapped (Bricker, Macke, Levin, and Simmons, 1982; Brown et al., 1976; White, 1980). Instructional content and consequently the skills to be evaluated as part of the educational assessment process should be developed from the perspective of those criteria. In addition, we suggest that analysis of skills or tasks be accomplished with reference to the level of cognitive development implicit in performance of the task. Thus a cognitive model is one in which information from theories or from a framework of cognitive development is used as the basis for an analysis of the component skills of a specific task.

Application of a Cognitive Model

It is possible that some may interpret and possibly dismiss an analysis of tasks by cognitive level on the basis that it represents the developmental model. Certo (1983) and Brown, Branston, Hamre-Nietupski, Pumpian, Certo, and Grunewald (1979) appropriately challenge much that has been done in the name of the developmental model as the basis for selecting instructional content for severely and profoundly handicapped pupils. Specifically, they object to the frequent use of materials such as infant and toddler toys in settings that use developmental checklists as the reference basis for their curricula. Such an objection is well founded: the use of infant materials by older severely and profoundly handicapped persons is stigmatizing and is not instructionally sound. It is essential, however, to distinguish the useful instructional information that may be derived from the documentation of the typical course of development from inappropriate practices, such as those cited by Certo (1983), that have been carried out in the name of the developmental model. The metaphorical admonition not to "throw the baby out with the bathwater" seems an appropriate message to those who would ignore the benefits of considering normal developmental sequences when designing instruction. It is important that the teacher develop good problem-solving skills in order to combine the benefits of different approaches to the selection of instructional content.

Determining Conceptual Level.   Observation is the best basis on which to determine the nature of relationships among development in different functional domains of behavior. We have found a Piagetian framework useful in much of our work with severely and profoundly handicapped pupils. However, the use of a developmental framework at a descriptive level does not require the acceptance of any of the assumptions of that framework, whether it be Piagetian, Gesellian, or any other. Rather, a developmental framework provides a validated sequence of skills that can indicate how a pupil functions and helps us to predict related behaviors.

For example, a term such as "object permanence" can serve as a form of shorthand: it tells us that a given individual will demonstrate the behavior of looking for someone or something with which he has lost sensory contact. The term in and of itself does not say all that we need to know about that person's searching behavior, but the added qualifier of sensorimotor stage level will give considerable additional information. If the level is Stage Four, for instance, we know that a person will probably search only for an object or person with whom he or she has just lost contact seconds before, and that he or she will probably only search in one location. If the person is at Stage Six, we know he or she can probably search through several locations.

Why should we even be concerned with object permanence? It is a conceptual foundation for many activities of daily living. Object permanence is not operationalized simply as search behavior; it is also implicit in the recognition that object properties serve particular functions. It underlies our day-to-day confidence in the predictability and dependability of environmental events. We usually look for any object that we need in the place where we last remember having it; we approach a sink and turn a faucet in the expectation that water will come out. If we are teaching someone with a severe or profound learning handicap to use public facilities to wash his or her hands, we include experience with turning taps on at the beginning and off at the end of the sequence as part of the task. If the person turns a faucet and nothing comes out, we may not expect him or her to have a strategy for finding a different source of water, such as another sink, but we do not expect him or her to engage in the remainder of the hand-washing routine if there is no water.

Whether one wishes to use the term "object permanence" or "causality," or any other "cognitive" term, in one's analysis of skills required in a given task, unifying requirements underlie performance in different situations. Knowledge of the conceptual level implicit in a given person's performance in one situation will help one analyze the level of contextual support necessary to support performance in another situation. Returning to the hand-washing example, if the person's level of object permanence is Stage Four, which is shorthand for, "will engage in search behavior only for an object that has been gone momentarily," we would not expect any evidence of spontaneous searching for another source of water. However, if the person had demonstrated Stage-Six behavior (systematic search for an invisibly displaced object) in another situation, we would expect the person to try another tap. If he or she did not do so spontaneously, we would attempt to develop such behavior through a systematic instructional process.

Developing Task Analyses of Conceptual Level. There are two major types of task analyses that are used to specify task components: procedural task analysis and hierarchical task analysis (Dick and Carey, 1978). Both types can be used to assess pupils' skill levels. Procedural analyses entail determining the sequence of steps that must be performed to complete a behavior. For example, to open a door with a doorknob, a pupil would locate the knob, extend his or her hand to the knob, grasp the knob, turn the knob, and pull or push the door open. Hierarchical task analyses, by contrast, entail determining a sequence of skills to be learned successively in order to attain a goal. For example, to learn how to walk, a pupil might learn the following skills: pull to stand, cruise along furniture, walk with assistance from an adult for balance, walk independently. Note that hierarchical task analyses are the basis for many curricula.

For each of these procedures, a teacher can incorporate information about pupils' conceptual skills. In a procedural analysis, the level of cognitive ability required to perform the steps can be noted. For example, if a pupil demonstrated the ability to look at an object in the distance, to roll to it, and to obtain it, the teacher could infer that the pupil had a certain level of means-ends cognitive abilities.

Hierarchical task analyses can be designed to reflect the acquisition of skills at successively higher cognitive levels. For example, a pupil could first be taught to engage in a leisure activity when all the materials were visible. Later, he or she could be asked to locate and gather the materials before engaging in the activity. This level of performance represents more sophisticated problem solving because the materials are not directly visible and the pupil must move about the environment to get them. As another example, a task seemingly as simple as opening a door represents different levels of causality performance. A pupil could open a swinging door by pushing, thus using a simple level of causality; whereas a door with a knob requires using a sequence of steps that must be done in the proper order for successful task completion, thus requiring a higher level of causality.

Analyses of Conceptual Level of Sorting Skills. The relevance of a cognitive organizational framework can be exemplified by examining the skill of sorting a group of items into categories. A sorting task can be designed to use any type of material, such as tools (e.g., eating implements), types of clothing, or any type of object. It is a functional skill that is called upon across the life span. The specific behavior identified for the pupil to complete can represent one of numerous levels of cognitive complexity. For example, a predefined classification task is cognitively simpler than a sorting task in which the pupil has to identify the categories and thus define the sort. The level of difficulty of sorting is defined by a host of other dimensions, among them the number of categories, whether all of the objects within a category are identical or simply similar but varied on irrelevant dimensions, whether all the items are in the same location or have to be collected first, whether sorting of the particular material is a daily or a monthly task.

Selection of Materials. While sorting wooden discs of different colors and shapes is a typical preschool activity, this is probably not an appropriate choice of materials for accomplishing an instructional goal of learning to classify objects for any severely or profoundly retarded pupil even if he is of preschool age. The reason the material is said to be less appropriate than, for example, functional materials such as eating implements relates to the issue of the overall deficit in generalization of learning from one situation to another seen among persons who are severely or profoundly retarded. The assumption made in the use of abstract play materials is that the activity of sorting and particularly the ability to define the categories for classification spontaneously is a generalizable skill. The instructional implication of this point is that there is no particular advantage to be obtained from the use of one type of material over another, so long as the person learning to do the sorting can discriminate between or among the categories represented. The assumption of generalizability is not tenable with the severely or profoundly handicapped pupil. Therefore, because classification of a specific set of items is a skill that will be required for a given individual in an environment where he or she spends or should be spending time on a routine basis, the assessment of the ability and instruction on the task should use the material(s) and setting(s) that call for the skill.

Selection of Response. In addition, the manner in which the pupil actually executes the task must be specified. Sensory and physical abilities in particular may affect the responses in the pupil's repertoire. A totally blind pupil will sort objects on the basis of tactile recognition; a physically disabled pupil may need to use jigs or an eye point or to ask for assistance from another person in the physical placement of materials to complete a sort.

Analysis of the cognitive level or implicit conceptual demands of any task will provide the most efficient means for task analysis, whether it be as part of the assessment or of the instructional process (remember that the two processes are argued here to be more appropriately viewed as interactive). Learning theorists agree that instructional process can be made more efficient by planning activities so that tasks with similar demands are presented in such a way that the similarities and differences in their demands are accentuated and made explicit. We believe that the most relevant dimension of analysis of similarities and differences across demands of various tasks is the cognitive demands. The conceptual organization that Piaget offers at the sensorimotor and preoperational levels is especially useful. To reiterate at the risk of belaboring the point, acceptance of the first premise, the utility of an analysis of tasks by conceptual requirements, does not demand acceptance of the Piagetian view as the organizational framework to be used.

Summary

In a recent presentation, Chess (1983) used the metaphor of "different roads to Rome" to make the point that we must recognize the impact specific disabilities can have on developmental progress. This metaphor emphasizes the principal issue that must be recognized in the assessment of severely and profoundly handicapped persons. Although we need to use the content of typical developmental sequences and the functional demands of typical settings in our assessment and instructional approaches to severely and profoundly handicapped persons (i.e., Rome is the goal), we must value the roads taken by these pupils as viable ones even though they are not the roads we have traveled. Thus our assessment efforts must be highly individualized and oriented to process.

Educational assessment of severely and profoundly handicapped pupils presents a challenge to the educator. The multiple handicaps of the typical severely and profoundly handicapped pupil make the use of existing norm-referenced instruments in their present form an untenable practice. Adaptations are always necessary. The skilled use of existing instruments and the ability to make adaptations for the handicaps of the individual pupil are most typically thought of as demanding the skills of an experienced clinical psychoeducator. However, if assessment is to inform the implementation of educational programs, the classroom teacher must be able to make this type of highly skilled observation at the level of the educational setting. A specific purpose of this chapter was to acquaint you with a rationale for a particular approach to assessment, that of a conceptual analysis of task requirements, and to acquaint you also with some of the specific skills you will need in an educational program in which severely and profoundly handicapped pupils are served. A summary of major points covered in this chapter follows.

1. The objectives of this chapter relate to procedures for psychoeducational assessment of the severely or profoundly handicapped learner.
2. Severely and profoundly handicapped pupils are defined on the basis of their functioning levels and of the difficulty in serving them in typical educational settings. They have been served in public educational facilities only since the passage of the "right-to-education" legislation, P.L. 94–142.
3. The primary issue in the assessment and education of the severely or profoundly handicapped pupil is the thoughtful application of the "criterion of ultimate functioning," which has implications for the selection of skills to be taught, the conditions of instruction, and the assessment of the generalizability of the skills assessed and taught.
4. The primary implications of multiple handicaps in this area of assessment are the need to adapt assessment procedures in accordance with the specific disabilities of the pupil and with the form of performance of which the pupil is capable. The need for an integrated, fully interdisciplinary approach is discussed.
5. The benefits and limitations of several assessment procedures were presented. The severe limitations of using norm-referenced assessments with this population were emphasized. The teacher of severely and profoundly handicapped pupils needs skills in the areas of criterion- and curriculum-referenced assessments and in the direct observation and recording of behaviors.
6. The use of task analysis within the framework of a cognitive-developmental model was discussed. Examples of how the cognitive level of a task can form the basis for the most meaningful type of task analysis were included. The issue of use of age-appropriate settings and materials was discussed, and the point was made that a primary emphasis on functional instructional goals does not have to be antagonistic to a cognitive model.

Mastery Review

I. Recall

1. The most frequent characteristic of pupils who are severely and profoundly handicapped is:

   a. undiagnosed sensory handicaps that are severe in degrees.

   b. severe emotional disturbance such as autism.

   c. a measured I.Q. of less than 40.

   d. significant motor impairments with implications for both gross and fine motor development.

2. A functional definition of severely and profoundly handicapped pupils includes which of the following characteristics?

   a. brittle medical existence.

   b. no imitiation skills.

   c. not toilet trained.

   d. all of the above.

3. The emphasis on the development of basic skills as the primary emphasis of educational programs for severely handicapped pupils derives from which of the following of their characteristics?

   a. Severe physical disability.

   b. Uncontrolled seizure disorders.

   c. Intellectual retardation.

   d. Severe visual impairment.

4. The "criterion of ultimate functioning" is:

   a. a strategy for assessing skills of severely and profoundly handicapped persons.

   b. a guideline to be used in the education of severely and profoundly handicapped persons.

   c. a basis for defining students who meet the criteria of severe or profound handicaps.

   d. a strategy for designing instructional environments.

5. Basic skills critical for severely and profoundly handicapped pupils include:

   a. functional reading.

   b. use of a communication system.

   c. self-care skills.

   d. all of the above.

6. Of the following statements regarding norm-referenced assessment procedures, which are most applicable to severely and profoundly handicapped pupils?

   a. Behaviors can be predicted from testing in a representative sample of situations.

   b. The person being assessed is represented in the standardization sample.

   c. Information provided is often not relevant for the instructional process.

   d. All of the above.

7. Which of the following statements regarding adapted testing procedures and their use is inaccurate?

   a. Adapted testing represents an attempt to evaluate underlying abilities.
   b. Adapted testing procedures represent an effort to minimize the impact of a specific disability on an individual's performance.
   c. Reliability and validity of the testing procedure are not important with adapted testing techniques.
   d. Adapted testing may involve altering the presentation of items or modification of the mode of the response.

8. A major reason for using an interdisciplinary approach with severely and profoundly handicapped pupils rather than a multidisciplinary one is that:

   a. the high incidence of multiple handicaps among persons who are severely or profoundly retarded makes either an interdisciplinary or a multidisciplinary approach desirable.
   b. each member of a team can perform the others' functions.
   c. the approach calls for integration of the information each discipline brings to the team.
   d. none of the above.

9. Criterion-referenced assessments can be useful in educating severely and profoundly handicapped persons in which of the following ways?

   a. In setting performance criteria against an ultimate standard.
   b. In setting performance criteria against a relative standard.
   c. In determining progress made.
   d. All of the above.

10. Which of the following is likely to be least important to note in using direct observation of behavior as an assessment strategy with severely or profoundly handicapped students?

    a. The specific location.
    b. Persons present.
    c. Time of day.
    d. The weather.

11. Which of the following statements is not a primary consideration for selecting a tool for use in the design of educational programs for severely and profoundly handicapped persons?

    a. The predictive validity of the instrument.
    b. The assumption underlying the development of the tool.
    c. The population for whom the instrument was developed.
    d. The reliability of the instrument.

12. Which of the following are included in generally accepted guidelines for selecting curricula content for severely and profoundly handicapped pupils?

    a. age appropriate appropriateness of the tasks.
    b. functional utility of the skill.
    c. level of cognitive development required for performance of the tasks.
    d. all of the above.

13. A developmental framework does which of the following?
    a. Helps predict related behaviors.
    b. Can provide information regarding how the student is currently functioning.
    c. Can indicate how uneducable the student is.
    d. Both a and b.

14. Procedural task analysis:
    a. is the basis for many curricula.
    b. involves determining the sequence of steps required to complete a behavior.
    c. involves determining the sequence of skills to be learned successively to attain a goal.
    d. Both a and b.

15. The instructional process can be made more efficient by:
    a. the use of environmental analysis.
    b. the use of a cognitive-developmental model.
    c. presenting tasks so that similarities and differences in demands are accentuated.
    d. all of the above.

II. Comprehension

1. Describe the "criterion of ultimate functioning" and its application to assessment and instructional programming.
2. Discuss the implications of multiple handicaps for assessment and ways to deal with them.
3. Compare the usefulness of norm-referenced, criterion-referenced, and curriculum-referenced assessment with severely and profoundly handicapped pupils.
4. Referring back to your answer for Section II, Question 4, in the previous chapter, discuss the similarities and differences among assessment of pupils with mild handicaps, T.M.H. pupils, and severely and profoundly handicapped pupils.
5. In this chapter, criteria for instructional content and skills to be evaluated were suggested. Describe these criteria and give specific examples of their application.
6. Discuss why an interdisciplinary approach to assessment of severely and profoundly handicapped pupils is generally preferred. Give an example of its use.

III. Application

1. Pick a specific target skill. Task analyze this behavior and tie the steps to cognitive levels. In a two-to-three-page paper, describe how you would teach the skills in the task analysis.
2. Develop an instructional goal for a fictitious severely or profoundly handicapped pupil, applying the "criterion of ultimate functioning" as discussed in this chapter. In a three-to-five-page paper, describe the basis for your selection of this particular skill, how you will assess the instructional conditions, and how you will assess generalization of this skill.

IV. Alternate Task

If none of the Application exercises applies to your setting or curriculum, you can design two exercises of your own. They should demonstrate application of one or more of the principles or concepts described in the preceding chapter. Prior approval of both exercises should be obtained from your course instructor.

V. Answer Key

I.
1. c and d pp. 253–54
2. d p. 254
3. c p. 254, p. 255
4. b p. 255
5. d p. 254, p. 255
6. c pp. 259–60
7. c pp. 256–58
8. c pp. 258–59
9. d p. 260
10. d pp. 261–62
11. a pp. 263–64
12. d pp. 268–69
13. d pp. 269–70
14. b p. 270
15. c p. 271, p. 272

II.
1. pp. 255–56
2. pp. 256–58
3. pp. 259–61
4. p. 255, Chapters 7, 8, 9
5. pp. 268–72
6. pp. 258–59

Chapter 10

Assessment of the Physically Handicapped

Key Terms:

architectural barriers
developmental assessment
fine motor evaluation
gross motor evaluation
interdisciplinary assessment
medical examination
motor testing
multidisciplinary team
nonvocal communication
physically impaired and multiply
  handicapped
positioning
reflex testing
subscale scoring
task-analytic assessment
therapeutic evaluation

Chapter Objectives:

After reading this chapter and completing the Mastery Review, you will be able to:

1. Describe the unique characteristics of pupils who have motor or physical dysfunction that should be considered in the assessment process.
2. Describe the issues related to testing children with motor or physical dysfunction, including the limitations of standardized tests and the advantages of the specialized intelligence tests that have been developed.
3. Discuss issues and concerns related to the use of interdisciplinary team approaches in the assessment process.
4. Identify the unique aspects of assessing children who are physically impaired and multiply handicapped, including gross motor management, developmental evaluation, and task analysis.
5. List and briefly describe the factors to be considered before initiating testing of children with motor or physical dysfunction.
6. Discuss the specialized techniques used in assessing children with motor or physical dysfunction in the academic and behavioral areas, including methods of adapting and modifying the environment, the assessment procedures, and record forms.
7. Describe procedures for assessing motor ability and name at least three motor tests.

The children considered in this chapter are those who are physically or motorically handicapped to such an extent that special education services are required to meet their unique educational needs. These children make up a diverse group with a broad range of disabilities. Each disability presents a unique problem that requires specialized approaches in assessing academic, social, and motor levels of performance and in programming.

The nature of classes for children with motor or physical handicaps has changed rapidly in recent years because of progress in medical science, improved identification techniques, and changing attitudes. Historically, classes for physically handicapped children were composed of those whose primary problems were with ambulation or fine motor manipulation. Assessment procedures were much the same as those used in a class of nonhandicapped children except for the need to evaluate ways to eliminate architectural and equipment barriers that limited or prevented the child's regular classroom participation.

Today, most children placed in classes for the physically handicapped have problems in perception, cognition, and language as well as ambulation and manipulation. Assessment procedures include not only evaluating the classroom for architectural barriers but also identifying and evaluating adjustment and learning problems unique to the physically and motorically handicapped. Most children requiring special education for a physically handicapping condition are multiply handicapped. They have significant problems in related areas such as learning, social, self-help, and communication skills.

Defining the Population and Setting

There are a large range and variety of conditions, ranging from mild to severe, that result in physical or motor dysfunction. Most of them are the results of impairments occurring before, during, or very soon after birth, but physical and motor dysfunction can occur at any time in life. Assessment of children with physical impairments involves evaluating both their educational needs and their related needs, including such factors as medication impact, pain, functioning of orthotic devices, mobility status, and emotional needs. Each of the conditions that result in physical disabilities will be briefly described in this section.

Cerebral Palsy

Cerebral palsy is not one condition but a series of related conditions that frequently involve more than one specific motor disability. The disorder can be narrowly defined as motor disability caused by damage to the brain occurring before, during, or soon after birth. Cruickshank (1976) has described cerebral palsy as a comprehensive term covering a wide range of nonprogressive motor disabilities resulting from brain damage. In addition to motor disability or dysfunction, children with cerebral palsy frequently exhibit neurological, intellectual, and perceptual disorders.

One or more parts of the body can be affected by cerebral palsy, and various terms exist to describe the affected parts. These are: monoplegia, which means that one limb is affected; hemiplegia, which refers to the involvement of one side of the body; triplegia, which means that three limbs are involved; paraplegia, which refers to a condition affecting the legs only; and quadriplegia, which refers to the involvement of all four limbs.

Because cerebral palsy is such a broad category, it is usually described in terms of the type of motor impairment. The four major types of cerebral palsy are spasticity, athetosis, ataxia, and mixed. The first, spasticity, is the largest single type.

Spasticity. The most common type of cerebral palsy is spasticity, which is characterized by hypertonicity, or too much muscle tone. This means that opposing muscle groups receive stimulation from the brain to act at the same time, so that the affected part of the body is moved in a jerky manner. Hemiplegia is the most common type of spasticity.

Like all types of cerebral palsy, spasticity can range from mild to severe. In severe spasticity, the child may have little voluntary movement and may require braces, crutches, a specialized wheelchair, and other adaptive equipment to be able to stand, sit, and walk. In moderate spasticity, the child may walk with a scissoring gait and may hold one arm close to the body with the elbow flexed and the hand in a fist position. Mild spasticity may involve a slightly awkward walking pattern and some loss of fine motor control in one arm or hand. Such a child's spasticity may not be noticed except during close observation of a task such as walking or writing.

Athetosis. The second most common type of cerebral palsy is athetosis, in which the muscle tone is usually normal. The athetosis is seen during voluntary movement, when it is manifested as uncontrollable, jerky, irregular, writhing, and/or twisting movements. Children with athetosis walk in an uncoordinated, stumbling, lurching manner. A child with athetosis is able to eat a sandwich or write a letter, for example, but in doing so makes uncontrollable movements. As fatigue, tension, and effort increase, so do athetotic movements. This may be a particular problem in testing because anxiety about the test may trigger increased athetosis.

Ataxia. A type of cerebral palsy that is much less common than spasticity and athetosis is ataxia, which is characterized by problems in balance during movement and by a lack of muscle coordination. The child with ataxia walks with a high-stepping gait, falls easily, and usually has other gross motor movement problems, particularly in the area of balance.

Mixed. It is often possible to identify distinct types of cerebral palsy, but many individuals are handicapped by mixed types. These may involve, for example, spasticity and athetosis or spasticity and ataxia. Mixed cerebral palsy is more common in severe cases and is frequently associated with such impairments as mental retardation, sensory deficits, language problems, and convulsive disorders. These deficits may, however, accompany any type of cerebral palsy.

Spina Bifida

"Spina bifida" is a general term referring to three conditions: spina bifida occulta, meningocele, and mylomeningocele. All of these conditions are spinal-canal defects caused by the incomplete development of the spine during gestation. Spina bifida occulta is the mildest form of this condition and is not usually accompanied by neurological impairment. Meningocele is the moderate form of the condition and is characterized by a tumorlike sac protruding from the back along the vertebral column. This sac, which results from the incomplete development of the bony elements of the spine, is usually filled with cerebrospinal fluid.

Mylomeningocele is the most severe form of spina bifida. In this form, the meningeal sac is filled with nerve tissue from the spinal column and membrane as well as with fluid. Frequently, the sac is surgically removed soon after birth, but this impairment usually results in complete paralysis from the waist down.

Hydrocephalus and other impairments, including mental retardation and blindness, may be associated with spina bifida. Young children with the severe forms of the condition usually require lengthy medical treatment, including complex surgery.

Convulsive Disorders

The numerous disorders grouped under the general term "epilepsy" or "convulsive disorders" are the result of functional disturbances of the brain. They may take the form of mild seizures (often referred to as "partial seizures"), including petit-mal seizures, or of major seizures (often referred to as "generalized seizures"), including grand-mal seizures. Convulsive disorders are not associated only with the physically handicapped; they may be present both in children who have other handicaps and in those who are otherwise normal.

Special educators who are in direct, daily contact with these children may be the key professionals involved in initially identifying and referring a pupil with a convulsive disorder. This is the case especially with partial seizures, as they are usually characterized by brief losses of consciousness that may appear to be just a momentary stare into space or a few blinks. Diagnosis of a convulsive disorder is usually made by a pediatric neurologist, and treatment almost always involves medication to control the seizures. The teacher is often involved in assessing the child's convulsive activity level through observation. If the rate or severity of the convulsions changes, he or she may request, usually through the parent, that the type and dosage level of the current medication be reviewed.

Orthopedic and Health Impairments

The child with an orthopedic impairment has a crippling condition affecting the bones, joints, or muscles. Orthopedically impaired children include those born with handicaps and those who acquire them later in life through trauma or disease. Orthopedic birth defects include the absence of one or more limbs and defects in the legs, neck, hips, hands, or feet. The more common types of acquired orthopedic conditions are poliomyelitis, hemophilia, arthritis, and muscular dystrophy. The most frequently occurring muscular dystrophy in children is Duchenne muscular dystrophy, a hereditary, progressive, degenerative condition that causes the gradual loss of voluntary muscle control because of degeneration of the nerve endings in the muscles. Children with this syndrome usually do not live into adulthood, but improved treatment is increasing their life expectancy.

Other health impairments that cause motor or physical dysfunction include heart defects, diabetes, cystic fibrosis, kidney diseases, asthma, and tuberculosis. Although children who have these impairments are usually educated in the regular classroom, they may require some special services in the school setting. Among adolescents, there is an increased frequency of conditions related to spinal-cord injury resulting from accidents, such as diving and motorcycle accidents, and of insult to the central nervous system because of accidents resulting in head trauma and oxygen deprivation. These conditions may cause the student to require special services in school.

Defining the Service-Delivery Settings

Since there are so many different kinds of physically handicapping conditions, children with physical handicaps are placed in a variety of settings, including classes for the gifted. Whenever possible, placement is made in a regular class. Sometimes it is in self-contained or resource-room classes specifically designed for children who are physically handicapped. In other cases, children are placed in classes designed for the multiply handicapped. Homebound and hospital placement is an alternative for children who have such severe medical problems that they are physically unable to attend school. Because of the diversity of placement options, diagnosis and assessment provide important information concerning optimal placement for each child. Assessment information may include data on the pupil's intellectual level, levels of educational performance, medical status, type of physical impairment, and special needs.

Placement in the Least Restrictive Environment. The present philosophy of educating children with physical disabilities is that they should be placed in an environment as close to that of nonhandicapped children as possible. Many pupils with physical or motor disabilities are otherwise normal and are placed in regular grades through mainstreaming. In these settings, they usually receive the same kind of academic assessment that the other children in the class receive. At the same time, the regular class teacher needs to communicate with the professionals who provide supportive services to ensure that there is carryover and coordination between ancillary programs and the regular class. Supportive help may come from consultants, including the special education teacher, the school nurse, the occupational therapist, and/or the physical therapist. In other cases, one or more therapists may serve the child on an itinerant or resource basis. For example, a child who is physically handicapped may receive itinerant speech therapy and also physical therapy weekly.

Children with more severe physical and motor impairments and multiply handicapped children with physical disability as one of their primary handicaps may be placed in more restrictive settings. They are primarily the responsibility of the special education teacher, who usually works together with a team of professionals who provide ancillary support services. In some settings, a comprehensive team of professionals — including the special education teacher, the physical therapist, the speech therapist, the occupational therapist, the school nurse, the social worker, and sometimes other professionals — provides direct service to a child. There is a tremendous need in these cases to coordinate the assessment process in such a way as to facilitate the establishment of an integrated instructional or intervention program for each child. For this reason, an interdisciplinary team model for assessment is often preferred in working with the physically handicapped.

Sometimes physically handicapped children require lengthy hospitalization or convalescence lasting weeks or months. Specially prepared hospital teachers and itinerant homebound teachers teach in these settings. The teacher's caseload and amount of contact time with each pupil varies according to each child's individual needs. Because the teacher in such cases may teach a child only briefly, there is a continued need here to evaluate children efficiently in order to develop optimal short-term educational programs that will prepare them for re-entry into long-term, school-based placement.

Defining the Issues and Special Problems

Two special problems in assessing children with motor and physical dysfunction occur so frequently that they have become issues of widespread concern. First, there is a variety of problems associated with standardized testing, particularly intelligence testing. A second series of problems is related to the use of a team approach in assessing children with motor and physical dysfunction. The problems of teaming have become a more intense issue as an increasing number of severely physically impaired and multiply handicapped children are being served in educational settings. The increasing severity of the handicaps in the population has created a need to change the methods used by the various interdisciplinary team members.

Standardized Testing

Standardized tests frequently have serious limitations when used with children who have motor and physical dysfunctions. For example, instruments that require good oral language may be inappropriate for children who are nonvocal because of physical handicaps. The intelligence tests most frequently used with children are the Wechsler Intelligence Scale for Children–Revised (WISC–R) and the Stanford-Binet Intelligence Scale. Both have limited usefulness with physically disabled children because many of their items require oral responses, are timed, or require good fine motor manipulation skills. Other tests have been developed that may be particularly useful with this population. These include the Columbia Mental Maturity Scale, the Peabody Picture Vocabulary Test, the Leiter International Performance Scale, and Raven's Progressive Matrices (Cruickshank and Hallahan, 1976). Standardized assessment instruments developed for measuring aptitude, academic achievement, and perceptual-motor skills have similar limitations and need to be adapted.

Administration Procedures

In some cases, modifications of administration procedures are not necessary for children who have mild physical or motor disabilities. Administration procedures that follow the standardized method precisely are obviously highly desirable because they allow comparison of the child's performance to that of the normative sample. (A detailed discussion of the process of establishing a normative sample is provided in Chapter 3.)

In cases involving children who have severe physical or motor dysfunction, the use of standardized administration procedures may result in depressed scores that simply confirm the impairment without providing any functional information regarding the potential for achievement. In such cases, it is appropriate to modify administration procedures. Modifications may include the elimination of verbal tests from a battery or of verbal subtests from a comprehensive test. For verbal children who have serious motor dysfunctions, the modification may be the elimination of performance tests or subtests that require either a fine or a gross motor skill that the child is physically unable to perform. In some standardized testing situations with children who have extreme physical limitations, it may be necessary to have a physical or occupational therapist present to assist the psychologist in handling and positioning techniques to maximize the child's performance.

Any time changes are made in the standard administration procedures of a test, they must be noted on the data sheets. Notes should state why modification was required and the precise nature of the changes made. (Additional information on the procedures used in standardizing an assessment instrument is found in Chapter 3.)

Use of Norm-Referenced Tests

Norm-referenced tests are widely used with children who are physically handicapped. The need to modify and adapt tests in some cases has already been discussed, but some norm-referenced tests may need to be administered according to the prescribed method. For example, a large percentage of children with physical handicaps talk well enough to be understood easily, so verbal tests should be administered to them without modification. Others have enough finger dexterity in one hand to be administered unmodified performance tests. Even with children who have more severe physical handicaps, it is often useful and necessary to use norm-referenced tests following standard procedures. Interpretation of them may provide assessment data useful for identification, placement, instructional planning, and measuring progress. Norm-referenced achievement test scores would be particularly helpful in making decisions about mainstreaming by giving an indication of how the child performs in relation to nonhandicapped peers.

The classic approach to using norm-referenced tests with the handicapped involves first administering a test item or group of items in the specified manner and then readministering it in a manner that takes the handicap into account. Possible changes during readministration include providing extra encouragement to obtain the best possible performance from the child who is self-conscious in test situations because of physical limitations, giving the child extra time to complete certain items, and working out a simple head-gesture code when using a picture test with the child who has difficulty pointing. Other possibilities for modifying norm-referenced tests are changing test materials and omitting certain subtests.

The standard administration indicates how well the child does relative to nonhandicapped children; the readministration is a clinical procedure that indicates the child's potential without placing constraints on the way the response is made or how long it takes the child to respond. More research needs to be done on clinical procedures in testing to attempt to determine the extent to which modifications in test administration invalidate norms. It is critical that the classroom teacher not be placed in the role of deciding how or what to change in a norm-referenced test to assure that the pupil's performance is not handicapped by a test's administration.

Intelligence Testing

Evaluating the intelligence of children with physical and motor dysfunctions is difficult. Few tests are specifically developed for this group, yet if the child's physical impairments are not considered, errors can be made in diagnosis and mislabeling can occur. The rigorous task of testing the intelligence of children who are physically limited requires specialized competencies. Simply obtaining a specific I.Q. score from a test does not necessarily provide any information that is meaningful for educational purposes. The goal of all testing is to obtain qualitative information that describes an individual's present levels of functioning and identifies strengths and weaknesses so that realistic educational planning can be developed to meet the pupil's needs (Cruickshank and Hallahan, 1976).

Picture Vocabulary Tests

A number of picture vocabulary tests are widely used to measure children's intelligence. These tests are useful with children who have physical and motor dysfunction that results in an inability to complete the performance tasks that require dexterity and the verbal tasks of the traditional intelligence tests. The picture vocabulary tests present hand-drawn pictures, and the child is asked to identify which drawing among four matches the spoken vocabulary word.

It is possible for the child to identify the correct picture using an adapted communication system if this is necessary. For example, a nonvocal child who has head control might use only a head pointer, a pointing-stick attached to a helmet. Tests of this type are not global measures of intelligence but gauge only one aspect of intellectual functioning, receptive language vocabulary. Despite this limitation, the picture vocabulary tests are a useful measure of a child's ability (Salvia and Ysseldyke, 1981). Of all the I.Q. tests' subscales, vocabulary has the highest correlation with full-scale intelligence.

Caution should be observed when evaluating a child who does not speak English, uses sign language, or has spoken English for less than five years. The words that have been part of these children's training may be different from those validated for inclusion for English speakers at a certain age level.

One of the most widely used picture vocabulary tests is the revised Peabody Picture Vocabulary Test (PPVT–R)(Dunn and Dunn, 1981).

The Peabody Picture Vocabulary Test–Revised (PPVT–R) (L. Dunn and L. Dunn, 1981). The PPVT–R is a standardized, individually administered assessment instrument designed to measure receptive language vocabulary that may be administered to individuals between 2½ and 40 years of age. It requires approximately 15 minutes to administer. An easellike format is used to present a series of pages, each containing four pictures. The individual being tested points to or otherwise identifies the picture that goes along with the vocabulary word spoken by the examiner. The PPVT–R is highly useful in assessing receptive vocabulary. It may provide one indication of the potential ability of a child who is physically impaired.

Although the standardization of the original PPVT was weak, the test was restandardized in 1979 on a national sample of five thousand people between 2½ and 40 years of age. No validity data are reported in the PPVT–R manual, but the test has demonstrated adequate reliability. Data on both split-half reliability and test-retest reliability using alternate forms are reported. The median split-half reliability coefficient is .80 on Form L and .81 on Form M. The test-retest reliability coefficients from four separate studies range from .52 to .90, with medians of .82, .79, .78, and .77. These reliability coefficients are adequate but sufficiently low to warrant further research. The classroom teacher will need to be somewhat cautious in interpreting the test data for purposes other than instructional development.

Specialized Intelligence Tests

A few instruments have been developed to measure the intelligence of children with physical and motor dysfunctions who are nonvocal and have limited finger dexterity. One of the most commonly used specialized tests is the Columbia Mental Maturity Scale.

The Columbia Mental Maturity Scale, Third Edition (CMMS) (B. B. Burgermeister, C. H. Blum, and I. Lorge, 1972). The CMMS is an individually administered assessment instrument designed to measure general reasoning ability that does not require verbal answers. The test consists of 92 cards depicting figures, colors, forms, symbols, and drawings. The child is required to make visual discriminations to classify and correlate the various pictures. He or she may select the correct figure or picture by pointing or using other nonvocal response modes, including eye blinks if necessary. The CMMS requires approximately 20 minutes to administer and is designed for children from 3 years, 6 months to 9 years, 11 months of age.

If the child does not understand similar and different, is unable to see a number of small drawings at one time, or is unable to focus on small details, this test may be inappropriate. Like other specialized tests, the CMMS measures only a limited set of behaviors within the construct of intelligence. It does not tap the same skills as do more comprehensive measures such as the WISC–R.

The CMMS has adequately developed norms, and reliability and validity data are reported in its administration manual. It was standardized on a national sample of twenty-six hundred children in the age range reported above. Its split-half reliability coefficients range from .85 to .91, and its test-retest reliability coefficients are between .84 and .86. Validity data from one reported study indicate that the scores of 353 children on the CMMS correlate .67 with their scores on the Stanford-Binet and .62 to .69 with their scores on the Otis Lennon Mental Ability Test. Other validity data include CMMS test scores correlated with scores on the Stanford Achievement Test (.31 to .61).

Although the CMMS has adequately developed norms, reliability, and validity, it is best suited to individuals who are unable to respond verbally because it measures only one type of intelligence, reasoning ability.

Other examples of potentially appropriate tests and test modifications include the Katz Pointing Scale for the Stanford-Binet (Katz, 1956) and the Arthur Adaptation of the Leiter International Performance Scale (Arthur, 1950).

Assessment Team Approaches

A second issue in assessment is how best to utilize the interdisciplinary team. As mentioned, the use of various types of professional teams to provide educational services is increasing as the number of severely physically handicapped children being served in the schools rises. In fact, teams are a key feature of the assessment process in many school settings. Medical, health-related, psychological, social, and educational service staff members evaluate a child and then share information and, along with parents, develop an appropriate individualized education plan. The use of the team approach in assessment entails both benefits and problems. The method is a critical aspect of the evaluation process because professionals from various disciplines are usually needed in assessing a child with physical handicaps (Golin and Ducanis, 1981).

Problems with Team Approaches.   It is difficult to coordinate and integrate the contributions of team members from various disciplines in an effective manner (Sternat et al., 1977). The issue of teaming is not confined to the field of physical disabilities, but in order to meet the specific needs of this population, one needs special knowledge of the vocabulary and procedures used by medical health-related professions (Darnell, 1976).

Specific problems in teaming include the fact that professionals from different disciplines may disagree on how to assess the child. Moreover, they may use different kinds of assessment tools and systems, resulting in discrepancies in diagnosis and prescription. Professionals often base their goals for a child based on data from their specific areas, creating widely varied goals among the team.

These kinds of problems may cause duplication of evaluation efforts and gaps in evaluation procedures. Smooth functioning of the team is based on good communication among all of its members. Formal communication channels and the recording of all team decisions should be clearly established, including regular meetings. Informal communication among members is also important, especially during evaluations. The coordination of evaluation efforts is critical in light of the needs of the child and his or her family. Parents are key members of the team, and they should be involved in the evaluation process. All evaluation results should be communicated to the parents carefully, because differing diagnoses from professionals can cause family disruptions and a host of problems concerning appropriate placement and intervention.

While there are other problems in the assessment of children who are physically handicapped, standardized testing and teaming stand out as critical issues today. There are no simple solutions. One of the first steps in dealing with these issues is awareness of their nature and scope.

Assessing the Physically Impaired and Multiply Handicapped

Several factors, including mandatory special education legislation, have resulted in the entry of increasing numbers of children who are physically impaired and multiply handicapped into our educational systems. These children usually require services, including specialized assessment services, beyond those traditionally offered in regular and special education classes to meet their unique learning needs.

Specialized Assessment Services

Intensive, specialized assessment may be provided by physical and occupational therapists in the areas of physical management, mobility, and self-help skills development and by speech and language therapists in the area of nonvocal communication. Other specialists may also be involved in the assessment process. However, the special education teacher has the key role in the daily assessment of children who are physically impaired and multiply handicapped. He or she may be directly involved, for example, in assessing the need for unique life-support services in the school setting on a daily basis.

Children who have severe medical problems may need to be evaluated in their need for life support, maintenance, or safety care. This may include the evaluations by physicians and other health professionals of the use and functioning of ileostomy and colostomy devices (prosthetic urinary and bowel diversion systems), tracheostomy and suctioning skills, gastrostomy and gavage (tube) feeding, and aspiration prevention for children with severe feeding problems such as hyperactive gag and bite reflexes, cleft palate, and tongue and lip dysfunction (Kohn, 1982).

Motor and Mobility Evaluation and Management Analysis

A large area of assessment is gross motor evaluation and management. This may involve the use of a combined medical, therapeutic, and educational team approach. Specialized areas of evaluation include range-of-motion testing, reflex testing, and assessing needs for equipment such as walking aids, exercise aids, and chairs. The team usually includes an orthopedic surgeon, who evaluates the need for braces, orthoses, therapy to enhance educational functioning, and surgery. Team members from the allied health (therapy) professions are responsible for the evaluation of joint range of motion, postural reflex patterns, gross motor skills, and appropriate positioning, and for the selection of adaptive equipment for the classroom. The education members of the team are involved in daily management of the child's program, which integrates the contributions of all the team members to provide a comprehensive, coordinated, consistent, effective education plan for each child (Fraser, Galka, and Hensinger, 1980).

The educator's role is a comprehensive and varied one. He or she is responsible for supervising paraprofessionals and assisting in the monitoring of the child's progress. Frequently the teacher serves as coordinator of the multidisciplinary team in the school and may be responsible for ensuring that communication occurs among team members, that all evaluations are initiated and completed as required, that priorities of the child's needs are used to determine daily schedules, such as times when various academic and therapeutic activities occur, and that all paperwork is completed and functional.

Once the physical and motor evaluations are completed, implications for classroom management and adaptive equipment need to be determined from the data they provide. Indications of appropriate expectations for physical functioning in school must be written up, as must indications and contradictions of the child's conditions that affect classroom practices.

Instruments such as the Vulpé Assessment Battery (Vulpé, 1977) and the Comprehensive Developmental Evaluation Chart (Cliff et al., 1975) may be most helpful in evaluating the level of motor skill. These protocols have been designed to measure the movement skills and mobility of young children, and the data gathered from them are easily translated into programming objectives and activities. A physical and occupational therapist and a teacher of the physically handicapped may be involved in conducting motor evaluations, as may a nurse or a physician.

Other Areas of Assessment

In addition to the specialized areas, there are other areas of assessment in a comprehensive diagnostic prescriptive program for children who are physically impaired and multiply handicapped. Self-help skills assessment includes identifying the child's level of functioning in toileting, dressing, eating, and hygiene. Assessment may also be conducted in the related area of daily-living skills. Fine motor skill development and cognitive skill development are also key areas in assessment. For some children, the area of functional academics is crucial. Comprehensive assessment in the areas of leisure-time, recreational, and vocational skill development is especially important for the pupil beyond age eight.

Developmental Assessment

Many younger children who are physically impaired and multiply handicapped function in the developmental age range of zero to six months for at least some skills. Developmental assessment is frequently the basis for determining programming priorities in these skill areas.

Because so many developmental assessment tools are available, it is important to use the tests that are effective with this group of children. The teacher who is in need of developmental data for programming should be specific about what information is required. This will help in selecting the shortest, most efficient tool for collecting the necessary data. At times a level screening instrument is all that is required. In these cases, the Developmental Activities Screening Inventory (DASI) (DuBose and Langley, 1977) or the Birth to Three Scale (Bangs and Dodsen, 1979) may be appropriate. When more specific and comprehensive data are needed, other measures, such as the Developmental Assessment for the Severely Handicapped (DASH) (Dykes, 1981a), the Learning Accomplishment Profile (LeMay, Griffin, and Sanford, 1977), or the Vulpé Assessment Battery (Vulpé, 1977) may be used. Additional screening instruments and procedures appropriate for use with young handicapped children are described in Chapter 5.

Characteristics of Developmental Assessment.   Several unique characteristics are important in the developmental assessment of the physically impaired and multiply handicapped child. Instruments with these characteristics provide more functional programming information and permit the daily reassessment of small increments of progress.

Multiple Samples and Partial Credit.   Effective instruments provide numerous pinpoints and opportunities to sample a wide range of observable behaviors. Tests with few items usually serve only to confirm the fact that the child cannot do very much, is severely handicapped, or lacks the skills to communicate what he or she knows. Useful assessment tools also permit the awarding of partial credit under certain conditions. Instruments that are scored on a pass-fail basis do not always give the kind of information about skill levels and small changes in behavior that is necessary for precise programming with this population.

Task Conditions.   A third desirable characteristic of developmental assessment systems is that they provide the opportunity to stipulate the conditions under which the behavior necessary to perform a task occurred. This is important because children who are physically impaired and multiply handicapped may perform certain tasks in an adaptive manner only when specialized equipment is provided. Tools that permit the evaluator to record the specifics of such conditions are helpful in providing a functional assessment that is useful in programming.

Multiple Presentations.   A fourth characteristic of effective assessment tools for children who are physically impaired and multiply handicapped is multiple presentations of tasks in the assessment process. Often these children will not respond to the best of their ability on the first or sometimes even the second presentation of a task, and it may not be until the third presentation that they begin to respond as well as possible. Therefore, scoring systems designed to allow multiple presentations tend to be more effective than those that do not.

Subscale Scoring.   A fifth characteristic of effective tools is that they emphasize subscale scoring instead of single scoring (the use of only one general score that reflects the average performance on all parts of the test). Because subscale scoring uses more than one score from a test, it expresses the specific performance on each skill area measured. Single developmental age scores are frequently extremely low and serve only to confirm that the child does not have a wide behavioral repertoire. During the early years, an impairment in motoric functioning greatly influences a comprehensive developmental age score. In contrast, subscale scoring in each developmental learning area — and sometimes in skill clusters within a learning area — can yield significant information about a child's strengths, weaknesses, developmental gaps, and splinter skills.

Other criteria the classroom teacher may want to consider regarding the usefulness and appropriateness of an assessment tool include its item validity, item specificity, usefulness to all team members, relevance for intervention, and usefulness to all levels of staff, from paraprofessionals to doctoral-level evaluators.

Functional Living Skills.   For older students who have been in school for several years and for whom years of education are limited, developmental assessments are generally less appropriate. Evaluation of these pupils should focus on functional adult living skills such as communication, recreation, social, and leisure-time skills rather than on a developmental continuum of skills. The discussion in Chapter 9 of the "criterion of ultimate functioning" applies to this aspect of assessment of the physically handicapped pupil.

Task-Analytic Assessment

Another type of assessment system frequently utilized in programming for students who are physically impaired and multiply handicapped is task analysis. This technique involves breaking a difficult task down into small steps to enable the pupil to learn it more easily. Task analysis is effective in making decisions about where and why students are having problems when they fail to complete tasks independently, what steps are needed to help students complete an entire task successfully, and what adaptations need to be made to facilitate the accomplishment of a task (Bigge, 1976).

Task analysis is useful in evaluating progress because it provides a system for gathering baseline data, keeping daily progress records, and monitoring success in achieving specific goals over time. It is also a powerful system for solving the most difficult learning problems because it provides a means of understanding the components of a task by breaking it down into small parts to facilitate teaching. (Chapter 2 provides a detailed description of the use of task analysis as an assessment tool.)

Task analysis is already a major component in many programs, including those for teenagers and adults who are physically impaired and multiply handicapped. Daily-living, leisure-time, recreational, and vocational skills are only a few of the areas particularly well suited to this approach. An example of a task-analytic assessment program is presented in Figure 10–1.

This task-analysis format is designed so that the pupil's progress can be displayed in graphic form on a data sheet. The task analysis was designed for a teenager who had paralyzed legs and was mentally handicapped. He was taught how to get out of his wheelchair and into the seat of his mother's car by himself. The teacher planned out the steps necessary to complete the task and used the task analysis as a teaching guide and as a way to measure progress. She taught the skill each afternoon when the boy's mother came to pick him up after school. The task-analysis data sheet lists the steps from last to first. Each time the student completed a step correctly a line was drawn through the number on the data sheet that represented that step. The total number of steps completed correctly for each trial was circled, and a line graph was drawn by connecting the circles.

Nontraditional Assessment Procedures

This section explores both traditional and nontraditional classroom procedures utilized in assessing children with motor and/or physical dysfunction. The focus is on what the teacher can accomplish in assessment designed to develop educational prescriptions to meet the needs of physically handicapped children. The types of procedures discussed are preparation and intervention; assessing the physical environment; classroom evaluation of braces, artificial limbs, and wheelchairs; academic and behavioral assessment; and assessing motor ability.

Preparation and Intervention Procedures in Testing

The techniques used in testing children who are physically handicapped are generally similar to those used with normal children, but there are some differences. One is that a number of factors must be considered before any assessment procedure is initiated. No child is untestable, but many testers are unskilled and incapable of establishing a means to allow the child to demonstrate what he or she knows.

Figure 10–1

A Task-Analysis Data Sheet Showing Task Learning after 11 Trials

Task: Wheelchair transfer

Program: High School

Student: Rodney

Teacher: Bonnie Fowler

Steps \ Date	10-1	10-3	10-5	10-8	10-10	10-12	10-15	10-18	10-19	10-22	10-24				
9. Fasten seat belt	9	9	9̸	9̸	9̸	9̸	9̸	9̸	9̸	9̸	⑨̸	9	9	9	9
8. Close car door after wheelchair has been placed in trunk of car	8	8	8̸	8̸	8̸	8̸	8̸	8̸	8̸	8̸	8̸	8	8	8	8
7. Use arms to lift legs inside of car	7	7	7	7	7	7	7	⑦	⑦	⑦	7̸	7	7	7	7
6. Push with arms to swing body onto car seat	6	6	6	6	6	⑥	6	6	6	6	6̸	6	6	6	6
5. Place left arm on left wheelchair arm	5	5	⑤	⑤	⑤	5	⑤	5̸	5̸	5̸	5̸	5	5	5	5
4. Place right arm on car seat	4	4	4	4	4	4̸	4	4̸	4̸	4̸	4̸	4	4	4	4
3. Lock brakes on wheelchair	③̸	③̸	3̸	3̸	3̸	3̸	3̸	3̸	3̸	3̸	3̸	3	3	3	3
2. Position wheelchair in front of car seat	2̸	2̸	2̸	2̸	2̸	2̸	2̸	2̸	2̸	2̸	2̸	2	2	2	2
1. Open car door	1̸	1̸	1̸	1̸	1̸	1̸	1̸	1̸	1̸	1̸	1̸	1	1	1	1

Primary Response Mode.   Before initiating testing, one must know the child's primary response mode. Some children with motor or physical dysfunction use speech that can be understood without difficulty; others communicate verbally but have speech problems. It may be difficult but possible for strangers to understand the speech of some children. That of those at a more severe level is unintelligible to strangers but may be understood by family members and others who know them well. In this situation, it may be necessary to have a family member present during formal testing to interpret for the child.

Finally, there are some children who have totally unintelligible speech but may be able to communicate using one of several nonvocal systems. These systems include communication boards of various types, the one-hand finger-spelling alphabet used by the deaf, electronic voice synthesizers, and, for some severely physically limited children, encoding systems using eye blinks and eye movements. One advantage of nonvocal communication systems such as direct-selection communication boards and electronic voice synthesizers is that the person communicating with the child need not have special knowledge or training to understand the message. With systems such as finger spelling and eye movements, an interpreter may be needed to translate the message.

Gathering information concerning the pupil's primary response mode is a vital part of the assessment process because the type of testing done will depend in part on it. It is important to have information from a speech and language therapist before beginning educational and psychological assessments.

Sensory Input.   A second thing to know before initiating testing of a child with a motor or physical dysfunction is how well the child uses his or her senses, including vision, hearing, and tactile input. This is important because a child with a vision impairment, for example, may need large-print or braille materials, while one with a hearing impairment may need to be tested in a quiet setting.

"Tactile input" refers to the sense of touch and is important in manipulation tasks such as the table-work activities that take place in the classroom. Some children with spastic cerebral palsy have a condition called "astereogenosis," characterized by the loss of ability to take in information through the sense of touch. Not only will this loss affect a child's performance on manipulative tests, but it also has direct implications for classroom programming.

Degree of Motor Impairment.   The degree of the child's motor-functioning impairment is another thing to know before initiating testing. This refers primarily to sitting balance, arm and hand use, and mobility. Tests should be selected on the basis of the child's physical strengths and weaknesses. It may be necessary to omit some test items or to test in shorter time periods because of the physical needs of the child. For example, a child who has very limited use of the upper extremities should not be expected to complete manipulative tasks such as drawing and block building, while the child with poor sitting balance and head control may need special positioning to perform such tasks. Table 10–1 lists areas for motor evaluation that need to be included in a comprehensive assessment.

Table 10–1

Areas of Motor-Skill Evaluation

. . . .

General

Alignment of the body in relation to the midline

Grasp and release

Mobility

Manual dexterity

Psychomotor precision, including speed

Psychomotor approximations, including eye-hand coordination

Reaction time

Range of motion of the major joints

Respiration

Stamina when performing movement tasks

Visual status, including fixation, rotation, and gaze

Oral musculature and feeding

Maintenance of appropriate position for eating

Suck

Swallow

Bite

Chew

Thrust or retraction of tongue, lips, and jaws

Saliva control

Fine motor

Grasp pressure control

Coordination of trunk, arm, and hand to perform tasks

Ability to reach

Manipulation skill for self-help and table-work tasks

Reflexes

Retention of normal reflexes

Presence of abnormal reflexes

Relationship of reflex activity to muscle tone and motor development

Level of integration of reflex into higher-level movement pattern

. . . .

Positioning.　"Positioning" refers to the positions that are best for maximizing a child's performance during testing. Most children perform best in a seated position at a desk appropriate for their height, but some children with motor or physical dysfunction may do best when positioned in special, adaptive ways. For example, children in wheelchairs may need special desks that their chairs will fit under; others may perform best when positioned on a prone board. Prone boards, barrel chairs, and corner-sitting chairs are adaptive equipment that may eliminate a child's need to work at maintaining stability and balance while working. The best position for some young children may be on a wedge or in a side-lying position on the floor. Information about the optimal positioning for a child needs to be gathered before testing is initiated. A physical or occupational therapist may need to position the child for optimal functioning and/or to be present during testing to help maintain appropriate positioning for each task.

Reflexes that are inappropriately present or absent have a significant effect on the child's motor performance. Resources such as Fiorentino (1972), Bobath and Bobath (1964), and Ulrey and Rogers (1982) may be helpful in determining the role of reflexes in performance.

Fatigue. There is considerable variation in the length of time physically handicapped children can work in one session, how easily they become tired, and the initial signs of fatigue; for example, children who have such conditions as muscular dystrophy and athetosis may become fatigued quickly. To deal with this problem, it may be necessary to schedule several short testing sessions over a few days rather than one long session. Testing during the morning hours when the child is less tired may be appropriate.

Medical Problems. Before testing, one should know whether there are any health-related problems such as convulsions that may occur during the testing. For example, partial seizures may seriously affect a child's performance. Other problems may be associated with gagging, coughing, or side effects of medication such as distractibility, inability to attend, or short attention span. In some cases, children may be in pain due to surgery or other factors.

Signs of Learning Disabilities. All of the classic signs of learning disabilities may be observed in children with motor or physical dysfunction. One of the conditions in which they frequently accompany a motoric handicap is cerebral palsy. The characteristics of learning disability include perseveration, rotations, reversals, short attention span, distractibility, and visual-perception problems. It is unusual for one child to present all of these problems, but a physically handicapped child often presents one or a group of them.

Recent Evaluations. It is common practice to review all available recent evaluations prior to initiating the testing of any child, and the types of evaluations that may be available for a child with motor or physical dysfunction may be more varied than usual. In some cases, a child may have recent evaluations from occupational therapy, physical therapy, speech and language therapy, neurology, orthopedics, psychology, and education. In conducting a comprehensive assessment, it is necessary to review them all in order to prevent the costly duplication of services and waste of time in assessment. The educational or psychological assessment specialist must request that such evaluations be conducted before educational assessments so that information is available concerning appropriate positioning, handling, adapted equipment used, and communication.

Developing a Positive Intervention Plan

It is important to develop a plan for testing to identify and describe the child's strengths and abilities rather than to merely put together test instruments to confirm nonfunctional skills and areas of disability. While there is no question that a child's weaknesses and deficit areas need to be clearly identified, testing should go beyond this level to give the child an opportunity to demonstrate skills that have been learned or are emerging. For example, a child should be given the Wechsler Intelligence Scale for Children–Revised (WISC–R) (Wechsler, 1974) or the Brigance Diagnostic Inventory (Brigance, 1977) only if it will provide the type of information desired and allow the child to demonstrate obtained skills. If a test's formal, standardized administration requirements are inappropriate for the child, then it should not be used. An examiner can cause a child to score significantly below his or her ability level by selecting the wrong measure.

These preparation and intervention procedures illustrate some of the unique aspects of testing a child with a physical or motor disability. They demonstrate the importance of planning and preparation to ensure successful comprehensive assessment. If the professionals involved consider these aspects in the testing stage, they will facilitate meeting the child's needs during the complete diagnostic assessment process.

Assessing the Physical Environment

An important aspect of assessment that the special education teacher should not forget to complete is an evaluation of pupils' physical environment. Assessing the physical environment involves both how the pupil interacts with the environment and how the physical environment itself affects the pupil's behavior. An excellent checklist that can be used as a guide for assessing the appropriateness of the physical environment has been developed by Baker (1980). See Figure 10–2.

Classroom Evaluation of Braces, Artificial Limbs, and Wheelchairs

Because of the heterogeneous characteristics of the population, children who have physical and motor disabilities are placed in a variety of educational settings which may include educational programs for the gifted, mentally handicapped, learning disabled, emotionally handicapped, hearing impaired, and visually impaired. Teachers in these programs may not have received technical training in the specialized areas related to teaching the physically handicapped. One of these is the care and maintenance of braces, artificial limbs, and wheelchairs (Venn, Dykes, and Morganstern, 1979).

Braces are orthopedic devices used to support body weight, control involuntary movements, and prevent deformities. There are lower-extremity braces for the hips, legs, and feet and upper-extremity braces for the arms and hands. Artificial limbs are prosthetic devices that replace absent body parts with artificial ones. They may provide for lost function as well as for cosmetic appeal. Wheelchairs are for

Figure 10–2

Accessibility Checklist

. . . .

	YES	NO
I. Are exterior spaces and passageways barrier-free?	____	____
Steep slopes and/or steps?	____	____
Ramps:		
Wherever needed?	____	____
1′ rise/12″ run?	____	____
Nonslip?	____	____
Handrails 32″ from floor, extending 1′ beyond top and bottom edges of ramp?	____	____
6′ base clearance?	____	____
5 × 5′ platforms where doors swing out?	____	____
4 × 5′ platforms where doors swing in?	____	____
⩾ 48″ wide?	____	____
Level rest platforms at 30′ intervals long ramps only?	____	____
Doors:		
⩾ 32″ clear openings?	____	____
Open with single effort?	____	____
Kickplates?	____	____
Level 5′ in direction of door swing?	____	____
Thresholds ⩽ ½″ and beveled at both edges?	____	____
Sidewalks:		
Materials smooth and homogenous, not slippery when wet?	____	____
Short walks ⩾ 44″ wide; long walks ⩾ 60″?	____	____
Small openings in gratings?	____	____
Curb cuts/ramps between street and sidewalk?	____	____
II. Are interior spaces and circulation paths barrier-free?	____	____
All spaces same level or connected with ramps?	____	____
Ramps meet specifications in I above?	____	____
Doors meet specifications in I above?	____	____
Furniture and space arranged to allow 60″ × 60″ average turning space wherever needed?	____	____
Floors:		
Smooth, nonslip (no wax)?	____	____
Carpeting (where used short, dense < ¼″ padding securely tacked, especially at seams)?	____	____
Drinking fountains:		
Hand and foot operated?	____	____
Spout and hand controls at front or side?	____	____
Basin 30″?	____	____
Not recessed?	____	____

Figure 10–2

Accessibility Checklist (*continued*)

. . . .

	YES	NO
Cafeteria:		
Serving line with ⩾ 36″ between food tray shelf and rail/wall?	_____	_____
Accessible tables?	_____	_____
Auditorium and assembly rooms with safe, level viewing space for wheelchair users?	_____	_____
Corridors:		
Short > 42″; long > 60″ wide?	_____	_____
III. Are alarm and evacuation systems accessible?	_____	_____
Emergency exit doors with > 32″ clearance?	_____	_____
Clear aisleway > to emergency exit?	_____	_____
60″ × 60″ turnaround space wherever necessary?	_____	_____
Evacuation route barrier-free to point of safety?	_____	_____
Specific plan developed to evacuate physically disabled persons?	_____	_____
Instructions given regarding alarm systems and evacuation procedures?	_____	_____
IV. Are areas for use and storage of equipment accessible for the physically disabled student?	_____	_____
Accessible storage areas for classroom learning materials?	_____	_____
Accessible hall lockers (if used)?	_____	_____
Accessible storage for personal possessions (e.g., coats, boots, lunchboxes) within and/or outside classroom?	_____	_____
Accessible gym locker (if used)?	_____	_____
V. Are restroom facilities accessible for the physically disabled student?	_____	_____
Entry door meets specifications in I above?	_____	_____
Open entry areas to allow wheelchair passage and turning (44″ if door opens out; 60″ if door opens in)?	_____	_____
At least one accessible stall per restroom?	_____	_____
3′ × 5′ (at least)?	_____	_____
Door on 3′ side swings out, has ⩾ 32″ clearance?	_____	_____
Located to permit easy wheelchair use?	_____	_____
Toilet:		
2′ 6″ from wall to front of seat?	_____	_____
Standard height toilet seat, or as required by law?	_____	_____
Grab-bars:		
Both side walls?	_____	_____
Pair 24″ and 48″ or single 13″ above toilet seat and parallel to floor?	_____	_____
Extending from 6″ from rear wall to 12″ in front of toilet?	_____	_____
Toilet paper dispenser below single grab-bar and within easy reach?	_____	_____

Figure 10–2

Accessibility Checklist (*continued*)

· ·

	YES	NO
Urinal bowl ≥ 18″ from floor?	_____	_____
At least one accessible lavatory per restroom?	_____	_____
Mounted ≥ 29″ from floor?	_____	_____
Lever-type faucets?	_____	_____
Soap dispenser within reach, operable with one hand?	_____	_____
Covered/insulated hot water and drain pipes?	_____	_____
Mirrors, towel racks, dispenser mounted ≥ 40″ from floor?	_____	_____

· ·

children who are unable to walk or for whom walking is unsteady or unsafe. They include motorized chairs and newly designed, lightweight wheelchairs for children.

Special educators need to be able to evaluate the condition and function of these devices. The classroom teacher, for example, may be the first person to observe that a child's leg brace is so tight that it is bruising the tissue. Children who are paralyzed may not feel any pain and thus may not know that severe injury is occurring. Another example is a situation in which the teacher observes that a child's wheelchair is damaged, resulting in an unsafe situation, or is causing the child difficulty in propelling it easily. In both of these examples, the teacher is primarily responsible for assessing the problem through daily observation and for making an appropriate referral to have the problem corrected. In order to do this, he or she needs to know how to evaluate the fit and function of the equipment.

Evaluating braces is a three-step process involving examination of the brace when it is off the student, with the student standing with the brace on, and with the student using the brace during movement. Points to look for include the condition and the fit of the brace. There should be no pressure that results in reddened areas that do not pale after a few minutes.

Examination of artificial limbs should focus on the condition and fit of the device. Identification of artificial limbs that are too small is particularly important with young children who may outgrow them quickly.

Evaluating the fit and function of a wheelchair involves examination of three conditions: with the student out of the chair, with the student sitting in the chair, and with the student pushing or riding in the chair. A wheelchair has many moving parts that need to be maintained, so their condition should be closely examined. Chairs that are too small or too large can seriously affect mobility and positioning; this aspect should also be carefully evaluated.

Several types of medical specialists are involved in prescribing, fitting, and maintaining braces, artificial limbs, and wheelchairs. They include occupational and physical therapists, orthotists, and prosthetists. These persons are valuable support personnel, and communication with them is especially important when new devices are provided and when special problems arise.

Academic and Behavioral Assessment

The types of academic, aptitude, and behavioral tests used with children who have physical or motor dysfunctions are the same as those used with all children. In fact, no specialized achievement or behavioral tests have been developed for physically handicapped pupils since the curriculum for such students is usually the same as that for those who are not handicapped. Differences between the academic and behavioral testing of most children and that of children with motor and physical dysfunctions are in the procedures used in administering the tests. Several adaptive procedures for academic and behavioral evaluation have been found useful with children who have motor or physical dysfunctions. Without the use of such procedures, evaluation results may not accurately reflect a child's true level of performance.

Suggestions for Academic Assessment

Achievement tests and other academic tests may need to be given orally or without time limits. A pupil's response to test items may sometimes need to be written by an adult or peer. Other modifications in academic assessment include taping paper or response sheets to a desk and modifying the writing activities involved in assessment. Pupils may need to use splints on the wrist or hand to hold a pencil or may be able to write well using a built-up pencil. Some may be unable to write by hand or may be so slow that handwriting is not feasible. In such cases, typing may facilitate optimal written communication.

In assessing mathematics skills, a calculator, especially a printing calculator, can be used successfully to speed the testing process and give the pupil the opportunity to perform independently (Dykes, 1981b). The record form for an achievement test, for example, may need to be adapted by including comments on the pupil's performance and notes about the modifications required to enable him or her to complete an item or cluster of items.

Suggestions for Behavioral Assessment

The observation and evaluation of the behavior of a pupil who has a physical or motor handicap is critically important because behavior is closely related to success in learning. Pupils with physical and motor dysfunction are especially sensitive to teasing and rejection by teachers and peers.

Adjustment and coping are especially difficult during adolescence. The teacher must be sensitive to and aware of each pupil's self-concept and attitudes as reflected in behavior so that problems can be identified early enough to prevent the development of maladaptive coping behaviors (Dykes, 1981b). Behavioral assessment is especially important with pupils who have terminal conditions such as muscular dystrophy. Teachers need to be aware of their special problems so that the school program supports the emotional needs of each child.

Learned helplessness is especially common among children who have physical handicaps. It is characterized by the lack of independent action, particularly in daily-living skills. In some cases, the child may expect that activities like dressing and eating should be done for him or her even when he or she is physically able to perform them with minimal help. Observation assessment can be used to identify such problems so that a positive intervention plan can be developed.

Calhoun and Hawisher (1979) suggest that behaviors that should be noted for the child with a physical handicap include a change in activity level; complaints concerning physical functioning such as headache, cramps, difficulty in breathing; tremor; changes in appetite or bathroom needs; sluggishness; changes in memory patterns; increased or decreased communication; and changes in muscle tension.

Assessing Motor Ability

All children must move to learn and learn to move. Movement ability is one of the foundations of early development; communications and language skills development, cognitive development, and the development of social skills are all based on the ability to move. Limitations in movement can affect development in all learning areas, from self-help skills development to vocational skills development. It is through movement that a child actively participates in the environment and learns from direct experience (Langley, 1979). For these reasons, the assessment of motor-skill development is a crucial area in programs for children with physical and motor dysfunctions that limit movement ability.

The term "motor-skill development" refers to movement controlled by the muscles. Motor development is divided into two broad areas: gross motor movement is that controlled by the large muscles, such as walking, throwing, catching, and balancing; and fine motor movement is that controlled by the small muscles, such as grasping, stringing beads, writing, and buttoning. The assessment of motor ability involves four major components: medical examinations, therapeutic evaluation, motor testing, and teacher assessment (Morris and Whiting, 1971). Information gathered from each component is necessary to the development of an educational plan to meet the child's needs.

Medical Examinations. Medical examinations provide assessment information relevant to a child's motor ability and performance. They may include orthopedic and neurological evaluations of reflexes, muscle coordination, muscle tone, balance, and gait. Electroencephalography (EEG) and other clinical tests may also be performed. Interventions based on medical evaluations may include medication, therapy, braces, and surgery.

Teacher Assessment.   The teacher should observe the child's motor performance in the classroom and the school environment and may also relate the information available in the child's school and other records — such as educational strengths and weaknesses, intelligence test results, medical history, and home background — to motor performance. He or she may also be involved in administering some motor tests for the purpose of developing educational objectives.

Therapeutic Evaluation.   Therapeutic evaluation of motor ability and performance may include assessment by a physical therapist, who measures gross motor strengths and weaknesses, range of joint motion, reflex development, and mobility. It may also include assessment by an occupational therapist, who measures fine motor ability as it relates to a range of functional daily-living, recreational, and leisure-time skills (Banus, 1971). Occupational therapists may also assess a child's sensory integration as a measure of perceptual–motor skill development.

Motor Testing.   Motor tests are used extensively with children who have physical or motor dysfunctions. Such testing is useful to determine present levels of motor development, strengths and weaknesses in motor ability, and priorities for intervention. In addition, the regular use of motor tests is a systematic method of measuring a child's progress in fine and gross motor skills development. Several widely used motor tests are reviewed to illustrate what is available.

Motor-Development Assessment Instruments

Many types of tests and scales are available for measuring motor-skill development and proficiency. When detailed, comprehensive assessment data are required, such measures as the Stanford Functional Developmental Assessment, the Peabody Developmental Motor Scales, and the Bruininks-Oseretsky Test of Motor Proficiency can be utilized. These three tools are examples of effective diagnostic-prescriptive motor skill development tests.

Stanford Functional Development Assessment (E. E. Bleck, 1982).   This instrument, a detailed developmental scale, provides a wide range of items for assessing both fine and gross motor skills. A criterion-referenced instrument, it is designed for use as a programming guide. The gross motor abilities evaluated include coordination/strength, balancing, locomotion, visual-motor–upper limbs, and visual-motor–lower limbs. The fine motor abilities evaluated include reach/ carry and bilateral coordination; grasp, placement, release, and eyelash coordination; prehension; thumb-finger manipulation; visual-motor and visual discriminations; spatial relations; and graphics, drawing, and writing. Age levels for each task are provided, as are multiple criteria for scoring each task. The scoring levels are pass; pass with equipment and/or adaptive technique; accomplished, but not in practical time; attempted, but required assistance to complete; and cannot attempt activity.

Peabody Developmental Motor Scales (R. Folio and R. Fewell, 1982).
These scales are individually administered tests designed to measure the gross and fine motor development of children from birth to seven years of age. They provide a comprehensive measure of the skills a child has mastered, those skills that are emerging, and those that have not yet been learned.

The Peabody Developmental Motor Scales are criterion-referenced assessment tools designed primarily for use in diagnostic and prescriptive programming. Programming activities provided describe how to teach each of the skills included in the scales. These activities permit the development of an individualized motor program for each child based upon strengths, weaknesses, and specific needs. One strong feature of the scales is that they provide a large number of items, giving the child many opportunities to demonstrate ability. The scales require approximately 45 minutes to administer, and five criteria are provided for rating performance on each item.

Bruininks-Oseretsky Test of Motor Proficiency (R. H. Bruininks, 1978).
This instrument is an individually administered test designed to measure the motor functioning of children from 4½ to 14 years of age. The complete battery consists of eight subtests that provide a comprehensive measure of both fine and gross motor skills. The short form is a screening-level survey of general motor proficiency.

The Bruininks-Oseretsky test is a standard assessment tool that can be useful in developing motor-skill acquisition programs for individual pupils and in evaluating motor disabilities and developmental delays. Test equipment is provided in the examiner's kit, and the administration of the complete battery requires approximately an hour. Administration time for the short form is about 20 minutes.

Four subtests measure the gross motor skills of running speed, agility, balance, bilateral coordination, and strength. Three subtests measure the fine motor skills of response speed, visual motor control, and upper-limb speed and dexterity. One subtest, upper-limb coordination, measures both gross and fine motor skills.

The technical adequacy of the Bruininks-Oseretsky is limited by its lack of validity data. The normative sample consisted of 765 children who were mostly from the north-central states. Test-retest reliability coefficients ranged from .68 to .89 for the gross motor, fine motor, and total test batteries. Test-retest reliability coefficients for the individual subtests ranged from .29 to .89. Validity data on the test are weak, though research studies on the earlier version of the test, the Lincoln-Oseretsky Test of Motor Proficiency, are available.

Summary

Assessment of pupils with physical handicaps has become a vital competency of the special education classroom teacher. More often than not, regardless of classification, the teacher of special education will be confronted with the necessity of conducting educational assessments of pupils exhibiting one or more of the handicapping conditions described in this chapter. Some of the topics and information discussed in this chapter include:

1. There is a wide range and variety of conditions that result in physical and motor dysfunction. This makes it necessary to use a broad variety of assessment procedures.
2. Cerebral palsy is a broad term used to describe the most common types of physically handicapping conditions.
3. One of the issues in testing children with motor or physical dysfunction is the limitations of standardized testing, especially intelligence testing.
4. The issue of how to use the interdisciplinary team approach most effectively in assessment is of increasing concern because the numbers of physically impaired and multiply handicapped children being served have increased rapidly.
5. Assessing children who are physically impaired and multiply handicapped requires specialized approaches to gross motor evaluation, developmental evaluation, and task-analytic assessment.
6. There are a number of factors to be considered before initiating testing of a child with a physical or motor dysfunction.
7. Specialized techniques have been developed for evaluating and modifying the physical environment to eliminate architectural barriers.
8. It is often necessary to evaluate the fit and function of braces, artificial limbs, wheelchairs, and other adaptive equipment as part of the assessment process.
9. Assessment of academic skills and behavior often involves modifying and adapting the assessment procedures, the record forms, and the environment.
10. A major area of assessment involves motor ability. There are a number of motor tests available for specialized assessment in this area.

Mastery Review

I. Recall

1. There are _____ conditions that cause physical handicaps.
   a. a large range and variety of
   b. very few
   c. two major
   d. three major

2. Cerebral palsy is:
   a. only one condition.
   b. a broad term for many conditions.
   c. a condition that only affects the arms and hands.
   d. a term used to describe two common types of physical impairment.

3. The most severe form of spina bifida, mylomeningocele, usually results in:
   a. mild motor impairment.
   b. complete paralysis of the arms and hands.

    c. complete paralysis from the waist down.

    d. none of the above.

4. Specialized intelligence tests such as the Columbia Mental Maturity Scale were designed for children who have physical handicaps and:

    a. use wheelchairs.

    b. use long leg braces.

    c. are nonvocal.

    d. have mobility problems.

5. The team approach in testing children with physical handicaps usually involves:

    a. only one or two professionals.

    b. only medical and health-related professionals.

    c. a number of professionals from various disciplines, including psychology, medicine, and education.

    d. the teacher as the primary team member.

6. The area of assessing the gross motor skills of children who have physical handicaps may include evaluation of all of the following *except*:

    a. reflexes.

    b. needs for walking aids such as crutches.

    c. range of motion.

    d. writing skills.

7. The type of assessment frequently used with younger children who are physically impaired and multiply handicapped is:

    a. academic.

    b. developmental.

    c. vocational.

    d. projective.

8. All of the following are desirable characteristics of good tests for children who are physically impaired and multiply handicapped *except*:

    a. numerous pinpoints.

    b. partial credit.

    c. single scoring.

    d. multiple presentation.

9. Subscale scoring refers to:

    a. obtaining a separate score for each major skill area of a test.

    b. scoring only part of a test.

    c. eliminating part of the test in computing the score.

    d. obtaining one global score from a test.

10. Assessment of older students who are physically impaired and multiply handicapped should focus on:

    a. academic skills.

    b. developmental skills.

    c. psychological skills.

    d. functional skills.

11. In testing a child with physical handicaps, the child's primary response mode should be identified:
    a. before the testing.
    b. during the testing.
    c. after the testing.
    d. after the testing but before making a placement decision.

12. If a teacher determines through evaluation that a child's wheelchair is too small for the child and in poor repair, the teacher should:
    a. fix the wheelchair.
    b. make a referral to the child's parents and physical therapist concerning the problem.
    c. order a new wheelchair.
    d. wait until the child's next appointment at the medical clinic.

13. Academic testing of children who have physical handicaps involves the use of:
    a. many specialized academic tests.
    b. the traditional academic tests without modification of administration procedures.
    c. traditional academic tests with modification of administration procedures.
    d. many specialized academic tests with modification of administration procedures.

14. Assessing fine motor ability involves evaluating movement skills in all of the following areas *except*:
    a. drawing.
    b. grasping.
    c. cutting with scissors.
    d. catching a ball.

15. All of the following are tests of motor development *except* the:
    a. Peabody Developmental Motor Scales.
    b. Bruininks-Oseretsky Test of Motor Proficiency.
    c. Stanford Functional Development Assessment.
    d. Brigance Inventory of Basic Skills.

II. Comprehension

1. Discuss the factors that must be considered before initiating any assessment procedures with physically handicapped pupils.
2. Describe the role of the classroom teacher in evaluating braces, artificial limbs, and wheelchairs.
3. What are the differences between assessment of typical pupils and of pupils with motor and physical dysfunctions? Discuss the implications of these differences.
4. Describe the four major components of assessment of motor ability.
5. Describe the use of developmental assessment with physically handicapped pupils.
6. Discuss tests used with pupils with physical and motor dysfunctions who have difficulty with verbal tasks. Describe one such test.

III. Application

1. Visit a local public facility (zoo, library, movie theater, museum, college, city hall, etc.) and complete an accessibility checklist as illustrated in Figure 9–2. Write a two-to-three-page paper discussing your findings.
2. Visit a facility serving physically handicapped pupils and arrange to observe a child for at least two hours on a typical day. During your observation time, determine the primary response modes of the pupil, and discuss the implications of each mode for instruction in a three-to-five-page paper.

IV. Alternate Task

If none of the Application exercises applies to your setting or curriculum, you can design two exercises of your own. They should demonstrate application of one or more of the principles or concepts described in the preceding chapter. Prior approval of both exercises should be obtained from your course instructor.

V. Answer Key

I.
1. a p. 279
2. b pp. 279–80
3. c p. 281
4. c pp. 286–87
5. c pp. 287–88
6. d pp. 289–90
7. b pp. 290–92
8. c p. 291
9. a p. 291
10. d p. 291
11. a p. 294
12. b pp. 300–01
13. c p. 301
14. d p. 302
15. d pp. 303–04

II.
1. pp. 288–96
2. pp. 297–301
3. pp. 301–02
4. pp. 302–03
5. pp. 301–03
6. pp. 303–04

Chapter 11

Assessment of the Gifted Learner

Chapter Objectives:

After reading this chapter and completing the Mastery Review, you will be able to:

1. List the various definitions of giftedness and identify the most frequently recognized types of giftedness.
2. Discuss the settings in which assessment of giftedness will usually occur.
3. Identify the types of assessment and information sources useful in answering assessment questions at each of the five stages.
4. List the major issues involved at each stage of assessment and with different assessment techniques.
5. Describe a variety of assessment procedures, identify the abilities they are designed to assess, identify the indicators of giftedness and questions to be asked, and match these indicators to the assessment questions at each stage.
6. List the characteristics indicating giftedness in intellectual, academic, and creative areas.
7. List the characteristics indicating a high degree of motivation, self-directedness, critical thinking, and leadership and social skills.
8. Identify the eight most common goals of programs for the gifted and describe an informal assessment procedure that can be used to evaluate skills related to each goal.

Key Terms:

academic aptitude
creativity
critical thinking
elaboration
eligibility criteria
flexibility
fluency
general intellectual ability
gifted
higher levels of thinking
independence
indicators of giftedness
instrument ceilings
leadership ability
learning styles
motivation
open-ended activities and
   questions
originality
out-of-level testing
problem-solving abilities
product assessment
productive thinking
screening and identification team
self-directedness
talented
task commitment

Recent public focus on education has resulted in, among other things, an increased interest in programs for the gifted learner. Unlike other fields in special education, gifted programs are not mandated by federal laws like P.L. 94–142, and the number and types of programs provided vary considerably from state to state. In fact, in many states programs for gifted learners are considered a part not of special education but of regular educational services. Because of the learning characteristics of this population of pupils and the variety of services provided, educational assessment of the gifted learner is somewhat different from that of other populations addressed in this text. However, the five-stage model for assessment described in Chapter 1 is applicable here, and its use with gifted learners will be described in this chapter.

Concepts of Giftedness

Definitions of giftedness are many and varied. They range from very narrow ones, such as "the top one percent level in general intellectual ability, as measured by the Stanford-Binet Intelligence Scale or a comparable instrument" (Terman, 1926, p. 43), to broader conceptions like this one: "About one-third of the students will be highly gifted in at least one of the multiple talent (academic, creative, planning, communication, forecasting, decision-making) areas" (Taylor, 1968, p. 2). What is perceived as a gift is often value laden and is determined by the needs of the culture. A person perceived as gifted in a tribal society, for example, may be an outstanding hunter or an excellent warrior. A complex society such as ours will have a multifaceted definition. And as a society's needs change, the definition of giftedness often changes too. Because of the complexity of these issues, there are no standard definitions of giftedness. Criteria often vary from state to state and from community to community.

In 1972, the U.S. Office of Education (U.S.O.E.) (Marland, 1972) attempted to develop a multifaceted definition of giftedness that could take into account the many points of view about who should be included in programs for the gifted:

Gifted and talented children are those identified by professionally qualified persons who by virtue of outstanding abilities are capable of high performance. These are children who require differentiated educational programs and services beyond those normally provided by the regular school programs in order to realize their contribution to self and society.

Children capable of high performance include those with demonstrated achievement and/or potential ability in any of the following areas:

1. General intellectual ability.
2. Specific academic aptitude.
3. Creative or productive thinking.
4. Leadership ability.

5. Visual and performing arts.
6. Psychomotor ability (Marland, 1972, p. 10).

In rules and regulations established later, psychomotor ability was deleted because many educators believe that students gifted in this area are well served in athletic programs and do not need to be included in other special education.

Gallagher (1975) asserts that "the ability to manipulate internally learned symbol systems is the *sine qua non* of giftedness" (pp. 10–11) because this ability allows individuals to learn on their own and to create new forms and products without waiting to be taught. Renzulli (1978), in contrast, proposes a definition that gives more weight to behavioral manifestations of ability. On the basis of his analysis of research on the qualities of eminent, productive adults, he presents the following definition:

> Giftedness consists of an interaction among three basic clusters of human traits — these clusters being above-average general abilities, high levels of task commitment, and high levels of creativity. Gifted and talented children are those possessing or capable of developing this composite set of traits and applying them to any potentially valuable area of human performance. Children who manifest or are capable of developing an interaction among the three clusters require a wide variety of educational opportunities and services that are not ordinarily provided through regular instructional programs (p. 6).

Evidence of these traits, according to Renzulli, emerges early in life, but simply possessing them is not enough. They must be applied to some potentially valuable field of endeavor, and one is gifted only when actively engaged in high-level, productive work.

The newest definition, proposed by Silverman (in press), places giftedness in a developmental framework and focuses on the learning needs that "prevent gifted students from functioning optimally in a regular instructional program" (p. 100). She defines the gifted child as "one who is developmentally advanced in one or more areas, and is therefore in need of differentiated programming in order to develop at his or her own accelerated pace" (p. 101).

Implications for Assessment

Although many definitions include several categories of giftedness, most programs focus on general intellectual ability or academic aptitude (Karnes and Collins, 1978). In general, the definitions and philosophies adopted by schools reflect their recognition that multiple types of talents exist, but that they must realistically limit their services to those related to the abilities most often exhibited in school. Those who use the Office of Education's definition would include general intellectual ability and specific academic aptitude, while those using Renzulli's definition would consider only intellectual ability and achievement in the cluster of behaviors labeled "above-average general abilities." If a school used Silverman's definition, it would focus on a child's intelligence or academic achievement in comparison to that of his or her peers.

The second most commonly recognized type of giftedness is creativity or productive thinking. In the Office of Education's definition, this is a separate category, while in Renzulli's it is considered an essential aspect of any kind of giftedness — a component of giftedness rather than a type. Using Silverman's definition, creativity would be one of the developmental areas assessed to determine whether children need services because they are more advanced than their peers. Schools are usually required to follow the guidelines developed by a particular state in its definition of giftedness, and most states have adopted the U.S.O.E. definition. Within that framework, however, a school district could choose an adaptation that more closely resembled Renzulli's (1978), Gallagher's (1975), or Silverman's (in press) concept. Because most schools focus on intellectual ability, academic aptitude, and creativity regardless of the specific definition they adopt, these three areas will be the focus of this chapter.

Defining the Setting

Depending on the state and sometimes the school district, gifted students may or may not be considered eligible for special educational services similar to those provided for handicapped children. Because the gifted are not included in the provisions of P.L. 94–142, the regulations and legal requirements that govern assessment of the other populations included in this text may not be followed in programs for the gifted, though other restrictions and guidelines may be in effect. In some states, however, the gifted are included as a category of exceptional children eligible to receive special education services, and in these cases the federal guidelines do apply.

Program-Delivery Models.   In states where services to gifted students and requirements of programs for them do not parallel those of other areas of special education, a variety of program types is used. The most common model at the elementary level is a resource room or "pullout" program (Gallagher et al., 1982). This model is often used with handicapped students, but differently. They usually attend the resource room every day and may spend from one-half hour to one-half day there, depending on the severity of their need. Groups are small — usually from 2 to 10 children — and often an aide is present. Gifted children, however, may spend one-half or one whole day each week in the resource room, may not attend each day, and may be part of a group of 30 to 50 children with one or two teachers. Very seldom are aides present in these classes.

Other common methods of serving the gifted are self-contained classes, independent study situations, special honors classes, seminars, internships, and group counseling. Often students are accelerated through grade-skipping; flexible grouping, with placement in one or more classrooms for different academic subject areas; special fast-paced classes; and early school entry. The methods described in this chapter will be those most appropriate to a resource room or a self-contained classroom but useful in many other settings as well.

Levels of Assessment

As described in Chapter 1, there are five stages or levels of assessment for exceptional children: One, Screening and Identification; Two, Eligibility and Diagnosis; Three, Placement and IEP Development; Four, Instructional Planning; and Five, Evaluation. Each stage asks a different set of questions, and these questions are answered by different tests or procedures. The issues, questions, and information sources in each of these levels will be discussed briefly in the next section. Specific tests, procedures, and characteristics to observe are summarized in Table 2 of Appendix III.

Level One: Screening and Identification

The major purpose of this stage of assessment is to collect information about a student's performance that indicates superior ability in areas that are included in the school district's definition of giftedness. This includes an examination of the results of tests given to all pupils, such as standardized achievement or aptitude tests, examination of cumulative record folders, and specific techniques designed to gather further information about a particular pupil thought to be gifted. In larger school districts, a diagnostician or program coordinator may have the major responsibility for developing specific procedures for screening and identification, but in small districts, this may be the task of the teacher of the gifted.

To gain information about a particular pupil's performance, the teacher can administer certain standardized group tests of intelligence, achievement, or creativity, or may request that a school psychologist or educational diagnostician administer individual tests. The teacher can also observe the student's performance in the regular classroom, interview the regular class teacher, the parents, and the pupil, assess the student's products or arrange for experts to evaluate them, review school records and patterns of achievement, compare expected performance (usually based on an I.Q. score) with actual achievement, or request that the regular classroom teacher make certain program modifications and then observe their effect on the child's performance.

The most important aspect of identification is to use a variety of sources to gain as much information as possible about children who may be gifted. Those who become a part of the pool of referrals through nomination by parents, teachers, or others are then administered additional tests and observed to determine whether they possess characteristics usually indicating giftedness.

Teachers and other staff members are often poor referral sources (Pegnato and Birch, 1959). They tend to identify well-behaved students who are high achievers and often miss highly gifted students who are troublemakers or do not achieve. Frequently, they are simply unfamiliar with the characteristics of gifted students.

Teachers asked to make referrals will be much more effective in spotting gifted pupils if they have received in-service training in identifying their characteristics (Gear, 1975). Checklists, rating scales, and nomination forms listing specific, observable characteristics are also helpful. Parents should not be given training in the characteristics indicative of giftedness or they may attempt to "stack the deck" because they want their child in the program, but they should be given checklists and rating scales or asked specific questions in an interview.

Appropriate Use of Tests.   A major issue at this level and the next is the maintenance of consistency between the definition of giftedness and the procedures used to identify children. The most important aspect of this issue is the appropriate use of tests. For example, if one has adopted the U.S.O.E. definition, which recognizes six separate categories of giftedness, one should use different tests or checklists for each area: intelligence tests should be used only to identify general intellectual ability, while creativity tests should be used only to identify creative and productive thinking, and achievement tests only to indicate academic ability. Although intelligence tests can provide some information about academic ability because they are considered good predictors of success in academic settings (Chronbach, 1970; Gallagher, 1966; Wallach, 1976), they are completely inappropriate for identifying ability in other areas such as the visual and performing arts.

If one adopts Renzulli's (1978) definition of giftedness, however, one must use measures of ability (achievement, intelligence, special aptitudes), creativity, and task commitment. Because the definition states that the gifted are those who possess all of these clusters, children selected should be given measures of all three and selected only if they show high ability or potential in all.

An increasingly popular practice, however, is to adopt a philosophy somewhat similar to Renzulli's. Many people believe that creativity and task commitment can be developed in children with high ability and that low creativity or motivation should not be used to exclude children from programs. Accordingly, they advocate the selection of children on the basis of high ability, with the two major goals of the program being the development of creativity and task commitment.

Regardless of the definition and philosophy adopted, there must be consistency among the stated definition, the identification procedures adopted to put the definition into practice, and the criteria used to determine eligibility for the program.

Level Two: Eligibility and Diagnosis

The most important question to be answered at this level is whether the child's performance and abilities are sufficiently superior to require a special program and to warrant the label "gifted." The decision about what scores on tests or on other assessment procedures are necessary for a child to be eligible for a gifted program are usually made by program directors or coordinators, but in small school districts this decision must often be made by the teacher.

In the past, the decision about entry into a gifted program was relatively simple: children were admitted if they scored 120 or above on a group-administered test of intelligence or 130 or above on an individually administered test. Achievement test scores and teachers' recommendations were sometimes also considered. However, the recent trend has been to consider a variety of factors and measures in making these decisions. Procedures such as case studies (Renzulli, 1978), the Baldwin Identification matrix (Baldwin and Wooster, 1977), and a modified matrix (Maker, Morris, and James, 1981) have been widely used to assist in the compilation of scores to be examined.

Multidisciplinary Approaches.   In most areas of special education, decisions about whether a child is eligible for the gifted program are made by a multidisciplinary placement and review team. Sometimes such procedures are followed for gifted children as well, but often, the teacher of the gifted is solely responsible for the decision. If that is the case, the teacher would be wise to request assistance from a group of individuals. For example, one could select a regular classroom teacher, the principal of the school, and a guidance counselor to serve on each school's screening and placement team. The teacher of the gifted could collect and organize all the information to be considered and then bring it to the team for consideration.

Unlike the parents of children considered for other special education programs, parents of potentially gifted pupils want very much for their children to be placed in a special program. They often put pressure on the teacher or others involved in the decision-making process to accept their child. For this reason, it is important to have clearly established criteria for eligibility and to follow an appropriate decision-making process. If a team makes such decisions, they are more acceptable to parents, removing the pressure from a single individual.

Service-Delivery Options.   After the teacher or team has decided that a student is gifted and thus eligible for special services, the nature of those services must be decided. As mentioned, the most common services available for students are resource room or "pullout" programs, but other options can be considered instead of or in addition to this more formalized program. Many of them require no more than an administrative agreement to allow a child to attend an advanced class rather than a required lower-level class. For example, a child with very high achievement in all areas who is socially mature and motivated might be placed in the resource room and also moved to the next-higher grade. One who has very high achievement in one subject area could be included in the resource room and also attend the next-highest grade during the period in which that subject is taught. Either of these pupils could be placed only in the resource room or only in the alternative placement depending on the goals and resources of the resource room and the particular characteristics of the child.

Other possible arrangements are enrichment and individualized instruction in the regular classroom, independent study, and advanced or honors classes. At the elementary level, the teacher of the gifted can assist regular classroom teachers in providing modifications that are more appropriate for the gifted students in the class. If teachers are interested and able to make special provisions, these changes may be sufficient to accommodate the needs of some gifted students.

At the secondary level, there are often many options. These can include internships, independent study, honors classes, advanced placement classes, and special seminars. The responsibility of the teacher or placement team is to work with the student, parents, and teachers to identify the program options that can best develop the student's strengths and permit the full expression of his or her ability.

Level Three: Placement and IEP Development

The major decisions to be made at this level of assessment are concerned with choosing the most appropriate goals for the student. For handicapped children, the goals are often clear-cut: we want to remediate the children's deficit areas, enable them to perform at the level usually expected of children their age, integrate them into the regular classroom, and help them to cope successfully in the mainstream of society. In other words, the aim is to "bring them up" to a certain standard. With gifted children, our purposes are less obvious; we want to enable them to *surpass* the usual standards because of their unusual abilities. How much and in what areas they should surpass standards are not easy questions to answer, and educators of the gifted do not always agree. Moreover, goals related to going beyond a standard are not easily measurable.

The usual purpose of a program for the gifted is to identify students with superior potential to make a positive contribution to society and to provide them with an education that provides them with challenges and experiences that maximize their development. A related goal is to develop in them certain characteristics that are likely to be important in achieving success as a productive adult in today's — or tomorrow's — world.

Program Objectives.   Although these overall purposes are certainly laudable and can be agreed upon by many educators, how they are actually translated into measurable objectives and individual outcomes constitutes a major problem in programs for the gifted. It is often difficult to choose assessment procedures that can provide definitive answers about what goals are most appropriate for a particular student. With these difficulties in mind, the reader should consider the following goals only as examples of those that might be developed; they are, however, objectives most commonly found in programs for the gifted.

1. Students will develop a high level of understanding of key concepts, ideas, methods, and significant individuals in an academic discipline or subject area.
2. Students will develop the ability to use and critically evaluate information rather than simply knowing that information.
3. Students will develop creative and divergent thinking or problem-solving abilities.
4. Students will become independent, self-directed learners.

5. Students will develop products that approximate or are similar to those produced by practicing professionals.
6. Students will develop the desire and ability to follow through on tasks or projects they initiate.
7. Students will develop social and leadership skills.
8. Students will develop self-knowledge and self-understanding that will enable them to become self-actualized, productive adults.

Assessing Goals. The achievement of a goal such as the first one, understanding in an academic discipline, can be assessed in part by traditional achievement tests. However, they need to be supplemented by teacher-made tests or informal measures that determine high-level understanding. The second goal would be assessed by tests of critical thinking, classroom observations, and informal assessments such as analysis of answers taped during a class discussion. Divergent thinking and problem-solving ability can be evaluated through tests of creativity, the assessment of products, observation at school and at home, and informal assessment procedures such as taping discussions or structured problem-solving exercises. The fourth goal, independence and self-direction, is best assessed through student interviews or self-reports, observation, and assessment of products. Interviews can be structured around discussion of the way a particular product was developed and the problems encountered in producing it. An assessment of products, using specific, consistent criteria, with products being completed independently and within agreed time, would be the major means of measuring both the fifth and sixth objective.

Assessment of the last two objectives is the most difficult since the measurement of social skills and self-knowledge is so subjective and value laden. Important assessment tools are observation; interviews with parents, pupils, and teachers; and the examination of anecdotal records kept by teachers, children, and parents.

Teachers are not always required to develop IEPs for gifted students as they are in other areas of special education, but IEPs are necessary where gifted programs are a part of special education. Unfortunately, because there is no such requirement in most states and because teachers of the gifted serve large numbers of pupils (sometimes as many as 30 each day or 150 children each week), individual goals for students often are not developed. Instead, the program goals become the pupil's goals. Regardless of the requirement or the numbers of children served, individual goals should be identified for each pupil. They can be common to several students, but they should reflect, to the extent possible, the individual strengths and weaknesses of each.

Level Four: Instructional Planning

Once the goals have been determined, individual assessment will determine the specific skills to be taught to each child and to the group of children. In addition, the methods used should respect pupils' interests and learning styles. Gifted students are much more likely to develop self-direction, motivation, and independence if they are working on projects of interest to them, and methods are much more effective if they take preferred learning styles into account. Techniques for determining interests and learning styles usually involve collecting self-reports from students, using an inventory or a more open-ended interview. Past and current teachers and parents are also good sources of information about interests and learning styles. (Chapters 2 and 8 provide additional discussion of learning-style preference.)

Level Five: Evaluation

One of the most difficult problems in the assessment of the gifted is evaluating progress. The two major difficulties are finding instruments with ceilings high enough to measure progress adequately and deciding how much progress constitutes a significant or adequate level. Assessment instruments often include very few items measuring higher levels of ability, making them inappropriate measures of progress for most gifted pupils, particularly those who were already performing at the 95th percentile or above when admitted to the program. A child with this level of achievement cannot show a great deal of progress on most tests.

Out-of-Level Testing. One way to resolve the test-ceiling problem is "out-of-level" testing, the administration of tests designed for older children or those at a higher grade level. One must exercise caution in interpreting the results of such testing, however, because they are normed for older students. If out-of-level tests are given to measure progress in a program, they should also be given at the beginning to establish a baseline. Raw scores or actual percentages of items correct are more appropriate to record than are percentiles or grade equivalents because the latter are related to the normative sample. (See Chapter 3 for a detailed discussion of raw scores and normative samples.)

Determining Progress. The problem of deciding how much progress is acceptable or significant is not easily resolved. In ordinary academic settings, we expect children to make a year's progress annually; in other words, we expect a pupil to make about the same progress as most of those in the normative sample. Gifted students learn more rapidly and should make much more than a year's progress annually, but how much more is difficult to know.

Achievement alone, however, is not a satisfactory indicator of a pupil's progress in a gifted program. Goals in the other seven areas listed in Level Three should also provide guidelines for assessments. What constitutes significant or acceptable progress in these areas is also difficult to determine, but one could begin by keeping careful records of each pupil's progress over a period of several years and then comparing present with past records and comparing progress across records.

The most important way to decide initially whether a child's progress indicates that the program and placement should be changed may be to ask for judgments by the student, regular classroom teachers, and parents and to compare them to the objective data collected on the student. As the program becomes better established and past records are available for comparison, subjective judgments may play a lesser role in decisions, but they will still continue to be important. (A detailed outline providing information for assessment at each level of the five-stage model described in Chapter 1 is provided in Table 1 of Appendix III.)

Assessment Procedures

A variety of methods can be used to assess the abilities and characteristics of gifted students. These range from formal assessment, such as norm-referenced standardized tests of intelligence, to more informal classroom procedures and subjective methods, such as interviews and rating scales. Each of these methods can be used to assess several abilities or characteristics and answer questions at several levels of the assessment schema presented.

Issues Related to Formal Testing

One of the first considerations is the use of group-administered intelligence tests versus that of individually administered tests. Even though individual tests are widely used, many school districts, unfortunately, employ group-administered I.Q. tests as a means of identifying gifted pupils (Richert, 1982). Such tests are inappropriate due to their low ceilings, low predictive validity, and low reliability — especially in the higher ranges of intelligence — and the limited range of abilities that can be assessed by a paper-and-pencil test. Many items are ambiguous, but the examiner cannot discuss them. Often a wrong answer is given because the child has too much knowledge of the subject or looks at an item with a creative perspective (Gallagher, 1966; Richert, 1982). One child, for example, consistently missed items on a test because she saw none of the variants as being different; the item that was supposed to be different was to her "the same as the others, but turned upside down." Martinson and Lessinger (1960) report that in one group I.Q. test, a student must get 96 percent of the items correct to obtain a score of 125; in another, it is impossible to obtain an I.Q. of 125 no matter how many items are correct. Scores on these group tests are very often equated with those on individual tests, but in reality a child's score on an individual test may be 20 to 40 I.Q. points higher.

Limitations of Intelligence Tests. Research on individual intelligence tests indicates that they have high validity as predictors of success in academic settings (Chronbach, 1970; Gallagher, 1966; Wallach, 1976) and that their scores are relatively stable over time. However, their limitations must also be recognized: they may be more appropriate as tests of achievement than of ability (Horn, 1978); they do not predict who will be successful in the nonacademic adult world of writing, business, teaching, and other pursuits (Wallach, 1976); I.Q. scores change with age and the environment (Bayley, 1970; Sprinthall and Sprinthall, 1981); scores on different types of tests or even different forms of the same test are not comparable

(Bayley, 1970; Martinson, 1974; Sattler, 1974); and the age at which an intelligence test is taken affects the score — the younger the child, the greater the possibility of achieving a high score (Silverman, in press). Intelligence tests are also limited in the range of abilities they can assess. Meeker (1969) reports that the Stanford-Binet measures little more than half the intellectual abilities identified in J. P. Guilford's research on the structure-of-intellect model. The Wechsler scales measure even fewer of these abilities.

Total I.Q. Scores.   In the past, educators have relied heavily on the use of total or "global" I.Q. score as a criterion for giftedness. We have become increasingly aware, however, of the mistakes that can be made and the available information that can be lost by using a sole criterion. Children from low-income homes or cultural or linguistic minorities and those who have certain handicaps will suffer most from the use of a single criterion (Maker, 1976; Maker, Morris, and James, 1981; Whitmore, 1981). High scores in areas that are unaffected by the handicap or lack of experience may be indicators of superior ability, but scores on abilities negatively affected by these factors will lower the child's total score.

Patterns of ability — specifically, the different scores on separate subtests or types of items — should be considered in addition to the total score. Generally, for instance, scores on nonverbal tests or nonverbal items on tests of intelligence are more accurate indicators of ability for children from non–English-speaking homes and children who have poor language skills because of economic or cultural background or because of a hearing loss. Items requiring auditory memory are useful indicators of ability in children with visual difficulties and are good nonbiased measures for use with children from deprived or culturally different backgrounds. Tests of learning rate are also useful in overcoming test bias against children who lack experiences that contribute to the learning drawn on by intelligence tests.

Supplements to Intelligence Tests.   Other standardized and criterion-referenced tests should be used as a supplement to intelligence tests. Such measures are designed to assess a child's more specific intellectual strengths and weaknesses rather than to yield one criterion score. Some examples are tests of critical thinking, tests of higher levels of thinking, and learning-abilities tests based on particular theories of intelligence. Some problem-solving programs and critical and higher-level thinking development curricula are keyed to diagnostic tests that provide suggested levels for beginning an individualized program. Language differences and disabilities should also be taken into account when these tests are given.

Tests of creativity generally do not suffer from the bias against certain cultural, ethnic, socioeconomic, and handicapped groups (Torrance, 1974, 1981); in fact, such children often have an advantage because scores for originality are based on how different the answers are from those usually given. The major criticisms of creativity tests are in the areas of validity and reliability: they may not yield similar scores each time they are administered, and they may not actually predict adult creative achievement (Crockenberg, 1972; Petrosko, 1978; Wallach, 1970; Yamamoto, 1966). However, Barron and Harrington (1981) and Torrance (1966, 1974, 1981) report studies showing high predictive validity and reliability. Clearly, more research needs to be conducted to resolve these arguments. It is also clear, however, that tests of creativity can be used as important indicators of abilities not assessed by intelligence tests but necessary for productive accomplishment and for problem solving.

Informal Assessment Procedures

Numerous informal methods of assessment can be used with gifted students; space does not permit a comprehensive listing and description of them. Because they are most appropriately used in relation to specific program goals, one example will be given for each of the common goals.

Develop a High Level of Understanding of Key Concepts, Ideas, Methods, and Significant Individuals. A teacher of the gifted in a middle school designed a procedure in which she asked students to use certain concepts in sentences and then assessed how closely the students' statements approximated her original generalizations. Here are some examples of her exercise:

Original: Many difficulties and problems are encountered when interacting with people who are different from you.

Student-generated: Humans have strange customs and superstitions that an onlooker might find confusing. Humans react differently at different times. All humans don't act well when they are under stress.

Original: Concrete remnants of a culture do not accurately reflect the abstract beliefs of a culture.

Student-generated: Artifacts tell about cultures of the past and can often be misinterpreted. All artifacts may be interpreted incorrectly.

Original: All people, past and present, have shaped their behavior and beliefs in the face of universal human problems and needs.

Student-generated: All artifacts represent something from the universals of culture. Universal human needs show how even the most different people have things in common (Maker, 1982b, p. 278).

Students Will Develop the Ability to Use Information and Evaluate It Critically Rather than Simply Knowing that Information. The critical-thinking–skills materials developed by Midwest Publications (Harnadek, 1976, 1979, 1980) are excellent sources of exercises to test and develop critical-thinking skills. The materials are designed to develop such skills as recognizing assumptions, distinguishing between fact and opinion, recognizing propaganda techniques, inductive reasoning (e.g., cause and effect, figure patterns, figure relations, inferences, reasoning by analogy, spatial perception), and deductive reasoning. Activities selected from the various areas can be used to assess children's reasoning ability. An example of an activity that could be used to test or develop the inductive-thinking skill of inference follows:

> Pupils are instructed to read the story and the statements, and then to indicate whether each statement is True (T), False (F), or Questionable (?). In making these decisions, students are also directed to (a) assume the story is true, (b) ignore any past knowledge of the story, and (c) assume the story is reported in good English. Emphasis is placed on defending answers and not changing them until absolutely certain one is wrong.

Jack and Jill

Jack and Jill went up the hill to fetch a pail of water. Jack fell down and broke his crown, and Jill came tumbling after.

1. Jack and Jill were the only two people who went up the hill.
2. All people who go up hills fall down.
3. Jack and Jill took a pail with them.
4. Jack and Jill walked up the hill.
5. Since Jill "came tumbling down," Jill must have been fat.
6. If Jack and Jill were the only people near the hill during the story, then Jack fell first, and Jill fell second.
7. The water spilled as a result of their falling.
8. Jack was angry at Jill.
9. Because they went up the hill, they fell down.
10. There was water obtainable at the top of the hill (Harnadek, 1979, p. 8).

When using this activity as a diagnostic tool, one should ask students to explain why they decided that a statement was true, false, or questionable in order to obtain more information about their thinking skills. Answers and explanations for the statements appear below. A "true" answer means that the statement is true under all conceivable circumstances or according to the story. A "false" answer means that the statement is false under all conceivable circumstances or according to the story. A "questionable" answer means that according to the story, the statement might either be true or false. In other words, one cannot tell from the information presented, but if something were added without changing the story, the statement could be true or false, depending on what was added.

1. ? Maybe there were others, but the story did not list them.
2. ? Although this statement could be false, it is marked as questionable because the author has never known anyone who has *never* fallen down. However, the statement does not follow from the story.
3. ? Maybe the pail was at the top of the hill.
4. ? The story says "went" which may mean ran, skipped, walked, or a number of other ways of going up.

5. F   Jill did not need to be fat.

6. ?   Maybe Jill tripped and fell first, Jack tripped over her (broke his crown), and then started Jill tumbling.

7. ?   Perhaps they did not get the water.

8. ?   We do not know how he felt based on what is included in the story.

9. ?   If the word "because" implies an indirect cause (e.g., they went up the hill, the hill was steep and/or had some rocks on it, and they tripped on the rocks, then tumbled down because the hill was steep), the statement is questionable.

10. ?   We only know they went up the hill for that purpose. We do not know whether there was water there.

If students answer "true" or "false" to the questionable statements, they have a tendency to "overgeneralize" or read more into the story than what is there. Other mistakes in logic can be determined from the reasons given for their answers (Harnadek, 1979, p. 8).

Students Will Develop Creative and Divergent Thinking or Problem-Solving Abilities.   One problem-solving task that has been used extensively in research is the "Twenty Questions Game" (Mosher and Hornsby, 1966). It begins with an array of pictures of common objects or with the names of items belonging to various categories, arranged in rows and columns. A player attempts to discover which picture in the array the experimenter has in mind by asking questions that can be answered yes or no. An example of an array follows (Robson, 1977, p. 154):

Eagle	Ball	Monkey	Knife
Apple	Rake	Balloon	Sparrow
Owl	Orange	Cat	*Duck*
Pail	Spoon	Kite	Wagon
Pear	Shovel	Cup	Banana
Dog	Coffee Pot	Zebra	Sprinkling Can

The categories are birds (eagle, owl, sparrow, duck), mammals (dog, cat, monkey, zebra), fruit (apple, pear, orange, banana), toys (ball, kite, balloon, wagon), eating utensils (spoon, coffee pot, knife, cup), and tools (rake, pail, shovel, sprinkling can). The tester observes and records the types of questions asked. A question that includes only one picture at a time (e.g., "Is it a cup?") is considered a hypothesis-seeking question and is not very efficient as a problem-solving strategy because it includes only one possible solution. A constraint-seeking question, such as, "Is it a bird?" is more efficient because it considers several possible solutions at once.

The game can be made more complicated by varying the items according to perceptual as well as abstract categories. In the above array, for example, there are three color groups — brown (eagle, sparrow, dog, monkey), black and white (owl, duck, cat, zebra), and yellow (pear, banana, kite, wagon). One group of items is round (apple, orange, ball, balloon), one has straight handles (spoon, knife, rake, shovel), and one has round handles (coffee pot, cup, pail, sprinkling can). If the student uses a questioning strategy in which either the abstract or the perceptual categories are eliminated one by one, it is possible to eliminate all but one picture from the array in seven questions. With the most efficient strategy possible, one that uses both types of categories for elimination, all but one picture could be eliminated in four questions.

When using this task, the teacher should record the questions asked, categorize them according to type, and note the total number of questions asked before the solution was discovered. After the game is over, the student should be asked to explain the process used to solve the problem.

Students Will Become Independent, Self-Directed Learners.   For the class-room teacher working with pupils exhibiting gifted learning skills, fostering focused, self-directed learning, independent of the need for continual monitoring, is very important. This goal is somewhat related to a later one involving leadership, but different in that it requires initiating and carrying out learning activities that may principally satisfy individuals' interests and not necessarily those of others. Methods that facilitate this include assigned independent studies, field practica, and tutorials working under a person with expertise in the pupils' areas of interest.

Students Will Develop Products that Are Similar to Those Produced by Practicing Professionals.   An integral part of the gifted pupil's education should include an exposure to the vocational expectations and work conditions regarding their occupational aspirations. Independent studies with practicing professionals, and opportunities to meet and discuss issues of common interest between pupil and practitioner, can facilitate this goal's attainment.

Students Will Develop the Desire and Ability to Follow Through on Tasks or Projects They Initiate.   These goals can be assessed together by having a student choose a topic and create a product that meets certain predetermined criteria related to professionalism. Observations of the student's progress, documentation of the frequency and type of assistance requested, interviews, and product-assessment procedures can be combined to provide data on progress toward all three objectives.

During interviews, students can be asked questions about the methods they used to produce a certain product, the problems they encountered, and the solutions they developed for these problems.

Students Will Develop Social and Leadership Skills.   Checklists and observation forms can be used in conjunction with structured activities designed to allow leadership characteristics to emerge, such as group-project planning efforts in which the teacher does not appoint a leader, assume the leadership, or provide a great deal of assistance to the students. Even though observation within a classroom is important, it is essential that observations to assess leadership ability occur in situations outside the classroom as well. More valuable information can be obtained by observing students in the playground and in their clubs or other extra-curricular activities, where the influence of adults is at a minimum.

Peer referral and nomination are also valuable techniques, especially if the children are asked specific questions about behaviors they can observe in other children. Maker and her colleagues (Maker, Morris, and James, 1981) found two questions especially valuable in soliciting the names of children with leadership ability:

1. Which boys or girls are the first to explain to others in your class how games are played or how things are done?
2. Which boys or girls are usually the first to suggest new games to play or new things to do? (p. 134)

Other, similar questions could be asked:

3. Who in the group usually has the best ideas for ways to complete a project?
4. Who in the group seems to be the best at organizing the others to get things done?
5. If you were to choose one person in this class as the best at getting things done and making people feel good about what they are doing, who would you choose? Why?

Students Will Develop Self-Knowledge and Self-Understanding that Will Enable Them to Become Self-Actualized, Productive Adults. Assessment of skills related to this goal is perhaps the most subjective. One of the best techniques is to have students write or talk about themselves and then compare their self-perceptions with the perceptions of their peers and of adults. One very simple activity is to have students write descriptions of their three or four major strengths and weaknesses. These can be compared with similar descriptions requested from regular classroom teachers, parents, friends, and the teacher of the gifted.

Summary

This chapter has presented many ideas regarding educational assessment with gifted learners. Emphasis was given to the role of the classroom teacher in collecting gifted-learner performance data. The major points covered were:

1. The many conceptions and definitions of giftedness are determined by society's needs.
2. Most current definitions emphasize a multifaceted view of giftedness.
3. Programs for the gifted usually focus on general intellectual ability, specific academic aptitude, and/or creativity.

4. Gifted-student programs or services may or may not be included with other special education services, depending on state and local funding patterns.

5. The gifted are not included in the provisions and regulations of P.L. 94–142, so the requirements of this law do not apply to them.

6. The most common program-delivery model is the resource room, but it may be very different from resource rooms in other areas of special education. Other options are usually available.

7. The five levels of assessment ask different questions, but most types of assessment can be used to answer questions at several levels.

8. Unlike teachers in other areas of special education, the teacher of the gifted may have the sole responsibility for all levels of assessment of gifted students.

9. The most important aspect of Level One, Screening and Identification, is the gathering of as much information as possible about children who may be gifted.

10. Assessment procedures at Levels One (Screening and Identification) and Two (Eligibility and Diagnosis) must be consistent with the district's definition of giftedness.

11. There are difficult decisions to be made with regard to placement, and parents often put pressure on the teacher to accept their child into the program. Therefore teachers would be wise to appoint a selection committee to assist in decision making.

12. At Level Two, Eligibility and Diagnosis, the teacher or selection committee should consider a variety of options.

13. It is difficult to agree upon the individual and program goals for gifted students since we are not bringing them up to a particular standard but attempting to enable them to surpass it.

14. The usual purposes of gifted programs are to develop characteristics enabling gifted students to reach their maximum potential as productive adult members of society and to provide an educational program that facilitates rather than inhibiting their normal rapid development.

15. The most common goals of gifted programs include the development of a high level of understanding of a subject area, critical and higher levels of thinking, creative or divergent thinking, self-directedness, the ability to create professional-quality products, task commitment or motivation, leadership and social skills, and self-knowledge and self-understanding.

16. Teachers are not always required to develop IEPs for gifted students.

17. The most difficult assessment problems to resolve at Level Five, Evaluation, are finding instruments with high enough ceilings to measure the progress of gifted students and deciding how much progress to expect.

18. Group-administered tests of intelligence are best used as screening instruments and individually administered tests as confirmation of giftedness, because tests given individually are more accurate.

19. Subtest scores, scores on subsections, and scores on particular types of items should be considered in addition to the total score on an intelligence test, especially if the child is handicapped, from a low socioeconomic background, or has poor English skills.

20. Nonverbal tests of intelligence are more appropriate than verbal measures for certain children.

21. Tests of creativity are not usually culturally biased, and they measure abilities important for productive accomplishment that are not measured by intelligence tests. However, their reliability and validity have been criticized.

22. Lists of characteristics of giftedness do not contain all possible traits, and one would not expect a gifted student to possess all the characteristics listed.

23. The many informal classroom assessment procedures are most appropriately used in Levels Three (Placement and IEP Development), Four (Instructional Planning), and Five (Evaluation) of the assessment schema presented in this book.

Mastery Review

I. Recall

1. The categories of giftedness usually served by special programs are:
   a. intellectual, visual and performing arts, and mechanical.
   b. intellectual, creative, and psychomotor.
   c. intellectual, academic, and creative.
   d. intellectual, academic, and visual and performing arts.
   e. creative, athletic, and academic.

2. The major questions to be asked at the first level of the assessment of giftedness address which of the following concepts?
   a. Performance on tests that is significantly different from that of age peers.
   b. Behaviors at home that are different from those of most children of the same age and background.
   c. Behaviors in the classroom that are superior to those of others of the same age and background.
   d. A comparison of expected performance with actual achievement.
   e. All of the above.

3. The major questions to be asked at the second level of assessment of giftedness address which of the following concepts?
   a. Behaviors and abilities that are superior and indicate the need for a special education.
   b. Determining which of the pupil's abilities are the most important to his or her success.
   c. Superior abilities that warrent the label "gifted".
   d. All of the above.

4. The major questions to be asked at the third level of assessment of giftedness address which of the following concepts?
   a. The importance of program goals in developing the pupil's abilities.
   b. The importance of program goals in remediating the pupil's weaknesses.
   c. Establishing goals that will allow the pupils to surpass the usual standards.
   d. a and c.
   e. b and c.

5. Which of the following statements does not describe the appropriate use of intelligence tests in the assessment of gifted students?

   a. Group-administered tests are equally valid as individually administered tests.

   b. I.Q. scores are good predictors of success.

   c. An individual's score is generally the same regardless of the test taken, the child's age when the test was taken, and the child's language skills.

   d. Intelligence tests measure all abilities necessary for success in school.

   e. All of the above.

6. Difficulties in evaluating progress in programs for the gifted include which of the following?

   a. Locating assessment instruments with ceilings high enough to measure progress.

   b. Deciding how much progress is acceptable.

   c. Deciding how to evaluate progress in areas other than academic achievement.

   d. A and c.

   e. All of the above.

7. Acceptable supplements to intelligence tests include which of the following?

   a. Tests of creativity.

   b. Out-of-level testing.

   c. Test of critical thinking.

   d. A and c.

   e. All of the above.

8. Evaluations of social and leadership skills should include:

   a. Peer referrals.

   b. Group projects.

   c. Checklists.

   d. A and b.

   e. All of the above.

9. According to the U.S. Office of Education, students identified as gifted include those with demonstrated ability in which of the following areas?

   a. Creativity.

   b. Performing arts.

   c. General intellectual ability.

   d. Leadership.

   e. All of the above.

10. The most common program delivery model for gifted elementary pupils is:

   a. Self-contained classroom.

   b. Honors classes.

   c. Grade skipping.

   d. Resource room.

   e. Flexible grouping.

11. Which of the following are among objectives commonly found in educational programs for the gifted?

    a. To develop problem-solving skills.

    b. To become self-directed learners.

    c. To develop the ability to use and evaluate information.

    d. To develop age appropriate social skills.

    e. All of the above.

12. Problem-solving abilities of gifted pupils can be assessed through:

    a. Structured problem-solving exercises.

    b. Student interviews.

    c. A and c.

    d. A and b.

13. Group-administered I.Q. tests are inappropriate as a means of identifying gifted pupils due to:

    a. Low reliability.

    b. Low predictive validity.

    c. A and c.

    d. All of the above.

14. The use of a total or global I.Q. score as the single criterion for placement in an education program for gifted pupils will most effect:

    a. Students from low income families.

    b. Students with some form of developmental impairment.

    c. Linguistic minorities.

    d. Hearing impaired pupils.

    e. All of the above.

15. Creativity tests have been criticized because:

    a. They do not predict achievement reliably.

    b. They often have low validity.

    c. They have high validity but low reliability.

    d. A and b.

    e. A and c.

II. Comprehension

1. List the various definitions of giftedness and identify the most frequently recognized types of giftedness.

2. Discuss the major difficulties of Level Five, Evaluation, of the assessment model for gifted pupils.

3. List and discuss in terms of their instructional implications the characteristics indicating giftedness in intellectual, academic, and creative areas.

4. Discuss the eight most common goals of programs for the gifted, including a brief description of an informal assessment procedure that a teacher could use to evaluate skills related to each goal.

5. Given that the gifted are not covered under P.L. 94–142, what implications does this have for the classroom teacher? Discuss both assessment and instructional issues.

6. Discuss the major issues regarding standardized testing and the assessment of giftedness.

III. Application

1. Contact your state department of education and determine whether gifted pupils are served in regular or special education programs or not at all. Write a three-to-five-page paper describing your state's service-delivery options or provisions for pupils assessed as gifted.

2. Visit a local shopping center or mall and obtain permission to interview shoppers. Randomly select 50 persons, approach them, identify yourself, and ask them if they can define what "gifted" means to them in regard to school-aged pupils and how they think it would be best to identify them. Write a three-to-five-page paper discussing your findings.

IV. Alternate Task

If none of the Application exercises applies to your setting or curriculum, you can design two exercises of your own. They should demonstrate application of one or more of the principles described in this chapter. Prior approval of both exercises should be obtained from your course instructor.

V. Answer Key

I.
- **1.** c pp. 310–11
- **2.** e p. 313
- **3.** d pp. 314–15
- **4.** d pp. 316–17
- **5.** e pp. 319–20
- **6.** e pp. 317–18
- **7.** d p. 320

- **8.** e pp. 324–25
- **9.** e p. 310
- **10.** d p. 312
- **11.** e p. 316
- **12.** d p. 317
- **13.** d p. 319
- **14.** e pp. 319–20
- **15.** d p. 320

II.
- **1.** pp. 310–311
- **2.** pp. 318–19
- **3.** Appendix III, Table 1
- **4.** pp. 316–17
- **5.** p. 312
- **6.** p. 311, p. 314, pp. 319–21

Part IV
Epilogue

Covering all of special education, as this book attempts to do, required the use of massive amounts of information, concepts, and materials, even with the self-imposed restriction of limiting the assessment procedures discussed to those that a classroom teacher could use efficiently and effectively. As a means of tying together this considerable array of information, a synthesis chapter is provided. Its purpose is at least twofold: first, to illustrate where among the book's chapters interaction and interplay are found with the five-level assessment model described in Chapter 1; and second, to provide a discussion of microcomputer applications in assessment and the emerging role that this technology may have in the field of special education assessment.

Chapter 12

Synthesis of Practices and Technological Innovations

Chapter Objectives:

After reading this chapter you will be able to:

1. Describe the purpose and utility of the educational assessment process.
2. Describe the political competencies required of the special education teacher in defining and fulfilling his or her role in the assessment process.
3. List and describe three procedural competency domains involved in the assessment process.
4. Describe the input required of the special education teacher during IEP development.
5. Describe the cycle of trial teaching, ongoing data collection, and program refinement involved in assessment for planning purposes.
6. Describe the uses of formative and summative data in answering questions at Levels Four and Five of the assessment model.
7. List and discuss the three major issues affecting assessment practices.
8. Describe several ways computer software can be used for assessment.
9. Describe the uses of telecommunications by special education teachers.

Key Terms:

classroom modification
false negatives
false positives
formative assessment
interactive video disk
microcomputer-administered
   assessment
prereferral assessment
prereferral intervention
social validation
summative assessment
telecommunications
test-generation programs

Recently, two special education teachers were overheard discussing the merits of a particular test. More attentive eavesdropping revealed that one of them, concerned about the test's instructional irrelevance, was carping about its uselessness in helping her develop a program for a pupil: "Basically, it just gives you a score; it doesn't tell you what the pupil can and cannot do."

This teacher had captured the essence of the purpose and utility of tests and, for that matter, of the educational assessment process as a whole: the gathering of data resulting in a profile of the pupil's present levels of performance that is sufficiently specific so as to lend itself to decision making about placement, program planning, and evaluation. Furthermore, in order to be useful, assessment should yield pupil-related data within environments that involve any part of the pupil's planned or current program. These environments include the home and the community as well as the classroom.

Many special education teachers-to-be view assessment with attitudes ranging from boredom to contempt. While for some, experience supports the former, an abundance of literature serving to chronicle the "testing movement" (e.g., Bersoff, 1979; Gould, 1981; Kamin, 1974; Kirp, 1974) underpins the latter perspective. When assessment is seen as nothing more than "giving a bunch of tests," certainly one could argue that it is a mechanistic activity; when it is viewed as a method for tracking and maintaining persons within various social strata, one could argue in favor of its contempt.

Neither perspective reflects an understanding of the changing role of assessment in special education today. There is no doubt that standardized tests continue to be used for social tracking purposes despite court rulings forbidding the practice (cf. *Hobson v. Hansen,* 1967). Nor is there any doubt that there are teachers practicing out there somewhere who give tests in perfunctory fashion at the beginning and end of the school year for "pre/post" purposes. But the study and use of the resources provided in this book should equip you with a more positive, useful approach to assessment — one that incorporates much more than the mere giving and scoring of tests, one that is wary of the potential power of tests to suppress rather than welcome human variability, and one that is workable and useful with respect to what really matters: designing and implementing appropriate programs for exceptional pupils in the least restrictive settings.

Toward this end, this chapter attempts to synthesize the implications of the many and varied material and procedural resources presented in the foregoing chapters. These implications reflect two themes that run throughout the text. The first relates to the special education teacher's role in the multidisciplinary assessment process. Although the contributions of other professionals and of parents are no less important, those of the special education teacher are critical if the gap between determining a child's eligibility for services and successfully achieving the goals of those services is to be bridged.

The second theme addressed in this chapter relates to the nuts and bolts of this bridge between entry into and exit from special education: namely, the application of quality assessment practices at each of the five assessment levels introduced in Chapter 1. Of particular importance are Levels Four (Instructional Planning) and Five (Evaluation), in which assessment practices serve as an ongoing part of the instructional process.

The next section of the chapter will address three key issues related to quality practices: prereferral assessment and classroom modification (Graden, Casey, and Christensen, 1985); improper test discrimination (Algozzine and Ysseldyke, 1982); and the assessment of adaptive behavior, especially in light of the emphasis on transition services (Halpern, 1985b). It is the special education teacher's stance in relation to these issues that ultimately determines the quality of assessment practices for any one pupil. The nature of such a stance is determined by the clarity and efficacy of the teacher's role in the assessment process.

The final section of this chapter focuses on microcomputer technology as applied to the assessment process. The microcomputer applications described include both currently useful ones and those indicative of future trends in assessment practices assisted by technological advances.

The Role of the Special Education Teacher in the Assessment Process

In proceeding to examine the special education teacher's role in the assessment process, a useful starting point is the model of assessment shown in Chapter 1 (see Table 1–1). Whether directly or indirectly, the teacher contributes to the process of answering each question within each level. He or she provides or assists in providing much of the information specified in the table's middle column, "Information Sources." In fact, the precise way in which these sources are selected and related to the questions is likely to be endemic to any one school district and, at a more specific level, to any one multidisciplinary team (Skrtic, Guba, and Knowlton, 1985). For example, with respect to the composition of the multidisciplinary team, P.L. 94–142 calls for inclusion, at minimum, of:

- A school or agency representative, other than the teacher, who is qualified to provide or supervise the provision of services.
- The child's teacher.
- One or both parents and, where appropriate, the child.

At the school's or parents' discretion, other interested parties may contribute. A person knowledgeable about assessment must participate as well if the child is being evaluated for the first time. In line with these minimal nationally mandated standards, states and local school districts within them have created their own IEP staffing routines within which most teachers will be in a position to apply our assessment model. To put it succinctly, each school's multidisciplinary team operates a little differently; some are effective and meet the intent of P.L. 94–142, and some do not. Using our model in any one of these environments requires that the special education teacher establish clarity with regard to his or her role in the assessment process. This role clarity requires two interdependent levels of competency: political and procedural.

Political Competency and the Special Education Teacher's Role

Preliminary to being competent in assessment procedures per se, the teacher must be able to size up the interrelationships among the various multidisciplinary team members and between the team and the overall functioning of the school and district. This often subtle and complex task is not accomplished in a day, a week, or in some cases even in a year. The process is known colloquially as "getting the lay of the land" or "scoping the place out." All of the procedural skills known to the field are moot without a knowledge of the philosophies of other team members, their biases, and their respective positions in the overall pecking order. Within this ecosystem, screening, diagnosis, IEP development, instructional planning, and evaluation for any one pupil take place.

Screening. In regard to screening, the special education teacher must develop and maintain good working relationships with one or a combination of multidisciplinary personnel depending on his or her categorical or cross-categorical emphasis. For any one teacher, such personnel could include a nurse, a physician, an occupational therapist, a physical therapist, a social worker, a regular classroom teacher, a school psychologist, and an administrator, to name some.

Recall the goal of the screening process: determination of who could be eligible for special education and who is not. Although he or she may not contribute to this process directly, the special education teacher should interact with screening team members in ways that provide him or her with a head-start level of awareness of those pupils most likely eligible for special education — that is, children with physical or learning handicaps or with outstanding abilities. The teacher must also encourage and assist meaningfully in prereferral assessment and classroom modification activities for which the regular educator is responsible. In some schools, the special education teacher's execution of these informal role functions is a necessary requisite for an appropriate screening process even though he or she is not directly responsible for the process.

Diagnosis and IEP Development. These informal role functions are critical at the diagnostic and IEP development levels as well. Here the goals are to determine eligibility, develop a total service plan, and reach consensus on an appropriate placement. The team's functioning relative to these goals is predicated on state-specific guidelines pursuant to the state's special education laws and to P.L. 94–142, the resources available to the school district, and the logistics involved in arranging for the use of those resources.

In determining present performance levels, the special education teacher and school psychologist must be in sync, not at loggerheads, about their respective duties regarding specific assessment tasks. In some cases, for example, the school psychologist handles the administration and scoring of formal tests, while the special education teacher gathers relevant work samples and observational data. In other instances, the psychologist administers intelligence tests and the teacher administers achievement and criterion-referenced measures. In developing the total-service-plan component of the IEP, the team must have designated personnel responsible for these tasks. Having good working relationships with key staffers enables the teacher to negotiate such specific role functions in a way that allows him or her to practice some of the necessary procedural competencies to be discussed in the next section.

Program Planning and Evaluation.   In regard to the planning and evaluation levels of assessment, the special educator may find him- or herself functioning as a "lone ranger" if political tasks are not addressed. Clearly, the lion's share of the work required at these levels is handled by the teacher. The short-term objectives specified in the total service plan are broken down into specific behavioral objectives and further analyzed along appropriate dimensions such as an instructional sequence designed in terms of the levels-of-assistance continuum described in Chapter 2. The integrity of the teacher's specific instructional design dictates how well he or she will be able to evaluate instructional programs, as called for in Level Five of the model (Utley, 1982).

Though he or she is responsible for these Level-Four and -Five tasks, the teacher's success in answering the relevant evaluative questions depends again on working relationships with other team members. The highly adaptive and specialized nature of assessing a pupil with severe developmental disabilities, for example, requires expertise from a variety of team members. Modern curricula and methodology often call for intricate sequencing of objectives across rather than within global domains and environments (Holvoet et al., 1984). This sequencing in turn requires ongoing data systems for planning and evaluation that must be maintained on a collaborative basis to be optimally effective. A teacher who cannot participate in — and at times instigate — the partnerships necessary to implement such programming is likely to be less effective than one who can.

While the political realities of bringing off special education in public schools are sometimes dismissed as frivolous, they are nonetheless integral to a successful program. With respect to assessment, the special education teacher's role is largely a political one if assessment is to fulfill the purposes outlined for it in this text. Within this context, the politically competent teacher has the "wiggle room" necessary to carry out the important procedural competencies.

Procedural Competency and the Special Education Teacher's Role

As mentioned, the 11 preceding chapters have presented a variety of practices that can contribute to a high-quality multidisciplinary assessment process. Regardless of one's interpersonal skills and knowledge of the political realities of schooling, the ability to apply these practices appropriately is required if the assessment is to meet its goals. These practices can be grouped, again, in relation to the assessment model — those relating to screening and diagnosis, IEP development, and instructional planning and evaluation.

Screening and Diagnosis.   These practices are crucial to ensure fairness to and protection of any pupil who is referred. As this level of the assessment process begins, decision making involves the determination of who is and who is not eligible for special education. Decision making geared toward the elimination of false positives (declaring a child eligible when he or she is not) and false negatives (declaring a child ineligible when he or she is) depends on the three competency domains outlined below (See note 1, p. 355).

1. *Proper Interpersonal Comparisons*

   Many standardized tests used with exceptional pupils have clearly inadequate standardization samples, validity, and reliability (Algozzine and Ysseldyke, 1982). A large number of tests do not include in their samples any groups representative of exceptional populations, thus rendering inappropriate in most cases any comparisons of the child being tested with the standardization sample. Problems with validity make many tests more costly and troublesome than they are worth, and low reliability coefficients increase the chances of false negatives and positives.

   The special education teacher's knowledge of tests and their strengths and weaknesses is paramount to appropriate diagnosis. Knowledge of direct-observation techniques can facilitate a more valid and reliable interpretation of formal adaptive behavior measures that typically depend on the subjective impressions of informants. The direct observation of behaviors within selective domains enhances the screening and diagnostic process if in no other way than by contributing more samples of behavior upon which decisions at these two levels are made.

2. *Regular Classroom Assessment and Modification Before Referral*

   Of late, many states and local districts are implementing prereferral routines (Graden, Casey, and Christensen, 1985) that include procedures to document the specific nature of the problem a child is encountering as well as any instructional techniques or modifications attempted by the referring teacher in the regular classroom. Potentially, these initiatives can enhance the assessment process by decreasing capricious referrals and by providing the team with a variety of directly observed, noninferential data to supplement and help interpret standardized test data. Ysseldyke (1980) observed that unbiased assessment must be part and parcel of the instructional process. Assessment data on daily regular-classroom performance in light of the teacher's curricular and instructional approaches at worst can provide useful special education programming information later on, and at best such data may furnish insights into approaches that can maintain the pupil in the regular classroom.

   The special education teacher can assist in this process by providing time-efficient observation techniques and by assisting in the use of trial teaching procedures and other modifications. These might include peer tutoring, a change in seating, or self-charting, to name just three.

3. ***Determination of Special Education Eligibility***

With the possible exception of "visible" handicaps, the decision to formalize an IEP and place a pupil in a special education program is, in the final analysis, a judgment call. Many school districts have voting methods to be used in cases where team consensus is elusive. The special education teacher's role in interpreting the data and arriving at answers to key questions often tilts the scale one way or the other. In essence, the teacher's competency in the previous two areas, comparisons and prereferral assessment, dictates the nature and degree of his or her contribution to the question of eligibility. Teachers' facility in the formal testing end of the assessment process, their skills in direct, periodic measurement, and their knowledge of the prereferral status of the pupil in question will enhance the validity of the eligibility decision.

IEP Development. The blueprint for an appropriate education is the IEP. Though its format and process vary from state to state and school to school, compliance with P.L. 94–142 dictates that the total service plan consist of the pupil's present performance levels; annual goals and short-term objectives; objective evaluative criteria; descriptions of special education and related services, including dates of initiation and duration; and the percentage of time to be spent in the regular classroom. As reflected in the questions asked in the assessment model, these are the decisions made by the multidisciplinary team at Levels One through Three. At Level Three, Placement and IEP Development, the key decisions involve goals and objectives, services, and percentage of time spent in regular classroom placement. The special education teacher's input at each of these decision-making junctures determines the nature of the pupil's "special education."

1. ***Delineation of Goals and Objectives***

One of the first indicators of the utility of the assessment process emerges when goals and objectives are delineated. For moderately and severely handicapped pupils, physically handicapped pupils, and behaviorally handicapped pupils, most standardized test results will have little to contribute. Even for mildly handicapped pupils, appropriate and useful long-term goals and short-term objectives are best derived from a prudent synthesis of formal test data with direct measurement of selected behaviors across selected environments, including but not limited to the classroom. In addition, pupil and parental preferences must be taken into account, especially in decisions addressing the prioritization of long-term goals and future planning.

2. ***Specification of Services Including Regular Classroom Placement***

Assessment data inclusive of a variety of environments (e.g., group and individual classroom instruction; prevocational, home, and selected community settings) will permit more reasonable decisions about services in light of available school and community resources. Recent literature has addressed the need for consideration of service resources beyond the confines of the classroom and school (Halpern, 1985; Wehman, 1981). Again, the best decision regarding services and *where* they should be administered ought to be a *data-based* decision.

Instructional Planning and Evaluation.   As mentioned previously, the special education teacher is primarily responsible for gathering and interpreting the data that lead to decisions at these two levels. These decisions and their resultant specifications as to exactly how programs are to be implemented and evaluated depend on the teacher's skills within the three competency domains outlined below.

1. *Designing Individual Implementation Programs (IIP)*

   The heart of teaching is the design and execution of an effective instructional program. Knowledge of methods of instructional sequencing and task analysis (see Chapter 2) combine with assessment skills in forming its organic parts. Currently, the special education teacher has access to a multitude of resources that assist in the translation of assessment data into valid instructional designs. Sugai (1985) describes ways in which the IIP's total-service-plan data are delineated to lend themselves to specific instructional designs and gives examples showing how a system for the ongoing assessment of IIPs can be created and maintained. Included are formats for data-based IIPs requiring minimal time and paperwork to maintain. Also, Utley (1982) presents an excellent assortment of hierarchical, time-based, and conceptual task-analysis methods. Specific procedures address objectives related to developmental skills, for example single and serial response sets, as well as higher-order objectives involving the discrimination of abstract concept attributes (See note 2, p. 355).

2. *Determining What Constitutes Mastery of Target IEP Skills*

   Since the implementation of the IEP concept in 1977, many problematic practices related to the IEP have been identified and addressed (Nevin, McCann, and Semmel, 1983). Among them is the problem of determining criteria on which mastery of specific skills — and ultimately a short-term objective —is evaluated. In some cases, mastery levels are designated arbitrarily; yet considerable thought must be given not only to the quantitative aspect of mastery but to its very nature. Kazdin (1977) and Kazdin and Matson (1981) offer guidelines related to this question. They propose two procedures by which treatment outcomes can be assessed. First, the special education teacher may want to develop rough norms of peer behavior relative to the target skill; or he or she could informally elicit the opinions of persons who would be competent to judge mastery of a given skill in a given environment. Either way, the teacher should be aware of school and community standards and be able to reflect these in the specification of mastery criteria.

3. *Tracking Pupil Performance Levels*

   If instructional design is the heart of teaching, the formative assessment of daily performance is the heart of assessment for program evaluation purposes (see Chapters 2, 6, and 7). Relative to these practices, the teacher must search deeply into his or her efficacy as a professional educator. To put it another way, what good is special education if it cannot at least bring about demonstrable improvement in a pupil's perceived problem or, if data so warrant, get the pupil *out* of the particular program with reasonable haste?

Among other resources (see Deno, Mirkin, and Wesson, 1984; Sugai, 1985), the special education teacher now has access to an ever-improving cache of microcomputer technology to aid in tracking performance levels. For example, Hasselbring and Hamlett (1983) have developed a program that maintains and projects data for multicycle semilogarythmic charts. The program, "Aimstar," (Hesselbring & Hamlett, 1983) decreases dramatically the amount of time necessary for keeping track of daily pupil performance. Additional information on microcomputer technology applications is provided in the final section of this chapter.

Assessment as an Ongoing Part of Instruction

Throughout this text, the various chapter authors have stressed the integral role assessment plays in the overall instructional process. Upon specification of an IEP and a decision about special education placement, the task is to implement the educational program according to the IEP blueprint. Assessment data related to IEP implementation are both formative and summative in their usefulness. Data derived from Level-Four questions are formative in the sense that they should contribute to accurate and relevant instructional planning on a continuous basis. Data collected toward decisions relative to Level-Five questions are more summative; that is, they lead toward an appraisal of how effective the program has been, whether it should be continued, and, if so, what refinements should be made. Such decision making can take place with regard to 12-week, annual, or triennial IEP reviews and evaluations.

With this responsibility comes flexibility on the part of the teacher to use assessment in planning *what* to teach and *how* to teach it and in evaluating *how well* it was taught (Zigmond, Vallecorsa, and Silverman, 1983). By examining the model presented in this volume, one can see that assessment for these instructional purposes involves continuous attention to the eight questions contained in Levels Four and Five. Although for conceptual clarity they are presented as separate entities, assessment for instructional purposes can best be understood by attending to the interaction and recycling of the questions specified at each of these two levels.

Instructional Planning

Instructional planning must be accurate and relevant in order to result in educational outcomes that are more beneficial to today's pupils than the results of "seat-of-the-pants" teaching plans were to pupils in special education classes during the forties and fifties (Lazerson, 1983). Assessment for planning purposes involves a cycle of trial teaching, ongoing data collection, and program refinements that provides an accurate and relevant account of the teacher's decisions relative to the three questions specified in Level Four. Moreover, the teacher's consideration of these questions via the data he or she collects and interprets plays a major role in decision making centering on the more summative questions specified in Level Five.

What Skills Should Be Taught?   Teachers often approach this question with a mistaken assumption: they believe they must administer a host of developmental, academic, language, or vocational skill inventories before actually beginning instruction. Among the guidelines offered by Zigmond, Vallecorsa, and Silverman (1983), two are useful in this regard. First, it is most prudent to break down skill and response hierarchies related to short-term objectives into an "as-you-go" form, beginning to teach as soon as possible, even if just on a trial basis, and allowing pupils' responses and further assessment to guide the fine tuning of the instructional program. Second, for any skill or response hierarchy employed, it is more efficient to predict the highest possible functioning level and test down rather than to assume some basal performance level and test up until the pupil (almost literally in some cases) hits the ceiling. For example, correct responses reflecting more complex skills derived from hierarchical task analysis can sometimes indicate possession of the more basic skills of the hierarchy. More efficient identification of skills tends to allow for more teaching and for a more accurate and relevant appraisal of subsequent mastery.

How Does the Pupil Learn Best?   Among the factors discussed that relate to this question have been environmental, emotional, physical, sociological, and psychological elements. Again, consideration of these areas in planning specific programs is not a one-shot venture. As stressed in Chapter 2, teachers must, for example, pay continuing attention to the reinforcers, planned and unplanned, that are operating in the learning setting. This author remembers well the knotty pine–paneled time-out room used some years ago in a summer practicum he was directing. He noticed how often a particularly troublesome pupil was being placed there by his student teacher. Simple observation revealed that the pupil was literally "snorting" the walls of this room, ostensibly getting turned on by the smell of that knotty pine! Of the array of reinforcing objects and events available, this smell was indeed pleasantly powerful in the case of our "troublesome" pupil. In many instances, the determination of the way a pupil learns best relative to the five dimensions of learning style discussed in Chapter 2 is an empirical determination — one requiring ongoing probes and refinements by the teacher.

Resources that can assist in systematically matching the learner with appropriate instructional procedures abound for the industrious teacher. Teachers can gain access to resources through various professional networks, such as the Council for Exceptional Children (CEC), as well as through published-document computer searches. The best of the available resources and materials can stimulate, but do not necessarily provide, creative and workable instructional programs. Procedures for analyzing short-term objectives into skill and response hierarchies (Utley, 1982) and for organizing teaching and data-collection activities around them (Deno, Mirkin, and Wesson, 1984; Sugai, 1985) are crucial to appropriate instructional planning. Low cost (especially in terms of time) and high yield (especially in terms of instructional data) are the rules of thumb. Some short-term objectives, particularly those that address skill domains in oral reading (Knowlton, 1980, 1982a), written language (Graham and Miller, 1979, 1980), and mathematics (Knowlton, 1982b; Skrtic, Kvam, and Beals, 1983) can be broken down into data-based trial teaching designs. For example, Skrtic, Kvam, and Beals (1983) have described the clinical math interview, a procedure by which error-pattern analysis for any operation (e.g., subtraction) translates into step-wise programs that are graduated in presentation from concrete to symbolic levels. Procedures like this make deciding what and how to teach easier. The teacher should never be constrained by the perceived need to test first and wait on the initiation of instructional programming.

How Should Objectives Be Modified?   The multi- or interdisciplinary team should assume at the outset that short-term objectives are subject to a process of refinement not only during the three years between initial placement and reevaluation but also yearly and at appropriate times (e.g., every 12 weeks) between the initiation of IEP services and the annual IEP update. Because of regulatory requirements, short-term objectives and their mastery criteria (and the remainder of the IEP components) must be specified no longer than 30 days after diagnosis. It is unreasonable to expect that for any one pupil at least a few of the objectives will not be in need of refinement at some point during the school year. Their content and standards need to be scrutinized for realism and relevance (Kazdin and Matson, 1981). Ongoing assessment and instructional planning will yield new and clearer insights into the pupil's ultimate level of potential functioning, his or her most probable next placement, and the nature of his or her transition needs, whether from class to class or from school to independent living. Nothing in P.L. 94–142's legislative history or in its implementation during the past decade would lead one to the conclusion that the IEP should be a static document or that its objectives should be staid.

Program Evaluation

While the data pursuant to the Level-Four questions mentioned above are formative in nature, those derived from Level-Five questions are for the most part summative; that is, they are collected and interpreted for the purpose of drawing conclusions about the merits of the special education program, whether it should be continued, and, if it is continued, what refinements are necessary. Such refinements would include the degree and nature of programming for the handicapped pupil in regular classroom and/or community settings. The appropriateness of decisions regarding questions at the four earlier levels becomes apparent at this summative level. In particular, the teacher's daily planning habits and the relevance of his or her data management at Level Four serve decisions about program effectiveness and continuance quite well. These decisions and the nature of the data that support them are described below.

Mastery of Goals and Objectives.   Exactly what constitutes "mastery" of an objective is a matter best determined through systematic analysis — a process Kazdin

(1977) has termed "social validation." Introduced previously in this chapter, social-validation procedures assist teachers in maintaining the relevance of their instruction by assuring that the standards against which a pupil's behavior is assessed are normatively realistic and relevant. Crossing the street unassisted, paying the correct fare and riding the subway from Center City to Veterans' Stadium, balancing a checkbook, taking lecture notes, writing a thank-you note, reading and responding to a classified ad, and dealing with local government bureaucracies are but a handful of "goals" for which mastery is an elusive concept.

How facile a pupil is in the skills and behaviors associated with any one goal is a decision that should be made in light of socially valid mastery criteria. Whether one chooses to collect normative mastery data on a small scale — for example, the work rates of pupils in vocational programs (Scarlett and Latta, 1985) or ecological inventories of community settings (Sailor and Guess, 1984) — or to invite the subjective judgments of "experts" — for example, supermarket employees and customers or local government bureaucrats — ongoing social-validation procedures preclude irrelevance in instructional programming as well as assisting in making decisions about mastery.

Current Performance Levels. When the special education program is reviewed, it is tempting to make pre/post comparisons on the basis of, say, a standardized achievement test and proclaim the program a success or a failure. Yet, if Level-Four data have been collected continuously and in a manner consistent with the suggestions made above, the pupil's progress or lack of it can be analyzed, not merely judged. It is important to let such data contribute to postprogram decisions about current performance levels.

Regular Classroom Functioning. Again, proper decision making at this point depends heavily on decision making at previous levels. Specifically, what prereferral data were taken regarding classroom and instructional modification as part of Level-One assessment efforts? If pupils are placed in a regular classroom for the first time as part of their IEP services, this question should be included in data-collection efforts with regard to Level Four. Either way, regular and special education teachers' collaboration in the mainstreaming of handicapped pupils is discussed in some 20 books on the subject (one of the better ones is by Morsink [1984]) the scope of which is beyond the intent of the present chapter.

Continuation in Special Education. The purpose of the triennial re-evaluation of a pupil in special education is to make sure he or she continues to need a program and, if so, in what way his or her needs have changed. The IEP is evaluated annually with an eye on program changes also. Decisions at this juncture are among the most important that the multidisciplinary team must make, and the data relevant to them are among the most important that the special education teacher collects. Risking redundancy, it must be stressed that sole dependence on pre/post methods of making these decisions amounts to folly. The best decisions about program continuance are made in light of a thorough database and with substantive input from a teacher thoroughly familiar with that database.

A Summary of the Major Issues Affecting Assessment Practices

As stressed in the foregoing sections, the overriding issue affecting proper assessment in special education is the quality of school personnel; that is, their practices as they comply with P.L. 94–142 and corresponding state laws. Their ability to apply the practices discussed throughout this text in complying with requirements is critical, specifically in relation to the assessment process and generally to all facets of special education. Concerns about the quality and compliance of personnel lead to consideration of three specific issues that bear on quality-assessment practices: prereferral assessment and intervention, test discrimination, and assessment of adaptive behavior.

Prereferral Assessment and Intervention

Increasing concern has been voiced over the issue of pupil referrals for consideration of eligibility for special education services (Ysseldyke et al., 1983). This concern relates to practices specific to Levels One and Two of our model, whereby many pupils are referred for, and placed in, special education — some in an almost capricious manner (Algozzine, Ysseldyke, and Christensen, 1983).

In attempting to address this problem, many states are requiring schools to focus resources on prereferral interventions and to document these efforts. As mentioned, the special education teacher plays an important, albeit indirect, role in this process. Most statewide models and local efforts in this direction are variations of the model proposed by Graden, Casey, and Christensen (1985). In essence this model explicates question 4 in Level One, concerning regular classroom modifications.

In their model, Graden and her colleagues call for four stages of indirect services before a formal referral: request for consultation, consultation, observation, and either a repetition of consultation and observation or a formal referral. The consultation and observation stages involve increasing intensities of collaborative problem solving on the part of the special and regular educators. This problem solving addresses the pupil's particular interactions with a variety of teacher and classroom variables. The successful implementation of a prereferral model such as this in any given school will depend heavily on the aforementioned political and procedural competencies of the special education teacher (Skrtic, Guba, and Knowlton, 1985).

Improper Test Discrimination

The issue of bias in assessment practices is well documented (Algozzine and Ysseldyke, 1982; Flaugher, 1978; Kirp, 1974). Refer also to Chapter 3, "Basic Principles of Measurement and Test Development," for an in-depth discussion of issues involving bias in educational assessment practices and instrumentation. Ysseldyke (1980) cautions against viewing the issue from the perspective of tests per se. There is probably no such thing as a completely fair test for any one person being tested. Discrimination as a psychometric quality of a test is appropriate — as long as it is consistent with the test's purposes.

For example, if one were to discriminate between those who can and cannot walk a balance beam for the purpose of selecting persons to perform balance-beam stunts, the test's discrimination is potentially useful. If, however, the purposes of such testing were related to the formation of reading groups, one would be making an improper test discrimination. Similarly, if one were assessing intelligence by discriminating between those who can and those who cannot make appropriate verbal responses to questions, the proper basis for discrimination would be whether or not a person has the cognitive potential to know the answers, not whether the person's background equipped him or her with the answers.

The days of blatantly improper discrimination are waning. However, there is still evidence to indicate that pupils are being administered tests that reflect deficits in intelligence, achievement, or adaptive behavior that may be due to naturally occurring characteristics or to acculturation rather than to the factor the particular test is alleging (Algozzine and Ysseldyke, 1982). Improper test discrimination is an issue most practitioners will look squarely in the eye. And, as mentioned, the more directly samples of behavior related to the skill domain of interest are measured, the more likely the achievement of proper discrimination.

Assessment of Adaptive Behavior

Unfortunately, many practitioners believe adaptive behavior assessment is necessary only when a classification decision involves mental retardation (M.R.) as one possibility. This view stems from the inclusion of the component "deficit in adaptive behavior" in both the P.L. 94–142 and American Association on Mental Deficiency definitions of M.R. Because P.L. 94–142 requires that no one test serve as the sole criterion for special education placement, adaptive-behavior assessment and some type of intellectual assessment (most often an I.Q. test) have formed the typical approach when diagnostic decisions (Level Two) about M.R., especially the mild range, are being made.

Decisions regarding how adaptive or maladaptive a behavior is within a given environment are important at *all* levels of the assessment model. Furthermore, such decisions affect all pupils, not just those labeled "retarded." Adaptive behavior and its precursor notion, social competence, have comprised the more fuzzy "social factor" that formal tests have tried to capture for years. Today the most widely accepted definition of adaptive behavior is "the effectiveness or degree with which individuals meet the standards of personal independence and social responsibility expected for age and cultural groups" (Grossman, 1983, p. 1).

Currently the most promising use for adaptive-behavior assessment is in instruction and training geared toward the transition of mildly handicapped pupils from secondary education to community living (Halpern, 1985a). In addition to pupils labeled "mildly mentally handicapped," those labeled "learning disabled" and "behavior disordered" face a variety of tasks once they are no longer eligible for mandated secondary education programs. These include adjustment to competitive employment environments; the establishment of interpersonal networks; the maintenance of safe, useful, and personally satisfying independent-living skills; and the enjoyment of and satisfaction in avocational leisure activities (Halpern, 1985b).

Although it is clear that adaptive-behavior assessment has much to offer in longitudinal educational programming toward these ends, its current strength in validity and reliability is of concern. A key facet of this problem relates to the format of adaptive behavior scales. Most scales — for example, the AAMD's Adaptive Behavior Scale (Nihira et al., 1974) — use an informant-based format in which a parent or someone who knows the pupil is interviewed about the pupil's functioning and, to a degree, developmental levels across a variety of domains such as self-help, motor, communication, and so on. The potential uses of such information are undermined by threats both to validity (a one-shot judgment regarding an aspect of functioning about which the informant may or may not know is solicited) and to reliability (direct, periodic observation by persons qualified to do so are not typically called for).

Although a few teachers and psychologists supplement formal tests of adaptive behavior with more useful assessment practices, most administer one formal scale, usually for diagnostic purposes. Until there are tests with more desirable psychometric characteristics, and until practitioners supplement formal testing with more direct data-gathering procedures, many instructionally meaningful data will remain uncovered.

If assessment for instructional decision making on the basis of our model is to be achieved and practices made exemplary rather than seen as suspect, the multidisciplinary team and the special education teacher in particular need to be equipped with an effective combination of professional training and political, procedural, and technological competencies.

The final portion of this chapter will describe some applications of microcomputer technology that have been found currently useful and that are believed to be indicative of future trends in the area of technology application to educational assessment.

Microcomputers and Related Technologies in Assessment

An emerging trend in assessment in special education is the use of microcomputer and microcomputer-related technology. To date, most of the software has been used to organize and retrieve records and data after initial assessment has taken place. Increasingly, however, educators and diagnosticians are using computers *during* the assessment process.

Microcomputer-Administered Assessment and Test-Generation Programs

Microcomputer-administered assessment involves direct use of the computer and software by the examinee. Programs using speech synthesis have been developed to assess comprehension of prepositional concepts by exceptional pupils with limited English proficiency (Wilson and Fox, 1982). Other direct-assessment programs provide career or vocational counseling. "Job Readiness — Assessment and Development" (Microcomputer Educational Products, 1982) is a four-disk program that provides pupils in grades 7 through 12 with vocational guidance for job hunting, interviewing, filling out job applications, and determining job-hunting resources.

Records Management.   One way special education teachers can continually assess pupils' academic skills is through software packages that contain records-management systems, such as the Milliken Math Sequences (Johnston, 1980). This software allows the teacher to make individual and class assignments, review individual and class performances, establish personalized performance levels for each pupil, and receive printed records of pupils' performances. Basic math skills are covered for kindergarten through the eighth grade in number readiness, addition, subtraction, multiplication, division, equations, decimals, percentages, fractions, integers, laws of arithmetic, and formulas for measurement. Because problem levels are not stated as grade levels, the program can be used in a wide range of school settings and tailored to individual pupils' needs for basic skills review.

Adapting IEP Goals.   Existing software can also be used in assessment to create various goals for a particular program. These goals need not relate to those intended by the software's author. For example, several activities can be organized around a program for language and literacy development (Boyer, 1985) using the teacher's own observational techniques and activity results for assessment. After using a particular program, pupils can be instructed to discuss the content and write a review or strategy for the program. This allows the instructor to assess reading, writing, and strategy formulation, none of which is intended by the program authors.

Videodisk Technology.   The use of videodisk technology provides another assessment alternative for the special education teacher. This technology can carry both audio and video information. The video portion is a single track with a capacity of 54,000 frames per side, and any individual frame can be found within one to two seconds either by entering the frame number into a prewritten computer program or by punching it in on the videodisk player. The audio portion is made up of two separate tracks, so two separate verbal descriptions could accompany

Figure 12–1

A Diagram of an Interactive Video System

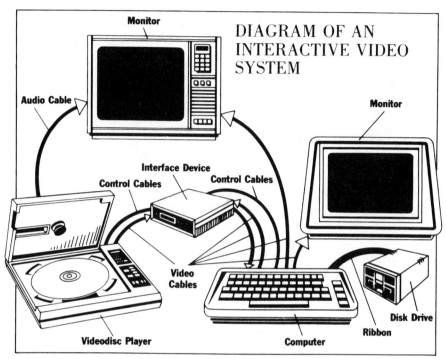

DIAGRAM OF AN INTERACTIVE VIDEO SYSTEM

Although systems will vary, usually video signals from the computer and the videodisc player have to pass through the interface device and go back to the computer in order to be modulated by the computer and sent on to the monitors.

Illustration by Bill Gilbert reprinted by permission of the artist.

each video frame, making possible two different descriptions of the same event or descriptions of it in two different languages.

Videodisk technology consists of three main parts: any equipment needed to produce the video, the video cassette, and the video cassette player (see Figure 12–1). Pupils could be assessed with it in a variety of ways. With the use of this technology, the testing situation would be more standardized than most because all pupils would be viewing and responding to the same presentation of the instrument. Because of the high cost of a videodisk, about $4,000, video cassette tapes are more commonly used.

Interactive Video. Technology that allows pupils to interact with the videodisk is called "interactive video." The most sophisticated form of interactive video is controlled by a computer programmed to present the lesson, ask questions, and process responses. The potential for use of interactive video in assessment within many special education settings is promising because of the many adaptations available for computer input. Touch-sensitive screens, for example, facilitate responding for physically handicapped pupils who might not be able to use the keyboard. Using fingers or a pointer, the child touches the screen at the desired answer. Responses could be recorded, analyzed, and reported quickly from the standardized input and output facilitated by the machine. Formative, summative, and criterion-referenced evaluations could be easily administered through videodisk technology.

In a study by Friedman (1985), a videocassette prototype math assessment program was used to evaluate pupils on seven strands of math in grades 1 through 4. The program was field-tested in El Paso, Texas, on Spanish-speaking pupils. This capability, when it is further developed, should have significant implications for assessment of pupils with whom language may be a barrier. The SuperPILOT authoring language (Apple Computer, 1982) supports the programming of microcomputer-controlled interactive video. A teacher who knows this language could write assessment programs using this versatile and promising combination of technology.

Test-Generation Programs.   For teachers with little computer or programming experience, commercial test-generation programs are available. They are sold as separate software packages and, depending on the program, allow the teacher to enter questions, mastery criteria, and other information important to test generation. "Tests Made Easy" (Compu-Tations Incorporated, 1984) is a menu-driven program that allows the teacher to enter, store, review, revise, and delete questions on any subject by making choices or entering information in each phase of the menu. Specific questions from a previously created file may be selected, or the computer can randomly choose a specified number of questions. Essay questions may be interspersed with fill-in questions.

The use of microcomputer and related technology in assessment is a controversial emerging practice. Software packages with built-in record-keeping systems can provide the special educator with continual assessment information, and using software for purposes other than the authors' original program goals may fill the same function. Videodisk and related computer-controlled technology may well be the teaching and assessment methodology of the future, while test-generation programs provide an immediate, user-friendly way of assessing pupils.

Data Collection, Assessment-Analysis Programs, and IEP Development

As previously mentioned, the most common use of computers in assessment is in post-assessment data management. The computer's ability to handle much of the clerical work and data analysis involved saves valuable time for teachers, diagnosticians, and administrators. Records and data management are handled more efficiently by the computer, and with the use of security systems, the confidentiality of pupil information is easier to maintain.

Data Recording. Small, lap-sized computers can be used to record data in the form of coded responses that represent observed behaviors. The person collecting the information enters it and has almost immediate feedback for data analysis.

There are many gradebook or record-keeping programs available. "Record Keeper" (Sky, 1984), for example, provides educators with a grade-keeping program that computes pupils' averages and provides them with personal progress reports. Up to nine subjects with 250 pupils each can be entered. This program allows the teacher to determine criteria for grading, the weight each criterion carries, and the grading range.

Analyzing Assessment Data. A valuable assessment-analysis program for teachers needing to modify pupils' behavior is "Aimstar" (Hasselbring and Hamlett, 1983). "Aimstar" is also effective for educators who wish to make decisions about the effectiveness and efficiency of instructional programs on the basis of predetermined criteria. This program develops graphs and charts of pupil-performance data and can be used in a wide variety of instructional approaches. "Aimstar" can simulate a standard six-cycle behavior chart or be adjusted to make charts with fewer cycles. Time spans of 30 to 270 days can be included, and a "line of progress" provides the learning trend line for the six most recent days of data.

Computer-Generated IEPs. Probably the most promising time saver for special education teachers and administrators is the improving capability and sophistication of computer-generated IEPs. These programs allow the user to generate an individualized education plan by entering pertinent personal and assessment data. They then analyze this information and print out an IEP. The first IEP programs available on disk contained banks of goals and objectives, but many of the goals on the printout had already been reached and needed to be deleted. These unneeded goals had to be crossed out, producing an unprofessional-looking document, an overwhelming amount of information for parents, and unnecessary paperwork in a pupil's file.

However, newer programs, such as the "TALLEY Goals and Objectives Writer" (Talley, 1985a), have a completely flexible bank of goals. Thus goals can be entered as they were intended, on an individual basis. Also available are supplementary objectives on floppy disk (Talley, 1985) for all levels of the Brigance Diagnostic Inventories (Brigance, 1977, 1978, 1980, 1983), including a Spanish version of the Diagnostic Inventory of Basic Skills (Brigance, 1983). Objectives for the Enright Diagnostic Inventory of Basic Arithmetic Skills (Enright, 1985) are also available. The "TALLEY Goals and Objectives Writer" (Talley, 1985) is a flexible, district-wide system for pupil data and IEP management. It accommodates important pupil information, IEPs, monthly updates, instructional objectives and annual goals, statistical summaries, cross-tabulation capabilities, and correspondence.

Post-assessment computer use can save valuable time for special education teachers and others involved in assessment, freeing them for direct interaction with pupils. Data collection during assessment, pupil-records management, gradebook programs, behavior management, and IEP programs are among the many capabilities of assessment management through computers.

Using Technology to Support Assessment

Among the many ways special educators can get and give support in the assessment of pupils is by using telecommunications and evaluation service centers.

Telecommunications Technology. Using the computer and telephone lines for sending and receiving information is referred to as "telecommunications." SpecialNet is an educational communication network sponsored by the National Association of State Directors of Special Education that processes information through electronic mail or electronic bulletin boards. The assessment bulletin board is one among many and was established in response to requests from SpecialNet subscribers. It provides a means for special educators to communicate directly with publishers and test developers concerning assessment instruments. Publishers post information about new instruments and are available for consultation on target populations, test standardization, test administration, and the availability of training. Special education teachers can take advantage of this readily available information to select assessment instruments, learn about the most recent methodologies, and obtain training for themselves and others involved in educational assessment.

Another resource for assessment information is the Special Education Software Center in Menlo Park, California, which provides information on the selection of assessment software packages and technical assistance on their use. It can also provide database listings of assessment packages. The Center's software-information telephone number is 1–800–327–5892; the technical-assistance number is 1–800–223–2711; and the TTY number for the deaf is 1–800–435–7639. The Special Education Software Center can also be reached via modem and telecommunications through a local call to a computer telephone network called "TYMNET."

Applications Where Language May Be a Factor. Some organizations, such as the Intercultural Development Research Association (IDRA), help school districts manage assessment through the use of computers. A disproportionate number of pupils labeled as "limited English proficient" (L.E.P.) have been represented in special education programs. Several probable reasons for this disproportionate representation include inaccurate assessment of a pupil's language proficiency. L.E.P. pupils have often been identified as needing special education services when, in fact, their problems were the result of language differences rather than language or cognitive deficits. Conversely, many pupils are denied quality special education services because there are no teachers available with the appropriate combination of language and special education skills to deliver the services.

Texas now requires all pupils who may be classified as limited English proficient to be assessed for language proficiency and language dominance (IDRA Staff, 1984). The IDRA currently offers a variety of services related to the most widely used language assessment tests, the Language Assessment Scales (LAS) (DeAvila and Duncan, 1979). A team of highly trained test scorers can grade the production section of the test, a portion that is often difficult to score objectively. This large-scale grading insures greater reliability and accuracy within and across school districts. The IDRA will also train personnel in the scoring of this instrument and provide computerized management of the LAS. Data included in the listings provided to campuses, teachers, and districts summarize breakdowns of the various test sections. This information is used for planning, reporting, and proposal-development purposes.

Those using the IDRA's scoring services cite many advantages, including saving valuable teacher time, scoring accuracy, the availability of computer listings, and summary data for easier record keeping, reporting, program planning, and management. Computer listings also lend themselves to more efficient review and evaluation of school district programs provided for L.E.P. pupils. Support services that utilize various forms of computer technology can benefit and support the special educator, not to mention the pupil.

The Need for More Data.   The use of microcomputer-administered assessments is controversial. Many say it is the best, most standardized way to test, while others oppose the loss of human interaction in assessment (Boyer, 1985). Those supporting the use of assessment software maintain that microcomputers may offer the best opportunity to date for nondiscriminatory, objective testing (Boyer, 1985). Others emphasize the accuracy of computer assessment and point out that people are often able to respond to the computer before they respond to other human beings (Wilson and Fox [1982]). In fact, after exposure to the computer in one research study dealing with the language comprehension of exceptional limited-English-proficient pupils, only one examinee out of fourteen chose not to use the computer for further testing (Wilson and Fox, 1982). The rest preferred to use the computer combined with speech synthesis.

Those opposing computer assessment argue that it entails a loss of clinical observation and human interaction. They see the kinds of data that can be accepted by the computer as limited and inflexible, posing a threat to accurate assessment and diagnosis. However, microcomputer applications in data collection, assessment-analysis programs, and IEP development, to be used after assessment occurs, are very popular. These programs can save the teacher or diagnostician valuable time in data analysis and record keeping.

Summary

This chapter has synthesized the essential attributes of the educational assessment model utilized in this volume and has explored the use of microcomputers and related technologies in assessment. Some of the major topics and issues dealt with in this chapter include:

1. Contemporary roles of the special education teacher in educational assessment practices.
2. Political and procedural competencies the special education classroom teacher needs in order to play an integral role in the educational assessment process.
3. How assessment serves ongoing classroom instruction.
4. The critical function of prereferral assessment and intervention in special education.
5. Issues involving test development, administration, and interpretation biases.
6. Issues involving the assessment of adaptive behavior.
7. How the use of microcomputers and related technology *during* assessment is controversial.
8. Some of the ways computers are used during assessment, including the use of record-keeping systems that are an integral part of a drill and practice.
9. The most common use of computers and related technologies in assessment is in data collection, assessment-analysis programs, and IEP development.
10. Computerized IEP programs are now more flexible. Some can take currently popular assessment instruments and generate IEP goals.
11. Emerging uses of computers in assessment include the exchange of information about assessment through telecommunications and organizations that offer assessment analysis and management.

You may have been wondering about the two teachers whose discussion was described at this chapter's outset. Well, the second teacher's reply to the first one's concern about the utility of a particular test consisted of some sage advice: "When we have to think about assessment as apart from teaching — that is, stopping to give a test — we've missed the boat on its potential uses. Successful teaching is informed teaching — the two are one."

Notes

1. It should be noted that comparisons of the exceptional person with age peers in a standardization sample *could* be appropriate with respect to certain pupils if one were interested in decisions related, for example, to the evaluation of the special education program and its possible cessation. Nevertheless, such comparisons at the screening and diagnosis level of decision making increase the probability of false positives.
2. Individual Implementation Plans (IIPs) are instructional designs for any one short-term objective specified in the IEP's total service plan.

Appendix I

Appendix I

Test Review Form[1]

1.) Title	2.) Author(s)
3.) Publisher, Publisher's address, Copyright	4.) Type of test
	5.) Age range
6.) Purpose of test	
7.) Time requirements	
8.) Validity	9.) Reliability
10.) Standardization described	
11.) Norm population	
12.) Examiner qualifications	
13.) Response modalities required	
14.) Can test be adapted? (Briefly state how.)	
15.) Other important features	
16.) Critique	

[1]Adapted from Test Review Form, developed by D. Cross, Department of Special Education, Educational Assessment Clinic, University of Kentucky, Lexington, KY 40506. Used with permission.

Appendix II

Appendix II
Table 1

Informal Inventories, Norm- and Criterion-Referenced Reading Tests

Test, Publisher, and Grades	Type of Test

Advanced Reading Inventory (Johns, 1981),
  William C. Brown
  Grades 7–College
	Informal reading inventory with graded word lists.

Analytic Reading Inventory (Woods & Moe, 1981),
  Charles E. Merrill
  Preprimer–Grade 9
	Informal reading inventory with graded word lists.

Botel Reading Inventory (Botel, 1962),
  Follett Educational Corporation
  Grades 1–12
	Informal reading inventory with graded word lists.

Brigance Diagnostic Inventory of Basic Skills (Brigance, 1977),
  Curriculum Associates
  Kindergarten–Grade 7
	Criterion-referenced; some subtests yield grade equivalents.

Brigance Diagnostic Inventory of Essential Skills (Brigance, 1980),
  Curriculum Associates
  Grades 7–12
	Criterion-referenced; some subtests yield grade equivalents.

Classroom Reading Inventory (Silvaroli, 1976),
  William C. Brown
  Preprimer–Grade 8
	Informal reading inventory with graded word lists and spelling lists.

Criterion Reading (Hackett, 1974),
  Random House
  Grades 1–12
	Criterion-referenced.

Diagnosis: An Instructional Aid (Shub, Carlin, Friedman, Kaplan, & Katien, 1973),
  SRA
  Kindergarten–Grade 6
	Criterion-referenced.

Diagnostic Reading Scales (Spache, 1972),
  CTB/McGraw-Hill
  Grades 1–8
	Norm-referenced but technically inadequate; best used as a criterion-referenced device.

Durrell Analysis of Reading Difficulty (Durrell, 1955),
  Harcourt Brace Jovanovich, Inc.
  Preprimer–Grade 6
	Norm-referenced but technically inadequate; best used as a criterion-referenced device.

| | Skills | | | | | | | |
| Word recognition | | | Comprehension | | | | | |
Word attack	Sight vocabulary	Fluency	Vocabulary	Literal	Inferential	Evaluative	Listening	Applications
	X	X		X	X	X		
	X	X		X	X	X		
X	X		X					
X	X	X	X	X				X
X	X	X	X	X				X
X	X	X	X	X	X		X	
X	X		X	X	X			
X	X		X	X	X			
X	X	X		X	X		X	
X	X	X		X			X	

Table 1

Informal Inventories, Norm- and Criterion-Referenced Reading Tests (*continued*)

Test, Publisher, and Grades	Type of Test
Gates-McKillop Reading Diagnostic Tests (Gates & McKillop, 1962), Teachers College Press Grades 1–7	Norm-referenced but technically inadequate; best used as criterion-referenced device.
Gilmore Oral Reading Test (Gilmore & Gilmore, 1968), Harcourt Brace Jovanovich Grades 1–8	Norm-referenced but technical adequacy is questionable; best used as a criterion-referenced device.
Gray Oral Reading Test (Gray & Robinson, 1967), Bobbs-Merrill Grades 1–12	Norm-referenced but technical adequacy is questionable; best used as a criterion-referenced device.
Individual Reading Placement Inventory (Smith & Bradtmueller, 1969), Follett Grade 5–Adult	Informal reading inventory with graded word lists.
Informal Reading Diagnosis (Rae & Potter, 1981), Prentice-Hall Preprimer–Grade 8	Informal reading inventory with graded word lists; available in English and Spanish.
Iowa Silent Reading Tests (Farr, 1973), Houghton Mifflin Grade 6–College	Norm-referenced.
McCollough Word Analysis Tests (McCollough, 1963), Ginn All grades	Norm-referenced test, but standardized on small sample; norms should be used with caution.
On the Spot Reading Diagnosis File (LePray, 1978), Center for Applied Research in Education Primer–Grade 11	Informal reading inventory with graded word lists.
Reading Miscue Inventory (Goodman & Burke, 1972), Macmillan	Criterion-referenced.
Roswell-Chall Diagnostic Test of Word Analysis (Roswell & Chall, 1959), Essay Press Grades 2–6	Criterion-referenced.

| | Skills | | | | | | | |
| Word recognition | | | Comprehension | | | | | |
Word attack	Sight vocabulary	Fluency	Vocabulary	Literal	Inferential	Evaluative	Listening	Applications
X	X	X	X					
		X		X				
		X		X				
X	X	X		X	X			
	X	X		X	X			
			X	X	X	X		
X								
X		X		X	X			
X	X	X		X				
X								

Table 1

Informal Inventories, Norm- and Criterion-Referenced Reading Tests (*continued*)

Test, Publisher, and Grades	Type of Test
Silent Reading Diagnostic Tests (Bond, Balow, & Hoyt, 1970), Meredith Grades 2–6	Norm-referenced.
Stanford Diagnostic Reading Tests (Karlsen, Madden, & Gardner, 1978), Harcourt Brace Jovanovich Grades 1–13	May be used as both a norm-referenced and a criterion-referenced test.
Sucher-Allred Reading Placement Inventory (Sucher & Allred, 1973), Economy Primer–Grade 9	Informal reading inventory.
System Fore (Bagaie & Bagai, 1979), Foreworks Preschool–High school	Criterion-referenced.
Test of Reading Comprehension (Brown, Hammill, & Wiederholt, 1978), Pro-Ed Grade 2–High school	Norm-referenced.
Wisconsin Tests of Reading Skill Development (Kamon, Miles, Van Blaricom, Harris, & Stewart, 1972), National Computer Systems Kindergarten–Grade 6	Criterion-referenced.
Woodcock Reading Mastery Tests (Woodcock, 1974), American Guidance Service Kindergarten–Grade 12	Norm-referenced.

Skills								
Word recognition			Comprehension					
Word attack	Sight vocabulary	Fluency	Vocabulary	Literal	Inferential	Evaluative	Listening	Applications
X	X							
	X	X	X	X	X			
	X	X		X	X	X		
X								
			X	X	X			X
X	X		X	X	X	X		
X	X		X	X	X	X		

Appendix II
Table 2

Norm- and Criterion-Referenced Tests of Written Language

Test, Publisher, and Grades	Type of Test
Basic School Skills Inventory (Hammill & Lehigh, 1982), Pro-Ed Kindergarten–Grade 3	Norm-referenced.
Brigance Diagnostic Inventory of Basic Skills (Brigance, 1977), Curriculum Associates Kindergarten–Grade 7	Criterion-referenced; some subtests yield grade equivalents.
Brigance Diagnostic Inventory of Essential Skills (Brigance, 1980), Curriculum Associates Grades 7–12	Criterion-referenced; some subtests yield grade equivalents.
Kottmeyer Diagnostic Spelling Test (Kottmeyer, 1959), Webster Publishing Grades 1–6	Criterion-referenced; yields a grade-level score.
Picture Story Language Test (Myklebust, 1965), Grune & Stratton Grade 2–High school	Norm-referenced but technical adequacy is questionable; best used as a criterion-referenced device.
Sequential Test of Educational Progress (1958), Educational Testing Service Grades 1–6	Norm-referenced.
Spellmaster (Cohen & Abrams, 1976), Publishers Test Service Grades 1–8	Norm-referenced but technically inadequate; best used as criterion-referenced device.
Test of Adolescent Language (Hammill, Brown, Larsen, & Wiederholt, 1980), Pro-Ed Grades 5–High school	Norm-referenced (also assesses oral language skills).
Test of Written Language (Hammill & Larsen, 1978), Pro-Ed Grades 3–8	Norm-referenced.
Test of Written Spelling (Larsen & Hammill, 1976), Pro-Ed Grades 1–9	Norm-referenced; but analysis of spelling errors may yield criterion-referenced information.
Zaner-Bloser Evaluation Scales (1979), Zaner-Bloser Grades 1–8	Criterion-referenced; yields quality ratings in reference to grade-level expectancies.

	Skills			
Generation of ideas	Handwriting	Conventions of print	Spelling	
	X			
	X	X	X	
	X	X	X	
			X	
X		X		
X		X	X	
			X	
X				
X	X	X	X	
			X	
	X			

Appendix II
Table 3

Norm- and Criterion-Referenced Mathematics Tests

Test, Publisher, and Grades	Type of Test	Skills	
		Problem Solving	
		Word problems	Applications
Basic Educational Skills Inventory: Math (Adamson, Shrago, & Van Etten, 1972), Brad Winch Grades 1–6	Norm-referenced.		
Brigance Diagnostic Inventory of Basic Skills (Brigance, 1977), Curriculum Associates Kindergarten–Grade 7	Criterion-referenced; some subtests yield grade equivalents.		X
Brigance Diagnostic Inventory of Essential Skills (Brigance, 1980), Curriculum Associates Grades 7–12	Criterion-referenced; some subtests yield grade equivalents.	X	X
Diagnosis: An Instructional Aid in Mathematics (Guzaitis, Carlin, & Juda, 1972), SRA Kindergarten–Grade 6	Criterion-referenced.	X	
Diagnostic Chart for Fundamental Processes in Arithmetic (Buswell & John, 1925), Bobbs-Merrill All grades	Criterion-referenced; assesses computational strategies.		
Diagnostic Mathematics Inventory (Gessell, 1977), CTB/McGraw-Hill Grades 1–9	Criterion-referenced.		
Diagnostic Test of Arithmetic Strategies (Ginsburg & Mathews, 1983), Pro-Ed Grades 1–6	Criterion-referenced.		
Diagnostic Tests and Self-Help in Arithmetic (Brueckner, 1955), CTB/McGraw-Hill Grades 3–8	Criterion-referenced.		
KeyMath Diagnostic Arithmetic Test (Connolly, Nachtman, & Pritchett, 1976), American Guidance Service Grades 1–9	Norm-referenced; may also be used as a criterion-referenced device by referring to table of objectives.	X	

				Skills								
		Concepts						Computation				
Math readiness	Whole numbers	Time	Money	Measurement	Geometry	Algebra	Addi-tion	Subtrac-tion	Multipli-cation	Divi-sion	Decimals	Frac-tions
X	X	X	X				X	X	X	X	X	X
X	X	X	X	X	X		X	X	X	X	X	X
	X	X	X	X	X		X	X	X	X	X	X
	X			X	X		X	X	X	X	X	X
							X	X	X	X	X	X
							X	X	X	X	X	X
							X	X	X	X	X	X
							X	X	X	X		
	X	X	X	X	X	X	X	X	X	X	X	X

Table 3

Norm- and Criterion-Referenced Mathematics Tests (*continued*)

		Skills	
		Problem Solving	
Test, Publisher, and Grades	Type of Test	Word problems	Applications
Stanford Diagnostic Mathematics Test (Beatty, Madden, Gardner, & Karlsen, 1976), Harcourt Brace Jovanovich Grades 2–High School	Norm-referenced and criterion-referenced.	X	X
Test of Early Mathematics Ability (Ginsburg & Baroody, 1983), Pro-Ed Kindergarten–Grade 4	Norm-referenced and criterion-referenced.		
Test of Mathematical Abilities (Brown & McEntire, 1983), Pro-Ed Grades 1–6	Norm-referenced; also assesses attitudes toward mathematics.	X	
Wisconsin Design for Math Skill Development Test (Armenia, Kamp, McDonald, & Von Kuster, 1975), Educational Systems Kindergarten–Grade 6	Criterion-referenced.	X	X

								Skills				
			Concepts						Computation			
Math readiness	Whole numbers	Time	Money	Measurement	Geometry	Algebra	Addi-tion	Subtrac-tion	Multipli-cation	Divi-sion	Decimals	Frac-tions
	X	X	X	X	X	X	X	X	X	X	X	X
X	X						X	X	X	X		
							X	X	X	X		
	X	X	X	X		X	X	X	X	X	X	X

Appendix III

Introduction

Appendix III provides an overview of the different assessment methods used with gifted learners, the ability areas covered in these assessments, and the indicators teachers should be aware of when answering the assessment questions presented in the five-level assessment model used throughout this volume.

Table 1 provides a series of questions useful in clarifying gifted-pupil assessment. Table 2 of Appendix III lists characteristics of giftedness and high abilities. Not all students who are gifted in a certain area will exhibit all the characteristics listed; and some characteristics indicative of giftedness are not included in the list. Those included are merely indicators and are intended as examples.

The procedures labeled "Classroom modifications and observation of results" in Table 2 can actually be used for two purposes. When attempting to decide whether a child is gifted, you can use them as ways to approximate the methods shown to be successful with the gifted. If the child is successful, shows interest, and performs like other gifted students, this information can be used in deciding whether the child is eligible for a program. However, use of methods such as these in the regular classroom may meet the needs of the student and reduce the necessity for a special program. Only a few examples of such methods have been given. Others can be found in textbooks describing methods for teaching gifted students (Gallagher, 1975; Maker, 1982a, 1982b; Whitmore, 1980).

Appendix III
Table 1

Levels of Assessment, Questions, and Information Sources

Questions to be Answered	Information Sources	Persons Responsible
Level 1: Screening and Identification		
a) Is the student's performance on standardized tests significantly different from that of peers?	Group-administered tests Individually administered tests	Teacher of the gifted Regular classroom teacher Diagnostician School psychologist
b) Does the student's performance in the classroom indicate superior abilities or talents?	Classroom observations Product assessment Checklists for rating student characteristics	Teacher of the gifted Various experts in product areas Regular classroom teacher
c) Does the child's behavior at home indicate superior abilities or talents?	Interviews with parents Observation of child at home Checklists and rating scales Assessment of products developed at home	Teacher of the gifted Diagnostician
d) Does the student have a history of superior performance?	Examination of school records Interviews with past teachers Interviews with parents	Teacher of the gifted Regular classroom teachers Diagnostician
e) Do modifications within the regular classroom provide enough challenges or opportunities for the child to develop his or her superior abilities?	Systematic modifications in the regular classroom program Observation of the effects of modifications Interviews with past and present teachers Interviews with parents Student interview	Regular classroom teacher Teacher of the gifted
f) What are the differences between the child's performance on standardized tests and his or her behavior in the classroom or at home?	Comparison of expected levels of performance with actual levels of performance	Teacher of the gifted Diagnostician
Level 2: Eligibility and Diagnosis		
a) What are the behaviors or skills that indicate superior ability?	Standard tests Referral instruments (e.g., checklists, nomination forms) Classroom observations Student interview	Teacher of the gifted Regular classroom teacher Parent Child Peers Other professionals or community members familiar with the child

Table 1

Levels of Assessment, Questions, and Information Sources (*continued*)

Questions to be Answered	Information Sources	Persons Responsible
b) What are the behaviors, characteristics, or experiences that limit or inhibit the expression of superior ability?	Classroom observations Referral instruments (e.g., checklists, nomination forms) Student interview Standardized tests	Regular classroom teacher Teacher of the gifted Diagnostician Parent, child, peers Other professionals or community members familiar with the child
c) What are the student's present levels of strength and weakness?	Standardized tests Criterion-referenced tests	Teacher of the gifted Diagnostician
d) Does the student meet the district's criteria for entrance into the program for the gifted?	Examination of all previously collected information	Teacher of the gifted Screening and identification team
e) How does the student perform in the regular class?	Classroom observations Product assessment Examination of cumulative records	Regular classroom teacher Teacher of the gifted Various experts in product areas
f) Can the student's needs for development of strengths and remediation of weaknesses be met by the existing program(s)?	Examination of all previously collected information	Screening and identification team Teacher of the gifted
g) What program option(s) would be the best for meeting the student's needs?	Examination of all previously collected information	Teacher of the gifted Screening and identification team
h) Are the student's abilities and talents in areas that can be developed by existing staff and resources?	Examination of all previously collected information	Screening and identification team Teacher of the gifted
Level 3: Placement and IEP Development		
a) Which of the program goals are most important for developing the student's abilities and talents?	Interview with regular classroom teacher Student interview Parent interview Standardized tests Criterion-referenced tests Classroom observations Informal assessment procedures	Teacher of the gifted

Table 1

Levels of Assessment, Questions, and Information Sources (*continued*)

Questions to be Answered	Information Sources	Persons Responsible
b) Which of the program goals are most important for remediating the student's weak areas?	Interview with regular classroom teacher Student interview Parent interview Standardized tests Criterion-referenced tests Classroom observations Informal assessment procedures	Teacher of the gifted
c) What additional goals should be developed to meet the child's individual needs?	Interview with regular classroom teacher Student interview Parent interview Standardized tests Criterion-referenced tests Classroom observations Informal assessment procedures	Teacher of the gifted
d) How are the additional goals best met (e.g., in the regular classroom, at home, in an alternative program placement for part of the day, through acceleration)?	Interview with regular classroom teacher Student interview Parent interview Standardized tests Criterion-referenced tests Classroom observations Informal assessment procedures Interviews with teachers and others responsible for alternative placements being considered Classroom modifications and observations of results	Teacher of the gifted Screening and identification team
Level 4: Instructional Planning a) What specific skills should be taught?	Product assessment Criterion-referenced tests Informal assessment procedures Classroom observation Standardized tests	Teacher of the gifted Regular classroom teacher

Table 1

Levels of Assessment, Questions, and Information Sources (*continued*)

Questions to be Answered	Information Sources	Persons Responsible
b) What are the student's interests?	Student interview Interest inventory Interviews with past and present teachers Parent interview	Teacher of the gifted Regular classroom teacher
c) What is the student's preferred learning style?	Learning-style inventory Interviews with past and present teachers Parent interview	Teacher of the gifted
Level 5: Evaluation		
a) Which of the student's goals have been mastered?	Criterion-referenced tests Product assessment Standardized tests Classroom observations Informal assessment procedures	Teacher of the gifted
b) What progress has the student made toward meeting identified objectives?	Criterion-referenced tests Product assessment Standardized tests Classroom observations Informal assessment procedures	Teacher of the gifted
c) How is the student performing in the regular class and at home?	Parent interview Interview with regular classroom teacher Examination of cumulative records	Teacher of the gifted Regular classroom teacher
d) Should the student continue in the current programs?	Criterion-referenced tests Product assessment Standardized tests Classroom observations Informal assessment procedures Parent interview Student interview Interview with all teachers and counselors involved	Teacher of the gifted Screening and identification team

Table 1

Levels of Assessment, Questions, and Information Sources (*continued*)

Questions to be Answered	Information Sources	Persons Responsible
e) Should the student's placement be changed?	Criterion-referenced tests Product assessment Standardized tests Classroom observations Informal assessment procedures Parent interview Student interview Interview with all teachers and counselors involved	Teacher of the gifted Screening and identification team
f) How should the student's or the program's goals be changed?	Criterion-referenced tests Product assessment Standardized tests Classroom observations Informal assessment procedures Parent interview Student interview Interview with all teachers and counselors involved	Teacher of the gifted Screening and identification team

Appendix III
Table 2

Assessment Procedures, Indicators to Consider, and Questions Addressed

Test, Method, or Procedure	Ability or Characteristic	Indicators and Questions Answered
Standardized test of intelligence (group administered)	Intellectual	A score of 115 or above on the total battery, any subtest, or any subsection (1a, 2a)*
		A score of 125 or above on a subsection or the total battery (2d, 2f)
		High abilities in areas addressed by the program (2f, 2g, 2h, 2d)
		All subtest scores in comparison with the student's own average (2c)
Standardized test of intelligence (individually administered)	Intellectual	A subtest total, or subsection score, at least two standard deviations above the mean (1a, 1f, 2a, 2g)
		High abilities in areas addressed by the program (2f, 2g, 2h, 2d)
		A total score of at least two standard deviations above the mean (2d)
		A subtest or subsection score one standard deviation below the mean (2b)
		A subtest or subsection score two standard deviations below the student's own average scores (2b)
		All subtest scores in comparison with the student's own average (2c)
Standardized test of achievement (group administered)	Academic	A score at or above the 90th percentile in total score or any subsection (1a, 2a)
		A score at or above the 95th percentile in total score or any subsection (2d, 2f, 3a, 3c, 3d)
		High abilities in areas addressed by the program (2f, 2g, 2h, 2d)
		All subtest scores in comparison with the student's own average (2c, 3a, 3b, 3c, 3d)
		A subtest or subsection score two standard deviations below the student's own average scores (2b, 3b, 3c, 3d)
		A subtest or subsection score at the 40th percentile (2b, 3b, 3c, 3d)
		Scores much lower than those predicted by scores on an intelligence test (1f, 1c, 1d)
		Extremely high scores in areas not addressed by the program (3c, 3d)
		Scores indicate that criterion level has been reached (5a, 5b, 5d, 5e, 5f)
		Scores indicate significant progress in areas addressed by the program (5b, 5d, 5e, 5f)

*Numbers 1a and 2a refer to Table 1 of this Appendix.

Table 2

Assessment Procedures, Indicators to Consider, and Questions Addressed (*continued*)

Test, Method, or Procedure	Ability or Characteristic	Indicators and Questions Answered
Standardized test of achievement (individually administered)	Academic	A score at or above the 90th percentile in total score or any subsection (1a, 2a)
		A score at or above the 95th percentile in total score or any subsection (2d, 2f, 3a, 3c, 3d)
		High abilities in areas addressed by the program (2f, 2g, 2h, 2d)
		All subtest scores in comparison with the student's own average (2c, 3a, 3b, 3c, 3d)
		A subtest or subsection score two standard deviations below the student's own average scores (2b, 3b, 3c, 3d)
		A subtest or subsection score at the 40th percentile (2b, 3b, 3c, 3d)
		Scores much lower than those predicted by scores on an intelligence test (1f, 1c, 1d)
		Extremely high scores in areas not addressed by the program (3c, 3d)
		Scores indicate that criterion level has been reached (5a, 5b, 5d, 5e, 5f)
		Scores indicate significant progress in areas addressed by the program (5b, 5d, 5e, 5f)
Standardized test of creativity	Creativity	A score of 115 or above on the total battery, any subtest, or any subsection (1a, 2a)
		A score of 125 or above on a subsection or the total battery (2d, 3f)
		High abilities in areas addressed by the program (2f, 2g, 2h, 2d)
		All subtest scores in comparison with the student's own average (2c)
		A subtest total, or subsection score, at least two standard deviations above the mean (1a, 1f, 2a, 2g)
		High abilities in areas addressed by the program (2f, 2g, 2h, 2d)
		A total score of at least two standard deviations above the mean (2d)
		A subtest or subsection score one standard deviation below the mean (2b)
		A subtest or subsection score two standard deviations below the student's own average scores (2b)
		All subtest scores in comparison with the student's own average (2c)
		Extremely high scores in areas not addressed by the program (3c, 3d)

Table 2

Assessment Procedures, Indicators to Consider, and Questions Addressed (*continued*)

Test, Method, or Procedure	Ability or Characteristic	Indicators and Questions Answered
		Scores indicate that criterion level has been reached (5a, 5b, 5d, 5e, 5f)
		Scores indicate significant progress in areas addressed by the program (5b, 5d, 5e, 5f)
Standardized test of aptitude	Intellectual, academic, or specific talents such as mechanical	A score at or above the 90th percentile in total score or any subsection (1a, 2a)
		A score at or above the 95th percentile in total score or any subsection (2d, 2f, 3a, 3c, 3d)
		High abilities in areas addressed by the program (2f, 2g, 2h, 2d)
		All subtest scores in comparison with the student's own average (2c, 3a, 3b, 3c, 3d)
		A subtest or subsection score two standard deviations below the student's own average scores (2b, 3b, 3c, 3d)
		A subtest or subsection score at the 40th percentile (2b, 3b, 3c, 3d)
		Scores much lower than those predicted by scores on an intelligence test (1f, 1c, 1d)
		Extremely high scores in areas not addressed by the program (3c, 3d)
		Scores indicate that criterion level has been reached (5a, 5b, 5d, 5e, 5f)
		Scores indicate significant progress in areas addressed by the program (5b, 5d, 5e, 5f)
Standardized test of critical or "higher-level" thinking	Intellectual	Patterns of ability indicating specific strengths and weaknesses in areas measured by the test (2a, 2b, 2c, 3a, 3b, 3c, 4a)
		Student shows significant progress in specific areas assessed by the test (5a, 5b, 5d, 5e, 5f)
Examination of cumulative records	Intellectual, academic	Achievement is consistently high, even though there may be occasional years or periods of time when performance is low (1d, 1e, 2d, 2e, 2f, 2g, 2h, 3a, 3d)
	Intellectual, academic	Teacher's anecdotal records indicate that child shows unusual abilities in one or more areas (1d, 1e, 2d, 2e, 2f, 2g, 2h, 3a, 3d)
	Intellectual, academic	Records indicate high achievement on standardized tests, but classroom performance (e.g., tests, grades) is not as high as one would expect from a child with high achievement scores (1d, 1e, 1f, 2d, 2e, 2f, 2g, 2h, 3c, 3d)

Table 2

Assessment Procedures, Indicators to Consider, and Questions Addressed (*continued*)

Test, Method, or Procedure	Ability or Characteristic	Indicators and Questions Answered
	Intellectual, academic	Achievement was high when the child entered school, but has been gradually declining (1d, 1e, 1f, 2e, 2f, 2g, 2h, 3b, 3c, 3d)
	Intellectual	Teacher's anecdotal records indicate that child has behavior problems or academic difficulties that seem unusual for someone with high achievement (1e, 1f, 2d, 2e, 2f, 2g, 2h, 3b, 3c, 3d)
	Creativity	Anecdotal records indicate nonconforming behavior (1d, 1e, 2e, 2g, 2h, 3a, 3b, 3c, 3d)
	Motivation	Teacher's records indicate high degree of achievement motivation and internal standards (1e, 1f, 2e, 2f, 2g, 2h, 3a)
	Creativity	Anecdotal records indicate that child produces unusual ideas or products (1d, 1e, 2d, 2e, 2f, 2g, 2h, 3a, 3d)
Classroom observation	Intellectual (general)	Demonstrates understanding of cause-effect relationships (Renzulli et al., 1976)
		Has rapid mastery and easy recall of information (Renzulli et al., 1976)
		Has rapid insight into underlying principles and ability to make valid generalizations quickly (Renzulli et al., 1976)
		Reasons in more sophisticated ways than age-mates, including the use of logic and common sense (Renzulli et al., 1976)
		Cognitive development is faster than that of age-mates (Renzulli et al., 1976)
		(1b, 2a, 2b, 2d, 2e, 2f, 2g, 3a, 3b, 3c, 3d)
	Creative	Generates many ideas, solutions to problems, and answers to questions (Renzulli et al., 1976)
		Shows curiosity about many things, and asks many questions (Renzulli et al., 1976)
		Demonstrates concern with changing, improving, and modifying objects, systems, and institutions (Renzulli et al., 1976)
		Prefers complexity (e.g., rich, dynamic, and asymmetrical) rather than simplicity (Dellas & Gaier, 1970)
		Possesses cognitive flexibility, or the ability to use perceptions and processes typical of several developmental levels in the development of products or ideas (Dellas & Gaier, 1970)

Table 2

Assessment Procedures, Indicators to Consider, and Questions Addressed (*continued*)

Test, Method, or Procedure	Ability or Characteristic	Indicators and Questions Answered
		Possesses a greater degree of perceptual openness or an awareness of and openness to both the outer world and the inner self (Dellas & Gaier, 1976)
		Is uninhibited in expressions of opinion and is nonconforming; does not fear being different (Renzulli et al., 1976)
		Shows unusual sensitivity to beauty, aesthetics, details in the environment (Dellas & Gaier, 1970)
		Shows ambivalence toward traditional sex roles, interests, and characteristics (Dellas & Gaier, 1970)
		(1b, 2a, 2b, 2d, 2e, 2f, 2g, 3a, 3b, 3c, 3d, 4a, 5a, 5b, 5d, 5e, 5f)
	Intellectual (critical thinking)	Shows ability to: judge whether a statement follows from the premises, judge whether something is an assumption, judge whether an observation statement is reliable, judge whether a simple generalization is warranted, judge whether a hypothesis is warranted, judge whether a theory is warranted, judge whether an argument depends on an ambiguity, judge whether a statement is overly vague or specific, judge whether an alleged authority is reliable (Ennis, 1964, pp. 600–610)
		(1b, 2a, 2b, 2d, 2e, 2f, 2g, 3a, 3b, 3c, 3d, 4a, 5a, 5b, 5d, 5e, 5f)
	Academic	Possesses a large store of information about the subject
		Has an advanced vocabulary and uses terms in a meaningful way within the subject area
		Understands abstract concepts or key ideas important to the structure of the subject area
		Makes valid generalizations about information and ideas in the subject area
		Understands and effectively uses the problem-solving methods or inquiry techniques characteristic of the field of study
		Recognizes and uses major sources of information in the subject area
		Possesses advanced skills in the use of reference tools related to the subject area
		(1b, 2a, 2b, 2d, 2e, 2f, 2g, 3a, 3b, 3c, 3d)

Table 2

Assessment Procedures, Indicators to Consider, and Questions Addressed (*continued*)

Test, Method, or Procedure	Ability or Characteristic	Indicators and Questions Answered
	Self-directedness	Prefers to work independently (Renzulli et al., 1976)
		Requires little direction from teachers (Renzulli et al., 1976)
		Likes to organize and bring structure to things, people, and situations (Renzulli et al., 1976)
		Possesses skills in using a variety of techniques for investigation (Atwood, 1974)
		Knows what sources of information and reference materials are available, and can use them appropriately (Atwood, 1974)
		Possesses skills in determining realistic goals and objectives for own work (Treffinger, 1975)
		Able to assess own skills and needs related to objectives (Treffinger, 1975)
		Can organize own work and plan realistically for completion of a project (Treffinger, 1975)
		Possesses skills in evaluating own work (Treffinger, 1975)
		(1e, 1f, 2b, 2f, 2g, 3a, 3b, 3c, 3d, 4a, 5a, 5b, 5d, 5e, 5f)
	Motivation	Becomes absorbed and truly involved in certain topics or problems; is persistent in seeking task completion (It is sometimes difficult to get student to move on to another topic.)
		Is easily bored with routine tasks
		Needs little external motivation to follow through in work that initially excites him
		Strives toward perfection; is self-critical; is not easily satisfied with own speed or products
		Prefers to work independently; requires little direction from teachers
		Is interested in many "adult" problems such as religion, politics, sex, race—more than usual for age level
		Is often self-assertive (sometimes even aggressive); stubborn in beliefs
		Likes to organize and bring structure to things, people, and situations
		Is quite concerned with right and wrong, good and bad; often evaluates and passes judgment on events, people, and things (Renzulli et al., 1976)
		(1e, 1f, 2b, 2f, 2g, 3a, 3b, 3c, 3d, 4a, 5a, 5b, 5d, 5e, 5f)

Table 2

Assessment Procedures, Indicators to Consider, and Questions Addressed (*continued*)

Test, Method, or Procedure	Ability or Characteristic	Indicators and Questions Answered
	Leadership and social skills	Ability to make positive and productive change (i.e., one who makes things happen that otherwise would not have occurred (McFarland, 1969)
		Ability to make decisions that militate in favor of positive and productive change
		Ability to effect change that is self-enhancing and group-enhancing in terms of the tasks assigned; for example, changes caused by the leader result in satisfaction, reward, or attainment of a goal in the group
		Empathy and sensitivity, personality, and proficiency. These characteristics are elaborated by Bass (1960):
		Empathy and social sensitivity. Included in ability to solve the group's problems is the ability to understand, appreciate, and exhibit sensitivity to those problems
		Personality. The character of the leader is important; leaders regularly exhibit such traits as persistence, consistency, self-confidence, sociability
		Proficiency. Touched on above, this characteristic can be described simply: the leader must be able to do what is to be done
		Charisma. The ability to actualize one's values to the extent that dynamic group change is effected; the ability to transform the group through one's own enthusiasm, energy
		(Lindsay, 1978)
		Carries responsibility well; can be counted on to do what has promised and usually does it well
		Is self-confident with children his or her own age as well as adults; seems comfortable when asked to show work to the class
		Seems to be well liked by classmates
		Is cooperative with teacher and classmates; tends to avoid bickering and is generally easy to get along with
		Can express self well; has good verbal facility and is usually well understood
		Adapts readily to new situations; is flexible in thought and action and does not seem disturbed when the normal routine is changed
		Seems to enjoy being around other people; is sociable and prefers not to be alone
		Tends to dominate others when they are around; generally directs the activity in which is involved

Table 2

Assessment Procedures, Indicators to Consider, and Questions Addressed (*continued*)

Test, Method, or Procedure	Ability or Characteristic	Indicators and Questions Answered
		Participates in most social activities connected with the school; can be counted on to be there if anyone is
		Excels in athletic activities; is well coordinated and enjoys all sorts of athletic games
		(Renzulli et al., 1976)
		(1e, 2b, 2f, 2g, 3a, 3b, 3c, 3d, 4a, 5a, 5b, 5d, 5e, 5f)
Product assessment (A student is asked to submit a product that is an example of his or her creative or academic work. This product, in any form, is either evaluated by a teacher or other program personnel or submitted to an expert in the area of assessment for an evaluation.)	Creative	Evidence of the following:
		Viewing from a different perspective (e.g., visual, philosophical, historical, theoretical, logical, emotional)
		Reinterpreting (e.g., adapting objects to new ideas, shifts in meaning; redefining a problem, illustrating ideas; "highlighting the essence"
		Elaborating (e.g., contributing details, adding to richness and color of a visual image, enhancing the product's appeal and uniqueness)
		Extending or "going beyond" (e.g., predicting, extrapolating, generalizing)
		(Maker, 1982b)
		(1e, 2d, 2e, 2f, 2g, 2h, 4a, 5a, 5b, 5d, 5e, 5f)
	Intellectual, academic	Product demonstrates an application of basic information and methodology appropriate to the problem or question being investigated
		Product extends or transforms the student's existing knowledge, the general principles in the applicable area of study, and/or raw data
		Product demonstrates the use of critical and higher-level thinking skills
		Product is designed for effective communication to an appropriate audience (e.g., organized, interesting, utilizes acceptable standards)
		Product acknowledges information sources in a suitable way
		Product demonstrates consideration of varying points of view, conflicting data, and primary sources; student has made a reasonably thorough search of relevant sources
		Product demonstrates the use of details or explanations that enhance their meaning or appeal to the audience
		(1b, 2d, 2e, 2f, 2g, 2h, 4a, 5a, 5b, 5d, 5e, 5f)

Table 2

Assessment Procedures, Indicators to Consider, and Questions Addressed (*continued*)

Test, Method, or Procedure	Ability or Characteristic	Indicators and Questions Answered
Checklists and rating scales (Use scales that contain characteristics such as those listed above for classroom observation.)	Intellectual, academic, creative, self-directedness, motivation, leadership and social skills	See indicators and questions addressed above for classroom observation.
Interviews with past and present teachers	Intellectual, academic, creative, self-directedness, motivation, leadership and social skills	Ask questions such as the following: a. What strengths do you believe are most important for _____ to develop? (3a, 3c) b. How can these strengths be developed in the special program? (3a, 3c) c. What weaknesses do you believe are most important for _____ to improve? (3b, 3c) d. How can these weaknesses be developed in the special program? (3b, 3c) e. Which of _____'s strengths and weaknesses can be developed in the regular classroom? (3d) f. What other programs or methods could be used to develop _____'s strengths and weaknesses? (3d) g. What are some of _____'s major interests? (4b) h. How does _____ seem to learn best? (4c) i. What differences do you notice in _____'s classroom performance and/or behavior after being in the special program? (5c, 5d, 5e, 5f) j. What factors suggest that _____ should remain in the current program? (5d, 5f) k. What factors suggest that _____'s placement should be changed? (5e, 5f) l. What changes do you believe should be made if _____ stays in the program? (5f)
Interviews with parents	Intellectual, academic, creative, self-directedness, motivation, leadership and social skills	Ask parents questions such as the following: a. What unusual abilities or skills have you noticed in _____? Describe them in as much detail as you can. (1c, 1f) b. When did you begin to notice these abilities? (1d) c. Do you believe _____ needs to be in a special program? Why? (1c, 1e)

Table 2

Assessment Procedures, Indicators to Consider, and Questions Addressed (*continued*)

Test, Method, or Procedure	Ability or Characteristic	Indicators and Questions Answered
		d. What are some of _____'s hobbies, collections, and interests? (1c, 1d, 1f)
		e. What does _____ prefer to do in spare time? (1c, 1d, 1f)
		(All of the above questions can also be used to provide information to answer questions 2d, 2f, 2g, 2h.)
		f. What strengths do you believe are most important for _____ to develop? (3a, 3c)
		g. How can these strengths be developed in the special program? (3a, 3c)
		h. What weaknesses do you believe are most important for _____ to improve? (3b, 3c)
		i. How can these weaknesses be developed in the special program? (3b, 3c)
		j. What other programs or methods could be used to develop _____'s strengths and weaknesses? (3d)
		k. What are some of _____'s major interests? (4b)
		l. How does _____ seem to learn best? (4c)
		m. What differences do you notice in _____'s behavior at home after being in the special program? (5c, 5d, 5e, 5f)
		n. What factors suggest that _____ should remain in the current program? (5d, 5f)
		o. What factors suggest that _____'s placement should be changed? (5e, 5f)
		p. What changes do you believe should be made if _____ stays in the program? (5f)
Classroom modifications and observation of effects	Intellectual	Include more teacher questions or activities that require critical thinking or higher levels of thinking; observe the child's ability to answer, levels of excitement and interest (1e, 1b, 1f, 2a, 2b, 2f, 2g, 2h, 3d, 4b, 5c)
	Intellectual, academic	Teach more abstract and sophisticated ideas or concepts; observe the child's ability to comprehend the ideas, levels of excitement and interest. (1e, 1b, 1f, 2a, 2b, 2f, 2g, 2h, 3d, 4b, 5c)
	Academic, intellectual	Accelerate the teaching of content and/or allow the student to progress at his or her own rate alone, with a tutor, or with a small group. Observe the student's learning rate, excitement, success, and interest (1e, 1b, 1f, 2a, 2b, 2f, 2g, 2h, 3d, 4b, 5c)

Table 2

Assessment Procedures, Indicators to Consider, and Questions Addressed (*continued*)

Test, Method, or Procedure	Ability or Characteristic	Indicators and Questions Answered
	Creative	Include more teacher questions or activities that are open-ended and require the production of unusual ideas or products. Observe the student's originality, flexibility, and elaboration in these ideas or products (1e, 1b, 1f, 2a, 2b, 2f, 2g, 2h, 3d, 5c)
	Creative	Include more teacher questions or activities that are open-ended and require the production of many different ideas or products. Observe the student's fluency (number of different ideas or different products) and flexibility (number of different categories of ideas or products) (1e, 1b, 1f, 2a, 2b, 2f, 2g, 2h, 3d, 4b, 5c)
	Self-Directedness, motivation, interests	Allow student more opportunities to choose activities, determine products to be developed, and set own schedule. Observe willingness to choose, clarity of own goals, willingness to complete self-chosen tasks, ability to meet self-chosen schedules, types of activities chosen (1e, 1f, 2b, 2f, 2h, 3d, 4b, 5c)
	Leadership and social skills	Provide more opportunities to work in small groups and to be group leader. Observe ability to lead and follow, excitement, and interest (1e, 1f, 2b, 2f, 2h, 3d, 4b, 5c)
Interviews with students	Intellectual, academic, creative, self-directedness, motivation, interests, leadership and social skills	Ask the students questions such as the following: a. What things do you do the best? (1e, 2a, 2f, 2g) b. How could your educational program be improved? (1e, 2a, 2b, 2f, 2g) c. What problems or frustrations do you encounter in school? (1e, 2b, 2f, 2g) d. How do you usually handle these problems or frustrations? (1e, 2b, 2f, 2g) e. What could teachers do to help you with your problems or frustrations? (1e, 2f, 2g) f. What projects are you currently involved in? (1e, 2a, 2f, 2g, 3a, 3b, 3c, 3d, 4d) g. What abilities or strengths would you most like to develop further in the special program? (3a, 3c, 4b) h. What weaknesses or problems would you most like to improve while in the special program? (3b, 3c, 4b) i. How has the special program helped you? (5d, 5e, 5f) j. How has the special program hurt you? (5d, 5e, 5f)

Table 2

Assessment Procedures, Indicators to Consider, and Questions Addressed (*continued*)

Test, Method, or Procedure	Ability or Characteristic	Indicators and Questions Answered
Comparison of expected levels of performance with actual performance	Intellectual, academic	If tests show an I.Q. of approximately 115–120, achievement should be one to one-and-a-half years above grade level (1f, 2f, 2g)
		If intelligence tests show an I.Q. of approximately 125–135, achievement should be one-and-a-half to two years above grade level (1f, 2f, 2g)
		If intelligence tests show an I.Q. of over 140–145, achievement should be more than two years above grade level (1f, 2f, 2g)
		Achievement after placement in the special program is higher than or closer to expected levels (5b, 5c, 5d)
		Achievement after placement in the special program is lower than or further from expected levels (5b, 5c, 5e)
Nomination forms (Use forms that contain characteristics such as those listed for classroom observation of intellectual, academic, and creative abilities)	Intellectual, academic, creative	See indicators and questions addressed above for classroom observation of these abilities
Criterion-referenced tests	Academic	Performance is at or above mastery level (2c, 2f, 2g, 2h, 3a, 3b, 3c, 3d, 3a, 4a, 5a, 5b, 5d, 5e, 5f)
Interest inventories	Interests	Specific academic or career interests (2g, 4b, 5a, 5b, 5d, 5e, 5f)
		Wide range of interests (2a, 2g, 4b)
		Range of interests has increased (5a, 5b, 5d, 5e, 5f)
		Interests are more sophisticated than those of peers (2a, 2g, 4b)
		Interests have become more sophisticated (5a, 5b, 5d, 5e, 5f)
Learning-style inventories	Learning style	Specific preferences for ways to learn (2g, 4c)
		Learning styles can be accommodated in existing program (2g, 4c, 5d, 5e, 5f)
		Learning styles are similar to learning styles of other gifted students (2g, 4c, 5d, 5e, 5f)

Table 2

Assessment Procedures, Indicators to Consider, and Questions Addressed (*continued*)

Test, Method, or Procedure	Ability or Characteristic	Indicators and Questions Answered
Informal assessment procedures (Procedures will vary depending on the goals and objectives being assessed. See pages 21 to 31 of Chapter 11 for examples.)	Intellectual (critical and higher-level thinking), academic, creative, motivation, self-directedness	Indicators will vary depending on the goals being assessed, but information would be used to address the following questions: 3a, 3b, 3c, 3d, 4a, 5a, 5b, 5d, 5e, 5f

References

Abeson, A. (Ed.) (1973). A continuing summary of pending and completed litigation regarding the education of handicapped children. Arlington, VA: Council for Exceptional Children's State-Federal Clearinghouse for Exceptional Children.

Adler, S. (1979). *Poverty children and their language.* New York: Grune & Stratton.

Alberto, P. A., & Troutman, A. C. (1982). *Applied behavior analysis for teachers.* Columbus, OH: Charles E. Merrill.

Algozzine, R. (1976). The disturbing child: What you see is what you get? *Alberta Journal of Educational Research, 22*(4), 330–333.

Algozzine, R., Whorton, J. E., & Reid, W. (1979). Special class exit criteria: A modest beginning. *Journal of special education, 13,* 131–135.

Algozzine, R., & Ysseldyke, J. (1982). *Critical issues in special and remedial education.* Boston: Houghton Mifflin.

Algozzine, R., Ysseldyke, J., & Christensen, S. (1983). An analysis of the incidence of special class placement: The masses are burgeoning. *Journal of Special Education, 17,* 141–147.

Alley, G., & Deshler, D. (1979). *Teaching the learning disabled adolescent: Strategies and methods.* Denver: Love.

Alley, G. R., Deshler, D. D., Clark, F. L., Schumaker, J. B., & Warner, M. (1983). Learning disabilities in adolescent and adult populations: research implications (Part II). *Focus on Exceptional Children. 15*(9), 1–4.

Alley, G., & Foster, C. (1978). Nondiscriminatory testing of minority and exceptional children. *Focus on Exceptional Children, 9,* 1–14.

Alpern, G. D., Boll, T. J., & Shearer, M. S. (1980). *Developmental profile II.* Aspen, CO: Psychological Development Publications.

American Psychiatric Association (1980). *Diagnostic and statistical manual of mental disorders* (3rd ed.). Washington, D.C.: American Psychiatric Association.

Anastasi, A. (1976). *Psychological testing.* New York: Macmillan.

Anderson, N., Kaufman, A., & Kaufman, N. (1976). Use of the WISCR with a learning disabled population: Some diagnostic implications. *Psychology in the Schools, 13,* 381–386.

Anderson, Z. (1982). Review of adaptive performance inventory, experimental edition. In A. Seital, A. Jung, & N. Fieber (Eds.), *A compendium of severe/profound special education resources.* Omaha, NE: Media Resource Center, Meyer Children's Rehabilitation Institute, University of Nebraska Medical Center.

Apple Computer Incorporated (1982). *Apple SuperPILOT.* Cupertino, CA: Author.

Aram, D., and Nation, J. E. (1982). *Child language disorders.* St. Louis: Mosby.

Arthur, G. (1950). *The Arthur adaptation of the Leiter international performance scale.* Chicago, IL: C. H. Stoelting.

Ashlock, R. B. (1982). Error patterns in computation: A semi-programmed approach (3rd ed.). Columbus, OH: Charles E. Merrill.

Ashlock, R. B. (1983). *Guiding each child's learning of mathematics: A diagnostic approach to instruction.* Columbus, OH: Charles E. Merrill.

Atkeson, B. M., & Forehand, R. (1981). Conduct disorders. In E. J. Mash and L. G. Terdal (Eds.), *Behavioral assessment of childhood disorders* (pp. 185–220). New York: Guilford.

Atwood, B. S. (1974). *Building independent learning skills.* Palo Alto, CA: Education Today.

Bagnato, S. J., & Neisworth, J. T. (1981). *Linking developmental assessment and curricula.* Rockville, MD: Aspen Systems.

Bailey, D. B., Clifford, R. M., & Harms, T. (1982). Comparison of preschool environment for handicapped and nonhandicapped children. *Topics in Early Childhood Special Education, 2,* 9–20.

Bailey, D., & Harbin, G. L. (1980). Nondiscriminatory evaluation. *Exceptional children, 46*(8), 590–596.

Bailey, D. B., Harms, T., & Clifford, R. M. (in press). Social and educational aspects of mealtimes for handicapped preschoolers: Observation and analysis. *Topics in Early Childhood Special Education.*

Bailey, D., & Wolery, M. (1984). *Teaching infant and preschool children with handicaps.* Columbus, OH: Charles E. Merrill.

Baker, D. B. (1980). Guidelines for evaluating and modifying the physical environment. In J. Umbreit & P. Cardullias (Eds.), *Educating the severely physically handicapped: Modifying the physical environment.* Vol. III (pp. 7–9). Columbus, OH: Special Press.

Baker, H. J., & Leland, B. (1967). *Detroit test of learning aptitude* (1967 ed.). Indianapolis, IN: Bobbs-Merrill.

Baldwin, A., & Wooster, J. (1977). *Baldwin identification matrix: Inservice kit for the identification of gifted and talented students.* Buffalo, NY: DOK Publishers.

Balthazar, E. E. (1976). *Balthazar scales of adaptive behavior.* Palo Alto, CA: Consulting Psychologists Press.

Bandura, A. (1969). *Principles of behavior modification.* New York: Holt, Rinehart & Winston.

Bangs, T. E., & Dodsen, S. (1979). *Birth to three developmental scale.* Hingham, MA: Teaching Resources.

Bankson, N. (1977). *Bankson language screening test.* Baltimore, MD: University Park Press.

Banus, B. S. (1971). *The developmental therapist.* Thorofare, N.J.: Charles B. Slack.

Barron, F., & Harrington, D. M. (1981). Creativity, intelligence, and personality. *Annual Review of Psychology, 32,* 439–476.

Bass, Bernard M. (1960). *Leadership, psychology, and organizational behavior.* New York: Harper & Brothers.

Bates, E. (1976). *Language and context: The acquisition of pragmatics.* New York: Academic Press.

Bayley, N. (1969). *Bayley scales of infant development.* New York: Psychological Corporation.

Bayley, N. (1970). Development of mental abilities. In P. H. Mussen (Ed.), *Carmichael's manual of child psychology (Vol. 1).* (3rd ed.) New York: John Wiley.

Belmont, I., & Belmont, H. (1980). Is the slow learner in the classroom learning disabled? *Journal of Learning Disabilities, 13*(9), 32–35.

Berdine, W. H. (1985). Mental retardation. In W. H. Berdine and A. E. Blackhurst (Eds.), *An introduction to special education* (2nd ed.). Boston: Little, Brown.

Berdine, W. H., & Cegelka, P. T. (1980). *Teaching the trainable retarded.* Columbus, OH: Charles E. Merrill.

Bergen, J. R., & Smith, J. O. (1966). Effects of socioeconomic status and sex on prospective teacher judgements. *Mental Retardation, 4,* 13–15.

Bernknoph, L. A. (1980). Responses of adolescents on a masculinity-femininity scale and a stereotyping questionnaire. *Exceptional Children, 47*(1), 59–61.

Bersoff, D. N. (1979). Regarding psychologists testily: Legal regulation of psychological assessment in the public schools. *Maryland Law Review, 32,* 671–679.

Bigge, J. (1976). Task analysis. In J. Bigge & P. A. O'Donnell (Eds.), *Teaching individuals with physical and multiple disabilities* (pp. 5–22). Columbus, OH: Charles E. Merrill.

Blackhurst, A. E. (1985). Issues in special education. In W. H. Berdine & A. E. Blackhurst (Eds.), *An introduction to special education* (2nd. ed.) (pp. 45–88). Boston: Little, Brown.

Blackhurst, A. E., & Berdine, W. H. (1981). *An introduction to special education.* Boston: Little, Brown.

Blankenship, C. S. (1985). Using curriculum-based assessment data to make instructional decisions. *Exceptional Children, 52,* 233–238.

Bleck, E. E. (1982). Cerebral palsy. In E. E. Bleck & D. A. Nagel (Eds.), *Physically handicapped children: A medical atlas for teachers* (2nd ed.) (pp. 37–90). New York: Grune & Stratton.

Bloom, B. S., Engelhart, M. D., Furst, E. J., Hill, W. H., & Krathwohl, D. R. (1956). *A taxonomy of educational objectives: The classification of educational goals.* In Handbook 1: Cognitive Domain. London: Longmans, Green & Co.

Bloom, L., and Lahey, M. (1978). *Language development and language disorders.* New York: John Wiley.

Bluma, S. M., Shearer, M. S., Froham, A. H., & Hilliard, J. M. (1976). *Portage guide to early education.* Portage, WI: Cooperative Educational Agency.

Bobath, D., & Bobath, B. (1964). The facilitation of normal postural reactions and movements in the treatment of cerebral palsy. *Physiotherapy, 50,* 246–262.

Borkowski, J. G., & Konarski, E. A. (1981). Educational implications of efforts to train intelligence. *Journal of Special Education, 15,* 289–305.

Bower, E. M. (1961). *The education of emotionally handicapped children.* Sacramento: California State Department of Education.

Boyer, A. (1985). The software need of exceptional limited English proficient students. An unpublished manuscript. Available from Ann Boyer, Department of Special Education, The University of Kentucky, Lexington, KY.

Bradley, R. H., & Caldwell, B. M. (1976). Relation of infants' home environments to mental test performance at fifty-four months: A follow-up study. *Child Development, 47,* 1172–1174.

Brandes, P. J., & Ehinger, D. N. (1981). The effects of middle ear pathology on auditory perception and academic achievement. *Journal of Speech and Hearing Disorders, 46*(3), 301–307.

Bricker, W., Macke, P., Levin, J., & Simmons, T. (1982). Assessment and modification of cognitive processes of handicapped children. In M. Stevens-Dominquez & K. Stremel-Campbell (Eds.), *Ongoing data collection for measuring child progress* (pp. 41–57). Special Education Programs, United States Department of Education. Seattle: WESTAR.

Brigance, A. H. (1977). *Brigance diagnostic inventory of basic skills.* North Billerica, MA: Curriculum Associates.

Brigance, A. H. (1978). *Brigance diagnostic inventory of early development.* Woburn, MA: Curriculum Associates.

Brigance, A. H. (1980). *Brigance diagnostic inventory of essential skills.* Woburn, MA: Curriculum Associates.

Brigance, A. H. (1983a). *Brigance diagnostic inventory of basic skills.* Woburn, MA: Curriculum Associates.

Brigance, A. H. (1983b) *Diagnostic inventory of basic skills (Spanish version).* North Billerica, MA: Curriculum Associates.

Brinker, R., & Lewis, M. (1982). Contingency intervention in infancy. In J. Anderson (Ed.), *Curricula for high risk and handicapped infants* (pp. 37–41). Chapel Hill, NC: Technical Assistance and Development System.

Bromwich, R. M. (1981). *Working with parents and infants: An interactional approach.* Baltimore: University Park Press.

Bronefenbrenner, V. (1974). Is early intervention effective? A report on longitudinal evaluations of preschool programs. Washington, DC: DHEW vs. Government Printing Office.

Brown, A. (1978). Knowing when, where, and how to remember: A problem of metacognition. In R. Glaser (Ed.), *Advances in instructional psychology* (pp. 77–165). Hillsdale, NJ: Lawrence Erlbaum.

Brown, L., Nietupski, J., & Hamre-Nietupski, S. (1976). The criterion of ultimate functioning and public school services for severely handicapped students. In *Hey don't forget about me: Education's investment in the severely, profoundly and multiply handicapped* (pp. 8–12). Reston, VA: Council for Exceptional Children.

Bruininks, R. H. (1978). *Bruininks-Oseretsky test of motor proficiency.* Circle Pines, MN: American Guidance.

Burgemeister, B. B., Blum, C. H., & Lorge, I. (1972). *Columbia mental maturity scale* (3rd ed.). New York: Harcourt Brace Jovanovich.

Burkhardt, L. (1982). *More homemade battery devices for severely handicapped children with suggested activities.* Millville, PA: Author.

Buros, O. K. (Ed.) (1978). *The eighth mental measurements yearbook.* Highland Park, NJ: Gryphon.

Butterfield, E. C. (1979). *Instructional improvements that produce generalized improvements in cognition.* Paper presented at the Congress of the International Association for the Scientific Study of Mental Deficiency, Jerusalem.

Butterfield, E. C., Wambold, C., & Belmont, J. M. (1973). On the theory and practice of improving short-term memory. *American Journal of Mental Deficiency, 77,* 654–669.

Bzoch, K. R., & League, R. (1970). *Receptive-expressive emergent language scale.* Gainesville, FL: Anhinga.

Caldwell, B. M., & Bradley, R. H. (1978). *Home observation and measurement of the environment.* Little Rock: University of Arkansas.

Calhoun, M. L., & Hawisher, M. (1979). *Teaching and learning strategies for the physically handicapped student.* Baltimore: University Park Press.

Carrow, E. (1973). *Test of auditory comprehension of language.* Austin, TX: Learning Concepts.

Cartwright, C. A., & Cartwright, G. P. (1974) *Developing observations skills.* New York: McGraw-Hill.

Cegelka, P. (1976). Sex role stereotyping in special education: A look at secondary work study programs. *Exceptional Children, 42,* 323–328.

Certo, N. (1983). Characteristics of educational services. In M. Snell (Ed.), *Systematic instruction of the moderately and severely handicapped* (2nd ed.) (pp. 2–16). Columbus, OH: Charles E. Merrill.

Charles, C. M. (1976). *Individualizing instruction.* New York: Mosby.

Cherkes-Julkowski, M., Davis, L., Fimian, M., McGuire, J., Okolo, C., & Zoback, M. (1983). The effects of dual strategy training on performance in average and handicapped learners. Unpublished manuscript.

Chess, N. (1983). Temperament, handicaps, and the vulnerable child. Annual Mary Elaine Meyer O'Neal lecture in developmental disabilities. Omaha, NE: Meyer Children's Rehabilitation Institute, University of Nebraska Medical Center.

Chomsky, N. (1965). *Aspects of the theory of syntax.* Cambridge: M.I.T. Press.

Christenson, S., Ysseldyke, J. E., & Algozzine, B. (1982). Influencing referral decisions. *Psychology in the Schools, 19,* 341–345.

Chronbach, L. J. (1970). *Essentials of psychological testing* (3rd ed.). New York: Harper & Row.

Clements, S., & Peters, J. (1962). Minimal brain dysfunction in the school aged child. *Archives of General Psychiatry, 61,* 185–197.

Cliff, S., Carr, D., Gray, J., Nymann, C., & Redding, S. (1975). *Institutional manual for the comprehensive developmental evaluation chart.* El Paso: El Paso Rehabilitation Center.

Compton, A. (1977). *Compton speech and language screening evaluation.* San Francisco: Carousel Publishing.

Compu-Tations Incorporated (1984). Tests made easy [Computer program]. Troy, MI: Author.

Connolly, A., Nachtman, W., & Pritchett, E. (1973). *Keymath diagnostic arithmetic test.* Circle Pines, MN: American Guidance Service.

Cooper, J.O. (1981). *Measurement of behavior* (2nd ed.). Columbus, OH: Charles E. Merrill.

Crockenberg, S. B. (1972). Creativity tests: A boon or boondoggle for education. *Review of Educational Research, 42,* 55–73.

Cruickshank, W. M. (1976). The problem and its scope. In W. M. Cruickshank (Ed.), *Cerebral palsy: A developmental disability* (3rd ed.) (pp. 1–29). Syracuse: Syracuse University Press.

Cruickshank, W. M., Bice, H. B., & Hallahan, D. P. (1976). The evaluation of intelligence. In W. M. Cruickshank (Ed.), *Cerebral palsy: A developmental disability* (3rd ed.). Syracuse: Syracuse University Press.

Curriculum Associates (1985a). Objectives for the Brigance [Computer program]. North Billerica, MA: Author.

Curriculum Associates (1985b). Enright diagnostic inventory of basic arithmetic skills [Computer program]. North Billerica, MA: Author.

Dale, P. S. (1976). *Language development: Structure and function.* New York: Holt, Rinehart and Winston.

Darby, B. L., & May, M. J. (1979). *Infant assessment: Issues and applications.* Seattle: WESTAR.

Darnell, R. E. (1976). Collaborative approaches to professional intervention. In W. M. Cruickshank (Ed.), *Cerebral palsy: A developmental disability* (3rd ed.) (pp. 535–86). Syracuse: Syracuse University Press.

Davis, C. (1980). *Perkins-Binet tests of intelligence for the blind: Manual.* Boston: Houghton Mifflin.

DeAvila, E. A., & Duncan, S. E. (1979). *Language Assessment Scales.* Corte Madera, CA: Linguametrics Group.

Dellas, M., & Gaier, E. L. (1976). Identification of creative: to individual. *Psychological Bulletin,* Vol. 73, pp. 55–73.

Deno, S. L., Lowry, L., Mirkin, P. K., & Kuehnle, K. (1980). *Relationships among simple measures of spelling and performance on standardized achievement tests* (Research Report No. 21). Minneapolis: University of Minnesota, Institute for Research on Learning Disabilities.

Deno, S., Mirkin, P., & Wesson, C. C. (1984). How to write effective, data-based IEPs. *Teaching Exceptional Children, 16*(2), 99–104.

Deno, S. L., Marston, D., & Mirkin, P. (1982). Valid measurement procedures for continuous evaluation of written expression. *Exceptional Children, 48,* 368–370.

Deno, S. L., Mirkin, P. K., Chiang, B., & Lowry, L. (1979). *Relationships among simple measures of reading and performance on standardized achievement tests* (Research Report No. 20). Minneapolis: University of Minnesota, Institute for Research on Learning Disabilities.

Deshler, D. D. & Schumaker, J. B. (1986). Learning strategies: an instructional alternative for low-achieving adolescents. *Exceptional Children. 52*(6), 583–590.

Diana v. State Board of Education, N. C–70–37 (N.D. Calif., 1970).

Dick, W., & Carey, L. (1978). *The system design of instruction.* Glenview, IL: Scott, Foresman.

Dietz, D. E. D., & Repp, A. C. (1983). Reducing behavior through reinforcement. *Exceptional Education Quarterly, 3,* 34–47.

Dinola, A. J., Kaminsky, B. P., & Sternfield, A. E. (1968). *TMR performance profile for the severely and moderately retarded.* Ridgefield, NJ: Reporting Service for Children.

Dion, K. (1972). Physical attractiveness and evaluations of children's transgressions. *Journal of Personality and Social Psychology, 24,* 207–214.

Doll, E. (1965). *Vineland social maturity scale.* Circle Pines, MN: American Guidance Service.

Doll, E. A. (1966). *Preschool attainment record.* Circle Pines, MN: American Guidance Service.

Doll, E. (1983). *Vineland social maturity scale–revised.* Circle Pines, MN: American Guidance Service.

Dore, J. (1974). A pragmatic description of early language development. *Journal of Psycholinguistic Research, 3,* 343–350.

Dore, J. (1975). Hosophrases, speech acts and language universals. *Journal of Child Language, 2,* 21–40.

Doucette, J., and Freedman, R. (1980). *Progress tests for the developmentally disabled: An evaluation.* Cambridge, MA: Abt Books.

DuBose, R. (1983). Identification. In M. Snell (Ed.), *Systematic instruction of the moderately and severely handicapped* (2nd ed.). Columbus, OH: Charles E. Merrill.

DuBose, R., & Langley, M. B. (1977). *Developmental activities screening inventory.* Hingham, MA: Teaching Resources.

Duffey, J. B., Salvia, J., Tucker, J., & Ysseldyke, J. (1981). Nonbiased assessment: A need for operationalism. *Exceptional Children, 47*(6), 427–434.

Dunn, L. M., & Dunn, L. M. (1981). *Peabody picture vocabulary test–revised.* Circle Pines, MN: American Guidance Service.

Dunn, L. M., & Markwardt, F. C. (1970). *Peabody individual achievement test.* Circle Pines, MN: American Guidance Service.

Dunn, L. M., & Markwardt, F. C. (1978). *Peabody individual achievement test.* Circle Pines, MN: American Guidance Service.

Dunn, R. (1983). Learning style and its relation to exceptionality at both ends of the spectrum. *Exceptional Children, 49*(6), 496–506.

Dunn, R., Cavanaugh, D., Eberle, B., & Zenhausern, R. (1982). Hemispheric preference: The newest element of learning style. *American Biology Teacher, 44*(5), 291–294.

Dunn, R., & Dunn, K. (1978). *Teaching students through their individual learning styles: A practical approach.* Reston, VA: Reston Publishing.

Dunn, R., Dunn, K., & Price, G. (1979). *Learning style inventory.* Lawrence, KS: Price Systems.

Dunn, R., & Price, G. (1980). Identifying the learning style characteristics of gifted children. *Gifted Children Quarterly, 24*(1), 33–36.

Dunst, C. J., & Rheingrover, R. M. (1981). An analysis of the efficacy of infant intervention programs with organically handicapped children. *Evaluation and Program Planning, 4,* 287–323.

Dykes, M. K. (1981a). *The developmental assessment for the severely handicapped.* Austin, TX: Exceptional Resources.

Dykes, M. K. (1981b). Teaching students with physical disabilities and health impairments. In J. Hardman, M. Egan, & E. Landau (Eds.), *What will we do in the morning?* Dubuque, IA: William C. Brown.

Eisenson, J. (1972). *Aphasia in children.* New York: Harper & Row.

Ennis, R. H. (1964). A definition of critical thinking. *The Reading Teacher, 18,* 599–612.

Enright, B. E. (1985). *Enright diagnostic inventory of basic arithmetic skills.* North Billerica, MA: Curriculum Associates.

Evans, I. M., & Nelson, R. O. (1977). Assessment of child behavior problems. In A. R. Ciminero, K. S. Calhoun, & H. E. Adams (Eds.) (pp. 603–682), *Handbook of behavioral assessment.* New York: John Wiley.

Fieber, N. (1982). Review of Callier-Azusa Scale. In A. Seitel, A. Jung, & N. Fieber (Eds.), *Compendium of severe/profound special education resources.* Omaha, NE: Media Resource Center, Meyer Children's Rehabilitation Institute, University of Nebraska Medical Center.

Fieber, N., & Robinson, C. (1982). Introduction to assessment. In A. Seitel, A. Jung, & N. Fieber (Eds.), *A compendium of severe/profound special education resources.* Omaha, NE: Media Resource Center, Meyer Children's Rehabilitation Institute, University of Nebraska Medical Center.

Fieber, N., & Robinson, C. (in press). Cognitive assessment with motorically impaired infants and preschoolers. In T. Wachs & R. Sheehan (Eds.), *Assessment of developmentally disabled children.* New York: Plenum Publishing.

Feuerstein, R., Rand, Y., & Hoffman, M. B. (1979). *The dynamic assessment of retarded performers. The learning potential assessment device: Theory, instruments, and the techniques.* Baltimore: University Park Press.

Feuerstein, R., Rand, R., Hoffman, M. B., & Miller, R. (1980). *Instrumental enrichment.* Baltimore: University Park Press.

Fewell, R., & Cone, J. (1983). Identification and placement of severely handicapped children. In M. E. Snell (Ed.), *Systematic instruction of the moderately and severely handicapped* (2nd ed.) (pp. 46–70). Columbus, OH: Charles E. Merrill.

Fiorentino, M. R. (1972). *Normal and abnormal development — Influences of primitive reflexes on motor development.* Springfield, IL: C. C. Thomas.

Flashcard vision test for children (1966). NY: New York Association for the Blind.

Flaugher, R. (1978). The many definitions of test bias. *American Psychologist, 32,* 671–679.

Flavell, J. H. (1976). Metacognitive aspects of problem solving. In L. B. Resnick (Ed.), *The nature of intelligence* (pp. 231–235). Hillsdale, NJ: Lawrence Erlbaum.

Fluharty, N. B. (1978). *Fluharty preschool speech and language screening test.* Boston: Teaching Resources.

Fodor, J. A., & Katz, J. J. (1964). *The structure of language: Readings in the philosophy of language.* Englewood Cliffs, NJ: Prentice-Hall.

Folio, R., & DuBose, R. F. (1974). *Peabody developmental motor scales.* Nashville: Institute on Mental Retardation and Intellectual Development.

Folio, R., & Fewell, R. F. (1982). *Peabody developmental motor scales and activity cards.* Hingham, MA: Teaching Resources.

Foster, R. (1977). *Camelot behavioral checklist.* Lawrence, KS: Camelot Behavioral Systems.

Frank, C. (1979). *The effects of self-graphing, drill, and free time on an emotionally handicapped child's mastery of basic multiplication facts.* Unpublished manuscript.

Frankenburg, W. K., Dodds, J. B., Fandal, A., Kazuk, E., & Cohrs, M. (1975). *Denver developmental screening test — revised.* Denver: LADOCA Project and Publishing Foundation.

Fraser, B., Galka, G., & Hensinger, R. (1980). *Gross motor management of severely multiply impaired students.* Baltimore: University Park Press.

Friedman, S. G. (1985). Testing language: Language dominance and math scores of bilingual Hispanic students. Unpublished doctoral dissertation, Utah State University, Logan.

Fudala, J. B. (1981). *Quickscreen.* Los Angeles: Western Psychological Services.

Furuno, S., O'Reilly, K. A., Hosaka, C. M., Inatsuka, T. T., Allman, T. L., & Zeisloft, B. (1979). *Hawaii early learning profile.* Palo Alto, CA: VORT.

Gajar, A. H. (1980). Characteristics across exceptional categories: EMR, LD and ED. *The Journal of Special Education, 14,* 165–173.

Gallagher, J. J. (1966). *Research summary on gifted child education.* Springfield, IL: Office of the Illinois Superintendent of Public Instruction.

Gallagher, J. J. (1975). *Teaching the gifted child* (2nd ed.). Boston: Allyn & Bacon.

Gallagher, J. J., Weiss, P., Oglesby, K., & Thomas, T. (1982). *Report on education of the gifted (Vol. 1).* Unpublished manuscript. (Available from Frank Porter Graham Child Development Center, University of North Carolina, Chapel Hill, NC 27514.)

Gauthier, S. V., & Madison, C. L. (1978). *Kindergarten language screening test.* Tigard, OR: CC Publications.

Gay, L. R. (1985). *Educational evaluation and measurement: Competencies for analysis and application* (2nd ed.). Columbus, OH: Charles E. Merrill.

Gear, G. H. (1975). Teacher judgement in identification of gifted children. *Gifted Child Quarterly, 20,* 478–489.

Gelfand, D. M., & Hartmann, D. P. (1984). *Child behavior analysis and therapy* (2nd ed.). New York: Pergamon.

Gentry, D. (1980). *The Adaptive Performance Inventory (A.P.I.) Experiential Edition.* Moscow, ID: Consortium on the Adaptive Performance Evaluation (CAPE), Department of Special Education, College of Education, University of Idaho.

Germann, G., & Tindal, G. (1985). An application of curriculum-based assessment: The use of direct and repeated measurement. *Exceptional Children, 52,* 244–265.

Gickling, E. E., & Thompson, V. P. (1985). A personal view of curriculum-based assessment. *Exceptional Children, 52,* 205–218.

Ginsburg, H. (1977). *Children's arithmetic.* Cincinnati, OH: Van Nostrand.

Glover, M. E., Preminger, J. L., & Sanford, A. R. (1978). *The learning accomplishment profile for developmentally young children (LAP-E).* Winston-Salem, NC: Kaplan Press.

Goldsworthy, C. L. (1982). *Multilevel informal language inventory.* Columbus, OH: Charles E. Merrill.

Golin, A., & Ducanis, A. (1981). *The interdisciplinary team.* Rockville, MD: Aspen Systems.

Goodman, K. S. (1970). Reading: A psycholinguistic guessing game. In H. Singer & B. B. Ruddell (Eds.), *Theoretical models and processes of reading* (pp. 279–308). Newark, DE: International Reading Association.

Goodwin, W. L., & Driscoll, L. A. (1980). *Handbook for measurement and evaluation in early childhood education.* San Francisco: Jossey-Bass.

Gould, S. J. (1981). *The mismeasure of man.* New York: Norton.

Graden, J. L., Casey, A., & Christensen, S. L. (1985). Implementing a prereferral intervention system: Part I. The model. *Exceptional Children, 51*(5), 377–384.

Graebner, D. (1972). A decade of sexism in readers. *The Reading Teacher, 26,* 52–58.

Graham, S., & Miller, L. (1979). Spelling research and practice: A unified approach. *Focus on Exceptional Children, 12*(2), 1–16.

Graham, S., & Miller, L. (1980). Handwriting research and practice: A unified approach. *Focus on Exceptional Children, 13*(2), 1–16.

Gray, B. B., & Ryan, B. (1973). *A language program for the nonlanguage child.* Champaign, IL: Research Press.

Griffiths, R. (1978). *Revised Manual: Griffiths mental development scales.* High Wycombe, Buckinghamshire, England: The Test Agency.

Griggs, S. A. (1984). Counseling the gifted and talented based on learning styles. *Exceptional Children, 50*(5), 429–432.

Grossman, H. J. (Ed.) (1977). *Manual on terminology and classification in mental retardation.* Washington, DC: American Association on Mental Deficiency.

Grossman, H. J. (Ed.) (1983). *Manual on terminology and classification in mental retardation* (3rd. ed. rev.). Washington, DC: American Association on Mental Deficiency.

Haeussermann, E. (1958). *Developmental potential of preschool children.* New York: Grune & Stratton.

Hallahan, D. B., & Kauffman, J. W. (1978). *Exceptional children.* Englewood Cliffs, NJ: Prentice-Hall.

Halliday, M. A. K. (1977). *Learning how to mean: Exploration in the development of language.* London: Edward Arnold.

Halpern, A. S. (1985). Transition: A look at the foundations. *Exceptional Children, 51*(6), 479–486.

Hamlett, C., and Hasselbring, T. (1983). Aimstar [Computer program]. Portland, OR: ASIEP Educational Computing.

Hammill, D., & Larsen, S. (1978). *Test of written language.* Austin, TX: Pro-Ed.

Hannah, E. P., and Gardner, J. O. (1974). *Preschool language screening test.* Northridge, CA: Joyce.

Haring, N. G., White, O. R., Edgar, E. B., Affleck, J. Q., Hayden, A. H., Munson, R. G., & Bendersky, M. (1981). *Uniform performance assessment system.* Columbus, OH: Charles E. Merrill.

Harms, T., & Clifford, R. M. (1980). *Early childhood environment rating scale.* New York: Teachers College, Columbia University.

Harnadek, A. (1976). *Critical thinking: Book one.* Pacific Grove, CA: Midwest.

Harnadek, A. (1979). *Inferences — A: Inductive thinking skills.* Pacific Grove, CA: Midwest.

Harnadek, A. (1980). *Critical thinking: Book two.* Pacific Grove, CA: Midwest.

Harris, F. R., Wolf, M. M., & Baer, D. M. (1964). Effects of adult social reinforcement on child behavior. *Young Children, 20,* 8–17.

Hasselbring, T., & Hamlett, C. (1983). *Aimstar: A computer software program.* Portland, OR: Applied Systems.

Hayes, S. (1943). A second test scale for the mental measurement of the visually handicapped. *The New Outlook for the Blind, 37,* 37–41.

Hedrick, D. L., Prather, E. M., & Tobin, A. R. (1975). *Sequenced inventory of communication development.* Seattle: University of Washington Press.

Helton, G. B., Workman, E. A., & Matuszek, P. A. (1982). *Psychoeducational assessment: Integrating concepts and techniques.* New York: Grune & Stratton.

Henker, B., Whalen, C. K., & Hinshaw, S. P. (1980). The attributional contexts of cognitive intervention strategies. *Exceptional Education Quarterly, 1,* 17–30.

Heron, T. E., & Skinner, M. E. (1981). Criteria for defining the regular classroom as the least restrictive environment for LD students. *Learning Disability Quarterly, 4,* 115–121.

Hersen, M., & Bellack, A. S. (1976). *Behavioral assessment.* New York: Pergamon.

Hiskey, M. (1966). *Hiskey-Nebraska test of learning aptitude.* Lincoln, NE: College Press.

Hobbs, N. (1975). *The futures of children.* San Francisco: Jossey-Bass.

Hoepfner, R., Stern, C., & Nummedal, S. G. (1971). *CSE–ECRC preschool/kindergarten test evaluations.* Los Angeles: UCLA Graduate School of Education.

Hobson V. Hansen. 269 F. Supp, 401 (D.D.C. 1967).

Holvoet, J., Mulligan, M., Schussler, N., Lacy, L., & Guess, P. (1984). *Kansas individualized curriculum sequencing model.* Portland, OR: Applied Systems.

Hopkins, C. D., & Antes, R. (1979). *Classroom testing: Administration, scoring and score interpretation.* Itasca, IL: Peacock Publishing Co., Inc.

Hopkins, C. D., & Nages, R. L. (1978). *Classroom measurement and evaluation.* Itasca, IL: Peacock.

Hops, H., Beickel, S. L., & Walker, H. M. (1976). *Contingencies for learning academic and social skills: Manual for consultants.* Eugene, OR: Center at Oregon for Research in the Behavioral Education of the Handicapped, University of Oregon, Center on Human Development.

Hops, H., & Greenwood, C. R. (1981). Social skills deficits. In E. J. Mash & L. G. Terdal (Eds.), *Behavioral assessment of childhood disorders* (pp. 347–396). New York: Guilford.

Horn, J. L. (1978). The nature and development of intellectual abilities. In R. T. Osborn, C. E. Noble, & N. Weyl (Eds.), *Human variation: The biopsychology of age, race and sex.* New York: Academic Press.

Hresko, W. P., Reid, D. K., & Hammill, D. D. (1981). *Test of early language development.* Los Angeles: Western Psychologists.

Huelsman, C. (1970). The WISC subtest syndrome for disabled readers. *Perceptual and Motor Skills, 30,* 535–550.

Hupp, S., & Donofrio, M. (1983). Assessment of multiply and severely handicapped learners for the development of cross-referenced objectives. *Journal of the Association for the Severely Handicapped, 8,* 17–28.

IDRA Staff (1984, September). IDRA LAS scoring and LAS computer-related services. *Intercultural Development Research Association Newsletter,* p. 7.

Jastak, J. E., & Jastak, S. R. (1978). *Wide range achievement tests.* Wilmington, DE: Guidance Associates.

Jenkins, J. R., Deno, S. L., & Mirkin, P. K. (1979). Measuring pupil progress toward the least restrictive alternative. *Learning Disability Quarterly, 2,* 81–92.

Jenkins, J. R., & Mayhall, W. F. (1976). Development and evaluation of a resource teacher program. *Exceptional Children, 43,* 21–29.

Johnston, C. (1980). Milliken math sequences [Computer program]. St. Louis: Milliken Publishing.

Kamin, L. J. (1974). *The science and politics of IQ.* Hillsdale, NJ: Lawrence Erlbaum.

Kanfer, F. H., & Saslow, G. (1969). Behavioral diagnosis. In C. M. Franks (Ed.), *Behavior therapy: Appraisal and status* (pp. 417–444). New York: McGraw-Hill.

Karnes, F. A., & Collins, E. C. (1978). State definitions on the gifted and talented: A report and analysis. *Journal for the Education of the Gifted, 1*(1), 44.

Katz, E. (1956). The pointing scale method: A modification of the Stanford-Binet procedure for use with cerebral palsied children. *American Journal of Mental Deficiency, 42,* 1341–1360.

Kauffman, J. M. (1981). *Characteristics of children's behavior disorders.* Columbus, OH: Charles E. Merrill.

Kauffman, J. M. (1984). *Characteristics of children's behavior disorders* (3rd ed.). Columbus, OH: Charles E. Merrill.

Kaufman, A. S. (1976a). A new approach to interpretation of test scatter on the WISC–R. *Journal of Learning Disabilities, 9,* 160–168.

Kaufman, A. S. (1976b). Verbal-performance IQ discrepancies on the WISC–R. *Journal of Consulting and Clinic Psychology, 44,* 739–744.

Kaufman, A. S., & Kaufman, N. L. (1983). *Kaufman assessment battery for children.* Circle Pines, MN: American Guidance Service.

Kavale, K. A. (1981). Meta-analysis of the relationship between visual perceptual skills and reading achievement. *Learning Disabilities Quarterly, 4,* 383–388.

Kazdin, A. E. (1977). Assessing the clinical or applied significance of behavior change through social validation. *Behavior Modification, 1,* 427–452.

Kazdin, A., & Matson, J. (1981). Social validation in mental retardation. *Applied Research in Mental Retardation, 2,* 39–53.

Keogh, B. K. (1973). Perceptual and cognitive styles: Implications for special education. In L. Mann & D. A. Sabatino (Eds.), *The first review of special education* (pp. 83–111). Philadelphia: JSE.

Keogh, B. K., & Becker, L. D. (1973). Early detection of learning problems: Questions, cautions and guidelines. *Exceptional Children, 40,* 5–11.

Kerr, M. M., & Nelson, C. M. (1983). *Strategies for managing behavior problems in the classroom.* Columbus, OH: Charles E. Merrill.

Killalea Associates (1980). State, regional, and national summaries of data from the 1978 civil rights survey of elementary and secondary schools. Report prepared for the U.S. Office of Civil Rights. Alexandria, VA: Author.

Kirby, P. (1982). *Cognitive style, learning style, and transfer skill acquisition.* Columbus, OH: Ohio State University's National Center for Research in Vocational Education.

Kirp, D. L. (1974). Student classification, public policy, and the courts. *Harvard Educational Review, 44*(1), 7–52.

Kohn, J. (1982). Multiply handicapped child: Severe physical and mental disability. In E. Bleck & D. Nagel (Eds.), *Physically handicapped children: A medical atlas for teachers* (2nd ed.). New York: Grune & Stratton.

Knowlton, H. E. (1980). The effects of picture fading on sight word acquisition of two learning disabled children. *Learning Disability Quarterly, 3,* 88–96.

Knowlton, H. E. (1982a, September). Effects of equivalent and analogous instruction on oral reading rates of LD students. Paper presented at the First Annual Conference on Behavioral Analysis in Education, Columbus, OH.

Knowlton, H. E. (1982b). The QC approach to teaching basic skills. *Directive Teacher, 4,* 20–24.

Krenzer, G. (1980). Preschool children's performance on standard and adapted test items of the Stanford-Binet Intelligence Scale (Form L-M). Unpublished doctoral dissertation. Lincoln, NE: University of Nebraska-Lincoln.

Krimsky, J. S. (1982). A comparative analysis of the effects of matching and mismatching fourth grade students with their learning style preferences for the environmental element of light and their subsequent reading speed and accuracy scores. Unpublished doctoral dissertation, St. John's University, Jamaica, NY.

Lambert, N., Windmiller, M., Cole, L., & Figueroa, R. (1975). *Manual: AAMD adaptive behavior scale, public school version (1974 rev.).* Washington, DC: American Association on Mental Deficiency.

Langley, M. B. (1979). Working with young physically-impaired children: Part B—Educational programming. In S. G. Garwood (Ed.), *Educating young handicapped children: A developmental approach* (pp. 109–150). Germantown, MD: Aspen Systems.

Larry P. v. Riles, 495 F. Supp. 926 (N.D. Cal. 1979).

LaVoie, J., & Adams, G. (1974). Teacher expectancy and its relation to physical and interpersonal characteristics of the child. *Alberta Journal of Educational Research, 20,* 122–132.

Lazar, I., & Darlington, R. (1982). *Lasting effects of early education: A report from the consortium for longitudinal studies* (pp. 47–195). Monographs of the Society for Research in Child Development, The University of Chicago Press for the Society for Research in Child Development, Chicago, IL.

Lazerson, M. (1983). The origins of special education. In J. G. Chambers & W. T. Hartman (Eds.), *Special education policies: Their history, implementation, and finance* (pp. 15–47). Philadelphia: Temple University Press.

LeMay, D. W., Griffin, P. M., & Sanford, A. R. (1977). *Learning accomplishment profile: Diagnostic edition (revised).* Winston Salem, NC: Kaplan School Supply.

Leonard, L. (1972). What is deviant language? *Journal of Speech and Hearing Disorders, 37,* 427–446.

Levine, M. (1976). The academic achievement test. *American Psychologist, 31,* 288–337.

Liebert, R. M., & Wicks-Nelson, R. (1981). *Developmental psychology.* Englewood Cliffs, NJ: Prentice-Hall.

Lillie, D. L. (1975). *Carolina developmental profile.* Chicago: Science Research Associates.

Lindsay, B. (1978). Leadership giftedness: Developing a profile. *Journal for the Education of the Gifted, 1,* 63–69.

Lubert, N. (1981). Auditory perceptual impairments in children with specific language disorders: A review of the literature. *Journal of Speech and Hearing Disorders, 47,* 3–9.

Lucas, E. V. (1980). *Semantic and pragmatic disorders: Assessment and remediation.* Rockville, MD: Aspen Systems.

Ludlow, B. C. (1981). Parent-infant interaction research: The argument for earlier intervention programs. *Journal of the Division of Early Childhood, 3,* 34–41.

Lynch, P. K. (1981). An analysis of the relationship among academic achievement, attendance, and the individual learning style time preferences of eleventh and twelfth grade students identified as initial or chronic truants in a suburban New York school district. Unpublished doctoral dissertation, St. John's University, Jamaica, NY.

MacMillan, D. L. (1982). *Mental retardation in school and society* (2nd ed.). Boston: Little, Brown.

Maker, C. J. (1976). Searching for giftedness and talent in children with handicaps. *The School Psychology Digest, 5,* 24–36.

Maker, C. J. (1982a). *Curriculum development for the gifted.* Rockville, MD: Aspen Systems.

Maker, C. J. (1982b). *Teaching models in education of the gifted.* Rockville, MD: Aspen Systems.

Maker, C. J., Morris, E., & James, J. (1981). The Eugene Field project: A program for potentially gifted children. In *Balancing the scale for the disadvantaged gifted.* Los Angeles: National/State Leadership Training Institute on the Gifted and Talented.

Malcom, P. J., Lutz, W. C., & Hoeltke, G. M. (1981). *Learning style identification scale.* Monterey, CA: Publishers Test Service.

Marland, S., Jr. (1972). *Education of the gifted and talented.* Report to the Congress of the United States by the U.S. Commissioner of Education. Washington, DC: U.S. Government Printing Office.

Marsh, G. E., Price, B. J., & Smith, T. E. C. (1983). *Teaching mildly handicapped children.* St. Louis: Mosby.

Marston, D., & Magnusson, D. (1985). Implementing curriculum-based measurement in special and regular education settings. *Exceptional Children, 52,* 266–276.

Marston, D., Mirkin, P. K., & Deno, S. (1984). Curriculum-based measurement: An alternative to traditional screening, referral and identification. *Journal of Special Education, 18,* 109–118.

Marston, D., Tindal, G., & Deno, S. L. (1982). Predictive efficiency of direct, repeated measurement: An analysis of cost and accuracy in classification (Research Report No. 104). Minneapolis: University of Minnesota, Institute for Research on Learning Disabilities.

Marten, L. A., & Matlin, M.W. (1976). Does sexism in elementary readers still exist? *Reading Teacher, 29,* 764–767.

Martinson, R. (1974). *The identification of the gifted and talented.* Ventura, CA: Ventura County Superintendent of Schools.

Martinson, R., & Lessinger, L. M. (1960). Problems in the identification of intellectually gifted pupils. *Exceptional Children, 26,* 227–242.

Mash, E. J., & Terdal, L. G. (Eds.) (1981). *Behavioral assessment of childhood disorders.* New York: Guilford.

Maxfield, K., & Bucholz, S. (1958). *A social maturity scale for blind preschool children: A guide to its use.* New York: American Foundation for the Blind.

McCarthy, D. (1972a). *Manual for the McCarthy scales of children's abilities.* New York: Psychological Corporation.

McCarthy, D. (1972b). *McCarthy scales of children's abilities.* New York: Psychological Corporation.

McFall, R. M. (1982). A review and reformulation of the concept of social skills. *Behavioral Assessment, 4,* 1–34.

McFarland, A. S. (1969). *Power and leadership in pluralist systems.* Stanford, CA: Stanford University Press.

McLean, J. E., & Snyder-McLean, L. K. (1978). *A transactional approach to early language training.* Columbus, OH: Charles E. Merrill.

McLoughlin, J., & Lewis, R. B. (1981). *Assessing special students: Strategies and procedures.* Columbus, OH: Charles E. Merrill.

McNeill, D. (1970). *The acquisition of language.* New York: Grune & Stratton.

Meeker, M. N. (1969). *The structure of intellect: Its interpretation and uses.* Columbus, OH: Charles E. Merrill.

Meichenbaum, D. (1977). *Cognitive behavior modification: An integrated approach.* New York: Plenum.

Meichenbaum, D. M., & Arsarnow, J. (1979). Cognitive-behavioral modification and metacognitive development: Implications for the classroom. In P. C. Kendall & S. D. Hollon (Eds.), *Cognitive-behavioral interventions* (pp. 11–35). New York: Academic Press.

Menyuk, P. (1964). Comparison of grammar of children with functionally deviant and normal speech. *Journal of Speech and Hearing Research, 8,* 109–121.

Menyuk, P. (1971). *The acquisition and development of language.* Englewood Cliffs, NJ: Prentice-Hall.

Mercer, J. R. (1972). Statement in *Environment, intelligence, and scholastic achievement: A compilation of testimony to the select committee on equal educational opportunity, United States Senate,* 433–437. Washington, DC: United States Government Printing Office.

Mercer, J. R., & Lewis, J. F. (1978). *The system of multicultural pluralistic assessment.* New York: Psychological Corporation.

Microcomputer Educational Products (1982). Job readiness—assessment and development [Computer program]. Kalamazoo, MI: Author.

Miller, J. (1981). *Assessing language production in children.* Baltimore: University Park Press.

Milliken Publishing Company (1980). Milliken math sequences [Computer program]. St. Louis, MO: Author.

Mirkin, P. K., Deno, S. L., Tindall, G., & Kuehnle, K. (1980). *Formative evaluation: Continued development of data utilization systems* (Research Report No. 23). Minneapolis: University of Minnesota, Institute for Research on Learning Disabilities.

Morehead, D., & Ingram, D. (1973). The development of base syntax in normal and linguistically deviant children. *Journal of Speech and Hearing Research, 16,* 330–353.

Morris, P. R., & Whiting, H. (1971). *Motor impairment and compensatory education.* London: G. Bell.

Mosher, F. A., & Hornsby, J. R. (1966). On asking questions. In J. S. Bruner, R. R. Oliver, & P. M. Greenfield (Eds.), *Studies in cognitive growth.* New York: John Wiley.

Morsink, C. V. (1984). *Teaching special needs students in regular classrooms.* Boston: Little, Brown.

Muma, J. R. (1978). *Language handbook: Concepts, assessment, intervention.* Englewood Cliffs, NJ: Prentice-Hall.

Mumm, M., Secord, W., & Dykstra, K. (1980). *Merrill language screening test.* Columbus, OH: Charles E. Merrill.

Myklebust, H. (1954). *Auditory disorders in children.* New York: Grune & Stratton.

Myklebust, H. (1973). *Development and disorders of written language. Volume 2. Studies of normal and exceptional children.* New York: Grune & Stratton.

Nealis, J. (1983). Epilepsy. In J. Umbreit (Ed.), *Physical disabilities and health impairments: An introduction* (pp. 74–85). Columbus, OH: Charles E. Merrill.

Nelson, C. M. (1981). Behavior disorders. In A. E. & W. H. Berdine (Eds.), *An introduction to special education* (pp. 427–468). Boston: Little, Brown.

Nelson, C. M., & Polsgrove, L. (1982). The etiology of adolescent behavior disorders. In G. Brown, R. L. McDowel, & J. Smith (Eds.), *Educating adolescents* (pp. 30–59). Columbus, OH: Charles E. Merrill.

Nevin, A., McCann, S., & Semmel, M. (1983). An empirical analysis of the regular classroom teacher's role in implementing IEPs: Training implications. *Teacher Education and Special Education, 6*(4), 235–247.

Newborg, J., Stock, J. R., & Wnek, L. (1984). *Battelle developmental inventory.* Allen, TX: DLM Teaching Resources.

Newcomer, P., and Hammill, D. (1977). *Test of language development.* Los Angeles: Western Psychologists Press.

Nihira, K., Foster, R., Shellhaas, M., & Leland, H. (1969). *AAMD adaptive behavior scale.* Washington, DC: American Association on Mental Deficiency.

Nihira, K., Foster, R., Shellhaas, M., & Leland, H. (1974). *AAMD adaptive behavior scale manual* (rev. ed.). Washington, DC: American Association on Mental Deficiency.

Oakland, T. (1980). An evaluation of the ABIC, pluralistic norms, and estimated learning potential. *Journal of School Psychology, 18,* 3–11.

Office of the Santa Cruz County Superintendent of Schools. McCarthy, D. (1973). *Behavioral characteristics progression.* Palo Alto: VORT.

O'Leary, K. D., & Johnson, S. B. (1979). Psychological assessment. In H. C. Quay & J. S. Werry (Eds.), *Psychopathological disorders of childhood* (pp. 210–246). New York: John Wiley.

Paget, K. D., & Bracken, B. A. (Eds.) (1983). *The psychoeducational assessment of preschool children.* New York: Grune & Stratton.

Parents in Action on Special Education v. Hannon, No. 74–C–3556 (N. D. Ill., 1980).

Parten, M. B. (1932). Social participation among preschool children. *Journal of Abnormal and Social Psychology, 27,* 243–269.

Pasanella, A. L., & Volkman, C. B. (1977). *Coming back or never leaving.* Columbus, OH: Charles E. Merrill.

Patton, M. Q. (1980). *Qualitative evaluation methods.* New York: Sage.

Payne, J. S., & Patton, J. R. (1981). *Mental retardation.* Columbus, OH: Charles E. Merrill.

Pearson, P., & Williams, C. (Eds.) (1972). *Physical therapy services in the developmental disabilities.* Springfield, IL: Charles C. Thomas.

Pegnato, C. C., & Birch, J. W. (1959). Locating gifted children in junior high schools: A comparison of methods. *Exceptional Children, 25,* 300–304.

Perrin, J. (1982). *Learning style inventory: Primary version.* Jamaica, NY: St. John's University.

Peterson, J., Heistad, D., Peterson, D., & Reynolds, M. (1985). Montevideo individualized prescriptive instructional management system. *Exceptional Children, 52,* 239–243.

Petrosko, J. M. (1978). Measuring creativity in elementary school: The current state of the art. *Journal of Creative Behavior, 12,* 109–119.

Piaget, J. (1952). *The origins of intelligence in children.* New York: Norton.

Pizzo, J. (1981). An investigation of the relationship between selected acoustic environments and sound, an element of learning style, as they affect sixth grade students' reading achievement and attitudes. Unpublished doctoral dissertation, St. John's University, Jamaica, NY.

Polsgrove, L., & Reith, J. J. (1983). Procedures for reducing children's inappropriate behavior in special education settings. *Exceptional Education Quarterly, 3,* 20–33.

Popham, W. J. (1978). *Criterion-referenced measurement.* Englewood Cliffs, NJ: Prentice-Hall.

Poteet, J. A. (1980). Informal assessment of written expression. *Learning Disability Quarterly, 3,* 88–98.

Powell, M. L. (1981). *Assessment and management of developmental changes and problems in children.* St. Louis: Mosby.

Price, G. E., Dunn, K., Dunn, R., & Griggs, S. A. (1981). Studies in students' learning styles. *Roper Review, 4,* 38–40.

Project RHISE. (1979). *Rockford infant developmental evaluation scales.* Bensenville, IL: Scholastic Testing Service.

Public Law 94-142 (1975). Education for all handicapped children act.

Public Law 94-142 (1977). Rules and regulations.

Quay, H. C., & Peterson, D. R. (1975). Manual for the behavior problem checklist. Unpublished manuscript.

Quay, H. C., & Peterson, D. R. (1983). *Interim manual for the revised behavior problem checklist.* Coral Gables, FL: University of Miami.

Quay, H. C. (1977). Measuring dimensions of deviant behavior: The behavior problem checklist. *Journal of Abnormal Child Psychology, 5,* 277–289.

Quay, H. C. (1979). Classification. In H. C. Quay & J. S. Werry (Eds.), *Psychopathological disorders of childhood* (pp. 1–42). New York: John Wiley.

Quay, H. C. (1983). A dimensional approach to behavior disorders: The revised behavior problem checklist. *School Psychology Review, 12*(3), 244–249.

Radabaugh, M., & Yuckish, J. (1982). *Curriculum and methods for the mildly handicapped.* Boston: Allyn & Bacon.

Rees, N. (1973). Auditory processing factors in language disorders: The view from Procrustes' bed. *Journal of Speech and Hearing Disorders, 38,* 304–315.

Rees, N. (1981). Saying more than we know: Is auditory processing disorder a meaningful concept? In R. A. Keith (Ed.), *Central auditory and language disorders in children.* Houston, TX: College Hill Press.

Reiss, S., Levitan, G. W., & Szyszko, J. (1982). Emotional disturbance and mental retardation: Diagnostic overshadowing. *American Journal of Mental Deficiency, 86,* 567–574.

Renzulli, J. S. (1978). What makes giftedness? *Phi Delta Kappan, 60,* 180–184, 261.

Renzulli, J. S., & Smith, L. H. (1977). Two approaches to identification of gifted students. *Exceptional Children, 43,* 512–518.

Renzulli, J S., & Smith, L. (1978a). *Learning style inventory.* Mansfield, CT: Creative Learning Press.

Renzulli, J. S., & Smith, L. H. (1978b). *Learning styles inventory: A measure of student preference for instructional techniques.* Mansfield Center, CT: Creative Learning Press.

Renzulli, J. S., Smith, L. H., White, A. J., Callahan, C. M., & Hartman, R. K. (1976). *Scales for rating the behavioral characteristics of superior students.* Wethersfield, CT: Creative Learning Press.

Reschly, D. J. (1981). Evaluation of the effects of SOMPA measures on classification of students as mildly mentally retarded. *American Journal of Mental Deficiency, 86,* 16–20.

Richert, E. S. (1982). *National report on identification: Assessment and recommendations for comprehensive identification of gifted and talented youth.* Sewell, NJ: Educational Improvement Center.

Robins, L. (1979). Follow-up studies. In H. C. Quay & J. S. Werry (Eds.), *Psychopathological disorders of childhood* (pp. 483–514). New York: John Wiley.

Robinson, C., & Fieber, N. (in press). Use of scales of psychological development with motorically impaired infants. In I. Uzgiris & J. McVHunt (Eds.), *Research with scales of psychological development in infancy.* Urbana: University of Illinois Press.

Robinson, C., & Robinson, J. (1983). Sensorimotor function and cognitive development. In M. E. Snell (Ed.), *Systematic instruction of the moderately and severely handicapped* (2nd ed.) (pp. 227–266). Columbus, OH: Charles E. Merrill.

Robson, G. M. (1977). *Problem solving strategies in learning disabled and normal achieving children.* Unpublished doctoral dissertation, p. 153, University of California, Los Angeles.

Rogers, S. J., Donovan, C. M., & D'Eugenio, D. B. (1981). *Early intervention developmental profile*. Ann Arbor: University of Michigan Press.

Rose, J. (1982). Review of developmental programming for infants and young children. In A. Seitel, A. Jung, & N. Fieber (Eds.), *A compendium of severe/profound special education resources*. Omaha, NE: Media Resource Center, Meyer Children's Rehabilitation Institute, University of Nebraska Medical Center.

Rosenberg, S., & Robinson, C. (1983). *Development of a microprocessor based workstation for severely and profoundly handicapped students*. U.S. Department of Education, OSEP Field Initiated Research Grant (G008300312).

Ross, M. B., & Salvia, J. (1975). Attractiveness as a biasing factor in teacher judgements. *American Journal of Mental Deficiency, 80,* 96–98.

Sabatino, D., & Miller, T. (Eds.) (1979). *Describing learner characteristics of handicapped children and youth*. New York: Grune & Stratton.

Sailor, W., & Guess, P. D. (1983). *Severely handicapped students: An instructional design*. Boston: Houghton Mifflin.

Salvia, J., & Ysseldyke, J. E. (1985). *Assessment in special and remedial education* (3rd ed.). Boston: Houghton Mifflin.

Salvia, J., & Ysseldyke, J. E. (1981). *Assessment in special and remedial education* (2nd ed.). Boston: Houghton Mifflin.

Sanford, A. R., & Zelman, J. G. (1981). *Learning accomplishment profile*. Winston-Salem, NC: Kaplan Press.

Sattler, J. M. (1974). *Assessment of children's intelligence*. Philadelphia: W. B. Saunders.

Sattler, J. M. (1982). *The assessment of children's intelligence and special abilities*. Boston: Allyn & Bacon.

Scarlett, J., & Latta, D. (1985). Computing work sample norms for sub-contract jobs. Unpublished manuscript available from the second author. Developmental Learning Center, Olathe Public Schools, Olathe, KS.

Schafer, D. S., and Moersch, M. S. (Eds.) (1977). Developmental Programming for Infants and Young Children. Ann Arbor: University of Michigan Press.

Schafer, D. S., & Moersch, M. S. (Eds.) (1979). *Describing learner characteristics of handicapped children and youth*. New York: Grune & Stratton.

Schafer, D. S., & Moersch, M. S. (Eds.) (1982). *Developmental programming for infants and young children*. Ann Arbor: University of Michigan Press.

Schmidt, P. (1976). Feeding assessment and therapy for neurologically impaired. *AAESPH Review, 1,* 19–27.

Searle, J. R. (1969). *Speech acts: An essay on the philosophy of language.* Cambridge, England: Cambridge University Press.

Segal, E., & Gold, R. (1982). *Educating the learning disabled.* New York: Macmillan.

Seitel, A., Jung, A., & Fieber, N. (Eds.) (1982). *A compendium of severe/profound special education resources.* Omaha, NE: Media Resource Center, Meyer Children's Rehabilitation Institute, University of Nebraska Medical Center.

Semel, E., and Wiig, E. (1980). *Clinical evaluation of language functions.* Columbus, OH: Charles Merrill.

Shankweiler, D., & Liberman, I. Y. (1972). Misreading: A search for causes. In J. E. Kavanaugh & I. G. Mattingly (Eds.), *Language by ear and by eye* (pp. 293–312). Cambridge, MA: M.I.T. Press.

Shea, T. C. (1983). An investigation of the relationship among preference for the learning style element of design, selected instructional environments, and reading achievement of ninth grade students to improve administrative determinations concerning effective educational facilities. Unpublished doctoral dissertation, St. John's University, Jamaica, NY.

Simeonsson, R. J., Cooper, D. H., & Scheiner, A. P. (1982). A review and analysis of the effectiveness of early intervention programs. *Pediatrics, 69,* 635–641.

Silverman, L. (in press). *Gifted education: A developmental approach.* St. Louis: Mosby.

Silverman, R., & Zigmond, N. (1983). Assessment of mathematics. In N. Zigmond, A. Vallecorsa, & R. Silverman (Eds.), *Assessment for instructional planning in special education* (pp. 203–267). Englewood Cliffs, NJ: Prentice-Hall.

Skinner, B. F. (1953). *Science and human behavior.* New York: The Free Press.

Skrtic, T., Guba, E. G., & Knowlton, H. E. (1985). Interorganizational special education programming in rural areas: Technical report on the multisite naturalistic field study. Special education in rural America (Contract No. 400–81–0017). Washington, DC: National Institute of Education.

Skrtic, T., Kvam, N., & Beals, V. (1983). Identifying and remediating the subtraction errors of learning disabled adolescents. *Pointer, 27,* 32–38.

Sky, N. C. (1984). Record keeper [Computer program]. Portland, OR: ASIEP Educational Computing.

Smith, C. R. (1983). *Learning disabilities: The interaction of learner, task, and setting.* Boston: Little, Brown.

Smith, C. R., & Knoff, H. M. (1981). School psychology and special education students' placement decisions: IQ still tips the scale. *Journal for Special Education, 15*(1), 55–64.

Snell, M. (Ed.) (1978). *Systematic instruction of the moderately and severely handicapped.* Columbus, OH: Charles E. Merrill.

Snell, M. (Ed.) (1983). *Systematic instruction of the moderately and severely handicapped* (2nd ed.). Columbus, OH: Charles E. Merrill.

Sontag, E., Burke, P., & York, R. (1973). Considerations for serving the severely handicapped in the public schools. *Education and Training of the Mentally Retarded, 8,* 20–26.

Sontag, E., Smith, J., & Sailor, W. (1977). The severely and profoundly handicapped: Who are they? Where are we? *Journal of Special Education, 11,* 5–11.

Somwaru, J. P. (1979). *Test of early learning skills.* Bensenville, IL: Scholastic Testing Service.

Sparrow, S. S., Bala, D. A., & Cicchetti, D. V. (1984). *Vineland adaptive behavior scales.* Circle Pines, MN: American Guidance Service.

Sprinthall, R. C., & Sprinthall, N. A. (1981). *Educational psychology: A developmental approach* (3rd ed.). Reading, MA: Addison-Wesley.

Sroufe, A. (1979). The coherence of individual development: Early care attachment and subsequent development issues. *American Psychologist, 34,* 834–841.

Staab, C. (1983). Language functions elicited by meaningful activities: A new dimension in language programs. *Language, Speech, and Hearing Services in the Schools, 14,* 164–170.

Staffieri, J. (1967). A study of social stereotypes of body image in children. *Journal of Personality and Social Psychology, 7,* 101–104.

Stephens, I. (1977). *The Stephens oral language screening test.* Peninsula, OH: Interim Publishers.

Stephens, T. M., Blackhurst, A. E., & Magliocca, L. A. (1982). *Teaching mainstreamed students.* New York: John Wiley.

Sternat, J., Messina, R., Nietupski, J., Lyon, S., & Brown, L. (1977). Occupational and physical therapy services for severely handicapped students: Toward a naturalized public school service delivery model. In E. Sontag (Ed.), *Educational programming for the severely and profoundly handicapped.* Reston, VA: Council for Exceptional Children.

Stewart, E. D. (1981). Learning styles among gifted/talented students: Instructional technique preferences. *Exceptional Children, 48*(2), 134–138.

Stillman, R. (1978). *Callier-Azuza scale.* Dallas: University of Texas, Callier Center for Communication Disorders.

Sugai, G. (1985). Case study: Designing instruction from IEPs. *Teaching Exceptional Children, 17*(3), 232–239.

Sulzer-Azaroff, B., & Mayer, R. G. (1977). *Applying behavior analysis procedures with children and youth.* New York: Holt, Rinehart & Winston.

Swanson, H. L., & Watson, B. L. (1972). *Educational and psychological assessment of exceptional children: Theories, strategies, and applications.* St. Louis: Mosby.

Tallal, P., & Stark, R. (1980). Speech perception of language delayed children. In G. Komshian and C. Ferguson (Eds.), *Child Phonology: Volume 2. Perception* (pp. 155–172). New York: Academic Press.

Talley, M. (1985). Talley goals and objectives. [Unifer computer program.] North Billerica, MA: Curriculum Associates.

Tarjan, G., Wright, S. W., Eyman, R. K., & Kiernan, C. V. (1973). National history of mental retardation: Some aspects of epidemiology. *American Journal of Mental Deficiency, 77,* 369–379.

Tarver, S. G., & Hallahan, D. P. (1978). Attentional deficits in children with learning disabilities: A review. *Journal of Learning Disabilities, 11,* 5–17.

Taylor, C. W. (1968). Nearly all students are talented: Let's reach them. *Utah Parent Teacher* (February).

Terman, L. M. (Ed.) (1926). *Genetic studies of genius Vol. 1. Mental and physical traits of a thousand gifted children.* Palo Alto, CA: Stanford University Press.

Terman, L. M., & Merrill, M. A. (1973a). *The Stanford-Binet intelligence scale* (3rd ed.). Boston: Houghton Mifflin.

Terman, L., & Merrill, M. (1973b). *Stanford-Binet intelligence scale, 1972 norms edition.* Boston: Houghton Mifflin.

Thal, D. J., and Barone, P. (1983). Auditory processing and language impairment in children: Stimulus considerations for intervention. *Journal of Speech and Hearing Disorders, 48,* 18–25.

Thompson, P. (March 1974). Wednesday morning keynote address [untitled]. In J. Moore & V. Engleman (Eds.), *The severely, multiply handicapped: What are the issues?* (pp. 70–76). Proceedings of the Regional Topical Conference. University of Utah, Salt Lake City.

Todd, J., Coolidge, F., & Satz, P. (1977). The Wechsler adult intelligence scale discrepancy index: A neuropsychological evaluation. *Journal of Consulting and Clinical Psychology, 45,* 450–454.

Torgensen, J. K. (1980). Conceptual and educational implications for the use of efficient task strategies by learning disabled children. *Journal of Learning Disabilities, 13,* 364–371.

Torrance, E. P. (1966). *Torrance tests of creative thinking: Norms-technical manual.* Lexington, MA: Ginn, & Princeton, NJ: Personnel Press.

Torrance, E. P. (1974). *Torrance tests of creative thinking: Norms — technical manual.* Lexington, MA: Ginn.

Torrance, E. P. (1981). Predicting the creativity of elementary school children (1958–80) and the teacher who "made a difference." *Gifted Child Quarterly, 25,* 55–62.

Tough, J. (1977). *The development of meaning.* New York: Halsted Press.

Treffinger, D. J. (1975). Teaching for self-directed learning: A priority for the gifted and talented. *Gifted Child Quarterly, 19,* 46–59.

Tucker, J. A. (1980). Ethnic proportions in classes for the learning disabled issuing on non-biased assessment. *Journal of Special Education, 14,* 93–105.

Tucker, J. A. (1985). Curriculum-based assessment: An introduction. *Exceptional Children, 52,* 199–204.

Turnbull, A. P., Strickland, B. B., & Brantley, J. C. (1982). *Developing and implementing IEPs* (2nd ed.). Columbus, OH: Charles E. Merrill.

Tyack, D., and Gottesleben, R. (1977). *Language sampling, analysis, and training.* Palo Alto, CA: Consulting Psychologists Press.

Tymitz-Wolf, B. (1982). Guidelines for assessing IEP goals and objectives. *Teaching Exceptional Children, 14*(5), 198–201.

Tymitz, B. (1984). The case for reasonable intervention: Training implications for judicious referral and placement decisions. *Teacher Education and Special Education, 7*(1), 12–19.

Ulrey, G., & Rogers, S. (1982). *Psychological assessment of handicapped infants and young children.* New York: Thieme-Stratton.

Utley, B. (1982). Instructional analysis. Unpublished manuscript, University of Pittsburgh, Department of Special Education.

Ŭzgiris, I., & Hunt, J. M. (1975). *Assessment in infancy: Ordinal scales of psychological development.* Urbana: University of Illinois Press.

Vallercorsa, A., Silverman, R., & Zigmond, N. (1983). The assessment of written expression. In N. Zigmond, A. Vallercorsa, & R. Silverman (Eds.), *Assessment for instructional planning in special education* (pp. 127–202). Englewood Cliffs, NJ: Prentice-Hall.

Vellutino, F. R. (1977). Alternative conceptualization of dyslexia: Evidence in support of a verbal-deficit hypothesis. *Harvard Educational Review, 47,* 334–352.

Venn, J. J., Dykes, M. K., & Morganstern, L. (1979). Checklists to evaluate the fit and function of orthoses, prostheses, and wheelchairs for use in the classroom. *Teaching Exceptional Children, 22,* 51–56.

Vincent, L. J., Salisbury, C., Walter, G., Brown, P., Gruenwald, L. J., & Powers, M. (1980). Program evaluation and curriculum development in early childhood special education: Criteria of the next environment. In W. Sailor, B. Wilcox, & L. Brown (Eds.), *Methods of instruction for severely handicapped students* (pp. 303–328). Baltimore: Paul H. Brookes.

Vulpe, S. G. (1977). *Vulpe assessment battery.* Toronto: National Institute on Mental Retardation.

Wachs, T. (1979). Proximal experience and early cognitive-intellectual development: The physical environment. *Merrill-Palmer Quarterly, 25,* 3–41.

Wahler, R. G., & Cormier, W. H. (1970). The ecological interview: A first step in outpatient child behavior therapy. *Journal of Behavior Therapy and Experimental Psychiatry, 1,* 279–289.

Walker, H. M., & Hops, H. (1976). Use of normative peer data as a standard for evaluating classroom treatment effects. *Journal of Applied Behavior Analysis, 9,* 159–169.

Walker, H. M. (1983). *Walker problem behavior identification checklist.* Los Angeles: Western Psychological Services.

Wallace, G., & Kauffman, J. M. (1978). *Teaching children with learning problems.* Columbus, OH: Charles E. Merrill.

Wallach, M. A. (1970). Creativity. In P. H. Mussen (Ed.), *Carmichael's manual of child psychology: Vol. 1* (3rd ed.). New York: John Wiley.

Wallach, M. A. (1976). Tests tell us little about talent. *American Scientist, 64,* 57–63.

Wechsler, D. (1955). *The Wechsler adult intelligence scale.* New York: Psychological Corporation.

Wechsler, D. (1967). *Manual for the Wechsler preschool and primary scale of intelligence.* New York: Psychological Corporation.

Wechsler, D. (1974). *The Wechsler intelligence scale for children revised.* New York: Psychological Corporation.

Weffer, R. (1981). Factors to be considered when assessing bilingual Hispanic children. In H. Martinez (Ed.), *Special education and the Hispanic child: Proceedings from the second annual colloquium on Hispanic issues* (pp. 31–48). ERIC Clearinghouse on Urban Education, Institute for Urban and Minority Education, Teacher's College, Columbia University, New York.

Wehman, P. (1977). *Helping the mentally retarded acquire play skills.* Springfield, IL: Charles C. Thomas.

Wehman, P. (1981). *Competitive employment.* Baltimore: Paul Brookes.

Wehman, P., & Schleien. (1979). *Leisure skills curriculum for developmentally disabled persons: Virginia model* (Vols. 1–5). Richmond: Virginia Commonwealth University.

Weisler, A., & McCall, R. B. (1976). Exploration and play: Resume and redirection. *American Psychologist, 31,* 492–508.

Wesman, G. A. (1968). Intelligent testing. *American Psychologist, 23,* 267–274.

Westling, D. L., Koorland, M. A., & Rose, T. L. (1981). Characteristics of superior and average special education teachers. *Exceptional Children, 47,* 357–363.

White, O. (1980). Adaptive performance objectives: Form versus function. In W. Sailor, B. Wilcox, & L. Brown (Eds.) (pp. 47–70), *Methods of instruction for severely handicapped students.* Baltimore: Paul H. Brookes.

White, O. R., Edgar, E., Haring, N. G., Affleck, J., Hayden, A., & Bendersky, M. (1981). *Uniform performance assessment system.* Columbus, OH: Charles E. Merrill.

Whitmore, J. R. (1980). *Giftedness, conflict, and underachievement.* Boston: Allyn & Bacon.

Whitmore, J. R. (1981). Gifted children with handicapping conditions: A new frontier. *Exceptional Children, 48,* 106–114.

Widerholt, J. L., Hammill, D. D., & Brown, V. (1978). *The resource teacher.* Boston: Allyn & Bacon.

Wiig, E., & Secord, W. (1983). *Test of language competence.* Columbus, OH: Charles E. Merrill.

Wiig, E. H., & Semel, E. M. (1976). *Language disabilities in children and adolescents.* Columbus, OH: Charles E. Merrill.

Williams, F. (1970). *Language and poverty.* Chicago: Markham Press.

Williams, W., & Fox, T. (1977). *Minimum objective system for pupils with severe handicaps.* Vol. 4. Burlington: University of Vermont.

Wilson, M. S., & Fox, B. (1982). Computer administered bilingual language assessment and intervention. *Exceptional Children,* 145–149.

Wood, B. (1981). *Children and communication: Verbal and nonverbal language development.* Englewood Cliffs, NJ: Prentice-Hall.

Woodcock, R. W., & Johnson, M. B. (1973). *Woodcock reading mastery tests.* Circle Pines, MN: American Guidance Service.

Woodcock, R. W., & Johnson, M. B. (1978). *Woodcock-Johnson psychoeducational battery.* Boston: Teaching Resources.

Yamamoto, K. (1966). Do creativity tests really measure creativity? *Theory into Practice, 5,* 194–197.

Ysseldyke, J. (1980). Implementing the protection-in-evaluation provisions of P.L. 94–142. In Department of Health, Education & Welfare (Ed.), *PEP: Developing criteria for the evaluation of PEP provisions.* Philadelphia: Research for Better Schools.

Ysseldyke, J. E., Algozzine, B., Shinn, M. R., & McGue, M. (1982). Similarities and differences between low achievers and students classified learning disabled. *Journal of Special Education, 16*(1), 74–85.

Ysseldyke, J. E., & Regan, R. R. (1980). Nondiscriminatory assessment: A formative model. *Exceptional Children, 46,* 465–468.

Ysseldyke, J. E., & Salvia, J. (1980). Methodological considerations in aptitude-treatment interaction research with intact groups. *Diagnostique, 6*(1), 3–9.

Ysseldyke, J. E., Thurlow, M., Graden, J., Wesson, C., Algozzine, R., & Deno, S. (1983). Generalizations from five years of research on assessment and decision making: The University of Minnesota Institute. *Exceptional Education Quarterly, 4,* 75–93.

Ysseldyke, J., Algozzine, B., & Epps, S. (1983). A logical and empirical analysis of current practice in classifying students as handicapped. *Exceptional Children, 50,* 160–170.

Zachman, L., Huisingh, R., Jorgensen, C., and Barrett, M. (1976). *Oral language sentence imitation screening test.* Moline, IL: Linguisystems.

Zeaman, D., & House, B. J. (1963). The role of attention in retardate discriminative learning. In N. R. Ellis (Ed.), *Handbook of mental deficiency* (pp. 159–223). New York: McGraw-Hill.

Zeaman, D., & House, B. J. (1979). A review of attention theory. In N. R. Ellis (Ed.), *Handbook of mental deficiency, psychological theory and research* (pp. 159–223). Hillsdale, NJ: Lawrence Erlbaum.

Zehrbach, R. R. (1975). *Comprehensive Identification Process.* Bensenville, IL: Scholastic Testing Service.

Zigmond, N., Vallecorsa, A., & Silverman, R. (1983). *Assessment for instructional planning in special education.* Englewood Cliffs, NJ: Prentice-Hall.

Zimmerman, I. L., Steiner, V. G., & Pond, R. E. (1979). *Preschool language scale.* Columbus, OH: Charles E. Merrill.

Name Index

Abelson, A., 253
Abrams, 366
Adamson, 368
Adler, S., 97
Affleck, J.Q., 120, 125
Alberto, P.A., 168, 169
Algozzine, R., 9, 190, 335, 338, 335, 345, 346
Alley, G., 42, 199
Allmann, T.L., 125
Allred, 364
Alpern, G.D., 115
Anastasi, A., 193, 194
Anderson, N., 194
Anderson, Z., 266
Antes, R., 61, 65, 69
Apple Computer, 350
Aram, D., 93
Armenia, 370
Arsarnow, J., 151
Arthur, G., 287
Ashlock, R. B., 211
Atkeson, B.M., 170
Atwood, B. S., 383

Baer, D.M., 145
Bagai, 364
Bagaie, 364
Bagnato, S.J., 122
Bailey, D.B., 16, 17, 37, 44, 119, 131, 135
Baker, D.B., 297
Bala, D.A., 0
Bala, D.L., 229
Baldwin, A., 315
Balow, 364
Balthazar, E.E., 135
Bandura, A., 151

Bangs, T.E., 290
Bankson, N., 99
Banus, B.S., 303
Barone, P., 94
Baroody, 370
Barrett, M., 99, 101
Barron, F., 321
Bass, B.M., 384
Bayley, N., 122, 126, 319, 320
Beals, V., 343
Beatty, 370
Becker, L.D., 187
Beikel, S.L., 151
Bellack, A.S., 144
Belmont H., 188
Belmont I., 188
Belmont, J.M., 199
Bendersky, M., 120, 125
Berdine, W.H., 40, 191, 221, 222, 224, 233
Bernknoph, L.A., 44
Bersoff, D.N., 334
Bice, H.B., 0
Bigge, J., 0
Birch, J.W., 313
Blackhurst, A.E., 42, 221, 222
Blankenship, C.S., 33
Bleck, E.E., 303
Bloom, B.S., 53
Bloom, L., 83, 84, 86, 90, 104
Blum, C.H., 286
Bluma, S.M., 125
Bobath, B., 296
Bobath, D., 296
Boll, T.J., 115
Bond, 364
Borkowski, J.G., 192

Botel, 360
Bower, E.M., 142
Boyer, A., 348, 353
Bracken, B.A., 122
Bradley, R.H., 136
Bradmueller, 362
Brandes, P.J., 93
Branston, 269
Brantley, J.C., 42, 43
Bricker, W., 269
Brigance, A.H., 124, 230, 231, 297, 351, 360, 366, 368
Brinker, R., 263
Bromwich, R.M., 136
Bronefenbrenner, V., 0
Brown, 364, 366, 370
Brown, A., 199
Brown, L., 255, 269
Brown, P., 118
Brown, V., 0
Brueckner, 368
Bruininks, R.H., 304
Burgemeister, B.B., 286
Burke, P., 254, 362
Burkhardt, L., 263
Buros, O.K., 122
Buswell, 368
Butterfield, E.C., 197, 199
Bzoch, K.R., 130

Caldwell, B.M, 136
Calhoun, M.L., 302
Carey, L., 270
Carlin, 300, 368
Carrow, E., 130
Cartwright, C.A., 40
Cartwright, G.P., 40
Casey, A., 335, 338, 345
Cavanaugh, D., 32
Cegelka, P., 40, 44, 233
Certo, N., 255, 268, 269
Chall, 362
Cherkes-Julkowski, M., 197
Chess, N., 272
Chomsky, N., 90
Christensen, S., 335, 338, 345
Christenson, S.L., 190
Chronbach, L.J., 314
Cicchetti, D.V., 229

Clements. S., 193
Cliff, S., 289
Clifford, R.M., 131, 135
Cohen, 366
Collins, E.C., 311
Compton, A., 99, 100
Compu-tations Limited, 350
Cone, J., 258, 259
Connolly, A., 210, 368
Coolidge, F., 193
Cooper, J.O., 165
Cormier, W.H., 154, 163
Crockenberg, S.B., 320
Cronbach, 319
Cross, D., 358
Cruickshank, W.M., 279, 284, 285

Dale, P.S., 84, 97
Darby, B.L., 122
Darlington, R., 112
Darnell, R.E., 288
Davis, C., 257
DeAvila, E.A., 353
Deitz, 158
Dellas, M., 381, 382
Deno, S.L., 205, 209, 221, 340, 342
Deshler, D.D. 199
Dick, W., 270
Dinola, A.J., 232
Dodsen, S., 290
Doll, E., 45, 115
Donofrio, M., 264
Dore, J., 90, 128
Doucette, J., 122
Driscoll, K.A., 122
DuBose, R.F., 133, 290
Ducanis, A., 287
Duffey, J.B., 189, 190
Duncan, S.E., 353
Dunn, K., 27, 29, 30, 286
Dunn, L.M., 130, 200
Dunn, R., 27, 29, 30, 31, 32, 286
Dunst, C.J. 112
Durrell, 360
Dykes, M.K., 290, 297, 301, 302
Dykstra, K., 99, 101

Eberle, B., 32
Edgar, E.B., 120, 125

Ehinger, D.N., 93
Eisenson, J., 90
Engelhart, M.D., 53
Enright, B.E., 351
Evans, I.M., 170
Eyman, R.K., 0

Farr, 362
Feuerstein, R., 192
Fewell, R., 258, 259, 304
Fieber, N., 258, 260, 263, 264, 267
Fiorentino, M.R., 296
Flaugher, R., 345
Flavell, J.H., 199
Fluharty, N.B., 99, 100
Fodor, J.A., 90
Folio, R., 133, 304
Forehand, R., 170
Foster, R., 230
Foster, 42, 45
Fox, B., 348, 353
Fox, T., 255
Frankenberg, W.K., 45, 115
Fraser, B., 289
Freedman, R., 122
Friedman, S.G., 350, 360
Froham, A.H., 125
Fudala, J.B., 99, 101
Furst, E.J., 53
Furuno, S., 125

Gaier, E.L., 381, 382
Gajar, A.H., 185
Galka, G., 289
Gallagher, J.J., 311, 312, 314, 319, 372
Gardner, J.O., 99, 100, 364, 370
Gates, 362
Gauthier, S.V., 99, 100
Gay, L.R., 40
Gear, G.H., 314
Gelfand, D.M., 164, 166, 168
Gentry, D., 264
Germann, G., 35
Gessel, 368
Gickling, E.E., 33
Gilmore and Gilmore, 362
Ginsburg, H., 212, 368
Glover, M.E., 124, 231
Gold, R., 191

Goldsworthy, C., 99, 101
Golin, A., 287
Goodman, K.S., 202, 362
Goodwin, W.L., 122
Gottesleben, R., 90
Gould, S.J., 334
Graden, J.L., 335, 338, 345
Graebner, D., 44
Graham, S., 343
Gray, 362
Gray, B.B., 90
Greenwood, C.R., 147
Griffin, P.M., 231, 232
Griffiths, R., 126
Griggs, S.A., 27
Grossmann, H.J., 196, 218, 219, 253, 346
Gruenwald, L.J., 118, 269
Guba, E., 335, 345
Guess, P., 344
Guidubaldi, 115, 124
Guzaitis, 368

Hackett, 360
Haeussermann, E., 257
Hallahan, D. 185, 198, 284, 285
Halliday, M.A.K., 90, 103
Halpern, A.S., 335, 340, 347
Hamlett, 341
Hammill, D.D., 99, 207, 364, 366
Hamre-Nietupski, S., 255, 269
Hannah, E.P., 99, 100
Harbin, 44, 119
Haring, N.G., 120, 125
Harms, T., 131, 135
Harnadek, A., 321, 322, 323
Harrington, D.M., 321
Harris, F.R., 145, 364
Hartman, R.K., 0
Hartmann, D.P., 164, 166, 168
Hasselbring, T., 0
Hawisher, M., 302
Hayden, A.H., 120, 125
Hayes, S., 256, 257
Hedrich, D., 130
Heistad, 34
Helton, G.B., 224, 225
Henker, B., 159
Hensinger, R., 289
Heron, T.E., 10

Hersen, M., 144
Hesselbring, 341
Hill, W.H., 53
Hilliard, J.M., 125
Hinshaw, S.P., 159
Hiskey, M., 0
Hobbs, N., 143
Hoeltke, G.M., 32
Hoepfner, R., 122
Hoffman, M.B., 192
Holvoet, J., 337
Hopkins, C.D., 61, 65, 69
Hops, H., 145, 147, 151
Horn, J.L., 319
Hornsby, J.R., 323
Hosaka, C.M., 125
House, B.J., 198
Hoyt, 364
Hresko, W.P., 99
Huelsman, C., 193
Huisingh, R., 99, 101
Hunt, J.M., 122, 126
Hupp, S., 264

Inatsuka, T.T., 125
Ingram, D., 84, 86, 90
Intercultural Development Research
    Association, 352

James, 315, 320, 325
Jastak, J.E., 200
Jastak, S.R., 200
John, 368
Johns, 360
Johnson, M.B., 194
Johnson, S.B., 144
Johnston, C., 348
Jorgensen, C., 99, 101
Juda, 368

Kamin, L.J., 334
Kaminsky, B.P., 232
Kamon, 364
Kamp, 370
Kanfer, F.H., 143, 145, 170
Karlsen, 364, 370
Karnes, F.H., 311
Katz, E., 287
Katz, J.J., 90

Kauffman, J.W., 185
Kauffmann, J.M., 191
Kaufman, A.S., 193, 194, 195, 196
Kaufman, N., 194, 195, 196
Kavale, K.A., 192
Kazdin, A.E., 340, 343–344
Keogh, B.K., 187, 198
Kerr, M.M., 164, 165, 168, 169
Killalea Associates, 42
Kirby, P., 2
Kirp, D.L., 334, 345
Knoff, H.M., 192
Knowlton, H.E., 335, 343, 345
Kohn, J., 289
Konarski, E.A., 192
Kottmeyer, 366
Krathwohl, D.R., 53
Krenzer, G., 258
Krimsky, J., 32
Kvam, T., 343

Lahey, M., 83, 84, 86, 90, 97, 104
Lambert, N., 224, 227
Langley, M.B., 290, 302
Larsen, S., 207, 366
Latta, D., 344
Lazar, I., 112
Lazerson, M., 341
League, R., 130
Lehigh, 366
Leland, H., 45
Leland, 45
LeMay, D.W., 231, 232
Leonard, L., 90
LePray, 362
Lessinger, 319
Levin, J., 269
Levine, M., 193
Levitan, G.W., 191
Lewis, J.R., 224
Lewis, M., 263
Lewis, R.B., 44, 260
Liberman, I.Y., 202
Liebert, R.M., 142
Lillie, D.L., 124
Lorge, I., 286
Lovece, 349
Lowry, L., 0
Lubert, N., 94

Lucas, E.V., 90
Ludlow, B.C., 136
Lutz, W.C., 32
Lynch, P.K., 2

McCall, R.B., 131
McCann, S., 340
McCarthy, D., 117, 126
McClean, 120
McCollogh, 362
McDonald, 370
McEntire, 370
McFall, R.M., 145
McFarland, A.S., 384
McGue, M., 190
Mchoughlin, 44
Macke, P., 269
McKillop, 362
McLaughlin, 260
MacMillan, D.L., 222
McNeill, D., 90
Madden, 364, 370
Madison, C.L., 99, 100
Magnusson, D., 35
Maker, C.J., 315, 320, 321, 325, 372, 385
Malcolm, P.J., 32
Markwardt, F.C., 200
Marland, S., 310
Marsh, G.E., 185
Marston, D., 34, 35, 209
Marten, L.A., 44
Martinson, R., 319, 320
Mash, E.J., 144
Matlin, M.W., 44
Matson, J., 340, 343
Matthews, 368
Matuszek, P.A., 225
Maxfield-Bucholz, K., 257
May, 122
Mayer, R.G., 158
Meeker, M.N., 320
Meichelbaum, 151
Meichenbaum, D., 198
Menyuk, P., 90
Mercer, J.R., 190, 224
Merrill, M., 126, 194, 219
Miles, 364
Miller, J., 84
Miller, L., 343

Miller, R., 192
Miller, T., 257
Mirkin, P.K., 4, 205, 209, 341, 342
Moe, 360
Moersch, M.S., 267
Moersch, 124
Morehead, D., 84, 86, 90
Morganstern, L., 297
Morris, P.R., 302, 315, 320, 325
Morsink, C.V., 344
Mosher, F.A., 323
Muma, J.R., 88
Mumm, M., 99, 101
Munson, R.G., 120
Myklebust, H., 90, 206, 366

Nachtman, W., 210, 368
Nation, J.E., 93
Neisworth, J.T., 122
Nelson, C.M., 160, 164, 165, 168, 169
Nelson, R.O., 170
Nelson, 160, 164, 165, 168, 169
Nevin, A., 340
Newborg, J., 115, 124, 229
Newcomer, P., 99
Nietupski, J., 255
Nihira, K., 45, 196, 224, 347
Nummedal, S.G., 122

Oakland, T., 193
O'Leary, K.D., 144
O'Reilly, K.A., 125

Paget, K.D., 122
Parten, M.B., 131, 132
Pasanella, A.L., 186
Patton, 170
Pegnato, C.C., 313
Perrin, J., 33
Peters, J., 193
Peterson, J., 34, 145, 162, 163
Petrosko, J.M., 320
Piaget, J., 122
Pine County Special Education Cooperative, 35
Pizzo, J., 32
Polsgrove, L., 158, 160
Pond, R.E., 99, 130
Popham, W.J., 258

Poteet, J.A., 206
Potter, 362
Powell, M.L., 122
Powers, M., 118
Prather, E.M., 130
Preminger, J.L., 124, 231
Price, B.J., 185
Price, G., 27
Pritchett, E., 210, 368
Pumpian, 269

Quay, H.C., 145, 158, 162, 163

Radabaugh, M., 185
Rae, 362
Rand, Y., 192
Rees, N., 93
Regan, R.R., 44
Reid, D.K., 99
Reiss, S., 191
Renzulli, J., 32, 311, 312, 314, 315, 381, 383, 385
Repp, A.C., 158
Reschly, D.J., 190
Reynolds, M., 221
Rheingrover, R.M., 112
Richert, E.S., 319
Rieth, 158
Robins, L., 142
Robinson, C., 258, 260, 263, 264, 362
Robinson, J., 258
Robson, G.M., 323
Rogers, S., 296
Rose, J., 268
Rosenberg, S., 263
Roswell, 362
Ryan, B., 90

Sabatino, D., 257
Sailor, W., 254, 344
Salisbury, C., 118
Salvia, J., 34, 44, 71, 144, 226, 286
Sanford, A.R., 124, 125, 231, 232
Saslow, G., 143, 145, 170
Sattler, J.M., 194, 320
Satz, P., 193
Scarlett, J., 344
Schafer, D.S., 124, 267
Schafer, 124

Scheiner, A.P., 112
Schellhaas, M., 0
Schleien, 255
Schmidt, P., 135
Searle, J.R., 90
Secord, W., 99, 101, 99
Segal, E., 191
Semel, E., 99, 100, 205
Shankweiler, D., 202
Shea, T.C., 32
Shearer, M.S., 115, 125
Shellhaas, 45
Shinn, B., 190
Shrago, 368
Shub, 360
Silbert, 349
Silvaroli, 360
Silverman, L., 311, 312, 320
Silverman, R., 206, 211, 341, 342
Simeonsson, R.J., 112
Simmons, T., 269
Skinner, B.F., 0   10 51 ??
Skinner, M.E., 10, 151
Skrtic, T., 335, 343, 345
Sky, N.C., 351
Smith, 362
Smith, C.R., 192, 209
Smith, J., 254
Smith, L.H., 32
Smith, T.E.C., 185
Snell, M., 255
Snyder-McLean, L.K., 120
Somwaru, J.P., 126
Sontag, E., 254
Spache, 360
Sparrow, S.S., 229
Sprinthall, N.A., 319
Sprinthall, R.C., 319
Sroufe, A., 257
Staab, C., 103
Stark, R., 94
Steiner, V.G., 99, 130
Stephens, I., 99, 101
Stern, C., 122
Sternat, J., 287
Sternfield, A.E., 232
Stewart, E.D., 27, 364
Stillmann, R., 266
Stock, J.R., 115, 124, 229

Strickland, B.B., 42, 43
Sucher, 364
Sugai, G., 341, 342
Sulzer-Azaroff, B., 158
Svinicki, 115, 124
Szyszko, J., 191

Tallal, P., 94
Talley, M., 351
Tarjan, G., 222
Tarver, S.G., 198
Taylor, C.W., 310
Terdal, L.G., 144
Terman, L., 126, 194, 219, 310
Thal, D.J., 94
Thompson, P., 253
Thompson, V.P., 33
Tindall, G., 34, 35
Tobin, A.R., 130
Todd, J., 193
Torgensen, J.K., 199
Torrance, E.P., 320, 321
Tough, J., 128
Treffinger, D.J., 383
Troutman, A.C., 168, 169
Tucker, J., 35, 190
Turnbull, A.P., 42, 43
Tyack, D., 90
Tymitz, 188, 190
Tymitz-Wolf, B., 5

Ulrey, G., 296
Utley, B., 337, 342
Uzgiris, I., 122, 126

Vallecorsa, A., 206, 341, 342
Van Blaricom, 364
Van Etten, 368
Vellutino, F.R., 202
Venn, J.J., 297
Vincent, L.J., 118
Volkmann, C.B., 186
Von Kuster, 370
Vulpé, S.G., 125, 289, 290

Wachs, T., 136

Wahler, R.G., 163
Walker, H.M., 145, 151, 158, 162, 163
Wallace, G., 0
Wallach, M.A., 314, 319, 320
Walter, G., 118
Wambold, C., 199
Wechsler, D., 126, 219, 297
Weffer, R., 190
Wehman, P., 129, 255, 340
Weisler, A., 131
Wesson, C.C., 341, 342
Whalen, C.K., 159
Whaler, R.G., 153, 154
White, O., 120, 121, 125, 269
Whiting, H., 302
Whitmore, J.R., 320, 372
Wicks-Nelson, R., 142
Widerholt, J.L., 364
Wiig, E., 99, 100, 205
Williams, F., 97
Williams, W., 255
Wilson, M.S., 348, 353
Wnek, L., 115, 124, 229
Wolery, M., 16, 17, 37
Wolf, M.M., 145
Wood, B., 84, 87
Woodcock, R.W., 194, 200, 203, 364
Woods, 360
Wooster, J., 315
Workman, E.A., 224–225

Yamamoto, K., 320–321
Yorke, R., 254
Ysseldyke, J., 34, 44, 71, 144, 188, 190, 226, 286, 335, 338, 345, 346
Yuckish, J., 185

Zachman, R., 99, 101
Zaner-Boser, 366
Zeaman, D., 198
Zehrbach, R.R., 115
Zeisloft, B., 125
Zelman, J.G., 125, 213
Zenhausern, R., 32
Zigmond, N., 206, 211, 341, 342
Zimmermann, I.L., 99, 130

Index

ABC analysis, 164
Abstract problems, 185
Academic assessment
    of gifted learner, 318–319
    of mildly handicapped. *See* Mildly
        handicapped learner
    of physically handicapped, 301
Accessibility checklist, 298–300
Achievement tests, 53
Adaptive behavior assessment, 346–347
    commercially available tests, 228–232
    of mildly handicapped, 196–197
    with multiple handicaps, 226–227
    of trainable mentally handicapped, 219,
        224–225
Adaptive Behavior Inventory for Children,
    197
Adaptive Behavior Scale, 45, 196–197, 224–
    225, 227–228, 347
Adaptive equipment. *See* Physical
    equipment
Adaptive Performance Instrument-
    Experimental Edition, 264–266
Administration of tests
    interscorer reliability, 71
    modification of
        for multiply handicapped young child,
            120–121
        for physically handicapped, 284
    standard procedures, 54–55
    with multiple handicaps, 119–121
Administrators, 8
Adolescence, 300–301
Adults. *See also* Parents and guardians;
        Significant others

and problem behavior, 159–160
    interviewing, 172–173
    trainable mentally handicapped
        responses to, 245–246
Advanced Reading inventory, 360
Affect, with language disorders, 97
Age
    and language development, 84–85
    in normative samples, 56, 57.
Age equivalents, scoring as, 67–68
Agreement coefficient, 169
Alternate form reliability, 70–71
Alternative behavior, 161
American Association of Mental Deficiency,
        196
    Adaptive Behavior Scale, 45, 196–197,
        224–225, 227–228, 347
    classifications of mental retardation, 218–
        220
Analytical learning style, 31–32
Analytic Reading Inventory, 360
Antecedent events
    data collection procedures, 16, 17
    in problem behavior, 151–152
Appropriate behavior, defining, 143
Aptitude testing. *See* Tests
Artificial limbs, 297, 300–301
Assessment
    computer-assisted, 351–352
    definitions, 4–5
    five-stage model, 7–11
    language use, 89
    legal issues, 37–40
    levels of, 6–7, 373–377
    with multiple handicaps, 119–121

prereferral, 345
procedures, indicators, and questions addressed, 378–389
questions and information sources, 373–377
settings for, 5. *See also* Settings
steps in, 38
Assessment instruments. *See* Instruments, assessment; Tests
Assistance levels, 25–26, 238–239
Associative play, 131
Ataxia, 280
Athetosis, 280
Attention spans
difficulties with, 185
of mildly handicapped, 198
of young children, 116
Audiologists, 8
Auditory impairment, 89, 92–94. *See also* Multiple handicaps; Sensory deficits
Augmentative communication modes, 127
Autistic pupils, 253
Automatic reactions, 134

Baldwin Identification Matrix, 315
Bankson Language Screening Test, 99
Baseline
for behavior change programs, 161–162
problem behavior, 175
in task analysis, 23–25
Basic Educational Skills Inventory: Math, 368
Basic School Skills Inventory, 366
Battelle Developmental Inventory, 115, 124, 229–230
Bayley Scales of Infant Development, 56, 122, 126
Behavior
classes of, 158
defined, 143
strategies for changing, 161
Behavioral assessment. *See also* Adaptive behavior assessment
of gifted learner, 311
of physically handicapped, 301–302
of trainable mentally handicapped, 227
Behavioral Characteristics Progression, 124
Behavioral repertoires, 143

Behavior deficits, 145–147
Behavior domains, 53
Behavior excesses, 145
Behavior Problem Checklist, 145, 146, 162–163
Behavior problems
adaptive behavior assessment, 196–197, 346–347
assessment methods, 162–169
accuracy and reliability of observations, 168–169
direct observation, 164–168
ecological survey, 163–164
rating scales, 162–163
assessment process, 144–162
diagnosis, 149–157
program planning, 157–162
screening, 144
types of problem behaviors, 145–149
classification of, 145–149, 185, 190, 191
definitions, 142–143
of gifted learners, 313–314
intervention process, 175–176
interviews, 170–175
Bell curve, 61–62
Bias
in early childhood special education, 119
identifying, 43
and identification of mildly handicapped, 189–190
improper discrimination, 345–346
observer and procedural, 40–41
in tests, 57
Binet scale, Hayes adaptation of, 256
Blindness. *See* Multiple handicaps; Sensory deficits
Botel Reading inventory, 360
Braces, 297, 300–301
Brigance Diagnostic Inventories, computer software, 351
Brigance Diagnostic Inventory of Basic Skills, 231, 360, 366, 368
Brigance Diagnostic Inventory of Early Development, 124, 230–231
Brigance Diagnostic Inventory of Essential Skills, 360, 366, 368
Bruininks-Oseretsky Test of Motor Proficiency, 304

Callier-Azuza Scale, 266–267
Camelot Behavioral Checklist, 230
Carolina Developmental Profile, 124
Categorical classroom, 186
Categorical definitions, 185
Category sampling, 22
Causality, 123
CBA. *See* Curriculum-based assessment
Central nervous system, 32, 40
Central tendency errors, 40
Cerebral palsy, 253, 279–280
Charisma, 384
Children's Arithmetic, 212
Classroom
    accessibility checklist, 298–300
    for gifted learners, 312
    and learning style, 28
    program evaluation, 344
    structure in, 29–30
Classroom assessment, 23
    of language impairment, 95–96
    role of teacher, 338–339
    uses of and indications for, 381–385
Classroom Reading Inventory, 360
Classroom teachers. *See* Teachers
Clinical Evaluation of Language Functions:
        Advanced Level Screening, 100
Clinical Evaluation of Language Functions:
        Elementary Level Screening, 99–100
Cognitive development
    auditory processing, 93–94
    in early childhood, 122–123, 126–127
    language impairments, 86
Cognitive model, assessment of profoundly
        handicapped, 269–272
Columbia Mental Maturity Scale, 284, 286–
        287
Communication skills
    early childhood, 127–129, 130
    and intelligence testing, 193–194
    interview techniques, 172–175
    of mildly handicapped, 205–206
    with physical impairments, 283–284, 294
    of profoundly handicapped
        modes of, 257–258
        and test selection, 263–268
    trainable mentally handicapped learner
        pupil preferences, 244–245

testing considerations, 226–227
Communication game, 89
Community behavior checklist, 154
Competing behaviors, 158–159
Comprehension, reading, 202
Comprehensive Developmental Evaluation
        Chart, 289
Comprehensive Identification Process, 115
Compton Speech and Language Evaluation,
        100
Computers and microcomputers
    assessment of profoundly handicapped
        students, 258
    MIPIM, 35
    tracking performance levels, 341
    uses of, 347–353
Concurrent validity, 72
Consequent events
    in data collection, 16, 17
    in problem behavior, 152, 154–155
Consistency, of tests, 57
Construct validity, 72
Content category development, 87
Content validity, 72
Continuum of special education services,
        221
Contracts, as strategy for changing behavior,
        160
Conversation, assessment of, 103
Convulsive disorders, 281
Cooperative play, 131
Coping skills, of physically handicapped,
        300–301
Correlation coefficient, 69
Creativity, 320
Criteria of next educational environment,
        118
Criterion of ultimate functioning, 255–256
Criterion Reading, 360
Criterion-referenced assessment, 210–211
    mathematics, 368–371
    profoundly handicapped student, 260–
        261
    reading, 203–204, 360–365
    written language, 366–367
Critical functions, 120
Critical thinking, 321–322, 382
Cross-categorical approach, 10

Cuing, 26, 97–98
Cultural factors
    discrimination, 41–44
    in early childhood special education, 119
    in language impairment assessment, 96–98
    in normative samples, 57
    and problem behavior, 155
    System of Multicultural Pluralistic Assessment (SOMPA), 197
    and T.R.H. designation, 190, 223–224
Curriculum-based assessment
    data collection considerations, 33–35
    with profoundly handicapped student, 261

Daily-living skills
    of physically handicapped, 289, 290
    for profoundly handicapped students, 257
Data-based decision-making, 340, 345
Data collection
    computer-assisted, 350–352
    curriculum-based assessment, 33–35
    learning styles, 27–33
        classroom assessment of, 32–33
        emotional elements in, 28–30
        environmental elements in, 27–28
        physical elements in, 30–31
        psychological elements in, 31–32
        sociological elements in, 30
    legal and ethical issues, 36–46
        discrimination, 41–44
        parents' role, 44–46
        quality of assessment, 37–41
        teacher competence and IEP requirements, 36–37
    methods of
        direct observation, 15–16
        naturalistic observation, 16–22
        task analysis, 22–27
    selection of system, 15–27, 39
    steps in assessment process, 38
Data-gathering procedures, 5
Deafness. See also Hearing impairment; Multiple handicaps; Sensory deficits
Delays in onset, 85, 92

Denver Developmental Screening Test, 45, 115
Developmental assessment
    in early childhood special education, 117, 124–125, 126
    in language impairment, 84, 91–92
    of physically handicapped, 290–291
    of problem behavior, 159
Developmental period, defined, 220
Developmental Potential of Preschool Children, The, 257
Developmental Programming for Infants and Young Children, 267–268
Development Profile II, 115
Deviation score, 66–67
Diagnosis
    of gifted learner, 314–316
    of language impairment, 102
    of problem behavior, 149–157
    questions and information sources, 374–375
    role of teacher, 336–337, 338–339
    testing for, 5, 6, 8
Diagnosis: An Instructional Aid, 360
Diagnosis: An Instructional Aid in Mathematics, 368
Diagnostic Chart for Fundamental Processes in Arithmetic, 368
Diagnosticians, 8
Diagnostic Mathematics Inventory, 368
Diagnostic Reading Scales, 360
Diagnostic Test of Arithmetic Strategies, 368
Diagnostic Tests and Self-Help in Arithmetic, 368
Dialects, 97–98
Differential reinforcement, 160, 161
Differential Reinforcement of Omission Behavior, 158
Direct observation
    biases in, 40
    data gathering considerations, 15–16
    play skills, 131
    profoundly handicapped student, 261–263
    trainable mentally handicapped learner, 233–241
    uses of and indications for, 381–385
Discrimination (intellectual), 185

Discrimination issues. *See also* Bias
  areas of, 41–44
  improper, 345–346
Distraction
  as mildly handicapped learner problem, 185
  as trainable mentally handicapped learner problem, 246
Divergent thinking, 323–324
Domains
  adaptive behavior testing, 229–230
  identification for testing, 53
  of profoundly handicapped pupils, 260–261
    curriculum content, 268–269
    testing, 264–268
Dump and play, 89–90
Duration data, 18
  problem behavior observation, 165
  trainable mentally handicapped learner, 234–235, 236
Durrell Analysis of Reading Difficulty, 360

Early Childhood Environmental Rating Scale, 131
Early childhood special education
  areas for assessment, 121–135
    cognitive skills, 122–123
    communication skills, 127–129, 130
    family skills, 135
    gross and fine motor skills, 132–135
    play and social interaction, 129–132
    preacademic skills, 123–127
    tests covering more than one developmental area, 124–125, 126
  definitions, 112–113
  issues and special problems, 113–119
    assessing young children, 116–117
    cultural factors, 119
    family assessment, 119
    instructional targets, 117–118
    screening and early identification, 113–116
    multiple handicaps, 119–121
    modifying assessment procedures, 120–121
Early Intervention Developmental Profile, 124
Early Learning Accomplishment Profile, 125

Eating skills, 135
Ecological survey, 147–149, 150–151, 159, 163–164
Educable mentally retarded, 185, 191. *See also* Trainable mentally handicapped learner
Educational assessment. *See* Assessment
Elementary-aged children, mildly handicapped, 187
Eligibility for special education
  gifted learner, 314–316
  questions and information sources, 374–375
  role of teacher, 339
  testing for, 5, 6, 8
Emotional factors, in learning style, 28–30
Emotionally disturbed pupils, 253. *See also* Behavior problems
Empathy, 384
Enright Diagnostic Inventory of Basic Arithmetic Skills, 351
Environmental context
  antecedent and consequent events, 16, 17
  and learning style, 27–28
  of trainable mentally handicapped, 246
Environments
  classroom. *See* Classroom
  play, 131
Epilepsy, 281
Equipment. *See* Physical devices
Error, assessment, 189–190
  biases, 40–41, 43
  mislabeling or inaccurate referral, 190
Error-pattern analysis, 343
Ethical issues. *See* Legal and ethical issues
Ethnicity. *See also* Culture
  dialects, 97–98
  and intelligence testing, 194
  language proficiency, 352, 353
Etiology
  in language impairment, 92
  in mildly handicapping conditions, 191
Evaluation, program, 5, 7, 9–10, 343–345
  gifted learner, 318–319
  questions and information sources, 376–377
  role of teacher, 337, 340–341
  of test, 68–73
Event recording, 17–20

problem behavior observation, 165
timing, 19–20
trainable mentally handicapped learner, 234

Face validity, 72
Family. *See* Parents and guardians
Fatigue, and test performance, 296
Feedback, with language disorders, 97, 98
Fine motor skills, 129–132
Five-level assessment model, 7–11
    curriculum-based assessment and, 34–35
    for gifted learner, 313–318
    questions and information sources, 373–377
    role of teacher, 336–337
Fluharty Preschool Speech and Language Screening Test, 100
Food intake, and learning, 31
Formative assessment, 209
Functional approach
    in early childhood special education, 117–118
    with physically handicapped, 291
    with profoundly handicapped student, 254

Gates-McKillop Reading Diagnostic Tests, 362
Gender, in normative samples, 57
Gender issues, 44
General adaptation, 119
Generalization
    assessment of ability, 256
    difficulties with, 185
Generosity errors, 40
Gifted learners
    assessment levels, 313–319
        eligibility and diagnosis, 314–316
        evaluation of progress, 318–319
        goals, assessing, 317
        instructional planning, 317–318
        multidisciplinary approaches, 315
        placement and IEP development, 315–317
        program objectives, 316–317, 321–325
        screening and identification, 313–314
        service delivery options, 315–316
        tests, appropriate use of, 314

assessment procedures, 318–325
    formal testing issues, 319–321
    informal, 321–325
    I.Q. scores, 320
    definitions, 310–311
    learning style, 31–32
    settings, 312–313
Gillmore Oral Reading Test, 362
Global learning style, 31–32
Goals
    delineation of, 339
    gifted learner, 317
    mastery of, 343–344
Grade equivalent scores, 68
Grammar
    language impairments, 87–88
    oral language assessment, 205
Gray Oral Reading Test, 362
Griffiths Mental Development Scales, 126
Gross motor skills, 129–132
Guardians. *See* Parents and guardians

Halo effect, 40
Handwriting, 207
Hannah-Gardner Preschool Language Screening Test, 100
Hawaii Early Learning Profile, 125
Health problems
    with motor dysfunction, 281–282
    and test performance, 296
Hearing impairment, 89, 92–94. *See also* Multiple handicaps; Sensory deficits
Hemispheric preferences, 32
Hierarchical task analysis, 23, 270–271
High-risk children, 113
Home Observation and Measurement of the Environment, 136
Hydrocephalus, 281
Hypertonic, 134
Hypotonic, 134

Identification
    of gifted learner, 313–314
    questions and information sources, 374
    testing for, 5, 6, 8
IEP. *See* Individual education plan
Imitation, 26, 123
Impulsivity, 32
Inappropriate affect, 97

Inappropriate behaviors, 32
Inappropriate referrals, 189–190
Incidental learning, 186
Inconsistency, and problem behavior, 155, 159
Independence
adaptive behavior assessment, 196–197
of gifted learners, 324
with physical handicaps, 302
for profoundly handicapped students, 257
Independent study, 312
Individual education plan (IEP)
for gifted learner, 315–317
for language-impaired student, 103
microcomputer-assisted processes, 348, 351–352
modification of, 343
PL 94–142 requirement, 4
program evaluation, 345–346
questions and information sources, 375–376
role of teacher, 336–337, 339–340
teacher competence and, 36–37
testing for, 5, 6, 9
Individual implementation programs, 340
Individual Reading Placement Inventory, 362
Informal assessment
gifted learner, 321–325
of reading, 204–205
uses of and indications for, 390
Informal Reading Diagnosis, 362
Informal reading inventory, 203–204
Information use, of gifted students, 321–322
Instructional planning, 341–343
for gifted learner, 317–318
questions and information sources, 375–376
testing for, 5, 7, 9
Instruments, assessment. *See also* Tests
computer-assisted, 34
curriculum-based assessment, 34, 35
parent interview, 45
Integrated instructional program, 137
Intelligence tests and testing, 53
gifted learner, 319–321
of mildly handicapped, 192–196

of physically handicapped, 285–287
retardation categories, 219
scoring, 66–67
Interactive-behavioral system, 142–143
Interactive video, 349–350
Intercultural Development Research Association, 352–353
Interdisciplinary treatment
in early childhood special education, 113
with profoundly handicapped students, 258–259
Internal antecedents, 151
Interpretation of tests, 55
Interscorer reliability, 71
Interval recording
problem behavior observation, 166–168
time sampling, 19–20
Intervention
with physical handicaps, 292, 294–297
prereferral, 35, 345
Interviews
with behavior problems, 170–175
for math skills assessment, 212
parent, 45
Introduction to Special Education, 222
Iowa Silent Reading Tests, 362
Item bias, in tests, 57
Item pools, 53
Item selection, of test, 52–54
Item tryout, 53–54

Kaufman Assessment Battery for Children, 195, 196
Key concepts, 321
KeyMath Diagnostic Arithmetic Tests, 210–211, 368
Kindergarden Language Screening Test, 100–101
Kottmeyer Diagnostic Spelling test, 366

Labeling
as mildly handicapped, 189–190
mislabeling or inaccurate referral, 190
Language
early childhood education
assessment of communication skills, 127–129, 130
normal development, 83–85
limited English proficient, 352

of mildly handicapped learner, 201–209
oral, 205–206
reading, 201–205
written, 206–209
norm- and criterion-referenced tests
reading, 360–365
written language, 366–367
of profoundly handicapped pupils, 257
Language Assessment Scales, 353
Language content, 83
development sequence, 84
dialects, 97–98
language impairments, 86–87
Language form
development sequence, 84
dialects, 97–98
language impairments, 87–88
Language formulation
classification of disorders, 92
impairments of, 85
Language impairments
assessment formats, 98–105
conversational speech, evoking, 103
diagnostic measures, 102
informal, 99
minisamples, screening, 103–105
spontaneous language sampling, 102–103
tests, 99–102
classroom assessment, 95–96
controversies and issues with, 89–94
assessment vs. intervention, 90
auditory impairments, 92–94
delays vs. disorders, 91–92
etiologic vs. symptomatic classification, 92
patterns of impairment, 91
cultural and social factors in, 96–98
formal, 98–99
general characteristics of, 85–89
content problems, 86–87
form problems, 87–88
use problems, 88–89
Kaufman Assessment Battery with, 195
and intelligence testing, 193–194
normal development, 83–85
rule of six, 84–85
verbal language aspects, 83–84
with physical impairments, 283–284

role of special educator with, 94–96
Language processing
auditory, 93–94
impairments of, 85
Language sample, 128
Language structure
assessment of, 89
in minisample screening, 103–104
Language use
assessment of, 89
language impairments, 88–89
Latency data, 18–19
Leadership
of gifted learners, 324–325
indicators of, 384–385
Learned helplessness, 302
Learning Accomplishment Profile, 125
Learning Accomplishment Profile-Diagnostic Edition, 231–232
Learning disability
adaptive behavior assessment, 346–347
classification of, 185, 191
and intelligence testing, 193
with physical disability, 296
Learning set, 186
Learning strategies, 198
Learning style, 27–33
classroom assessment of, 32–33
emotional factors in, 28–30
environmental factors in, 27–28
of gifted learners, 318
and instructional planning, 342–343
physical factors in, 30–31
psychological factors in, 31–32
of trainable mentally handicapped learner, 241–247
Learning Style Inventory, 32
Least-restrictive environment, 282–283
Legal and ethical issues. See also Public Law 94–142
in assessment, 36–46
discrimination, 41–44
parent's role, 44–46
quality of assessment, 37–41
teacher competence, 36–37
Leisure skills curriculum, 255
Leiter International Performance Scale, 284
Levels of assistance
data collection considerations, 25–26

trainable mentally handicapped learner, 238–239
Limited English proficient (L.E.P.), 352, 353
Living skills. *See* Daily-living skills
Logic errors, 40
Low rate behavior, 161

McCarthy Scale of Children's Abilities, 66–67, 117, 126
McCollogh Word Analysis Tests, 362
Mainstream placement, 339–340
    evaluation for, 35
    of trainable mentally handicapped, 222
Mastery of target skills, 340, 344
Materials
    early childhood special education, 117
    for testing, 54
Mathematics
    microcomputer-assisted processes, 348, 350
    mildly handicapped learner, 209–211
    norm- and criterion-referenced tests, 366–367
Mean distribution, 59, 60, 61
Means-ends behavior, 123
Measurement. *See* Instruments, assessment; Tests
Measurement error, standard, 63–65
Median distribution, 59, 60, 61
Medical problems
    and hearing impairment, 92–93
    with physical handicaps, 302
    and test performance, 296
Medical professionals, 8, 302
Memory assessment, 186, 198
Meningocele, 281
Mental retardation classifications, 185
Merrill Language Screening Test, 100–101
Middle-ear infections, 92–93
Mildly behaviorally disordered, 185
Mildly handicapped learner
    academic achievement, 200–212
        math, 209–211
        oral language, 205–206
        reading skills, 201–209
        tests of, 201
        written language, 206–209
    adaptive behavior assessment, 346–347
    definitions, 185–186
    educational settings, 186
    issues and problems, 187–200
        aptitude measures, nontraditional, 197–200
        aptitude measures, traditional, 192–197
        classroom procedures, 191–200
        elementary-aged children, 187–188
        nondiscriminatory assessment, 189–191
        preschool-aged children, 187
        secondary-level youth, 187–189
(MIPIM) Montevideo Individualized Prescriptive Instructional Management System, 35
Mislabeling, 190
Modeling, 26
Moderately handicapped, 218
Moderate retardation, definitions, 218, 219
Modes, language, 127
Momentary time sampling, 20–21
Montevideo Individualized Prescriptive Instructional Management System (MIPIM), 35
Morphology, language, 83, 87
Motivation
    indicators of, 383
    in learning style, 28
Motor impairments. *See also* Multiple handicaps; Physically handicapped
    automatic reactions and reflexes with, 134
    with cerebral palsy, 280
    early childhood special education, 120
    of profoundly handicapped
        and approach to task, 272
        and test selection, 263
    in young children, 131
Motor skills
    in early childhood special education, 129–132
    with physical handicaps, 289, 302–304
    of profoundly handicapped, and approach to task, 272
Multidisciplinary approaches
    with gifted learner, 315
    with profoundly handicapped students, 258–259

role of teacher, 335–341
Multilevel Informal Language Inventory, 101
Multiple handicaps
    early childhood special education, 120–121
    of mildly handicapped, 190–191
    physical handicaps with, 288–292, 293
        developmental assessment, 290–291
        motor/mobility evaluation, 289
        other areas of assessment, 289–290
        specialized assessment services, 288–289
        task analytic assessment, 291–292, 293
    in profoundly handicapped, 256–259
        and approach to task, 272
        and test selection, 263–268
    of trainable mentally handicapped, 226–227
Multiple presentations, in developmental assessment, 291
Multiple samples, 290
Muscle tone, 133–134
Myelomeningocele, 281

Naturalistic observation, 16–22
Natural settings, observing in, 16
Negative reinforcement
    in problem behavior, 154–155, 157
    strategies for changing behavior, 161
Noncategorical setting, 112
Nondiscriminatory assessment, 41–44
    cultural issues, 42
    gender issues, 44
    of mildly handicapped, 187
    strategies for teacher, 42–44
Nonverbal communication, 26, 97–98, 286, 294
Normal distribution curve, 61–62
Normative sample, 55–57
Norm-referenced tests, 210–211
    of adaptive behavior, 227
    mathematics, 368–371
    and profoundly handicapped student, 259–260
    reading, 360–365
    written language, 366–367

Objectives
    delineation of, 339
    mastery of, 343–344
    modification of, 343
Object permanence
    developmental stage and, 122–123
    in profoundly handicapped, 269–270
Observation methods
    bias, 40–41
    direct, 15–16
    naturalistic, 16–22
Observee bias, 40
Obtained score, 63, 64, 65
Omission behavior, 161
Onlooking, 131
On the Spot Reading Diagnosis File, 362
Oral language. See also Communication skills
    of mildly handicapped, 205–206
    motor dysfunction and, 135, 294
    testing, 101
Oral Language Sentence Imitation Screening Test, 101
Oral-motor dysfunctions, 135
Oral reading tests, 203
Oral tests, with physical impairments, 283–284
Ordinal Scales of Psychological Development, 122, 126
Orthopedic impairment. See also Physically handicapped
    physical devices for assistance in, 297, 300–301
    types of, 281–282
Out-of-level testing, 318

Parallel play, 131
Parent-child interactions, 136
Parents and guardians. See also Adults
    in decision-making process, 8
    in early childhood special education, 116–117, 119, 135
    of gifted learners, 315
    legal and ethical issues, 44–46
    and problem behavior
        contributing factors, 155, 159–160
        defining problem, 143, 147
    and self-help skills, 134

Partial credit, 290
Peabody Developmental Motor Scale, 133, 304
Peabody Individual Achievement Test, 200, 201
Peabody Picture Vocabulary Test, 130, 284, 286
Peer groups
  of gifted learners, 325
  of trainable mentally handicapped, 246
Percentage recording, 235–236, 237
Percentile ranks, 65–66
Performance domains, 260–261
Performance I.Q., 193–194
Performance levels
  of gifted learner, 193–194
  microcomputer-assisted processes, 351
  of mildly handicapped learner, 186
  of profoundly handicapped learner, 260–261
  program evaluation, 344
  tracking, 340–341
Permanent products
  problem behavior observation, 164
  trainable mentally handicapped learner, 241
Persistence, in learning style, 28–29
Personality, 384
Phonology, 83, 127, 128
Physical ability. See Motor skills
Physical devices, with physical handicaps, 297, 300–301
  communication systems, 294
  positioning aids, 295–296
Physical factors
  hearing impairment, 92–94
  in learning style, 30–31
  in problem behavior, 151
Physically handicapped
  academic and behavioral assessment, 301–304
    academic areas, 301
    behavioral areas, 301–302
    motor ability, 302–304
  definitions, 279–282
  issues and special problems, 283–288
    assessment team approaches, 287–288
    intelligence testing, 285–287

    modification of test administration, 284
    norm-referenced tests, 284–285
    picture vocabulary tests, 285–286
    standardized tests, 283–284
  multiply handicapped, 288–292
    developmental assessment, 290–291
    motor/mobility evaluation and management analysis, 289
    other areas of assessment, 289–290
    specialized assessment services, 288–289
    task analysis, 291–292, 293
  nontraditional assessment, 292, 294–301
    developing indervention plan, 297
    physical devices, 297, 300–301
    physical environment, 297, 298–300
    preparation and intervention procedures, 292, 294–296
  settings, defining, 282–283
Physical prompting, 25–26
Picture Story Language Test, 366
Picture vocabulary test, 284, 285–286
P.L. 94–142. See Public law 94–142
Placement
  criteria of next educational environment, 118
  of gifted learner, 315–317
  questions and information sources, 375–376
  of student, 345–346
  testing for, 5, 6, 9
Planning, instructional program, 5, 7, 9, 341–343
  for gifted learner, 317–318
  questions and information sources, 375–376
  role of teacher, 337, 340–341
  schedule of observation, 16
  testing for, 5, 7, 9
Play, in early childhood education, 129–132
Portage Project Checklist, 125
Positioning, of physically handicapped, 295
Positive reinforcers, 154–155, 157. 162
Pragmatic approaches, in language impairment, 90
Pragmatics, 127
Preacademic skills, 123–127
Predictive validity, 72–73

Premath skills, 123
Prereading skills, 123
Prereferral intervention, 345
Preschool-aged children. *See also* Early
     childhood special education
     language development, 83–85
     mildly handicapped, 187
Preschool Attainment Record, 115
Preschool Language Scale, 130
Primary handicapping condition, 191, 226–
     227
Problem solving
     difficulties with, 185
     Kaufman Assessment Battery, 195
Procedural task analysis
     assessment considerations, 23, 24
     profoundly handicapped, 270–271
Product-assessment procedures, 324, 385
Proficiency, 384
Profoundly handicapped pupil
     definitions, 219, 253–254
     issues and special problems, 255–259
          criterion of ultimate functioning, 255–
          256
          multiple handicaps, 256–259
     P.L. 94–142, 253
     selection of instruments, 263–272
          analysis of skills assessed, 268–269
          cognitive model, 269–272
          materials, 264–268
     settings, 254
     types of assessment procedures, 259–263
          criterion-referenced, 260–261
          curriculum-referenced, 261
          direct observation, 261–263
          norm-referenced, 259–260
Program evaluation. *See* Evaluation,
     program
Program objectives, for gifted learner, 315–
     317
Program planning. *See* Planning,
     instructional program
Progress, of gifted learners, 318–319
Prompting, levels of, 25–26
Prostheses, 297, 300–301
Prosthetic adaptation, 119
Psychological elements
     in learning style, 31–32
     in problem behavior assessment, 144
Psychologists, 5, 8
Psychometricians, 5
Public Law 94–142. *See also* Legal and
     ethical issues
     evaluation requirements, 9–10
     and gifted learner, 312
     IEP requirements, 4
     on multidisciplinary team operation, 335
Pullout program, 312

Quality issues
     assessment validity, 37–41
     teacher competence, 36–37
Quickscreen, 101

Race. *See* Culture; Ethnicity
Range, test score distribution, 60–61
Rapport, and test performance, 117
Rating scale of social behavior, young child,
     131
Ratio score, 66–67
Raven's Progressive Matrices, 284
Raw scores, transformation of, 65–68
Reactions, 133–134
Reading
     and intelligence testing, 193
     of mildly handicapped, 201–205
     norm- and criterion-referenced tests,
          360–365
Reading Miscue Inventory, 362
Receptive-Expressive Emergent Language
     Scale, 130
Record Keeper, 351
Records
     levels-of-assistance data, 26
     microcomputer-assisted processes, 348,
          351
     problem behavior observation, 164–168
     of profoundly handicapped students
          responses, 262–263
     running, 17
     tracking pupil performance, 341
     trainable mentally handicapped learner
          observations, 234–241
Referral, 8
     curriculum-based assessment
          intervention before, 35

in early childhood special education, 113
of gifted learners, 313–314
intervention before, 345
with language impairment, 105
of mildly handicapped, 188
with problem behavior, 158
role of teacher, 338
Reflectivity, 32
Reflexes, 133–134, 296
Regular classroom placement, 339–340. *See also* Mainstream placement
Reinforcers
hierarchies of, 29, 30
instructional planning, 342–343
in problem behavior, 154–155, 157
with trainable mentally handicapped, 245
strategies for changing behavior, 161
Reliability
of assessment instruments, 224. *See also specific tests*
of behavioral observation, 168–171
of tests, 57
assessment of, 70–71
intelligence, 320–321
Reliability coefficient, 169
Resource room, 312
Resources, for teacher, 342
Response-latency requirements, 246
Response-set errors, 40
Responsibility, 29
Restrictive measures, 222
Retardation. *See also* Mildly handicapped learner; Profoundly handicapped pupil; Trainable mentally handicapped learner
classification of, 185
impulsivity vs. reflectivity, 32
levels of, 218–219
severe, 32
Rockford Infant Developmental Evaluation Scales, 125
Roswell-Chall Diagnostic Test of Word Analysis, 362
Rule of six, 84–85
Running records, 17

Sample, normative, 55–57
Sampling
category, 22

time, 19–21, 22
Scattergram, 69
Schedule of observation, 16
School behavior checklist, 153
Schoolroom. *See* Classroom; Settings
School settings. *See* Settings
Scoring
in developmental assessment, 291
tests, 65–68
test
deviation score, 66–67
distribution of, 59, 60, 61
grade equivalent scores, 68
normal distribution, 61–62
standard, 66–68
standard deviation, 62–63
standard error of measurement, 63–65
standard procedures, 55
z-score, 63
Screening, 5, 6, 8. *See also* Data collection
in early childhood special education
defined, 113–114
instruments for, 115
using data, 114, 116
gifted learner, 313–314
with language disorders, 99–102
language impairment assessment, 103–105
levels of assessment, questions and information sources, 373–377
procedures, indicators, and questions addressed, 378–389
role of teacher, 336, 338–339
Secondary handicapping condition, 226–227
Secondary school-aged youth, mildly handicapped, 187
Seizure disorders, 253
Seizures, 281
Self-directedness
of gifted learners, 324
indicators of, 383
Self-help skills
of physically handicapped, 289, 290
of profoundly handicapped students, 257
of young children, 134
Self-knowledge
of gifted learners, 325
of mildly handicapped pupil, 186

Semantics, 83, 85, 127
Sensorimotor skills. *See also* Motor
 impairments
 with mental retardation. *See specific*
  classes of retardation
 with physical disability. *See* Physically
  handicapped
 of young children, 122–123, 132, 133–134
Sensory deficits. *See also* Multiple
 handicaps
 with physical disability, test performance
  effects, 296
 in profoundly handicapped, 253
  and approach to task, 272
  and test selection, 263–268
 in young children, 131
Sensory input
 with physically handicapped, 294
 preferred, with trainable mentally
  handicapped learner, 245
Sentence patterns, 85, 86, 87
Sequenced Inventory of Communication
 Development, 130
Sequential problem solving, 195
Sequential Test of Educational Progress, 366
Settings
 for assessment, 5
 for early childhood special education,
  122
 for gifted learners, 312–313
 mildly handicapped learner, 186
 for observation, 16
 problem behavior, 163–164
 trainable mentally handicapped pupil
  preference, 247
Severely handicapped, 219, 253. *See also*
 Profoundly handicapped pupil
Severity errors, 40
Sexual stereotyping, 44
Significant others. *See also* Adults; Parents
 and guardians
 defining behavior problems, 143
 problem behavior definition, 147
Silent Reading Diagnostic Test, 364
Simultaneous problem solving, 195
Situational analysis, 147–149
Skills assessment
 in curriculum-based assessment, 35
 in early childhood special education, 118

instructional planning, 342
of profoundly handicapped students
 performance domains, 260–261
 task analysis, 270–271
 target, mastery of, 340
Skills selection, 255
Social factors. *See* Culture; Sociological
 factors
Social problems. *See* Behavior problems
Social sensitivity, 384
Social skills. *See also* Communication skills;
 Language
 in early childhood special education,
  129–132
 of gifted learners, 324–325
 indicators of, 384–385
 of mildly handicapped, 186
 and problem behavior, 152
 for profoundly hndicapped pupil, 254
Social tracking, 334
Social validation, 344
Sociological factors. *See also* Culture
 in intelligence testing, 193–194
 in language impairment assessment, 96–
  98
 in learning style, 30
Solitary independent play, 131
Sorting skills, 271
Spasticity, 280
Spatial relationships, 123
Special Education Software, 352
Speech deficits. *See* Communication skills;
 Oral language; Language
 impairment
Speech pathologists, 8
Speech sounds, 8
Spelling, 207, 209
Spellmaster, 366
Spina bifida, 281
Splinter skills, 260–261, 268
Split-half reliability, 71
Spontaneous language, 102–103
Standard deviation, 62–63
Standard error of measurement, 63–65
Standardization, of test, 54–55
Standardized tests. *See also* Instruments,
 assessment; Tests; *specific tests*
 microcomputer-administered, 353
 for physically impaired, 283–284

Standard materials, 54
Standard scores, 65–66
Stanford-Binet Intelligence Scale, 56, 126, 194, 310
  levels of retardation, 219
  with physical impairments, 283–284
  scoring, 66–67
Stanford Diagnostic Mathematics Test, 370
Stanford Diagnostic Reading Tests, 364
Stanford Functional Development Assessment, 303
Stephens Oral Language Screening Test, 101
Structure, in learning environment, 29–30
Subscale, 291
Sucher-Allred Reading Placement Inventory, 364
SuperPILOT, 350
Support adaptation, 119
Syntax, 83, 128
  development of, 127
  impairments of, 85, 87, 88
System Fore, 364
System of Multicultural Pluralistic Assessment, 197, 224

Tactile input, 294
TALLEY Goals and Objectives Writer, 351
Target behavior
  changing, 157–158
  duration data, 18
  environmental context, 16, 17
Target skills, mastery of, 340
Task analysis
  assessment considerations, 22–27
  in early childhood education, 118
  with physically handicapped student, 291–292, 293
  prerequisites to, 23–25
  of profoundly handicapped, 258, 270–271
  self-help skills, 135
  types of, 23, 24
Task approaches, of mildly handicapped, 186
Task conditions, in developmental assessment, 290–291
Teacher
  assessment by, 5, 8
  biases, 40–41, 189–190
  competence of, 36–37
  in decision-making process, 10
  discrimination, avoiding, 42, 43
  and labeling, 189–190
  levels of assistance from, 25–26
  as multidisciplinary team member, 8, 9
  problem behavior definition, 147
Teacher role, 335–341
Team approaches. See also Multidisciplinary team
  with gifted learner, 315
  with physically handicapped, 287–288
  with profoundly handicapped students, 258–259
  role of teacher, 335–341
Technology, 352–353
Telecommunications technology, 352
Termination of special education, 10, 339–340
Test of Adolescent Language, 366
Test of Auditory Comprehension of Language, 130
Test of Early Learning Skills, 126
Test of Early Mathematics Ability, 370
Test of Mathematical Abilities, 370
Test of Reading Comprehension, 364
Test of Written Language, 207–208, 366
Test of Written Spelling, 366
Test-retest reliability, 70
Test review form, 358
Tests. See also Assessment vehicles
  adaptive behavior assessment, for T.M.H. learner, 228–232
  biases
    improper discrimination, 345–346
    and labeling as mildly handicapped, 190
  in early childhood special education screening, 115
  for gifted learner, 319–321
  with language disorders, 99–102
  Learning Style Inventory, 33
  microcomputer-assisted processes, 348, 350, 353
  norm- and criterion-referenced
    mathematics, 366–367
    reading, 360–365
    written language, 366–367
  for physically handicapped, 283–286

intelligence, 285–287
modification of administration of, 284
standardized, 283–284
P.L. 94–142 requirements, 4, 334
principles of construction. *See* Tests,
    development of
problem behavior assessment, 144
for profoundly handicapped, 264–268
reasons for administering, 5–7
role of teacher, 338
trainable mentally handicapped learner,
    226–227, 228–232
uses of
    and indications for, 378–381
    for social tracking, 334
Tests, development of
evaluation of test, 68–73
    correlation coefficients, 69
    reliability, 70–71
    validity, 71–73
principles of construction, 52–65
    evaluation of test, 57
    item selection, 52–54
    normative sample, 55–57
    scores, distribution of, 58–60
    standardization, 54–55
    variability, measures of, 60–65
raw score transformation, 65–68
    percentile ranks, 65–66
    standard scores, 65–68
Thematic maturity, 207
Time of day, and pupil effectiveness, 31, 247
Time sampling, 19–21, 22
    problem behavior observation, 168
    trainable mentally handicapped learner,
        240–241
T.M.H., 220. *See also* Trainable mentally
    handicapped learner
TMR profile, 232
Toileting skills, 135
Total Special Education System, 35
Toy play, 129, 131
Trainable mentally handicapped learner
    assessment issues, 222–241
        cultural factors, 223–224
        direct-observation procedures, 233–
            241
        goals, 225
        methods, 224–225

methods, availability of, 224–225
methods, choosing, 225–228
multiple handicapping conditions,
    222–223, 226
testing materials, 228–232
definitions, 218–220
learning style preferences, 241–247
settings, 220–221
True score, 63, 64, 65
Twenty Questions Game, 323
TYMNET, 352

Uniform Performance Assessment Systems,
    125
Unoccupied behavior, defined, 131

Validation, social, 344
Validity
    of assessment, 37–41, 224
    of tests, 224
        assessment of, 71–73
        intelligence, 320–321
Variability, tests, 60–65
Variable-interval schedule, 19–20
Verbal cuing, 26
Verbal I.Q., 193–194
Verbal language. *See also* Communication
        skills; Oral language; Vocabulary
    aspects of, 83–85
    testing, 101
Verbal responses
    impulsivity vs. reflectivity, 32
    of physically handicapped, 283–284, 294
Videodisk technology, 348–350
Vineland Adaptive Behavior Scales -Revised,
    229
Vineland Social Maturity Scale, 225, 45, 257
Visual impairment. *See* Multiple handicaps;
        Sensory deficits
Vocabulary
    language impairments, 85, 86
    of mildly handicapped learner, 207
    picture tests of, 284, 285–286
Vulpe Assessment Battery, 125, 289

Walker Problem Behavior Identification and
        Checklist, 145, 150–151, 162, 163
Wechsler Adult Intelligence Scale, 193, 194
Wechsler Intelligence Scale, 219

Wechsler Intelligence Scale for Children-Revised, 193, 283
Wechsler Intelligence Scale-Revised, 56, 283
Wechsler Preschool and Primary Scale of Intelligence, 126, 193
Wechsler series, scoring, 66–67
Wheelchairs, 297, 300–301
Wide Range Achievement Tests, 200, 201
Wisconsin Design for Math Skill Development, 370
Wisconsin Tests of Reading Skill Development, 364
Woodcock-Johnson Psychoeducational Battery, 194–195, 200, 201
Woodcock Reading Mastery Test, 203, 364
Word forms, 83

Word meanings, 83
Word patterns, 83
Word recognition, 202
Work-sample analysis, 211
Written language
  of mildly handicapped, 206–209
  norm- and criterion-referenced tests, 366–367
Written language sample, 208–209

Young children. *See* Early childhood special education

Zaner-Bloser Evaluation Scales, 366
Z-score, 63, 64